Lecture Notes in Computer Science 6740

Commenced Publication in 1973
Founding and Former Series Editors:
Gerhard Goos, Juris Hartmanis, and Jan van Leeuwen

Jonathan M. McCune   Boris Balacheff
Adrian Perrig   Ahmad-Reza Sadeghi
Angela Sasse   Yolanta Beres (Eds.)

Trust
and Trustworthy
Computing

4th International Conference, TRUST 2011
Pittsburgh, PA, USA, June 22-24, 2011
Proceedings

 Springer

Volume Editors

Jonathan M. McCune
Carnegie Mellon University, 5000 Forbes Ave., Pittsburgh, PA 15213, USA
E-mail: jonmccune@cmu.edu

Boris Balacheff
Hewlett-Packard Labs, Long Down Ave., Stoke Gifford, Bristol BS34 8QZ, UK
E-mail: boris.balacheff@hp.com

Adrian Perrig
Carnegie Mellon University, 5000 Forbes Ave., Pittsburgh, PA 15213, USA
E-mail: adrian@ece.cmu.edu

Ahmad-Reza Sadeghi
TU Darmstadt / Fraunhofer SIT, Mornewegstr. 32, 64293 Darmstadt, Germany
E-mail: ahmad.sadeghi@trust.cased.de

Angela Sasse
University College London, Gower Street, London WC1E 6BT, UK
E-mail: a.sasse@cs.ucl.ac.uk

Yolanta Beres
Hewlett Packard Labs, Long Down Ave., Stoke Gifford, Bristol BS34 8QZ, UK
E-mail: yolanta.beres@hp.com

ISSN 0302-9743   e-ISSN 1611-3349
ISBN 978-3-642-21598-8   e-ISBN 978-3-642-21599-5
DOI 10.1007/978-3-642-21599-5
Springer Heidelberg Dordrecht London New York

Library of Congress Control Number: 2011928698

CR Subject Classification (1998): C.2, K.6.5, E.3, D.4.6, J.1, H.4

LNCS Sublibrary: SL 4 – Security and Cryptology

Typesetting: Camera-ready by author, data conversion by Scientific Publishing Services, Chennai, India

Printed on acid-free paper

Springer is part of Springer Science+Business Media (www.springer.com)

Preface

This volume contains the proceedings of the 4th International Conference on Trust and Trustworthy Computing (TRUST), held at Carnegie Mellon University, in Pittsburgh, Pennsylvania, USA, June 22–24, 2011.

TRUST is a rapidly growing forum for research on the technical and socio-economic aspects of trustworthy infrastructures. TRUST provides an interdisciplinary forum for researchers, practitioners, and decision makers to explore new ideas and discuss experiences in building, designing, using, and understanding trustworthy computing systems.

As in the previous edition, the fourth edition of TRUST welcomed manuscripts in two different strands: a technical strand and a socio-economic strand. We assembled an engaging program with 20 peer-reviewed technical papers and 3 peer-reviewed socio-economic papers; several keynotes from industry, academia, and government; and panel discussions. In addition, this year, TRUST was co-located with the Trusted Infrastructure Workshop (TIW), which is a 5-day Summer School in trustworthy computing.

We would like to thank numerous individuals for their effort and contribution to the conference and for making TRUST 2011 possible: the General Chairs Jonathan McCune (Carnegie Mellon University, USA) and Boris Balacheff (HP Labs, UK), as well as Marcel Winandy (Ruhr University Bochum, Germany) for their tremendous help with all aspects of the organization; the Technical and Socio-Economic Program Committees members, whose names are listed in the following pages and who helped us in the process of selecting manuscripts to be included in the conference proceedings; the keynote and invited speakers; and the invited panel speakers.

April 2011

Yolanta Beres
Adrian Perrig
Ahmad-Reza Sadeghi
Angela Sasse

Organization

TRUST 2011

The 4th International Conference on Trust and Trustworthy Computing was held at Carnegie Mellon University in Pittsburgh, PA, USA, June 22–24, 2011.

General Chairs

Jonathan McCune   Carnegie Mellon University, USA
Boris Balacheff   HP Labs, UK

Program Chairs

Technical Strand

Adrian Perrig   Carnegie Mellon University, USA
Ahmad-Reza Sadeghi   TU Darmstadt / Fraunhofer SIT, Germany

Socio-Economic Strand

Angela Sasse   University College London, UK
Yolanta Beres   HP Labs, UK

Program Committees

Technical Strand

Frederik Armknecht   University of Mannheim, Germany
Marina Blanton   University of Notre Dame, USA
Sergey Bratus   Dartmouth College, USA
Christian Cachin   IBM Research, Switzerland
Liqun Chen   HP Laboratories, UK
Xuhua Ding   Singapore Management University, Singapore
Paul England   Microsoft, USA
Michael Franz   University of California, Irvine, USA
Christian Gehrmann   Swedish Institute of Computer Science, Sweden
David Grawrock   Intel, USA
Helena Handschuh   Intrinsic-ID, USA / KU Leuven, Belgium
Gernot Heiser   NICTA, Australia
Thorsten Holz   Ruhr University Bochum, Germany
Cynthia Irvine   Naval Postgraduate School, USA
Stefan Katzenbeisser   TU Darmstadt, Germany

Steering Committee

Alessandro Acquisti	Carnegie Mellon University, USA
Boris Balacheff	Hewlett Packard, UK
Paul England	Microsoft, USA
Andrew Martin	University of Oxford, UK
Chris Mitchell	Royal Holloway University, UK
Sean Smith	Dartmouth College, USA
Ahmad-Reza Sadeghi	Ruhr University Bochum, Germany
Claire Vishik	Intel, UK

Additional Reviewers

Luigi Catuogno	Anbang Ruan
Hans Löhr	Ludwig Seitz
John Lyle	Anna Shubina
Emmanuel Owusu	Dave Singelée
Alfredo Rial	

Table of Contents

Session 5: Hardware Trust

Session 6: Access Control

Session 7: Privacy

Session 8: Trust Issues in Routing

Session 9: Crypto-Physical Protocols

Verifying Trustworthiness of Virtual Appliances in Collaborative Environments

Cornelius Namiluko[1], Jun Ho Huh[2], and Andrew Martin[1]

[1] Oxford University Computing Laboratory
Wolfson Building, Parks Road, Oxford OX1 3QD, UK
`firstname.lastname@comlab.ox.ac.uk`
[2] Information Trust Institute
University of Illinois at Urbana-Champaign
`jhhuh@illinois.edu`

Abstract. Often in collaborative research environments that are facilitated through virtual infrastructures, there are requirements for *sharing* virtual appliances and *verifying* their trustworthiness. Many researchers assume that virtual appliances — shared between known virtual organisations — are naturally safe to use. However, even if we assume that neither of the sharing parties are malicious, these virtual appliances could still be mis-configured (in terms of both security and experiment requirements) or have out-of-date software installed.

Based on formal methods, we propose a flexible method for specifying such security and software requirements, and verifying the virtual appliance events (captured through logs) against these requirements. The event logs are transformed into a process model that is checked against a pre-defined whitelist — a repository of formal specifications. Verification results indicate whether or not there is any breach of the requirements and if there is a breach, the exact steps leading to it are made explicit.

1 Introduction

With the growing influence of e-Research, a substantial quantity of research is being facilitated, recorded, and reported by means of cloud computing and various e-Infrastructures. In scenarios, where multiple virtual organisations (VOs) engage in collaborative research, researchers from one virtual organisation may want to use virtual appliances — these are ready-to-use virtual machine (VM) images with the required software installed — prepared by other virtual organisations for further experiments.

Sharing a virtual appliance across multiple virtual organisations, however, is not as easy as it sounds. Before using a virtual appliance prepared by another virtual organisation, a researcher needs to check its security configurations, integrity of the installed software and generated results, and input data and experiment models that have been used. Only those considered trustworthy and satisfying the researcher's software and security requirements should be used for further experiments.

J.M. McCune et al. (Eds.): TRUST 2011, LNCS 6740, pp. 1–15, 2011.

1.1   Motivational Case Study

Consider a publicly funded research project at an e-Research Centre, which involves collaboration between different virtual organisations such that results generated from one virtual organisation may be used by another. More specifically, the inputs, algorithms and configurations used in an experiment, as well as the generated outputs, may be used by another virtual organisation to perform the next series of experiments. One requirement is that each virtual organisation should contribute their experiment *setups* and *results* to the research community. These should be integrity-protected and accurate.

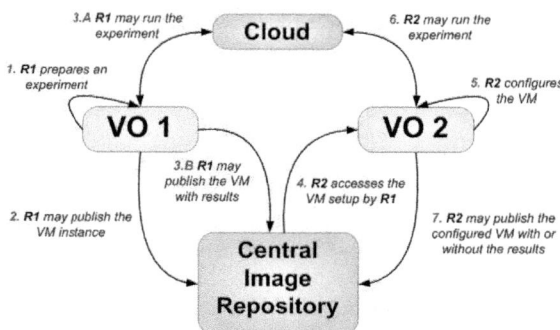

Fig. 1. Workflow showing how a virtual appliance is shared in a cloud

The collaboration works as follows. A researcher, $R1$, from virtual organisation 1, $VO1$, prepares an experiment (see Figure 1, workflow 1), installing and configuring the operating system, applications, their dependent libraries, input data and algorithms; security configurations, such as SELinux policies, are also configured during this stage. As a contribution to the project, $R1$ may publish this virtual machine instance — an initial experiment setup — to the central image repository (see Figure 1, workflow 2). Alternatively, $R1$ may run some experiments (workflow 3.A) and publish the virtual machine instance together with results of the experiments (workflow 3.B) as a virtual appliance ready for other researchers to use. $R1$ is willing to share this image with other researchers from a collaborating virtual organisation, $VO2$.

$R2$ from $VO2$ may design an experiment based on either the initial experiment setup published by $R1$ (workflow 4) or the results generated from running $R1$'s experiment (workflows 5 and 6). Since $R2$ is from a different virtual organisation, the downloaded virtual appliance needs to be configured to conform to the policies of $VO2$. At this stage, $R2$ may choose to publish this modified virtual appliance (specifying how it has changed) or choose to run the experiment and publish it with some results (workflow 7). Before setting up the experiment, $R2$ needs to be assured that the virtual appliance (downloaded from the central repository) contains the exact applications and settings she requires. Sufficient information about the source and history of the virtual machine and installed applications, their configurations, and the algorithms and inputs used for the experiment should be made available to potential users for analysis.

1.2   Paper Contributions and Structure

Motivated by the case study described above, this paper proposes a novel approach for verification of trustworthiness of virtual appliances based on formal methods. While a virtual appliance is up and running, all of the virtual appliance level events and configurations are captured through integrity-protected logs. These logs, shared with the collaborating virtual organisation, are transformed into a process model, which in turn, is checked against a pre-defined whitelist; this whitelist is captured as a repository of specifications. The specifications represent acceptable virtual appliance configurations and software environments. The results indicate whether the model (representing the virtual appliance configurations) satisfies the properties captured in the specifications.

We believe that our method will have wider implications for any system that requires high flexibility in constructing whitelists. For instance, Trusted Computing remote attestation/verification servers often require high flexibility in defining the application whitelists [4]: these whitelists need to model the acceptable combinations of software and dependencies between them, let alone the software configurations. Existing approaches for whitelisting [11], however, do not provide room for this flexibility. Our method on the other hand will allow the administrators to easily specify and manage acceptable software combinations and dependencies. More complex properties, such as acceptable system and application level events, can also be specified using our method.

In the following section, we identify the key requirements for trustworthy sharing of virtual appliances, and specify what information about virtual appliances should be captured through the logs. In Section 3, we give an overview of how our method works. This puts us in a position to describe, in Sections 4 and 5, the details of generating process models and verifying them against the given set of specifications. We describe a simple experiment performed to demonstrate the approach in Section 6. In Section 7 we evaluate our method against the requirements, and discuss how it could be generalised. We discuss related work in Section 8 and provide conclusions and discussions of future work in Section 9.

2   Requirements

Each virtual organisation, even in a collaborative research scenario, is likely to have different policies and requirements for running experiments. A single change made to the experiment environment by one virtual organisation may affect the integrity or validity of results. Hence, it is essential that all of the important events of a virtual appliance are captured accurately and such information made available to those who may be interested in using the virtual appliance.

Based on the case study above, we identify the key requirements for trustworthy sharing and analysis of virtual appliances:

1. Information about the source and history of a virtual appliance and installed applications, their configurations and the algorithms and inputs used should be recorded accurately.
2. The information described in `Requirement 1` should be integrity protected.
3. The information described in `Requirement 1` should be made available to subsequent users of the virtual appliance.
4. A researcher, before deploying the virtual appliance, should be able to verify whether the experiment environment conforms to her virtual organisation's policies and requirements — the information described in `Requirement 1` should be scrutinized to check that correct applications and configurations are present in the virtual appliance, and the results (outputs) have been generated through correct inputs and algorithms.
5. If the virtual appliance and its experiment environment does not conform to the policies and requirements of the researcher's virtual organisation, the researcher should be informed of the steps that led to the non-conformance to enable them decide the significance of the deviation from the policy.

2.1   What Information Should Be Logged?

This section further elaborates on `Requirement 1` to specify what information about a virtual appliance (when it is deployed and running) should be logged. Although the type of information required would vary between different collaborative projects, we believe that there will be a unifying set of events that all projects would want to keep track of. We identify some of these events here:

- *software installation/uninstallation* —details about software installed or uninstalled on the virtual appliance should be logged, keeping track of the software versions, security configurations used, permission levels given, and code signatures;
- *patch installation* — again, the details of any patch installed on the virtual appliance should be logged, capturing the patch names, descriptions, versions, sizes, and dependencies;
- *security configuration changes* — any change in the security configurations of the virtual appliance (e.g. SELinux, firewall and anti-virus settings) as well as the software level security configurations should be logged;
- *software execution* — the details of deployment and execution of any piece of software (e.g. experiment code) and the data/input used should be logged;
- and *operations on the file system* — any operation on the file system should be logged including the data accessed and used by software, results generated, modifications to data, and changes of file ownership and permissions.

The later sections discuss how the information listed here is transformed into a process model (a formal model representing the virtual appliance events) and how this model is checked against the whitelist.

2.2   Assumptions

Before describing our method, we first state the assumptions made:

- ASMP 1: A trustworthy logging system, capable of collecting the logs securely and protecting the log integrity, is available as part of the cloud infrastructure. Huh and Martin [2] proposed such a system based on Xen, which allows integrity-protected logs to be generated securely through an independent logging component. This component sits inside Domain-0, intercepting all I/O requests from guest virtual machines and logging the security-relevant information.
- ASMP 2: The logging system mentioned in ASMP 1 is capable of logging all of the events described in Section 2.1 and proving to remote entities that the logs are integrity (and totality) protected.
- ASMP 3: An access control mechanism is in place to ensure that only authorised entities can access the virtual appliances in the central image repository.

3 Overview of the Trustworthiness Verification Process

As outlined in Section 2, sharing of virtual appliances is a central requirement in a collaborative research environment. To support this, events collected from a running virtual machine instance are verified against policies defined by the VO before the virtual appliance can be used. This section gives an overview of the proposed trustworthiness verification process.

Our approach is based on the idea of modeling the trace of events as a process model and performing refinement checks against a pre-defined whitelist — a repository of specifications against which the trustworthiness of the virtual appliances can be verified. This process, illustrated in Figure 2, involves generating specifications and storing them in a repository and multiple runs of the trustworthiness verification process on the virtual appliances. The specification generation process (see Section 4.2) takes a dataset that conforms to the whitelist schema (see Section 4.1) and creates processes that capture intended properties together with a set of events relevant for proving each property.

Event logs are collected from a virtual machine while it is running using the logging system mentioned in ASMP 1. The logs are then integrity checked before unwanted events are filtered, based on the properties of interest. The filtered

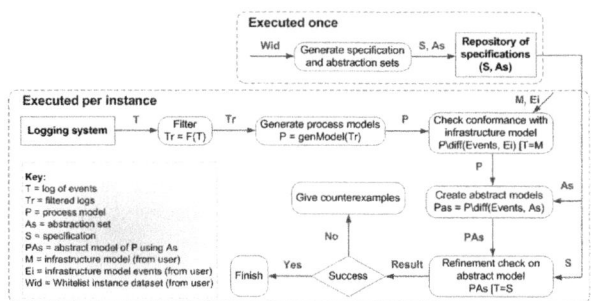

Fig. 2. Overview of the trustworthiness verification process

logs are then transformed into a process model (see Section 5.1) which is first
checked for conformance to the expected model of the infrastructure (see Section 5.3). The process model is then verified against the properties captured
by the specifications in the repository. This is achieved by creating system abstractions suitable for verifying specific properties, and checking whether the
system abstractions refine the specifications. When there is a refinement failure,
counter-examples are given, indicating the sequence of events that led to the
failure. These processes are described in more detail in the sections that follow.

4   Whitelist as a Repository of Specifications

A whitelist serves as a source of good values against which integrity measurements can be verified. Huh et al. [4] proposed how this notion of whitelisting
could be managed in a distributed environment while the Trusted Computing
Group[1] defines several schema to support interoperability of integrity measurement and verification. We extend this concept to enable the provision of refer-
ences for known-good *sequences of events* as well as *acceptable combinations of
configurations and events*. We thus define a whitelist as a repository of specifications, that capture intended properties, that can be used to verify whether the
observed traces of events on a virtual appliance indicate trustworthy operation.

In this section, we propose a formal schema of the whitelist and corresponding
specification generator, which accepts data corresponding to the defined schema
and generates a repository of specifications. Each specification process is associated with a set of events, which we call an *abstraction set*, that are considered
necessary to prove the property captured in the specification.

4.1   Specification of the Whitelist Schema

The TCG Infrastructure Working Group defines a Reference Manifest (RM)
Schema[2] — as an extension of the Core Integrity Schema — for specifying
reference measurements of components that may be used for verifying an operational environment. This schema, however, can not capture *inter-relations*
between components of a given environment. For example, the order in which
components must be loaded can not be captured. We extend the RM schema to
capture various forms of inter-relations that may exist between components of
a virtual appliance (see Figure 3). A component's behaviour not only depends
on its integrity but also on its configuration. To capture this, we define a map,
ConfigurationDataType, of all settings that may affect a component's behaviour
to the setting's values. For simplicity, we use Boolean expressions for specifying
these values, indicating whether a setting is activated or not.

In order to capture relationships between observed events in a system, we
identify three types of dependencies, *DependencyTypes*, that may exist between

---

[1] http://www.trustedcomputinggroup.org
[2] http://www.trustedcomputinggroup.org/files/static_page_files/
   20FB58C2-1D09-3519-AD9544FB0BC1F111/Reference_Manifest_v1_0.xsd

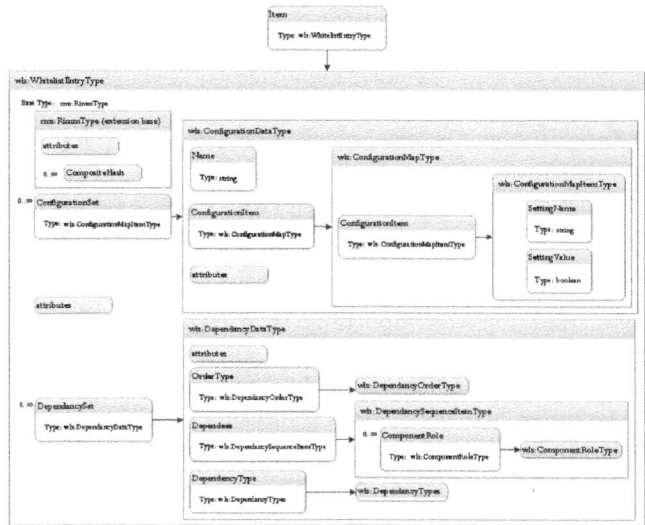

Fig. 3. Whitelist schema — an extension of *RimmType* from TCG RM Schema

components in the system: *Install, Execute* and *Config*. These capture the idea that a component may require another component to be installed, executed or configured in order for it to function correctly. Furthermore, a given dependency will be specified with *DependencyOrderType, Strict* or *Relaxed*, to indicate the constraints on the ordering of the dependencies.

We define *ComponentRoleType* to capture the roles in the system and *DependencyDataType* to represent the relationship of a component to other components that play given roles. *DependencyDataType* is captured as a sequence of roles (*Dependees*), the type of dependency (*DependenceTypes*), i.e. *Install. Config* or *Execute* and the order type (*Strict* or *Relaxed*).

We define *WhitelistEntryType* as a single entry on the whitelist, that extends the *RimmType* defined in the RM schema by adding a set of dependencies (*DependencySet*), a set of configuration settings (*ConfigurationSet*) and a unique identifier (*ID*). These entries are then combined into a set to complete the definition of the schema.

4.2   Specification Generation

The specifications in the repository are generated through a process that takes a dataset conforming to the whitelist schema, referred to as the *whitelist instance dataset*, and returns a set of specification processes and associated *abstraction sets*. It is divided into the following stages:

Instance decomposition. This stage involves extracting parts of the whitelist instance dataset that are required for a given property, and passing them on to an appropriate property-specific specification generator. Suppose we are interested in generating a specification that captures a property "every software component installed on a machine should be known". Given a whitelist instance dataset, WL_i, we first specify that unique identifiers, *UUIDs*, are required for this property. These are extracted from the parent *Rimm Type* of every *WhitelistEntry Type* and sent to the property-specific specification generator.

Property-specific specification generator. This generator takes parts of the *WhitelistEntry Type* and create processes that capture the intended property. In our example, the processor would take a set of *UUIDs*, S, and return a process which enforces that every *UUID* passed as data on the *install* channel must exist in S. This would be specified as a specification in CSP as follows:

$$SPEC_{exist\_on\_WL}(S) \;=\; \texttt{install.component:S} \;\rightarrow\; SPEC_{exist\_on\_WL}(S)$$

If the order of installation was important, then *Dependency Type* and *Order Type* would also be extracted and included in the specification.

Abstraction set generation. Checking a given process without careful consideration of the essential events would result in a refinement failure. Therefore, it is important that each specification is accompanied by an abstraction set. When creating an abstraction set, one must be careful not to hide information that may be required to prove (or disprove) a given property. In our example, an abstraction set, $A = \{\!|\texttt{install}|\!\}$, indicates that only the events that occurred on the *install* channel would be used. The abstraction sets are then combined with the related specifications as tuples $(SPEC, A)$, and stored in the repository.

5   Trace Analysis-Based Trustworthiness Verification

Our method for trustworthiness verification is based on analysing observed execution traces. Given an observed execution trace, S_o, a process model, P_s, that is capable of producing S_o is generated. P_s is then checked for refinement against the specifications in the repository. This section describes these steps in detail.

5.1   Trace-Process Transformation

The transformation of an execution trace into an equivalent process model can be done in multiple ways. One way would be to use denotational semantics of CSP, where the observed trace is transformed to the most non-deterministic process that chooses to perform the events in the given trace [7]. Roscoe [7] defines such a process, P, using the *traces* model, as follows:

```
P(<>)      = STOP
P(<tick>) = SKIP
P(<a>^s)  = a → P(s)
```

Furthermore, given any set of traces, S_o, a process, $P(S_o)$, capable of generating all the traces in the set can be defined as a non-deterministic choice of all the $P(s)$, where $s \in S_o$:

```
P(S_o) = ⊓ s:S_o • P(s)
```

For example, suppose the observed execution traces, S_o, is such that:

```
S_o = {<install.firewall, install.tomcat, config.firewall.default, reboot>,
        <start,install.java, install.scientific_app , shutdown>}
```

Then the resulting process would be:

```
P(Sₒ) = install.firewall → install.tomcat → config.firewall.default → SKIP
        ⊓ install.java → install.scientific_app → SKIP
```

Where '⊓' defines a non-deterministic choice operator which specifies a choice between the given events without regarding the events offered by the environment. Notice that some events in the trace such as *reboot* or *shutdown* may be translated to *SKIP*, while conditions such as *crash* may be translated to *STOP*, indicating successful operations or errors, respectively.

This approach may have limited practicality because the processes are not optimised for model checking. An alternative approach would be to use process mining techniques [13] to extract process models from the execution traces. A log file obtained from the virtual machine can be transformed into a process model using a framework such as the Process Mining (PROM) [15] and its associated toolkit [14]. A plug-in would be required to transform the log into a CSP model. Alternatively, the existing BPMN plug-in within the toolkit can be used to create a process model in BPMN, which in turn, can be translated into a CSP model using existing techniques proposed by Wong and Gibbons [6] or Flavio et al [1].

5.2   System Abstractions

Not every event that occurs on a running virtual machine is necessary to prove a given property. Therefore, we need to create representations of the system that would allow us to focus on the events necessary to reason about a given property. We propose the use of abstractions to generate these representations. For example, if we consider $P1$ (from the example above), then the system abstraction is a representation that hides all events other than those on the *install* channel. System abstractions are created using CSP's abstraction mechanisms with *abstraction sets* serving as the visible events. Suppose we have a process model P_S, and an abstraction set A, then the system abstraction, P_{S_A}, would be generated by hiding all the events that are not in A:

```
P_{S_A} = P_S \ diff(Events,A)
```

Where 'P \ x' is a CSP construct, implying that the resulting process behaves like P with all the events in the set X hidden.

5.3   Process Model Conformance to Infrastructure Model

Once the process model is generated, the next step is to verify whether the obtained model could have been generated by a system running within a given infrastructure. Conformance verification is performed in a similar way to conformance analysis in business processes [8,9]: system abstractions that hide all the events not represented within the infrastructure model are checked for refinement against the model of the infrastructure.

```
M [=T P\diff(Events,β)
```

Where, M is the model of the infrastructure with a set of possible events β, and P is the process model.

5.4   Refinements against the Whitelist

Finally, the abstract process model is checked for refinement against the specifications in the repository. The specifications used here must be mapped to the abstraction set that was used to create the system abstraction being checked. Given a mapping of specification to abstraction set, $(SPEC, A)$, the verification is performed as follows:

SPEC [=T P_{S_A}

The result will show whether the virtual appliance has executed any unacceptable event. If the process model fails a refinement check, *counterexamples* — explaining how that condition arises — are provided by the model checker.

6   Experiment

To demonstrate the feasibility and provide an easy-to-follow walkthrough of our method, we conducted a simple experiment: event logs were collected from two initially identical virtual machines that are running in a private cloud system setup using the Ubuntu Cloud Server[3].

Software installation events performed through the package manager were collected through *dkpg.log* and virtual machine management events through *nc.log* — the node controller log file. The list of events that were performed on both virtual machines is shown in Table 1.

Table 1. List of events performed on the virtual machines

events on VM1	events on VM2
1. install *firewall* firestarter	install *firewall* Lokkit
2. install *webserver* apache	config *firewall* (Custom settings)
3. config *firewall* (Default settings)	install *webserver* apache
4. config *webserver* (Webserver-Restricted)	config *webserver* (Webserver-Restricted)
5. install *app* Scientific Webapp	install *app* Scientific Webapp
6. execute *firewall*	execute *webserver*
7. execute *webserver*	execute *firewall*
8. execute *app*	execute *app*

where : Custom settings = {HTTP=1, SMTP=0, Telnet=1, SSH=0, FTP=1}

: Default settings = {HTTP=1, SMTP=0, Telnet=0, SSH=0, FTP=1)}

: Webserver-Restricted = {Includes=0, ConfigAccess=0, FollowSymLinks=0}

6.1   CSP Implementation of the Generator

A CSP implementation of the specification generator was developed according to the model described in Section 4.2. It was designed to generate specification processes that enable us to reason about the following properties:

1. A known firewall was installed with the correct configurations and activated before running the experiment.
2. The expected application was used to run the experiment.

---

[3] http://www.ubuntu.com/cloud/private

A whitelist instance dataset (not shown here given the space availability) was defined to include two firewalls, *Firestarter* and *Lokkit* with acceptable configurations (*Defaultsettings* = {*HTTP* = 1, *SMTP* = 0, *Telnet* = 0, *SSH* = 0, *FTP* = 1}) and a web server, *Apache*, with configuration (*Webserver* − *Restricted* = {*Includes* = 0, *ConfigAccess* = 0, *FollowSymLinks* = 0}). A simple application, which we called *Scientific webapp*, was defined to have dependencies on the installation and configuration of a firewall and the execution of a web server.

6.2   Extracted Processes

The collected logs were translated into CSP processes using a simple parser, which converts the individual entries in the log files into CSP events — channels with data. The events are then categorised according to the type, and arranged into a CSP process model. The generic model of the process models obtained is shown here:

```
VM_Extract(T) = start → (⊓ x : T ● x ....)
        [|vm_events_interface|]
        OrderEnforcement(T)
vm_events_interface = {|install, execute, config, uninstall, update|}
```

T is the trace of events obtained from a virtual machine, and *OrderEnforcement* is a function that enforces the order of events according to T.

6.3   Verification and Results

Verification was performed by checking the refinement of the extracted process models against the whitelist. We developed a model of the infrastructure which comprises of two virtual machines running in parallel, where each virtual machine interacts with a node controller process. The extracted process models were then checked for conformance against the infrastructure model. Each process model was abstracted using the abstraction set specified for a given specification and checked for refinement against the specifications in the repository (obtained from the generator implementation described in Section 6.1).

The results are shown in Table 2. Counterexamples obtained from the failed assertions show the divergence of events on *VM2* from the specifications. More specifically, the change in the firewall configuration, from *Telnet* = 0 to *Telnet* = 1, resulted in the failure of *SPEC_firewall_configured*; execution of the *webserver* before the *firewall* resulted in the failure of *SPEC_app_execute_dependence*.

Table 2. Results of assertions on the specifications

	VM1	VM2
1. *SPEC_firewall_installed*	pass	pass
2. *SPEC_firewall_configured*	pass	fail
3. *SPEC_app_installed*	pass	pass
4. *SPEC_app_execute_dependence*	pass	fail
5. *SPEC_app_config_dependence*	pass	pass

7 Observations

In this section, we make a number of observations and evaluate our method.

7.1 Satisfying the Requirements

Referring back to the case study in Section 1.1, our motivation was to make it possible for the users to verify the trustworthiness of virtual appliances before using them. Our method enables this by (1) recording the events of a running virtual machine, (2) translating the events into a process model, and finally, (3) verifying the model against specifications in a repository.

Requirement 1 (see Section 2) is satisfied by logging events on the virtual machine. For Requirement 2, we assumed that a trustworthy logging system is available to use. Requirement 3 is met by allowing the logs to be accessed by the verifiers. Requirement 4 is met by using the trace analysis approach that supports generation of the repository of specifications and process models of the virtual appliance events. The counterexamples in the verification process fulfill Requirement 5: if a virtual appliance does not satisfy a given property, counterexamples are provided, allowing the users to examine the steps leading to the failure.

7.2 Advantages over Traditional Whitelisting

Traditional whitelisting-based verification methods check whether an attested software component is listed on an application whitelist. These are restricted to specifications that consider each whitelist entry as an individual entity. Our method, on the other hand, is based on a formalism with semantics that facilitates reasoning about concurrency, enabling specification and verification of more powerful properties. For example, a database server might be required to conform to MYSQL configuration steps in Listing 1.1.

Listing 1.1. Example MYSQL configuration steps

```
+ yum install mysql-server mysql-connector-java
+ Configure to UTF-8
    + Modify /etc/my.conf
    + /etc/init.d/mysqld restart
+ run ''mysql'' to create the database and user
    + create database db_example;
    + use db_example;
    + grant all privileges on db_example.* to 'user'@'localhost';
```

Traditional whitelisting approach would enable one to verify that the expected version of MYSQL was installed and started, but will not that it was restarted after configuring the encoding (UTF-8) or that certain privileges were assigned to a given user. Our approach would allow one to verify that the exact process above has been performed in the required order and with the expected arguments passed to each step. In addition, it provides *counterexamples* upon failure to inform the users about the events that caused it.

7.3   Limitations of Common Log Files

During the experiment, we observed that the structure of common log files would only allow a small subset of properties (that are verifiable through our approach) to be verified. For instance, software integrity information is not recorded in the installation log files. To use our approach more effectively, the logging system would have to be configured to capture the information specified in Section 2.1. We intend to carry out further experiments to explore what kind of information would make the logs more useful for trustworthiness verification.

7.4   Custom Applications

In a collaborative research environment, custom applications may be developed and shared among collaborators. Custom applications as such may not exist in public repositories; hence, conventional installation mechanisms (e.g. package managers) may not be used. To solve this problem, our log analysis method can be combined with remote verification [3] to verify the compilation of applications.

7.5   Generalisation of Our Method

Our method is not limited to the verification of virtual appliances. The notion of having a repository of specifications can be applied to any application domain that requires verification of the observed traces of events against some desired properties. For example, events captured in a stored measurement log during the Trusted Computing authenticated boot process, could be translated into a process model; and used to verify a chain of trust against properties such as *measure before load, integrity and order of application execution.*

Although we used CSP in this work, our method can be applied to any other formalisms that has adequate semantics to handle possible concurrency in the execution, installation and configurations of applications. Our approach can also be used to verify events observed from processes that work together towards a common goal. For example, events observed from members of a trusted virtual domain [5] can be modeled as processes that work together to enforce a common policy, and verified against the specifications in the repository.

8   Related Work

A similar idea has been proposed by Ulrich et al. [12]. Their tracing-based analysis system checks security requirements of a distributed system by generating event logs at runtime and using them to reason about the implementation of the requirements. More specifically, the event logs (collected during system run) are processed into a specification of a system, which in turn, is checked against predefined security requirements using the SDL model checker.

Aalst et al. [13] have developed an algorithm for extracting a process model from a workflow log and a method for representing the model in terms of Petri net. Here, the workflow log contains information about the workflow process as it is being executed. Something like their approach, in our opinion, could be extended and used together with our approach to construct the process models representing the virtual machine executions.

Having realized the complexity of correctly configuring virtual infrastructures to conform to enterprise security policies, Bleikertz et al. [10] have described an automated virtual infrastructure validation and assurance system. Their system unifies the configurations of virtualization infrastructures (e.g. virtual machines) into a generic data model. This data model is then visualized through a data flow graph, which in turn, is used to detect any breach of security requirements.

9   Conclusions and Future Work

In collaborative research environments, a virtual appliance published through one virtual organisation may be used by another either as a basis for a new experiment or as an extension/rerun of an experiment. In such cases, the virtual appliance configuration is critical for both integrity and accuracy of the experiment results, and should be verified before using it.

To facilitate reliable sharing of virtual appliances, we proposed a formal methods based approach for verifying the events that occurred on virtual appliances. Using our method, the event logs are processed into a process model, which is, in turn, verified against properties captured in the repository of specifications — the whitelist. The verification results indicate whether or not the process model could have performed events that are not permitted by the specifications. Unlike the traditional whitelisting approaches, our method allows complex properties, including concurrency, order and dependency, to be modeled and checked.

We intend to develop a more generic method by simplifying the specification of properties and abstracting the finer details and to experiment with various virtual appliance usage scenarios and varying log data.

Acknowledgements

The work described here was supported by the Rhodes Trust and by a grant arising from a gift to the Computing Laboratory by Prof. Sir Tony Hoare. Presentation of this paper is supported by EU FP7 Project TClouds (project 257243) and by UK TSB Project Trust Domains (ref. TS/I002634/1). We would like to thank Dr. David Wallom from OeRC for insights on the requirements and his input on the case study.

References

1. Flavio, C., Alberto, A., Barbara, R., Damiano, F.: An eclipse plug-in for formal verification of bpmn processes. In: International Conference on Communication Theory, Reliability, and Quality of Service, vol. 0, pp. 144–149 (2010)
2. Huh, J., Martin, M.: Trusted logging for grid computing. In: Third Asia-Pacific Trusted Infrastructure Technologies Conference, October 2008, pp. 30–42. IEEE Computer Society, Los Alamitos (2008)

3. Lyle, J.: Trustable remote verification of web services. In: Chen, L., Mitchell, C.J., Martin, A. (eds.) Trust 2009. LNCS, vol. 5471, pp. 153–168. Springer, Heidelberg (2009)
4. Huh, J.H., Lyle, J., Namiluko, C., Martin, A.: Managing application whitelists in trusted distributed systems. Future Generation Computer Systems (2010), (in Press, accepted manuscript)
5. Griffin, J.L., Jaeger, T., Perez, R., Sailer, R., Doorn, L., Caceres, R.: Trusted virtual domains: Toward secure distributed services. In: 1st Workshop on Hot Topics in System Dependability (2005)
6. Wong, P.Y.H., Gibbons, J.: A Process Semantics for BPMN. In: Liu, S., Araki, K. (eds.) ICFEM 2008. LNCS, vol. 5256, pp. 355–374. Springer, Heidelberg (2008), 10.1007/978-3-540-88194-0_22
7. Roscoe, A.W.: The Theory and Practice of Concurrency. Prentice Hall PTR, Upper Saddle River (1997)
8. Rozinat, A., van der Aalst, W.M.P.: Conformance checking of processes based on monitoring real behavior. Inf. Syst. 33(1), 64–95 (2008)
9. Rozinat, A., van der Aalst, W.M.P.: Conformance Testing: Measuring the Fit and Appropriateness of Event Logs and Process Models. In: Bussler, C.J., Haller, A. (eds.) BPM 2005. LNCS, vol. 3812, pp. 163–176. Springer, Heidelberg (2006), 10.1007/11678564_15
10. Bleikertz, S., Gross, T., Schunter, M., Eriksson, K.: Automating Security Audits of Heterogeneous Virtual Infrastructures (August 2010), http://infrasightlabs.com/wp-content/uploads/2010/08/rz3786.pdf
11. Sailer, R., Zhang, X., Jaeger, T., Doorn, L.: Design and implementation of a TCG-based integrity measurement architecture. In: SSYM 2004: Proceedings of the 13th conference on USENIX Security Symposium, pages 16–16. USENIX Association, Berkeley (2004)
12. Ulrich, A., Hallal, H., Petrenko, A., Boroday, S.: Verifying trustworthiness requirements in distributed systems with formal log-file analysis. In: Hawaii International Conference on System Sciences, vol. 9, p. 337b (2003)
13. van der Aalst, W., Weijters, T., Maruster, L.: Workflow mining: Discovering process models from event logs. IEEE Trans. on Knowl. and Data Eng. 16(9), 1128–1142 (2004)
14. van der Aalst, W.M.P., van Dongen, B.F., Günther, C.W., Rozinat, A., Verbeek, E., Weijters, T.: Prom: The process mining toolkit. In: de Medeiros, A.K.A., Weber, B. (eds.) BPM (Demos), CEUR Workshop Proceedings, vol. 489 (2009), CEUR-WS.org
15. van Dongen, B.F., de Medeiros, A.K.A., Verbeek, H.M.W(E.), Weijters, A.J.M.M.T., van der Aalst, W.M.P.: The proM framework: A new era in process mining tool support. In: Ciardo, G., Darondeau, P. (eds.) ICATPN 2005. LNCS, vol. 3536, pp. 444–454. Springer, Berlin (2005)

Towards a Trustworthy, Lightweight Cloud Computing Framework for Embedded Systems

Kurt Dietrich and Johannes Winter

Institute for Applied Information Processing and Communications (IAIK)
Graz, University of Technology
Inffeldgasse 16a, 8010 Graz, Austria
{Kurt.Dietrich,Johannes.Winter}@iaik.tugraz.at

Abstract. Embedded systems are gradually evolving into alternatives to desktop and server systems in terms of performance, energy- and cost efficiency. Moreover, with the improvement of their performance and storage capabilities, they are about to enter the domain of desktop systems and cloud computing. However, the question remains whether such systems can be used in cloud computing scenarios in a secure and energy efficient way or not and, if this is not the case, how do they have to be enhanced and which components are missing. In this paper, we present an approach to how cloud computing can be realized securely on embedded systems by means of embedded Trusted Computing. We provide a reference design of a micro-data-center and present an analysis covering the topics of performance, security as well as energy consumption. Moreover, we discuss our concept for a light-weight virtualization framework which is specifically tailored to the requirements of embedded systems.

1 Introduction

Distributed computation and storage are major issues and applications in today's cloud computing scenarios. Moving services into the "cloud" allows flexibility in terms of service availability which means that more resources can be provided if the demand increases, or are reduced during idle times. Moreover, companies and end-users can reduce their overhead and their total costs by sharing resources. New cost-models may be employed, allowing services to be charged dependent on the user's resource consumption. Cloud services provide dynamical availability during crunch periods, enabling the service providers to further optimize their hardware resources.

Typical cloud-computing scenarios involve large data centers hosting applications on numerous servers and providing their capabilities to the cloud. Nevertheless, any kind of computing system has the possibility to provide its resources to the cloud - even resource constrained embedded systems. Most approaches and publications focus either on large data-centers for providing services to the cloud or they view data centers on embedded platforms as sets of home PCs with limitations in computational capabilities and availability. However, we want to investigate the idea of data centers on embedded systems and discuss their requirements in order to create secure and trustworthy *micro data centers*.

J.M. McCune et al. (Eds.): TRUST 2011, LNCS 6740, pp. 16–32, 2011.

Nowadays, embedded systems are used in many industrial and consumer devices. There is a broad range of use-cases and applications for such systems, starting from mobile phones to car electronics and remote sensor-nodes. In a futuristic vision and future use-case scenarios, all these embedded systems may act as micro data centers where information can be stored and processed and which are able to provide these services to the cloud. However, to achieve this goal we have to focus on major building blocks for this scenario which are security and trust. Establishing trust is important in order to convince the end-user that his data is stored or processed in a secure and trustworthy environment. Security is required to keep the processed information confidential, thereby further increasing the level of trust.

1.1 Our Contribution

There are several issues to be addressed and problems to be solved in order to create a secure embedded node that can be used in a cloud scenario like, e.g., the problem of energy efficiency. "Green IT" is one of the most popular areas in research today. Consequently, the question arises how cloud computing could be done in practice with the constraints of efficient energy utilization. Therefore, we use embedded systems for our micro data centers that are specially designed for low-power consumption and without the requirement of active cooling which would otherwise increase the overall power consumption.

From our point of view, a micro data center is a small embedded system with relatively strong computational powers (for a small system) and limited memory resources like the typical platforms that can be found in today's smart-phones, car- and consumer-electronics or remote sensor nodes. The hardware installed in these systems typically consists of a strong CPU - modern platforms already use multi core CPUs with a clock frequency of 1 GHz and beyond - and are equipped with memory of 64 MBytes and more. We present an approach which allows to use our definition of micro data centers in a secure and trustworthy way using state-of-the art security extensions on current embedded systems. We show how our approach can benefit from embedded trusted computing and which requirements in terms of hard- and software have to be fulfilled in order to get an embedded system platform that provides its resources to the cloud in a secure and trustworthy way. In addition, we provide an investigation of the power consumption of our approach in order to give an estimation of possible power savings in contrast to other approaches.

A key mechanism to cloud computing is *virtualization*. Virtualization allows the execution of applications in separated domains, thereby providing strong isolation between different processes. However, hardware supported virtualization as it is available on desktop and server systems is currently only available by the upcoming Cortex-A15 platform [1]. Hence, we address the topic of virtualization in our approach and provide a framework for light-weight virtualization which is especially designed to fit in small embedded environments. We give a discussion of the features of our framework and the required security mechanisms for implementing our concept.

1.2   Related Work

There are numerous publications on cloud computing available today. The most important ones with respect to our contribution are from Armbrust et al. [2] and Santos et al. [3]. Armbrust et al. provide an in-depth discussion of cloud computing. They provide a definition of what cloud computing is and how it emerged from grid-computing. Moreover, they discuss the economic effects of cloud computing and potential bottlenecks of this concept [2]. Santos et al. [3] give a definition of a trusted cloud computing platform and provide a discussion of the problem of how a user can verify the confidentiality and integrity of his data and computation. Moreover, they discuss how their trusted cloud platform can attest whether or not the service is secure before it launches a new virtual compartment.

Our approach can be used in different usage-scenarios. For example, one use-case addresses a single node that could be a cell phone or another embedded node which contributes its resources to the "cloud". The second use-case focuses on using micro data centers in smaller or medium-sized clusters, where many embedded nodes are connected in a center-like structure.

In the first scenario, we have a single node that is used and controlled by a specific device owner. In the second scenario, we have multiple nodes that offer their computational resources to the cloud. However, both scenarios share the requirement of, e.g, providing a proof of the trustworthiness of the platform. The single platforms have to provide a proof of their current configuration and the overall integrity of the platform. This can be achieved by means of trusted computing as we will discuss in the following sections.

The rest of the article is organized as follows. In section 2 we provide an overview of our concept. Section 3 deals with aspects of trust establishment and security requirements and how they can be met by our concept. Section 4 provides a discussion of our reference implementation and the measured results. Finally, section 5 concludes our contribution with a brief summary of our results.

2   Concept and Architecture Overview

In this section we discuss our concept of micro data centers starting with the description of our *μcompartment architecture*. Conceptually, each micro data center can be described as a container for managing and running one or more light-weight compartments. Each of these so-called μcompartments consists of executable code, static and dynamic data and a manifest describing the compartment's properties and security requirements.

Figure 1 visualizes the overall structure of the μcompartment architecture. Each individual μcompartment is based on an isolation container enclosing the code and data of the compartment. The realization of these light-weight containers on top of the Linux kernel is discussed in greater detail in section 2.1. Each compartment is monitored and managed by a per-compartment supervisor application. The responsibilities of the compartment supervisor (CSUP) include

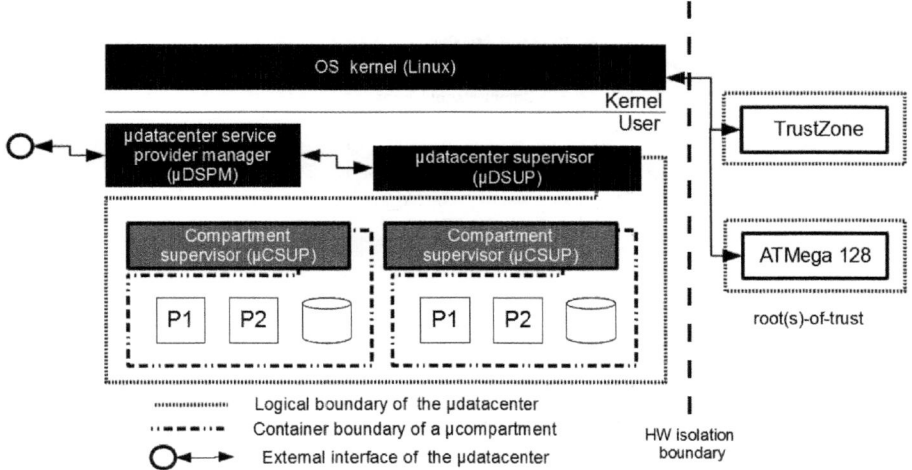

Fig. 1. Overview of the micro data center architecture

construction and destruction of the compartment as well as enforcement of security policies. By design, each compartment supervisor is responsible for exactly one μcompartment in order to keep the implementation of the supervisors small and simple. Support for handling multiple μcompartments is provided by the micro data center supervisor (DSUP) which defines the logical domain of a micro data center comprised by its child μcompartments. The DSUP is responsible for starting, stopping and monitoring the CSUPs of a micro data center. The μcompartment data center service provider manager (DSPM) is responsible for handling the communication of the node with the cloud. This communication may include requests to execute a certain image or information about the platform's configuration i.e. attestation information. Moreover, the DSPM verifies the integrity of the incoming compartments by verifying the signature that is attached to the immutable compartment image. This image contains the compartment executable code and further the signatures on compartments, manifest and static and dynamic data. After the verification of the signatures, the DSPM hands over the components of the compartment to the DSUP which afterwards initializes and launches the compartment.

Figure 2 shows the layout of a μcompartment when it is transferred to another node. The data associated with a μcompartment is classified in four categories according to its mutability and persistence properties.

Static, constant resources (immutable, persistent data). This resource type contains the static executable binary which is executed in the compartment.

Dynamic constant resources (immutable, transient data). This resource contains static data related to the compartment like the manifest.

Persistent compartment data (mutable, persistent data). This resource type contains dynamic data (e.g. data that is the result of a computation).

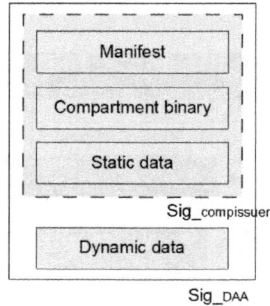

Fig. 2. μcompartment layout

This kind of data is attached to the satic compartment data before transfer to another micro data center.

Temporary compartment data (mutable, transient). Temporary compartment data is data that is used during execution on the platform. This kind of data is deleted when the compartment is closed, it is not transferred to other platform.

The immutable data and the executable binaries are signed by a trusted compartment issuer in order to guarantee authenticity and integrity of the compartment. The combination of dynamic data and the immutable data is signed by the node on which the data has been processed and which has generated the dynamic data before the compartment is sent to another node. One of the key requirements of micro data centers is to provide a reasonably strong level of isolation between individual compartments. Ideally, it should be impossible for any compartment to modify or observe the behavior of any other compartment in an unauthorized manner. Within our design, we try to fulfill this requirement by considering various light-weight mechanisms for strengthening isolation boundaries between individual compartments.

2.1 Reducing the Visible System Surface

We expect μcompartments to require access to local file system resources for the purposes of storing temporary computation results as well as persistent non-volatile data.

A large variety of access control mechanisms which are available in the Linux kernel and which could be used to implement the file system access control policies for μcompartments exist. The set of available mechanisms spans a broad range covering relatively simple UNIX file permissions to highly sophisticated (and complex) mandatory access control implementations like SELinux[1] or TO-MOYO Linux[2]. Support for Linux Security Modules (LSMs) providing a pluggable infrastructure suitable for implementing almost arbitrary custom security

---

[1] http://www.nsa.gov/research/selinux/
[2] http://tomoyo.sourceforge.jp/

models has been around for several years [4]. Security functionality implemented in LSMs is not restricted to access control, as demonstrated by the TPM-based Integrity Measurement Architecture [5] LSM which aims to implement TCG-style integrity reporting on top of an LSM.

On the first glance, it appears to be suitable to pick and use one of these security mechanisms, which are readily available as an LSM to implement isolation between compartments. However, there are issues when using these approaches in architectures like the μcompartment architecture where low-overhead and simple compartment setup are key design goals. The μcompartments envisioned by our architecture have highly dynamic semantics with a rather short life-cycle on the platform.

In case of one of the mandatory access control LSMs mentioned above, it would be required to reconfigure access control rules and policies each time a new μcompartment is about to be started. The performance overhead incurred by this step might be negligible. However, security implications of dynamically changing parts of the access control policies require particularly close consideration.

Namespaces. Linux provides namespaces as a low-overhead mechanism to build containers with a restricted view of the entire system. Basically, each of the five supported types of namespaces controls the visibility of a specific kind of system resource like IPC communication objects, networking stack properties, visible mount points, process IDs and system identification information.

In principle, Linux namespaces can be seen as a generalization of the `chroot` system call found on a large number of UNIX-like operating systems including Linux. The normal `chroot` system call allows privileged processes to select an alternate file system root directory ("/") before dropping their privileges. As such, `chroot` offers a coarse mechanism to restrict the view of an application on the file system independent of any other file and directory permissions.

Linux namespaces generalize this idea beyond simply changing the file system root directory with the intent to provide isolated containers. Using these containers it becomes possible to realize operating system level virtualization with a minimum amount of overhead.

2.2   Monitoring and Filtering System Calls

Like any other application, the μcompartments will request services from the operating system kernel via system calls. A simple, yet effective method to restrict the possible actions which can be performed by a compartment is to monitor its system call usage. When only considering single threaded applications, it seems appealing to simply intercept and check each potentially dangerous system call.

Security considerations. There are, however, serious problems with system call monitoring, as for example shown by [6] and [7]. In particular, system calls with complex arguments including (multiple) levels of pointer indirection and any kind of thread or process level parallelism complicate the task of properly implementing system call monitoring . The authors of [7] give a striking example of race conditions in system call monitoring software which can cause tools like ''sudo'' to lead to elevation of privileges.

Existing infrastructure. All recent Linux kernel versions contain seccomp which provides a very simple yet secure system call monitoring mechanism. Once seccomp mode is enabled for a process, the set of allowed system calls is closely restricted, usually to only write, read and return from signal handlers. Any attempt to invoke another system call causes immediate termination of the offending process.

Seccomp avoids issues with race conditions due to its special integration within the Linux kernel's system call dispatch mechanism and due to the restriction on only checking the system call number but not any of the call arguments.

The default system call restrictions of seccomp mode 1 (read, write, exit, sigreturn) were sufficient for crunching applications in the now defunct CPUShare[3] project. Unfortunately, the very limited set of system calls allowed in mode 1 makes it impractical to use seccomp for other real-world issues. The Linux kernel patch at [8] tries to rectify this situation by adding an alternate seccomp mode 2 with a per-process bitmap listing the allowed system calls.

Apart from seccomp, multiple other ways of monitoring or tracing system calls under Linux including the ptrace(2) system call or one of the in-kernel tracing mechanisms listed in [9] exist.

2.3 Simple Capabilities for μcompartments

As stated earlier, we want to to exercise control over system calls which processes inside a μcompartment might try to perform. The seccomp extension from [8] provides a lightweight tool to enforce simple restrictions and to exercise the principle of least privileges on μcompartments and on individual processes inside μcompartments.

Based upon the usage scenarios for micro data centers discussed in section 1 we can derive different sets of functionality required by μcompartments. More precisely it is possible to define capabilities of μcompartments which have a direct mapping to groups of related system calls, which might be executed by processes running within a compartment.

For our prototype realization of the μcompartment architecture we defined several capabilities which can be assigned to individual processes within μcompartments. In the remainder of this section, we discuss these capabilities and outlines associated problems.

Generic File I/O. The generic file input/output capability allows processes inside a μcompartment to create and manipulate files within the compartment. The capability group includes the standard I/O system calls like open, close, read, write, lseek and others. The use of filesystem namespaces, as discussed

---

[3] Archived at: http://web.archive.org/web/20080620091222/
   http://www.cpushare.com/

in section 2.1, automatically confines any file open and file create operations to the boundaries of the container spanned by a μcompartment.

There is one important caveat with granting file I/O operations to compartments: A malicious compartment could try to use the file descriptors passed in by the compartment manager application to break the boundaries of its enclosing container. A simple instantiation of this attack would be to execute a "file relative" system calls like `openat` against a file descriptor passed in by the compartment manager.

Subprocesses and multi-threading. This capability enables μcompartments to start, manage and kill their own subprocesses. Each μcompartment executes within a separate process-ID namespace,thus preventing malicious compartments to interfere with outside processes by sending signals to them. Mitigation of fork-bombs triggered by malicious compartments can be done by setting appropriate resource limits or by monitoring process creation and termination events from within the compartment manager application.

Full Network I/O. Another capability which can be granted to μcompartments is network input/output and access to the sockets interface. On several platform architectures (including ARM) Linux uses a *single* `socketcall` multiplexer system call for most socket operations due to historical reasons (see eg. [10]).

This multiplexer system call dispatches requests to most of the socket interface system calls including functions to create sockets, establish outgoing connection and accept incoming connections. Extracting the actual socket operation to be performed requires inspection of the system call parameters, which can be tricky to implement as discussed at the beginning of section 2.2.

In our prototype implementation, we experimented with strategies to tackle this problem. The simplest strategy we came up with is to establish outgoing network connections in the compartment manager application and to pass the corresponding socket file descriptors to the μcompartment on startup. Obviously this simple solution is only applicable to compartments for which a fixed set of stream (e.g. TCP) network connections is sufficient.

Another more complex strategy we experimented with is to actually investigate the system call parameters passed to the `socketcall` system call. We only need to investigate the first parameter of this system call to decide on the desired socket operation. Fortunately, the first call parameter is passed in a processor register which allows us to investigate it from within the compartment manager application without risking race-condition problems mentioned earlier. Section 4.4 describes a trick used in our prototype implementation to reduce the performance impact of system call monitoring using a simple pre-fitlering technique.

3   Trust Establishment

Our design relies on different roots-of-trust. The core components for establishing these roots in our concept are the root-of-trust for measurement (RTM), the root-of-trust for storage (RTS), root-of-trust for reporting (RTR), root-of-trust-for-enforcement (RTE) and the root-of-trust for verification as discussed in [11]. An additional requirement for building the roots-of-trust is the *Secure Boot* [11] concept. In our approach, we implement these roots either by means of the TrustZone CPU security extension [12] (e.g. the RTS, RTR, RTE can be enforced resp. implemented inside the TrustZone as discussed in [13]) or by means of a dedicated micro controller as discussed in section 3.2.

Furthermore, the secure boot can be established as discussed in [14], requiring at least a root-of-trust for verification installed on the platform as proposed in [15].

3.1 ARM TrustZone

The TrustZone architecture is a CPU security extension for smart-phones. Basically, it provides a separation of the memory resources and the CPU of a device, thereby creating two virtual domains which are the *secure-* and *normal world* [12]. This approach is an improvement to the basic concept of privileged/unprivileged-mode-split which can be found on many systems including earlier ARM cores. While user programs or any kind of untrusted applications are executed in the normal-world, security critical code is executed in the secure world. The isolation mechanisms of the TrustZone prohibit normal world applications from accessing the secure world. Furthermore, the data flow between both worlds is controlled by a *secure monitor*, which is under control of the secure world. The secure world may be controlled by a high-security operating system kernel. Typically, such a kernel is a small - in some cases security evaluated and certified - operating system core that fits into the memory of a TrustZone platform. The total memory available for software inside the TrustZone is vendor dependent and ranges from 64 kBytes up to 256 kBytes on typical systems. The security kernel may support the installation and execution of trusted executables inside the TrustZone, however, the security kernel and the trusted application must meet the memory constraints of the vendor.

One of the most important features for establishing trust is the knowledge of the actual manufacturer of the security extension. While TPMs provide this information via the endorsement-key (EK) and the endorsement certificate which clearly identifies the vendor and which allows the user of the TPM to assert certain trust assumptions on the TPM, TrustZone implementations lack this kind of certification. Best to our knowledge, existing TrustZone implementations are not equipped with a specific vendor identifier like the EK-certificate. Hence, it is hard to determine the genuinity of a certain TrustZone implementation for the verifier. Fortunately, TrustZone enabled systems allow to install keys for the purpose of authentication. As a consequence, micro data centers that are used in our scenario have to be equipped with a certified key that take over the role of an EK by a trusted third party prior to its deployment. Typically, TrustZone implementors provide a symmetric device-key for device identification and an asymmetric key for the purpose of secure boot. As a result, any further asymmetric key, like the EK from the trusted-third-party has to be stored outside the TrustZone. For security purposes, these keys may be encrypted and integrity protected by the symmetric device-key and stored on the platform outside the TrustZone environment [16].

With the EK, the EK-certificate and the RTR and RTS, the platform is now able to provide proof of the current configuration via remote-attestation as discussed in [17]. Summing up, our platform incorporates the different roots-of-trust and the secure boot by using the TrustZone security extension - the TrustZone and its software components basically takes of the functionality of a mobile TPM [18]. Moreover, we can conduct a secure boot process and remote-attestation as defined by the Trusted Computing Group (TCG).

3.2 Dedicated Micro-controller

A more traditional approach is to use a TPM-like approach such as the one used on desktop systems [17]. This approach involves a dedicated micro-controller which hosts the TPM functionality and executes the TPM functions separated from the main CPU, thereby providing not only a shielded location and protected capabilities. It also hosts the RTS and RTR. Moreover, this TPM like device may be used as a basis for for a secure boot process. Such a design can be realized by attaching an additional micro-controller to our platform. Details for this approach can be found in the prototype discussion in section 4.

However, the same drawbacks as for the TrustZone approach apply here. This dedicated micro-controller is typically not equipped with an EK nor with an EK-certificate. In addition, this platform also lacks a security security evaluation failing to provide an designated level of security-assurance.

Fortunately, the micro-controller is equipped with non-volatile memory, allowing permanent data, such as key material to be installed inside the device. Moreover, this data may locked by fuses in order to prevent overwriting the keys or the firmware of the controller. This way, the controller can be equipped with an EK and corresponding certificate.

Like the TrustZone approach, micro-controller approach allows easy update of the firmware respectively TPM functionality as discussed in [19].

Both approaches require a Trusted Software Stack (TSS) in order to allow the data center service provider manager to use their services. To provide this service for both approaches, we rely on the proposal of Dietrich and Winter [19].

The DSPM is responsible for handling requests to the platform like service requests that deal with the management of the software and provided resources and the management of our micro compartments (see section 2. Moreover, it is responsible for providing information about the trust status of the platform - in our scenario in the style of TCG remote-attestation TPM_QUOTE responses [20]. The integrity information collected during the boot process of the micro data center platform is then provided to the requester, proving the integrity of the system's hypervisor/supervisor.

In our prototype scenario, the integrity information of the single compartments is not included for two reasons: First, we assume that the applications running in the compartments are not able to break the compartment isolation, and second, the integrity and the authenticity of each of the compartment binaries is provided by a digital signature.

In our prototype environment, the single micro compartments and its applications are not able to access the TSS or TPM features at the moment.

3.3 Support for Privacy Protection

In some cloud computing scenarios, it is not necessary for the end-user to know where his data was moved to or where it has been processed. Moreover, the micro data centers do not need to know whose data they are processing and on which other micro data centers it has been processed before. Therefore, our design provides anonymity protection by means of anonymous group signatures. As discussed in section 2, the micro compartments have to be signed before they are moved from one node to the other in order to cryptographically bind the dynamic data to the compartment image and the manifest. This signature is created with a specific key which has been issued to the device previously which is in our concept an anonymous group signature key and certificate. Therefore, we use the direct-anonymous-attestation (DAA) feature of our TPM implementations, which allow us to create such a signature on the compartments before they are sent to another node. This can be done either by signing the compartment directly with an DAA signature or - because of performance reasons [21] - with an ephemeral key which is certified by a DAA signature prior to signing the compartment. The signature on the compartment enables the receiving node to check the integrity of the compartment and the authenticity of the sending node without revealing the sending node's identity. This approach requires that the nodes have obtained a group credential according to the DAA specification [17] and that they maintain a list with trusted DAA issuers.

3.4 Trust Layer

The service provider manager is responsible for managing the attestation process and DAA signature/verification creation process. Therefore, it requires a connection to one of our TPM implementations. For the interface, we use the light-weight TSS implementation discussed in [22] which provides a simple API and which is especially designed to fit the requirements of embedded systems. The layer is able to use either the TrustZone based TPM or the micro-controller based TPM.

4 Prototype Implementation and Test Setup

In this section, we discuss our proof-of-concept reference implementation and the hardware platforms used to evaluate it. We selected two hardware platforms with different capabilities and performance characteristics. The tiny hardware platform discussed in section 4.1 resembles a typical embedded system found in PDA and mobile phone platforms. These simple hardware platforms usually do not include dedicated security hardware which requires the use of a separate micro controller to provide a trust anchor. In context of the tiny hardware platform which resembles a battery powered device, power consumption becomes a major issue. Thus, we give some figures on current energy consumption with and without active micro data centers in section 4.5.

To demonstrate how the micro data center approach scales to more powerful next generation PDA and mobile phone platforms we also selected a "large" reference platform as described in section 4.2. This powerful platform provides dedicated hardware security building blocks which eliminate the need to implement the trust anchor in a separate micro controller.

4.1   Tiny Hardware Reference Platform

The tiny hardware reference platform for our prototype consists of a Gumstix Verdex XL6P embedded platform [23] which represents a typical embedded platform based on a 32-bit ARM processor. It is equipped with a Marvell PXA270 processor (ARMv5), 128 MBytes of RAM, 32 MBytes of flash memory (not used in our experiments) and a microSD card socket. For our experiments, we used a 1 GByte microSD card loaded with a minimal root filesystem image based on the Linux 2.6.31 kernel.

Fig. 3. Gumstix/Robostix reference platform

To model a dedicated micro-controller which hosts TPM-like functionality, we use the robostix expansion board [24]. This board is equipped with an Atmel ATMega128 micro-controller. The ATMega128 is an 8-bit AVR controller with 128 kBytes of flash memory, 4 kBytes of internal SRAM and 4 kBytes of EEP-ROM memory for holding non-volatile data. It supports a variety of interfaces including Bluetooth, the wifi standards 802.11(b) / 802.11(g), USB and ethernet.

Figure 3 depicts the tiny hardware reference platform with the Gumstix board containing the microSD slot on top and the Robostix motherboad below. The microSD card and the SD card adapter on top of the image are shown to give a reference for size comparison.

Communication between the ARM processor residing on the Gumstix board and the AVR controller on the Robostix daugther-board is done over a standard I^2C bus interface. The basic usage-scenario is similar to the usage scenario for trusted desktop systems as discussed in [25].

4.2   MHigh-End Mobile Phone Reference Platform

The mobile phone hardware reference platform for the micro data center prototype is a RealView Versatile Express [26] board fitted with an ARM Cortex-A9
quad-core processor. It is equipped with 1GB of dynamic RAM and various
non-volatile memories including NOR flash memory, an SD card reader and a
compact flash adapter. Depending on the detailed configuration this development platform can be used to model embedded systems like PDAs or mobile
phones.

Fig. 4. RealView Versatile Express reference platform

Figure 4 depicts the partly opened development platform, showing the μATX
motherboard fitted with an FPGA tile implementing base system peripherals in
front (the FPGA resides directly below the fan) and the quad-core Cortex-A9
tile in the back. For comparison of the physical size, the Gumstix board is shown
at the bottom of the picture.

The Cortex-A9 processor found on this development platform implements ARM
TrustZone technology which can be used effectively to eliminate the need for an external micro-controller as hardware anchor of trust. In our prototype micro data
center implementation on the RealView platform, we use a tiny secure monitor
running in the TrustZone secure-world to host TPM-like functionality required
for attestation and secure boot. The main Linux operating systems and the consequently, the μcompartments execute exclusively in TrustZone normal-world.

4.3   Prototype Software Implementation

The prototype software implementation of the μcompartment architecture consists of a small C library implementing a framework for handling μcompartments
and a simple compartment manager and monitor application. To start a
μcompartment it is sufficient to simply invoke the manager application and pass
a description of the compartment on the command line.

The total total code base of the compartment manager and its support framework library including basic system call monitoring and Linux name space support consists of approximately 1500 lines of C source code.

The core implementation of the secure monitor used on the platform discussed in 4.2 consists of approximately 1000 lines of C code and 780 lines of assembly code (excluding C runtime library support). The code required to implement TPM-like functionality largely depends on the used cryptographic libraries and the desired level of TCG-compatibility.

4.4 Pre-filtered System Call Monitoring

In section 2.2 we noted that it can be desirable to investigate some of the parameters of certain system calls like the socket call multiplexer to get a more detailed picture of the actions a μcompartment is trying to perform.

Unfortunately, the straightforward solution to intercept *all* system calls done by the processes of a single μcompartment has severe disadvantages. Each system call executed by any of the processes in a μcompartment would end up in two notifications of the compartment manager application on system call entry and exit. The resulting overhead would be at least four context switches between the compartment manager and the trapped process inside the μcompartment. Due to this extra overhead, performance would significantly decrease.

Within our prototype implementation, we found a simple yet very effective trick to reduce the overall number of switches into the compartment manager: With a slight modification, seccomp can be used to pre-filter the system calls issued by processes inside a μcompartment. In order to realize this pre-filtering mechanism we implemented an alternate error path for failed system call checks in seccomp. Instead of immediately killing the offending process our modification traps into the compartment manager application.

This way, we are able to use the seccomp system call white list to pre-filter the "uninteresting" system calls which should be directly handled by the Linux kernel without notifying the compartment manager. Notifications to the compartment manager application are only generated when a non white-listed system call is encountered. In those cases, the compartment manager can decide whether the system call should proceed or it can emulate the standard seccomp behavior and simply kill the offending process.

4.5 Prototype Results

In this section, we provide an overview of the energy and performance characteristics of our platform.

Table 5 shows the current consumption of the prototype reference platform under various configurations. All values shown in the table were measured at the maximum clock frequency (600 MHz) of the prototype platform. The first row gives the current consumption of the idle system with no compartments running. The second row shows the current consumption when our test application is run natively on the platform without any μcompartment support being activate. In contrast to the idle system, current (and consequently power) consumption have increased to more than twice the base value. Enclosing the test application in a simple μcompartment without explicit system call monitoring performed in

Test case	Current consumption
Idle system	120 mA
Application run natively	280 mA
μcompartment without syscall monitoring	280 mA
μcompartment with full syscall monitoring	290 mA

Fig. 5. Current consumption measured on the Gumstix prototype platform

user-space by the compartment manager application does not increase the power consumption as visible in the third row of table 5. If we additionally enable full user-space system call monitoring in the compartment manager application power consumption increases slightly due to the additional system load caused by the additional overhead incurred by the system call monitor.

5   Conclusion

Cloud computing and its applications are in the focus of a lot of researchers at the moment and will gain more and more attention in the near future. In addition, embedded systems are becoming more and more powerful computer systems with increased processing power and memory equipment allowing these platforms to carry out more and more computational and memory demanding tasks. Along with these increased capabilities comes the possibility to use these platforms in cloud computing scenarios. In this paper, we showed how the concept of cloud computing can be expanded to embedded systems like the ones that are used in today's mobile handsets and consumer electronics. We discussed the requirements for our concept concerning security and trust and how they can be achieved with these platforms. Moreover, we provided an analysis of the energy consumption of our concept in different situations and we discussed our concept of μcompartments which is especially tailored to the requirements of embedded systems. Furthermore, our approach shows a good balance between energy consumption and computational powers and our lightweight μcompartments concept allows a secure and simple approach to virtualization on embedded systems.

Acknowledgements. This work has been supported by the European Commission through project FP7-2009.1.4(c)-SEPIA, Grant agreement number 257433.

References

1. ARM Ltd.: Cortex-A15 Processor, http://www.arm.com/products/processors/cortex-a/cortex-a15.php5
2. Armbrust, M., Fox, A., Griffith, R., Joseph, A.D., Katz, R., Konwinski, A., Lee, G., Patterson, D., Rabkin, A., Stoica, I., Zaharia, M.: A view of cloud computing. Commun. ACM 53, 50–58 (2010)
3. Santos, N., Gummadi, K.P., Rodrigues, R.: Towards trusted cloud computing. In: Proceedings of the 2009 Conference on Hot Topics in Cloud Computing, HotCloud 2009, p. 3. USENIX Association, Berkeley (2009)

4. Loscocco, P., Smalley, S.: Integrating flexible support for security policies into the linux operating system. In: Proceedings of the FREENIX Track: 2001 USENIX Annual Technical Conference, pp. 29–42. USENIX Association, Berkeley (2001)
5. Sailer, R., Zhang, X., Jaeger, T., van Doorn, L.: Design and implementation of a tcg-based integrity measurement architecture. In: Proceedings of the 13th Conference on USENIX Security Symposium. SSYM 2004, vol. 13, p. 16. USENIX Association, Berkeley (2004)
6. Watson, R.N.M.: Exploiting concurrency vulnerabilities in system call wrappers. In: Proceedings of the First USENIX Workshop on Offensive Technologies, pp. 1–2. USENIX Association, Berkeley (2007)
7. Garfinkel, T.: Traps and Pitfalls: Practical Problems in in System Call Interposition based Security Tools. In: Proc. Network and Distributed Systems Security Symposium (February 2003)
8. Langley, A.: seccomp: Add bitmask of allowed system calls. Posted on linux kernel mailinglist (May 2009), http://lwn.net/Articles/332438/
9. Corbet, J.: Tracing: no shortage of options (July 2008), http://lwn.net/Articles/291091/
10. Noe, D.: sys socketcall: Network systems calls on Linux (April 2008), http://isoamerica.net/~dpn/socketcall1.pdf
11. Trusted Computing Group - Mobile Phone Working Group: TCG Mobile Reference Architecture, Specification version 1.0 Revision 1 (June 12, 2007)
12. Alves, T., Felton, D.: TrustZone: Integrated Hardware and Software Security - Enabling Trusted Computing in Embedded Systems (July 2004), http://www.arm.com/pdfs/TZ_Whitepaper.pdf
13. Dietrich, K., Winter, J.: Implementation aspects of mobile and embedded trusted computing. In: Chen, L., Mitchell, C.J., Martin, A. (eds.) Trust 2009. LNCS, vol. 5471, pp. 29–44. Springer, Heidelberg (2009)
14. Dietrich, K., Winter, J.: Secure boot revisited. In: The 9th International Conference for Young Computer Scientists, ICYCS 2008, pp. 2360–2365 (November 2008)
15. Jan-Erik Ekberg, M.K.: Mobile Trusted Module (MTM) - an introduction (November 14, 2007), http://research.nokia.com/files/NRCTR2007015.pdf
16. FreeScale: MCIMX51 Multimedia Applications Processor Reference Manual, http://cache.freescale.com/files/dsp/doc/ref_manual/MCIMX51RM.pdf?fsrch=1&sr=5
17. Trusted Computing Group - TPM Working Group: TPM Main Part 3 Commands, Specification version 1.2 Level 2 Revision 103 (July 9, 2007)
18. Winter, J.: Trusted computing building blocks for embedded linux-based arm trustzone platforms. In: STC 2008: Proceedings of the 3rd ACM workshop on Scalable Trusted Computing, pp. 21–30. ACM, New York (2008)
19. Dietrich, K., Winter, J.: Towards customizable, application specific mobile trusted modules. In: Proceedings of the Fifth ACM Workshop on Scalable Trusted Computing, STC 2010, pp. 31–40. ACM, New York (2010)
20. Trusted Computing Group, https://members.trustedcomputinggroup.org
21. Dietrich, K.: Anonymous client authentication for transport layer security. In: De Decker, B., Schaumüller-Bichl, I. (eds.) CMS 2010. LNCS, vol. 6109, pp. 268–280. Springer, Heidelberg (2010)
22. Reiter, A., Neubauer, G., Kapferberger, M., Winter, J., Dietrich, K.: Seamless integration of trusted computing into standard cryptographic frameworks. In: The Second International Conference on Trusted Systems, INTRUST 2010, pp. 21–30. Springer, New York (2011)

23. Gumstix inc.: Gumstix product specification, http://gumstix.com/)
24. Gumstix inc.: robostix-TH product description, http://www.gumstix.com/store/catalog/product_info.php?products_id=142
25. Trusted-Computing-Group-TSS-Working-Group: TCG Software Stack (TSS) Specification Version 1.2 Level 1. Specification available online at (2006), https://www.trustedcomputinggroup.org/specs/TSS/TSS_Version_1.2_Level_1_FINAL.pdf Part1: Commands and Structures
26. ARM Ltd.: RealView Versatile Express product specification

Side-Channel Analysis of PUFs
and Fuzzy Extractors

Dominik Merli[1], Dieter Schuster[1], Frederic Stumpf[1], and Georg Sigl[2]

[1] Fraunhofer Institute for Secure Information Technology
Munich, Germany
{dominik.merli,dieter.schuster,frederic.stumpf}@sit.fraunhofer.de
[2] Institute for Security in Information Technology
Technische Universität München, Munich, Germany
sigl@tum.de

Abstract. Embedded security systems based on Physical Unclonable Functions (PUFs) offer interesting protection properties, such as tamper resistance and unclonability. However, to establish PUFs as a high security primitive in the long run, their vulnerability to side-channel attacks has to be investigated. For this purpose, we analysed the side-channel leakage of PUF architectures and fuzzy extractor implementations. We identified several attack vectors within common PUF constructions and introduce two side-channel attacks on fuzzy extractors. Our proof-of-concept attack on an FPGA implementation of a fuzzy extractor shows that it is possible to extract the cryptographic key derived from a PUF by side-channel analysis.

Keywords: Physical Unclonable Function (PUF), Side-Channel Analysis (SCA), Fuzzy Extractor, Helper Data, FPGA.

1 Introduction

Smartcards and security microcontrollers can be found in a variety of applications. Among other things, they enable secure payment, protect the firmware of electronic control units in vehicles and control access to buildings and information. Their security is usually based on secret keys stored in non-volatile memory. During the last years, powerful attacks, e.g., with Focused Ion Beams (FIBs) [5] or Lasers [15], have been discovered. Countermeasures to resist tampering often imply significant resource overhead and protect devices only against specific attacks.

An approach towards holistic security are Physical Unclonable Functions (PUFs). PUFs are physical structures with a unique challenge-response behaviour, which depends on inevitable manufacturing variations. One advantage of PUFs is their unclonability, which means that even the original manufacturer cannot manufacture a second device or object that has the same behaviour. A second advantage compared to conventional security modules is that PUFs can be built in a way, that active tampering influences the physical structure and

J.M. McCune et al. (Eds.): TRUST 2011, LNCS 6740, pp. 33–47, 2011.

thereby destroys the corresponding secret. This can be seen as a natural counter-measure against invasive attacks. However, not all security properties of PUFs have been investigated in detail yet.

PUFs can be divided into Strong PUFs and Weak PUFs, as described by Rührmair et al. [13]. The security of Strong PUFs is based on their high entropy content providing a huge number of unique Challenge-Response Pairs (CRPs), which can be used in authentication protocols. On the other hand, Weak PUFs allow only a small number of challenges to be applied. Nevertheless, the corresponding responses can be used as a device unique key or seed for conventional encryption systems, while maintaining the advantages of tamper resistance and unclonability. In order to enable the extraction of cryptographic keys from PUFs, a fuzzy extractor is necessary. Fuzzy extractors were introduced by Dodis et al. [3].

Side-channel analysis operates on information leaked by the execution of an algorithm, such as, time, power consumption or electromagnetic emission. It is used to attack cryptographic devices to gain knowledge about integrated secrets. Both, Strong PUFs and Weak PUFs can be targets of side-channel attacks.

To the best of our knowledge, this is the first work that analyses side-channel leakage of PUFs and fuzzy extractors. In this contribution, we show that the side-channel leakage of PUFs needs to be considered. First, we analyse proposed PUF constructions theoretically regarding potential side-channels and assess requirements to exploit them. Further, we propose two side-channel attacks on fuzzy extractors, one on the Toeplitz hashing (TH-SCA) and one on the code-offset construction (CO-SCA) in general. For a proof-of-concept, we conducted an electro-magnetic analysis attack on a Toeplitz hashing hardware module which was designed as proposed in [1]. Therewith, we clearly demonstrate that side-channel attacks pose a real threat to fuzzy extractors.

The remainder of this paper is organised as follows. Section 2 gives a brief overview of previous work related to our contribution, while Section 3 describes necessary background information. An analysis of potential side-channels of proposed PUF structures can be found in Section 4. In Section 5, our developed attacks on the Toeplitz hashing and on the code-offset construction are explained. Section 6 presents the approach and the implementation results of the TH-SCA attack.

2   Related Work

Until now, only a small number of publications deals with vulnerabilities of PUFs and attacks targeting their weaknesses.

An information-theoretic analysis [18] of PUFs was conducted by Tuyls et al. in 2005. The number of necessary CRPs necessary to fully characterize an Optical PUF was analysed in the scenario of a brute force attack.

In [12], Rührmair et al. demonstrate PUF modeling attacks on Ring Oscillator PUFs, Arbiter PUFs, and arbiter-based variants by using machine learning techniques. Their approach allows to foresee PUF responses to a given challenge with prediction rates up to 99%. Since these methods need thousands of CRPs during their learning phase, they are targeted at PUFs providing a huge number of CRPs, but are not applicable to PUFs which are only used to generate a cryptographic key.

In contrast, our attacks are mostly targeted at Weak PUFs and their fuzzy extractors, but the identified weaknesses in PUF architectures might also be a source of information to support attacks on Strong PUFs, like, machine learning attacks or similar.

3   Background

This section gives relevant background information for the analyses presented in this paper.

3.1   Selected PUF Constructions

The first PUF construction, an optical PUF, was developed by Pappu et al. [10] in 2002. Reflecting particles are randomly brought into a transparent medium, which is stimulated by a laser beam. The resulting speckle pattern can be used to derive a PUF response. Later, Tuyls and Škorić described an integrated variant of this PUF architecture [17].

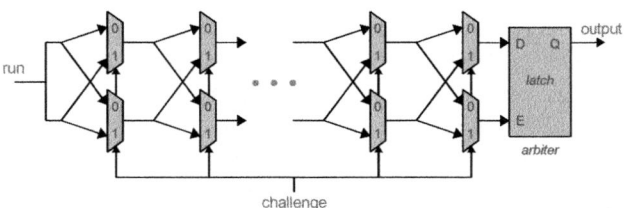

Fig. 1. Arbiter PUF architecture

The Arbiter PUF, shown in Figure 1, was introduced by Lim et al. [6]. Its principle is the difference in propagation delay between two signals on two symmetrically designed paths caused by manufacturing variations, e.g., material density and geometry. At the end of these paths, an arbiter circuit decides which signal was faster and outputs a binary result. This architecture and its enhanced variants have been shown to be susceptible to machine learning attacks [12].

Suh and Devadas introduced the Ring Oscillator PUF (RO PUF) [16] in 2007. As shown in Figure 2, it consists of an array of identical ring oscillators, which can be selected pairwise by a multiplexer. Two oscillators are enabled for a specified runtime, after which the values of the connected counters represent their material-dependent frequencies. Then, a comparison between both values yields a binary result.

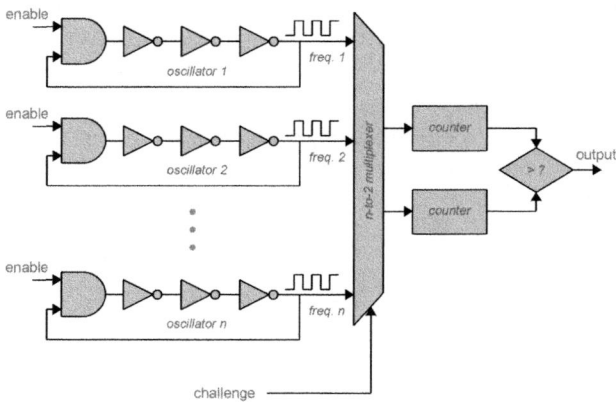

Fig. 2. RO PUF architecture

3.2 Fuzzy Extractors

Fuzzy extractors, as proposed by Dodis et al. [3], enable the generation of cryptographic keys out of data obtained from noisy and non-uniformly distributed sources such as PUFs or biometric measurements. The code-offset fuzzy extractor algorithm is the most suitable one for processing binary PUF responses. It consist of an enrolment phase where helper data is calculated and a reconstruction phase to recover the enrolled key.

During enrolment, a PUF response R and a randomly chosen codeword C_S of an error-correcting code C with length n, dimension k and minimum distance d are XORed to obtain helper data $W_1 = R \oplus C_S$. This helper data is needed for noise cancellation during the reconstruction phase. Helper data W_2 is a randomly chosen integer which defines the hash function h_{W_2} from a family of universal hash functions H. This hash function is used to obtain a uniform distribution of generated keys. Both helper data values, W_1 and W_2, can be stored publicly, because their information leakage about the secret R is sufficiently small.

The reconstruction procedure, as shown in Figure 3, is called every time the secret key is needed. It is separated into an information reconciliation phase to cancel noise and a privacy amplification step to ensure a uniformly distributed output. First, a noisy PUF response R' is acquired and XORed with the public helper data W_1 to obtain a codeword $C'_S = R' \oplus W_1$, containing errors. If C'_S has less than or exactly $t = \lfloor \frac{d-1}{2} \rfloor$ errors, it can be corrected by the decoder of code C. Afterwards, it is again XORed with the helper data W_1 to reconstruct the original PUF response $R = W_1 \oplus C_S$. According to the PUF's entropy, a part of the original response is hashed with the hash function h_{W_2} defined by helper data W_2 to generate a cryptographic key K.

Two efficient FPGA implementations of code-offset fuzzy extractors have been proposed in the literature. In [1], Bösch et al. recommend to implement concatenated repetition and Reed-Muller codes due to their low decoder complexity. The Toeplitz hash function was taken as a universal set of hash functions, because its

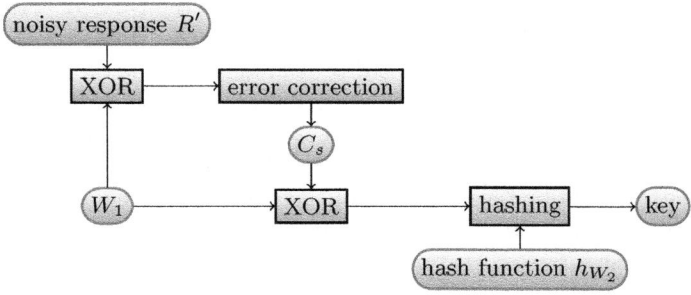

Fig. 3. Reconstruction algorithm

LFSR-based design can be implemented efficiently. Maes et al. [7] optimized the design of the Toeplitz hashing for FPGAs. They propose a soft-decision decoder to cancel noise in PUF responses.

Independent of the underlying PUF structure, the mentioned fuzzy extractors are vulnerable to side-channel attacks as shown in the following sections.

3.3 Side-Channel Analysis

Side-channel analysis based on power consumption was introduced by Kocher et al. in 1999 [4]. The basic form, Simple Power Analysis (SPA), is based on the leaked power consumption of an executed algorithm. SPA techniques were used for our analysis of fuzzy extractors. Differential Power Analysis (DPA), as introduced by Kocher, is a more powerful analysis method for encryption systems, but cannot be directly mapped to fuzzy extractors.

Peeters et al. [11] explained the advantages of using an electro-magnetic (EM) probe to record power traces of a device. Since non-invasive EM measurements can be focussed locally, an improved signal-to-noise ratio can be obtained, which is important for practical side-channel attacks.

4   Potential Side-Channels of PUFs

In the following paragraphs, we analyse three well-known PUF types, mainly Silicon PUFs, regarding potential side-channels like power consumption and electro-magnetic emission given by their architectures. Although the following analysis does not cover all published PUF architectures, most of the given approaches can be transferred to similar types of PUFs.

4.1   Arbiter PUFs

A potential side-channel of the Arbiter PUF originates from the power consumption or the electro-magnetic emission of the arbiter's output. In the common case of n parallel arbiters generating an n-bit response, the power consumption will not be informative enough to recover all n bits, therefore, EM emission is the only way to attack it. The difficulty is to locate each arbiter on the die of an ASIC or an FPGA and to focus the EM probe mainly on the radiation of its components. But since EM cartography methods [14] have been developed and are continuously improving, locating arbiters seems to be imaginable in the future. If enhanced tools allow to perform the described measurements, then Arbiter PUF responses could be recorded without actively attacking the PUF device or caring about how the generated bits are used.

Variants of the original Arbiter PUF [6,8] have been proposed to counteract machine learning attacks [12] by using XOR networks to obfuscate dependencies between output bits and path delays. However, side-channel information gathered by EM emission directly from the outputs of the arbiters could bypass these countermeasures and could be used as input to machine learning algorithms aimed at cloning Arbiter PUFs.

4.2   Ring Oscillator PUFs

The first side-channel of RO PUFs is represented by the oscillators themselves. During the time of comparison of two ring oscillators, they inevitably induce an electro-magnetic emission depending on their frequencies. Similar to arbiters, oscillators are quite tiny and hard to locate and separate on a chip. Finding oscillators by state-of-the-art EM cartography methods was not successful in our experiments, but as pointed out above, higher resolution cartography methods could enable these attacks in the future. As shown in one of our earlier experiments [9], the frequencies of ROs vary by several MHz over an FPGA die, which might be measurable with precise EM equipment. With this attack, RO PUFs could be cloned completely, because all information content, namely all RO frequencies, could be read out and an exact model could be generated.

The counters measuring RO frequencies are the second potential attack point for a side-channel analysis of RO PUFs. With each positive edge received from the oscillator signal, an incrementation operation takes place. In contrast to attacking every single oscillator, only the locations of the used counters have to be determined in order to monitor all comparisons during the PUF evaluation. This should at least allow to draw conclusions about which counter measured the higher frequency and therefore about the comparison's result representing the PUF response. It is not important to know the inequality used in the comparator, i.e., $Cnt1 > Cnt2 \rightarrow 1$ or $Cnt2 > Cnt1 \rightarrow 1$, because there are only these two possibilities to convert the comparison results into a binary string. Since the EM emission of counters is higher than of single oscillators and only the relatively few locations of these counters have to be found on a die, this attack scenario seems to achievable in practice. An effective countermeasure would be to mix the placement of the counter components on an FPGA or ASIC die, which renders a distinct localizing much harder.

The last potential information source is the binary signal generated by the comparator itself or the register storing this signal. If only one RO pair comparison takes place at a time, the impact of this signal change cannot only be found by using an EM probe, but also in the power trace of the PUF device. Exploitation of this side-channel would allow a direct extraction of the generated PUF response. Combined with machine learning attack, it would also allow to fully characterize and model a RO PUF.

4.3   Integrated Optical PUFs

In addition to all Silicon PUFs analysed above, we would like to mention the Integrated Optical PUF architecture. It was described by Tuyls and Škorić [17] as an integrated system, where a laser stimulates an Optical PUF which is extended by switchable liquid crystal pixels for applying challenges and a camera chip to transform the generated speckle pattern into a binary representation.

Of course, an optical system does not generate EM radiation in the way an electronic circuit does and optical side-channel attacks seem to be more or less impossible, but the crux of the matter is that the results of all optical effects have to be converted into electrical signals sooner or later. Although we cannot state a specific point of vulnerability for Optical PUFs, the implementation of camera sensors and post-processing units such as fuzzy extractors might still be susceptible to side-channel analysis.

4.4   A Note on Invasive Attacks

To the best of our knowledge, no analysis on the tamper resistance of Silicon PUFs and several other recently published PUF architectures has been conducted until now. Assuming that decapsulating a chip does not influence a PUF significantly, it would open the doors to laser injection attacks, probing and similar invasive attacks. Our analysis does not focus on invasive attacks, but we would like to emphasize that not every PUF architecture provides tamper resistance by default, but might be susceptible to invasive attacks of all kinds.

5   Side-Channel Attacks on Fuzzy Extractors

Independent of the underlying PUF technology, fuzzy extractors are required for generating a cryptographic key from noisy PUF responses. Therefore, these modules are a critical point of a PUF key generation system, because their weaknesses can lead to generic attacks independent of the security and properties of the implemented PUF structure.

We present two attacks on common implementations of fuzzy extractors which enable the unauthorized extraction of the cryptographic key derived from an arbitrary PUF structure.

5.1   Toeplitz Hashing Side-Channel Analysis (TH-SCA)

In Figure 3, the reconstruction process of a code-offset fuzzy extractor is depicted. The last step which outputs the generated key is a universal hash function, responsible for transforming part of the original PUF response into a uniformly distributed key. This universal hash function was proposed to be implemented as a Toeplitz hashing by Bösch et al. [1] as well as Maes et al. [7].

Our TH-SCA attack aims at recovering the input of this Toeplitz hashing algorithm, which is a part of the result of the $R = C_S \oplus W_1$ operation and therefore a part of the original PUF response.

The Toeplitz hashing is favoured in many applications because of its efficient implementation. The basic concept is shown in Figure 4. The shown LFSR generates the required Toeplitz matrix step by step. The content of the LFSR is XORed into the accumulator if the current input bit has the value 1 and neglected otherwise.

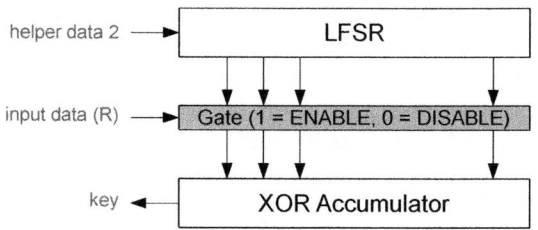

Fig. 4. LFSR-based Toeplitz hashing

TH-SCA exploits the fact that the input data to be hashed enables the XOR operation of the accumulator through a gate. The power consumption of the hashing module can be divided into one part depending on the shift operation, one part depending on the XOR accumulator operation and a constant part, formally described by $P_{hash} = P_{shift} + P_{xor} + P_{const}$. If the recent input bit of the input data (R) (see Figure 4) is 0, then only the shift operation takes place $(P_{xor} = 0)$, otherwise, the accumulator XOR operation is performed additionally $(P_{xor} > 0)$. Since an additional XOR operation causes an additional amount of power consumption, the input bits of this Toeplitz hashing implementation can be extracted from the side-channel information of the device's power traces or EM emission traces. Knowing these PUF response bits, the cryptographic key K can be computed using the Toeplitz hash function.

In practical attacks, measurements might be too noisy to achieve convincing results. Common techniques like alignment and averaging of several traces can be applied to cancel noise disturbances.

We propose a further way to enhance measurements by randomization of helper data W_2. The power consumption of the shift operation can be divided into two parts, i.e., $P_{shift} = P_{state} + P_{const}$. One part depends on the current state of the LFSR, the other part is constant. If an attacker is able to manipulate W_2, e.g., if it is stored in an external memory, then randomizing helper data W_2 and thereby randomizing the LFSR states, leads to a randomized state-dependent power consumption. After averaging the traces recorded with randomized W_2, noise introduced by P_{state} is canceled, leaving a constant offset of P_{state} no longer influencing the side-channel analysis of the Toeplitz hashing. Therefore, P_{shift} has a constant value, which leaves $P_{hash} = P_{xor} + P_{const}$. Although randomized W_2 alters the key generated in the PUF device, the input bits of the Toeplitz hashing, which matter for this attack, stay the same.

5.2   Code-Offset Side-Channel Analysis (CO-SCA)

During the reconstruction phase of the code-offset fuzzy extractor, as shown in Figure 3, helper data W_1 is involved into two operations. First, it contributes to the codeword $C'_S = R' \oplus W_1$ and afterwards, it is involved in computing the original PUF response $R = C_S \oplus W_1$.

The CO-SCA attack focuses on power analysis of the register storing the the result of the $R = C_S \oplus W_1$ operation. Since power consumption of CMOS devices mainly depends on switching activities, the power consumption of the mentioned register is proportional to the Hamming distance between its current and its following state. Then, the power consumption is also proportional to the Hamming weight of the current state XORed with the following state, i.e. $P_{register} \sim HD(Reg_{R(n)}; Reg_{R(n+1)}) = HW(Reg_{R(n)} \oplus Reg_{R(n+1)})$. Assuming that the register is initialized with zeros at power-up, i.e. $HW(Reg_{R(0)}) = 0$, the following power peak of this register is proportional to the Hamming weight $HW(C_S \oplus W_1)$.

If helper data W_1 is stored in external memory, which is allowed in terms of its information leakage regarding the secret R, the communication line between this memory and the PUF device could be compromised by an attacker, enabling the manipulation of W_1. Then, an attacker is able to brute force a bit sequence, e.g., the first byte, of W_1 while recording power or EM emission traces. The bit pattern corresponding to the lowest power consumption represents the correct bit sequence of the codeword C_S because $P_{register}$ reaches its minimum if the brute forced bits of W_1 match the corresponding bits of C_S, i.e., $P_{register} \sim HW(C_S \oplus W_1) = 0$.

Since W_1 also contributes to $C'_S = R' \oplus W_1$, the number of bits $t_{CO\text{-}SCA}$ allowed to be brute forced during CO-SCA is limited by the number of bits t_{noise} affected by PUF measurement noise and by the error-correcting code C, capable of correcting t_{ecc} errors in C_S. The codeword C_S has to be error-free to enable this attack, which means that CO-SCA can only manipulate $t_{CO\text{-}SCA} \le t_{ecc} - t_{noise}$ bits at a time.

The following steps explain the general approach of CO-SCA:

1. The first/next m bits of helper data W_1 are manipulated to represent the values 0 to $2^m - 1$ and the rest of W_1 is kept as given.
2. The reconstruction algorithm is run for each manipulated version of W_1 and the power consumption is recorded each time by power or EM measurements.
3. The value of $P_{register}$ is extracted from every power trace. Its variation increases by raising m.
4. The bit pattern corresponding to the minimum of $P_{register}$ is the correct respective bit pattern of the codeword C_S.

5. Steps 1 to 4 are repeated until the whole codeword C_S is revealed.
6. The operation $R = C_S \oplus W_1$ gives the secret PUF response R.
7. Hashing the computed response R leads to the secret key K.

Since this attack allows attacking most code-offset based fuzzy extractors, it is very critical, but it is only applicable if manipulation of helper data W_1 is possible.

5.3   Vulnerable Error-Correcting Codes

The attacks above concentrate on side-channels of the Toeplitz hashing and the code-offset construction, because these are popular in state-of-the-art fuzzy extractor implementations. Another important part is the error-correcting code used to cancel the PUF's noise. During our research, we did not focus on side-channel analysis of error-correcting codes, but as indicated by Dai and Wang [2], there seem to be usable side-channels in error-correcting codes, also.

6   Implementation of TH-SCA

In this section, we describe our proof-of-concept implementation for the TH-SCA attack, which was conducted on an FPGA prototype of a fuzzy extractor.

6.1   FPGA Prototype

Based on the architectures described in [16] and [3], we developed an FPGA fuzzy extractor prototype connected to a RO PUF with 511 oscillators. Since these architectures are the basis for diverse practical implementations, our implementation is representative for real implementations. The design is implemented on a Xilinx Spartan 3E FPGA. Note that side-channel analysis is always device dependent, but since TH-SCA focuses on architecture and implementation dependent side-channel leakage, device specific characteristics can be neglected in this case.

We chose to generate a 64-bit key from a 510-bit PUF response because of the limited resources of the FPGA. Of course, it would be possible to generate longer keys from more PUF response bits, but they would be as vulnerable to side-channel analysis as shorter keys. The error-correcting code C is implemented as a BCH (n=255,k=37,t=45) code. The Toeplitz hashing takes 74 bits as input and is implemented as described by Bösch et al. [1]. The clock frequency of our system is 50 MHz.

The helper data is stored on a PC at enrolment and sent to the PUF device with the respective reconstruction commands over a serial communication interface. Note that this implementation only simplifies the analysis of attacks where manipulated helper data is required, but does not simplify the attacks themselves. In a real world scenario, helper data could be manipulated by altering the connection lines between external memory and PUF device.

Fig. 5. EM measurement over FPGA package

6.2 Measurements

Because of the advantages of EM measurements mentioned in Section 3, our data was gathered using a Langer ICR HH 150 EM probe, as shown in Figure 5. In order to guarantee a sufficiently high resolution, the traces were recorded at a sample rate of 20 GS/s with a LeCroy wavePro 715Zi oscilloscope.

The EM probe was manually placed at a location on top of the FPGA package where it received signals with high information content without containing too much noise. Automated EM cartography methods [14] would contribute to finding even better locations.

The hashing operation of our prototype fits well in a 5 μs time frame. We recorded traces which captured the end of the reconstruction operation of the fuzzy extractor and contained 100,000 samples.

We gathered 10,000 traces for three different attack runs. First, the whole amplitude of the signal was recorded. Then, only the positive peaks of the signal were recorded to obtain a higher voltage resolution. In the third run, in addition to recording only the positive signal, helper data W_2 was randomized.

6.3 Processing and Analysis

Since we recognized a time shift between all captured traces, the first step in analysing the traces was to align them. For this purpose any outstanding peak or peak pattern can be used, as long as there is no clock drift present in the traces. In our case, the successful generation of a key was signalled by a trigger, which was used for alignment. Another possibility would have been a peak or a pattern at the end of the error correction phase, e.g., related to the performed XOR operation.

In every measured trace, a noise was present because of thermal noise and disturbance sources within the FPGA or related to components mounted to the same printed circuit board. In order to reduce these influences, every trace value was averaged over all sampled traces after alignment. Then, all peaks in the trace were extracted by looking for the local maxima surrounded by values lower than a specified delta, found by visual trace inspection or trial and error. This method

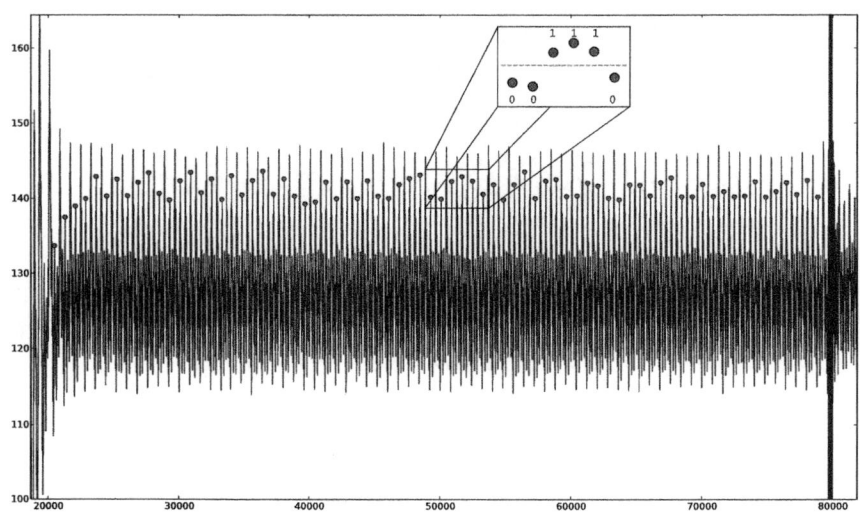

Fig. 6. EM emission trace and extracted peaks of the Toeplitz hashing

has the advantage of neglecting noise induced peaks automatically. The last step was to select only significant peaks, which was done by time range limitation and exploiting the average time delay between peaks.

Figure 6 shows the resulting trace after processing, which contains distinct detectable positive peaks in regular intervals which were covered by noise before. The higher and more or less constant peaks between the extracted points in the shown trace arise because of our implementation, but can be easily identified and neglected.

Algorithm 1. TH-SCA trace analysis

$traces \leftarrow$ read_traces()
for $trace$ in $traces$ **do**
    shift_trace($trace$)   ▷ shift traces for alignment
end for
$final\_trace \leftarrow$ average($traces$)
$peaks \leftarrow$ extract_peaks($final\_trace$)   ▷ detect peaks in the whole trace
$sig\_peaks \leftarrow$ select_significant_peaks($peaks$)   ▷ select important peaks
$threshold \leftarrow$ mean(sig_peaks)
$result \leftarrow$ list()
for $value$ in sig_peaks **do**
   if $value < threshold$ **then**
      $result$.append(0)
   else if $value \geq threshold$ **then**
      $result$.append(1)
   end if
end for
return $result$

Table 1. Bit errors (of 74 input bits) achieved by our TH-SCA

Number of Traces	TH-SCA Standard	TH-SCA Positive Signal	TH-SCA Positive Signal Randomized W_2
10000	0 (0%)	0 (0%)	0 (0%)
8000	0 (0%)	0 (0%)	0 (0%)
6000	1 (1.4%)	0 (0%)	0 (0%)
4000	1 (1.4%)	0 (0%)	0 (0%)
2000	1 (1.4%)	0 (0%)	0 (0%)
1000	1 (1.4%)	2 (2.7%)	1 (1.4%)
500	2 (2.7%)	4 (5.4%)	2 (2.7%)
200	10 (13.5%)	11 (14.9%)	6 (8.1%)

The average of all extracted peaks is taken as a threshold. The variations between the extracted peaks is like expected: peaks higher than the threshold indicate input bits, which are 1, peaks lower than the threshold represent input bits, which are 0.

The general steps for TH-SCA trace analysis are described in Algorithm 1.

6.4   Results

The results of our TH-SCA proof-of-concept attack are listed in Table 1. They clearly show that error-free extraction of a cryptographic key generated by a PUF is possible by analysing the EM emission side-channel of the Toeplitz hash function. When recording the whole amplitude of the EM signal, it was not possible to reveal the 74 input bits of the Toeplitz hash function without errors below 8,000 traces, even by manually adjusting analysis parameters. Since our attack only requires observing positive peaks, a higher resolution of power peaks can be achieved by recording only the positive part of the signal. This method decreased the required traces to 2,000. In our experiments, the additional randomization of helper data W_2 enhanced the quality of the captured traces only slightly, as indicated by the lower error rates for less then 2,000 traces in Table 1. Since capturing of even 10,000 traces can be achieved within a few hours, these results present a critical vulnerability of fuzzy extractor systems based on a Toeplitz hashing module. Although we restricted our design to a 64-bit key, the TH-SCA would also be applicable to systems generating 128-bit or larger keys with only little overhead, e.g. recording some more traces for noise cancellation.

7   Conclusion

We have shown that common PUF architectures are susceptible to side-channel attacks. While Arbiter PUFs inevitably leak information about their output signal by EM emission, RO PUFs additionally provide an attacker with leakage of oscillator frequencies and running counters. Optical systems are not directly prone to side-channel analysis, but their sensors might open the doors for attackers. Thus, potential side-channel leakage has to be considered already during the design of PUF architectures, and even more during implementation.

We also identified two attacks against fuzzy extractors, one for the popular Toeplitz Hashing (TH-SCA) and one for the code-offset construction (CO-SCA), the basis for most proposed fuzzy extractors. Our successful implementation of the TH-SCA attack on an FPGA fuzzy extractor prototype emphasizes the real threat of side-channel analysis for systems where a cryptographic key is generated by a fuzzy extractor. This threat is not limited to FPGAs but is also critical for ASIC and probably also software implementations of fuzzy extractors. As a result, Weak PUFs as well as Strong PUFs (especially when used with a fuzzy extractor) are not per se resistant against side-channel analysis.

References

1. Bösch, C., Guajardo, J., Sadeghi, A.-R., Shokrollahi, J., Tuyls, P.: Efficient helper data key extractor on fpgas. In: Oswald, E., Rohatgi, P. (eds.) CHES 2008. LNCS, vol. 5154, pp. 181–197. Springer, Heidelberg (2008)
2. Dai, J., Wang, L.: A study of side-channel effects in reliability-enhancing techniques. In: Proceedings of the 2009 24th IEEE International Symposium on Defect and Fault Tolerance in VLSI Systems, DFT 2009, pp. 236–244. IEEE Computer Society, Washington, DC (2009)
3. Dodis, Y., Ostrovsky, R., Reyzin, L., Smith, A.: Fuzzy extractors: How to generate strong keys from biometrics and other noisy data. SIAM J. Comput. 38(1), 97–139 (2008)
4. Kocher, P.C., Jaffe, J., Jun, B.: Differential power analysis. In: Wiener, M. (ed.) CRYPTO 1999. LNCS, vol. 1666, pp. 388–397. Springer, Heidelberg (1999)
5. Kömmerling, O., Kuhn, M.G.: Design principles for tamper-resistant smartcard processors. In: WOST 1999: Proceedings of the USENIX Workshop on Smartcard Technology on USENIX Workshop on Smartcard Technology, pages 2–2. USENIX Association, Berkeley (1999)
6. Lim, D., Lee, J.W., Gassend, B., Suh, G.E., van Dijk, M., Devadas, S.: Extracting secret keys from integrated circuits. IEEE Transactions on Very Large Scale Integration (VLSI) Systems 13(10), 1200–1205 (2005)
7. Maes, R., Tuyls, P., Verbauwhede, I.: Low-overhead implementation of a soft decision helper data algorithm for sram pufs. In: Clavier, C., Gaj, K. (eds.) CHES 2009. LNCS, vol. 5747, pp. 332–347. Springer, Heidelberg (2009)
8. Majzoobi, M., Koushanfar, F., Potkonjak, M.: Lightweight secure pufs. In: ICCAD 2008: Proceedings of the 2008 IEEE/ACM International Conference on Computer-Aided Design, pp. 670–673. IEEE Press, Piscataway (2008)
9. Merli, D., Stumpf, F., Eckert, C.: Improving the quality of ring oscillator pufs on fpgas. In: 5th Workshop on Embedded Systems Security (WESS 2010). ACM Press, Scottsdale (2010)
10. Pappu, R., Recht, B., Taylor, J., Gershenfeld, N.: Physical one-way functions. Science 297(5589), 2026–2030 (2002)
11. Peeters, E., Standaert, F.-X., Quisquater, J.-J.: Power and electromagnetic analysis: Improved model, consequences and comparisons. Integration 40(1), 52–60 (2007)

12. Rührmair, U., Sehnke, F., Sölter, J., Dror, G., Devadas, S., Schmidhuber, J.: Modeling attacks on physical unclonable functions. In: Proceedings of the 17th ACM Conference on Computer and Communications Security, CCS 2010, pp. 237–249. ACM Press, New York (2010)
13. Rührmair, U., Sölter, J., Sehnke, F.: On the foundations of physical unclonable functions. Cryptology ePrint Archive, Report 2009/277 (2009), http://eprint.iacr.org/
14. Sauvage, L., Guilley, S., Mathieu, Y.: Electromagnetic radiations of fpgas: High spatial resolution cartography and attack on a cryptographic module. ACM Trans. Reconfigurable Technol. Syst., 2:4:1–4:24 (March 2009)
15. Skorobogatov, S.: Flash memory 'Bumping" attacks. In: Mangard, S., Standaert, F.-X. (eds.) CHES 2010. LNCS, vol. 6225, pp. 158–172. Springer, Heidelberg (2010)
16. Suh, G.E., Devadas, S.: Physical unclonable functions for device authentication and secret key generation. In: 44th ACM/IEEE Design Automation Conference, DAC 2007, pp. 9–14 (2007)
17. Tuyls, P., Škorić, B.: Strong Authentication with Physical Unclonable Functions. In: Petkovi, M., Jonker, W. (eds.) Security, Privacy and Trust in Modern Data Management. Data-Centric Systems and Applications. Springer, Heidelberg (2007)
18. Tuyls, P., Škorić, B., Stallinga, S., Akkermans, A.H.M., Ophey, W.: Information-theoretic security analysis of physical uncloneable functions. In: S. Patrick, A., Yung, M. (eds.) FC 2005. LNCS, vol. 3570, pp. 141–155. Springer, Heidelberg (2005)

Coalition Resistant Anonymous Broadcast Encryption Scheme Based on PUF[*]

Łukasz Krzywiecki and Mirosław Kutyłowski

Institute of Mathematics and Computer Science, Wrocław University of Technology
firstname.secondname@pwr.wroc.pl

Abstract. We describe a broadcast encryption system with revocation, where security is based on PUF (Physical Unclonable Function) instead of a cryptographic problem. Our scheme is immune to advances of cryptography (which may suddenly ruin any system depending solely of cryptographic assumptions). It is resilient to collusion attacks, which are frequently the Achilles' heel of schemes based on cryptography. It provides a high level of privacy protection of the users. On the downside, it requires memory modules as well as time consuming initialization of PUFs by the broadcaster. Security of the scheme is based on the assumption of randomness of PUF's output and their unclonability.

Keywords: key broadcasting, exclusion protocol, anonymity, PUF.

1 Introduction

Broadcast Encryption (BE) is a scheme in which a single unit, called *broadcaster*, sends data to authorized users via a broadcast channel. By technical properties, the broadcast channel is accessible to everyone in its range, so BE has to ensure that:

- a non-authorized user cannot retrieve the data from the message broadcasted,
- each authorized user can read this data,
- the system supports changes of the set of authorized users.

The simplest way to achieve these properties is to broadcast data in an encrypted form, where the decryption key is given to the authorized users only. In this case the decryption key must be protected against duplication and forwarding to third persons – e.g. via an implementation on tamper-proof devices.

The hardest design problem of BE is how to change the set of authorized users. A standard solution is to change the decryption key and to inform the authorized users about the new key. The simplest way would be to send a separate message to each user, causing a flood of messages – hard to justify from the economic point of view, if a few devices are revoked. Usually we try to encode this information in a short broadcast message, called *enabling block*, so that only authorized users can derive the new key. "Short" could mean that its length is linear in the number of revoked devices.

BE systems are important for Pay-TV, TV-over-Internet, and local broadcasting in pervasive systems. Note that in these applications a set of authorized users changes in

---

[*] Partially supported by Polish MNiSzW, project NN206 36 9739.

J.M. McCune et al. (Eds.): TRUST 2011, LNCS 6740, pp. 48–62, 2011.

an unpredictable way, and in many cases only a small number of users must be excluded at a time.

Encoding based on Lagrangian interpolation is one of the fundamental techniques for BE revocation. It enables to revoke *any* subset of devices up to a given cardinality. There are many schemes based on this principle, however they share common threats:

- **Tampering and cloning:** Once a device is tampered, it can be duplicated and the adversary can pay once for enabling broadcast decryption for all clone devices.
- **Collusion:** a coalition of traitors attempts to extract cryptographic material from their devices. They use this material to build and solve a system of equations aiming to reconstruct the secret master key of the broadcaster (a polynomial or polynomial in the exponent) and produce a universal non-revocable device.
- **Privacy threats:** in regular polynomial based BE the behavioral patterns of users can be traced. Namely, by analyzing enabling blocks transmitted at different times it is possible to say if the same person has been revoked at these times.

In order to protect secret material we often use smart cards. However, there is a major difference between e.g. signature cards and BE: while compromising a smart card endangers solely its owner, in case of BE based on polynomials all users are endangered.

Physical unclonable functions (PUFs). PUF is a hardware primitive that extracts secrets from its physical characteristics acquired during inevitable random variation of fabrication process. Structural variations present in PUFs provide they cannot be cloned exactly, even by its original manufacturer. PUFs can be tested with external challenges, upon which (due to PUFs perplex structure) they react with corresponding responses which are extremely difficult to predict and are unique to each PUF.

There are several types of PUFs discussed in literature, one of them are Strong PUFs [1],[2],[3]. Strong PUFs, also referred to as Physical Random Functions [4],[2] or Physical One-Way Functions [5],[1], are hardware devices with very many possible challenge-response pairs (CRPs). Their requirements are: infeasibility of physical cloning, impossibility to determine all CRPs by any adversary who has unrestricted access to the tested PUF, infeasibility of response prediction for a randomly chosen challenge given a collection of previous CRPs. There are number of candidates for Strong PUFs implemented on integrated circuits proposed however the efforts in this area must be continued due to modeling attacks [6]. In the meantime Strong PUF features has been used for key establishment [1],[7], identification [1] and authentication [2].

Our Contribution. We propose to use PUFs to design BE systems. Clearly, PUFs is a remedy for tampering devices, however they are really independent of each other, so it is not obvious how to make them work in a common broadcasting system. This is much different in the solutions, where we install related secrets in all devices. Our scheme combines the features previously not achieved simultaneously by a single BE scheme:

- **Small communication overhead:** as for a typical polynomial based solution, the size of the enabling block is proportional to the number of revoked users.
- **Tampering and cloning resistance:** it is based on the assumption that physical cloning of the device is impossible by design.

- **Collusion resistance:** our scheme is resistant to arbitrary size coalition of traitors that would try to extract secrets from their devices in order to reconstruct the secret master key of the broadcaster and produce a universal non-revocable device. A substantial improvement against alluding revocation is also offered.
- **Unconditional anonymity:** in regular polynomial based BE enabling block shows whether the same device has been revoked at two different times. For anonymous BE *no* information on users' behaviour should be leaked (and not only very specific information that a certain device is revoked). For our scheme it is infeasible to determine if at different moments the same device has been revoked.
- **Small computational complexity:** our scheme does not require to hide secret polynomials in the exponent, neither in the user devices nor in the enabling block.

On the downside, it requires (unprotected) memory modules as well as time consuming initialization with PUFs.

Some Related Work. Renewing session keys for broadcast encryption systems was introduced in [8]. The first solution was not focused on revoking a small number of devices - communication complexity was linear in the number of authorized users.

The later case was addressed by several later papers. Many of them are based on Shamir's threshold secret sharing and Lagrangian interpolation in the exponent [9], [10], [11], [12]. These mechanisms turn out to be useful also for traitor tracing.

Privacy protection in broadcast encryption was studied in [13],[14] and [15]. The scheme [13] is based on Lagrangian interpolation, but shares of the excluded users need not to be included in the enabling block. Both schemes fail to use small size enabling blocks in case of small number of revoked devices.

2 PUF Based Broadcast Encryption Scheme

2.1 Preliminaries

First we fix some notation. Let:

- G be a finite group and let $g \in G$ be an element of prime order p, such that Discrete Logarithm Problem (DLP) in group $\langle g \rangle$ is hard,
- $\Omega \subset \mathbb{Z}_p$ be a set of indexes of all devices in the system,
- $\Phi \subset \Omega$ denote a set of indexes of the devices to be revoked,
- $BE(z, n)$ denote z-revocation broadcast encryption scheme, i.e. the scheme that enables to revoke up to z devices from a set of cardinality n,
- $\mathsf{Init}_{BE(z,n)}$, $\mathsf{Reg}_{BE(z,n)}$, $\mathsf{Enc}_{BE(z,n)}$, $\mathsf{Dec}_{BE(z,n)}$ denote, respectively, the initialization, registration, encryption, and decryption procedure of $BE(z, n)$ scheme,
- K denote a session key used to encrypt data,
- $\mathcal{B}$ denote a broadcaster – the entity that broadcasts session keys to users from Ω,
- $r \longleftarrow_R \mathbb{Z}_p$ mean that r is chosen uniformly at random from the set $\mathbb{Z}_p$.

Unless otherwise stated, from now on all arithmetic operations are executed in $\mathbb{Z}_p$.

2.2 Lagrangian Interpolation

Let $L : \mathbb{Z}_p \to \mathbb{Z}_p$ be a polynomial of degree z, and $A = \langle (x_0, L(x_0)), \ldots, (x_z, L(x_z)) \rangle$ be a set of pairs such that $x_i \neq x_j$ for $i \neq j$. Then we can reconstruct $L(x)$, for an arbitrary x, by *Lagrangian interpolation*. Namely, we compute a value

$$LI(x, A) = \sum_{i=0,(x_i,.)\in A}^{z} \left(L(x_i) \prod_{j=0, j \neq i, (x_j,.)\in A}^{z} \left(\frac{x - x_j}{x_i - x_j} \right) \right) \tag{1}$$

If interpolation set A is known from the context, $L(x)$ stands for $LI(x, A)$.

2.3 Revocation via Lagrangian Interpolation

Let us recall how Lagrangian interpolation can be used to revoke a subset of at most z devices. Typically a broadcaster chooses a private polynomial L and provides each registered device u with a share of the form $x_u, f(L(x_u))$. Here f is a function that somehow hides the polynomial L and prevents a device from learning it explicitly even if the same polynomial is used in subsequent sessions. A master example of such a function is $f(L(x_u)) = g^{L(x_u)}$, where all operations are performed in G.

The new session key is encoded as $f(rL(x_0))$ for a chosen x_0 and a random number r which additionally masks the polynomial L. The broadcaster composes an enabling block consisting of some auxiliary control parameters and z different pairs of the form $x, f(rL(x))$. Among these pairs there are:

– all shares of revoked devices and
– no share of authorized devices

(the number of devices is substantially smaller than p, so there are enough arguments x that may be used in this way). Note that the shares from the enabling block compose an incomplete interpolation set - just one pair is missing in order to perform Lagrangian interpolation.

After receiving the enabling block an authorized device

– prepares its share $x_u, f(rL(x_u))$ (some operations are necessary due to presence of r),
– uses its own share and the shares from the enabling block to perform Lagrangian interpolation for computing $f(rL(x_0))$.

No revoked device can perform Lagrangian interpolation - its share is already in the enabling block and it has no possibility to add one missing share.

When $f(L(x_u)) = g^{L(x_u)}$, then interpolation of $f(rL(x_0))$ is performed in the exponent, which is a straightforward modification of (1).

Although using the function f and masking the polynomial L by a fresh random nounce r prevents a single device from learning L, there is a threat that $z + 1$ users can collude to obtain a system of equations and learn L or at least $f(L)$. Therefore, a number of extensions with traitor tracing feature were discussed: traitor tracing means here possibility to learn identity of at least one traitor after capturing a pirate device.

3 PUF-Based BE

Now we describe a basic scheme. Later, in the Sect. 5, we sketch a complete system.

3.1 Scheme Overview

First let us describe the system from the point of view of a user (see Fig. 1). The user is equipped with a D-box for broadcast receiving and decoding. It must cooperate with an external PUF card, which is inserted to the slot of the D-box. The PUF card consists of a PUF module which serves as unclonable private function P_u of its user u. Additionally, there is a memory module where PUF answers for some input challenges are stored. The memory module can be implemented either on the PUF card or separately, e.g. on a removable flash card or in the D-box itself. It need not to be kept secret, so even downloading its contents per Internet is possible.

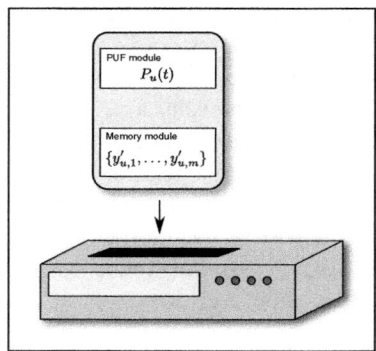

Fig. 1. D-box of a user u

Before the PUF card is given the user, it must be processed in a service-registration center (see Fig. 2). The PUF function P_u is queried for a number of challenges t_i, t_i'. The answers $x_{u,i} = P_u(t_i)$ are stored securely by the broadcaster in a dataset corresponding to the PUF queried. The values $y_{u,i} = L_i(x_{u,i})$ are computed, and in a masked form $y_{u,i}' = L_i(x_{u,i}) + P_u(t_i')$ they are recorded in the user's memory module.

3.2 Scheme Details

Definition 1. $BE(z, n)$ scheme is a 4-tuple of algorithms $(\text{Init}_{BE(z,n)}, \text{Reg}_{BE(z,n)}, \text{Enc}_{BE(z,n)}, \text{Dec}_{BE(z,n)})$ where:

- the initialization procedure $\text{Init}_{BE(z,n)}$ receives as an input at least the maximum number of revoked devices z out of n, and returns the master secret MK,
- the registration procedure $\text{Reg}_{BE(z,n)}$ receives as an input the master secret MK and an index u associated with the device to register; it returns the user's secret share SK_u,
- the encryption procedure $\text{Enc}_{BE(z,n)}$ receives as an input the master secret MK, a new session key K and a set of devices to revoke of cardinality at most z; it returns an enabling block H,
- the decryption procedure $\text{Dec}_{BE(z,n)}$ receives an enabling block H, and secret share SK_u of user u; it returns the session key K if u is an authorized device, and otherwise the failure symbol $\perp$.

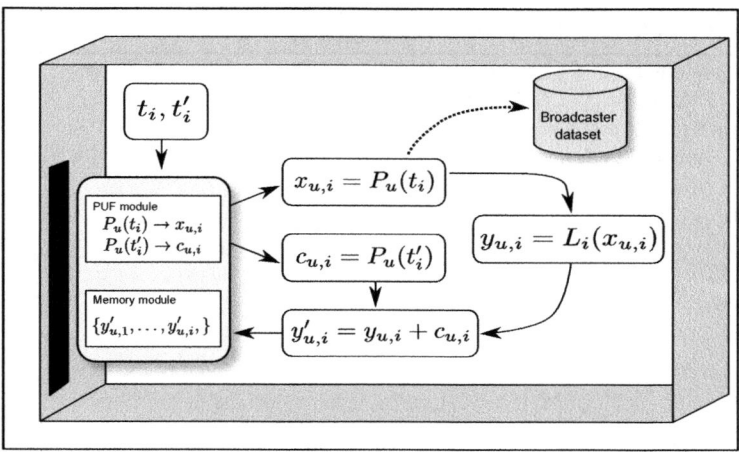

Fig. 2. Registration of a card of user u

Initialization procedure is performed by $\mathcal{B}$. It takes as an input the maximum number of revoked devices per round z, the total numbers of rounds T, the system security parameter ξ, and produces as output T random polynomials L_i of degree z altogether with $2T$ random challenges t_i, t'_i from the domain U of challenges of the PUF. We denote $MK_i = (L_i(x), t_i, t'_i)$ for each round i, and a master secret of the broadcaster as $MK = \{MK_i | i = 1, \dots, T\}$.

Algorithm 1. Initializing procedure $\mathsf{Init}_{\mathsf{BE}(z,n)}$

Data: the maximum number of revoked devices z, the maximum numbers of rounds T, system security parameter ξ

Result: the master secret polynomial $L_i(x)$, and challenges t_i, t'_i for each round: $MK = \{MK_i | i = 1, \dots, T\}$

I1. **begin**
I2.   choose $p \in PRIME$, such that $p > \xi$
I3.   **for** $i = 1, \dots, T$ **do**
I4.   **for** $j = 0, \dots, z$ **do**
I5. $a_{i,j} \longleftarrow_R \mathbb{Z}_p$
I6. $L_i(x) = \sum_{j=0}^{z} a_{i,j} x^j$
I7. $t_i, t'_i \longleftarrow_R U$
I8. $MK_i = (L_i(x), t_i, t'_i)$
I9. $MK \longleftarrow \{MK_i | i = 1, \dots, T\}$
I10.   **return** MK;

The registration procedure is executed when a PUF card is inserted into the broadcaster card profiling device. For each round i the device challenges the PUF against t_i, t'_i obtaining $x_{u,i} = P_u(t_i)$ and a mask $c_{u,i} = P_u(t'_i)$. Then $x_{u,i}$ is stored securely at the broadcaster dataset. The $y_{u,i} = L_i(x_{u,i})$ is computed and subsequently stored in a masked form as $y'_{u,i} = y_{u,i} + c_{u,i}$ in the memory module corresponding to the PUF card. $SK_u = \{y'_{u,1}, \dots, y'_{u,T}\}$ is a private secret key of the PUF card, and $BK_u = \{x_{u,1}, \dots, x_{u,T}\}$ is a private key of broadcaster $\mathcal{B}$ corresponding to this card.

Algorithm 2. Registration procedure $\text{Reg}_{\text{BE}(z,n)}$

Data: identifier u of the new device, PUF P_u of device u, master secret
  $MK = \{(L_i(x), t_i, t'_i) | i = 1, \ldots, T\}$ generated by Algorithm 1
Result: a private secret key $SK_u = \{y'_{u,1}, \ldots, y'_{u,T}\}$ of device u for each round, a
  private key $BK_u = \{x_{u,1}, \ldots, x_{u,T}\}$ of the broadcaster for device u for each
  round

R1. **begin**
R2. $BK_u = \emptyset$
R3. $SK_u = \emptyset$
R4.   **for** $i = 1, \ldots, T$ **do**
R5. $x_{u,i} \longleftarrow P_u(t_i)$
R6. $c_{u,i} \longleftarrow P_u(t'_i)$
R7. $y_{u,i} \longleftarrow L_i(x_{u,i})$
R8. $y'_{u,i} \longleftarrow y_{u,i} + c_{u,i}$
R9. $BK_u \longleftarrow BK_u \cup \{(i, x_{u,i})\}$
R10. $SK_u \longleftarrow SK_u \cup \{(i, y'_{u,i})\}$
R11.   **return** BK_u, SK_u;

Encoding procedure executed by broadcaster $\mathcal{B}$ takes a set of device indexes to revoke, say $\Phi \subsetneq \Omega$, and an index i of a round. For each device $\phi \in \Phi$, the broadcaster retrieves the key BK_ϕ from the secret dataset, locates $x_{\phi,i}$, and adds it to the set X. If $|\Phi| < z$, then the broadcaster randomly generates x_j for $j = 1, \ldots, z - |\Phi|$ and adds them to X as well. Then the broadcaster creates interpolation set $\Psi = \{(x, L_i(x)) | x \in X\}$.

Algorithm 3. Encoding procedure $\text{Enc}_{\text{BE}(z,n)}$

Data: the index i of the current round, the round key K_i, the master secret MK_i, the set
  of revoked devices $\Phi \subsetneq \Omega$
Result: $H = \langle i, t_i, t'_i, x_i, \Psi, K' \rangle$

E1. **begin**
E2. $X \longleftarrow \emptyset$
E3.   **foreach** $\phi \in \Phi$ **do**
E4. $X \longleftarrow X \cup \{x_{\phi,i}\}$
E5.   **if** $|\Phi| < z$ **then**
E6.   **for** $j = 1, \ldots, z - |\Phi|$ **do**
E7. $x_j \longleftarrow_R \mathbb{Z}_p$ s.t. $\forall_{(\phi \in \Phi)}(x_{\phi,i} \neq x_j)$
E8. $X \longleftarrow X \cup \{x_j\}$
E9. $\Psi \longleftarrow \emptyset$
E10.   **foreach** $x \in X$ **do**
E11. $\Psi \longleftarrow \Psi \cup \{(x, L_i(x))\}$
E12. $x_i \longleftarrow_R \mathbb{Z}_p$ s.t. $\forall_{(x \in X)}(x_i \neq x)$
E13. $K' \longleftarrow K_i \cdot L_i(x_i)$
E14. $H \longleftarrow \langle i, t_i, t'_i, x_i, \Psi, K' \rangle$
E15.   **return** H

He chooses randomly x_i such that $(x_i \neq x)$ for each $x \in X$, and encodes session key K_i as $K' = K_i \cdot L_i(x_i)$. Finally he creates an enabling block $H = \langle i, t_i, t'_i, x_i, \Psi, K' \rangle$ which is broadcast to all devices.

Decoding procedure is executed by each D-box with a PUF card. It takes as an input the enabling block $H = \langle i, t_i, t'_i, x_i, \Psi, K' \rangle$. It computes $x_{u,i} = P_u(t_i)$ for the challenge t_i. If $(x_{u,i}, -) \notin \Psi$, then it unmasks $y_{u,i} = y'_{u,i} - P_u(t'_i)$, constructs interpolation set $\Psi' = \Psi \cup \{(x_{u,i}, y_{u,i})\}$, interpolates the polynomial L_i at x_i, and computes session key $K_i = K'/LI(x_i, \Psi')$.

Algorithm 4. Decoding procedure $\mathsf{Dec}_{\mathsf{BE}(z,n)}(SK_u, H)$

Data: The secret key SK_u of device u, the enabling block $H = \langle i, t_i, t'_i, x_i, \Psi, K' \rangle$
Result: The session key K_i

D1. **begin**
D2. $x_{u,i} \longleftarrow P_u(t_i)$
D3. $c_{u,i} \longleftarrow P_u(t'_i)$
D4.   **if** $(x_{u,i}, y_{u,i}) \notin \Psi$ **then**
D5. $y_{u,i} \longleftarrow y'_{u,i} - c_{u,i}$
D6. $\psi_u \longleftarrow (x_{u,i}, y_{u,i})$
D7. $\Psi' \longleftarrow \Psi \cup \{\psi_u\}$
D8. $K_i \longleftarrow K'/LI(x_i, \Psi')$
D9.   **return** K_i;
D10.   **else**
D11.   **return** $\perp$;

---

4 Security Analysis

Security of the proposed scheme is based on the following assumption concerning PUF's unpredictability and unclonability.

Assumption 1 (PUF Assumption). *Each physical unclonable function (PUF) device realizes a separate and distinct instance of the random oracle model for a hash function.*

The consequences of the assumption are intuitive:

- There is a separate table of input-output pairs associated with each PUF device, empty at the end of the production stage, initialized on its first run and maintained throughout its lifetime. Every time the PUF is tested upon a new distinct input, it returns a new random output and the pair is stored in its table. For inputs previously queried the outputs are consistent with the pairs recorded to the table.
- The outputs are unpredictable, unless PUF has already been used for a given input.
- The PUF cannot be cloned in such a way that after cloning the answers for unqueried inputs would be consistent between the clones.

Now we show that it is impossible to find out an unknown broadcaster polynomial having only its values for unknown arguments, as it is in the case of a coalition of traitors that share their private keys.

Theorem 2. *Let L_i be the secret polynomial of round i that still has not been executed. Then the probability that any coalition of users learns any information about L_i making use of their private information is negligible.*

Proof. The only knowledge about the polynomial L_i accessible for a user u is $y'_{u,i}$ stored in the memory module. Indeed, the other polynomials L_j are chosen independently of L_i. Now, each $y'_{u,i}$ is a value of L_i in some unknown point but blinded by a pseudorandom value $c_{u,i}$. Since $c_{u,i} = P_u(t'_{u,i})$, and t'_i is unknown to u, according to Assumption 1 the number $y'_{u,i}$ is a one time pad ciphertext of $y_{u,i}$. The only way to break it is by probing with different inputs and checking that the shares obtained may belong to a single polynomial. However, probability of guessing t'_i is negligible. □

Note that each unrevoked user learns L_i at round i, but this is not a problem as L_i is used only once. Leaking L_i leads only to possibility to recover K_{i+1}, but K_{i+1} can be leaked directly as well. On the other hand, any coalition of revoked users cannot achieve much as all their knowledge on L_i is published in the enabling block.

Now we show that no adversary can link excluded users by examining the enabling blocks. W.l.o.g. we assume that an adversary has to distinguish only from two users u_0 and u_1, after challenging their PUFs for some arbitrary (but realistic) number of tests.

Theorem 3. *Assume that an adversary is given enabling blocks for rounds 1 through T, and knows identity of all revoked devices for all rounds except for round i as well as all PUF cards for devices u_j with $j \neq 0, 1$. Moreover, the adversary may determine which devices are to be revoked at all rounds except i. In round i the broadcaster revokes device u_d, where $d \in \{0, 1\}$ is chosen uniformly at random. The adversary wins, if he answers d. Then the advantage of the adversary is negligible.*

Proof. It follows directly from Assumption 1. Indeed, the enabling block from round i contains $x_{d,i} = P_d(t_i)$. So the adversary has to guess whether $x_{d,i} = P_0(t_i)$ or $x_{d,i} = P_1(t_i)$. However, P_0 and P_1 behave like in the Random Oracle Model, so conditional probabilities of the events $x_{d,i} = P_0(t_i)$ and $x_{d,i} = P_1(t_i)$ are the same. □

5 PUF Based Broadcasting System - An Example

Here we sketch a more complete system than described in Sect. 2. Our extension uses properties of PUF in a much broader way. Our goal now is is to show that the proposed architecture (a PUF module plus a memory module with matching data set stored in clear) is quite useful to deter problems that usually occur in BE with user revocation.

Collusion Problem. The standard technique based on polynomial interpolation gives the broadcaster freedom to revoke *any* subset of at most z users. In order to prevent deriving the new broadcast key K_{t+1} by users that have been already revoked, the enabling block should be encrypted with K_t.

The problem with this approach is that if decoding devices are not tamper resistant, then a malicious user can use two devices, say u_1, u_2, in order to prevent effective revocation. Namely, at time t, he asks the broadcaster to revoke u_1 (e.g. claiming that u_1 has been stolen). However, u_2 will recover the key K_t and can show this key to device u_1. Therefore, at time $t + 1$, device u_1 can derive K_{t+1}, since a device already revoked will not be revoked once again. Simultaneously, the malicious user demands revocation of u_2. As before, u_1 can help u_2 to escape exclusion via revocation procedure. If after revocation of the devices the malicious user is not obliged to pay for broadcasting service, this is a perfect scenario in which the user eventually gets the service for free. Below we sketch concepts which help to avoid this problem.

5.1 Building Blocks

Revocation groups. We assume that there are totally n receiver devices (n is not necessarily constant, by receiver devices we understand also the devices that have not been handed to the actual users, but only prepared for use). We assume that at each time step t the receiver devices are divided into μ groups, and allocation of devices to groups in different time steps are stochastically independent.

In each group revocation procedure is executed separately, with a different polynomial. Since there are at most z revoked users at a time, we have on average z/μ revoked users per group. However, almost always some groups will contain substantially more revoked users than z/μ. This effect has been intensively studied as *balls and bins problem*. For instance, if there are μ bins (groups) and μ balls (devices to be revoked), then with high probability there is a bin with as much as $(1 + o(1)) \ln \mu / \ln \ln \mu$ balls (see e.g. [16]), while the average number is 1. This effect occurs also when the number of balls is much higher than μ [17]. Therefore in our scheme:

- slightly more than z/μ devices can be revoked at a time in each group,
- since in average each group has some room for revoking, it can be used for devices that have not been revoked on time and placed on a *waiting list* for revocation.

Anyway, below we show another technique that increases effectiveness of revocation based on *power of two choices paradigm*.

It is worth to mention that dividing into groups has significant computational advantage in case of constructions based on Lagrangian interpolation of polynomials. Namely, instead of interpolating a global polynomial of degree z a device has to interpolate a polynomial of a much smaller degree η.

Power of two choices. In our scheme each device participates in two different groups at each round. As before, the pair is chosen at random. When the broadcast key changes from K_t to K_{t+1}, then we assign each group a share of K_{t+1} according to a threshold 2-out-of-μ scheme. So, in order to get K_{t+1} the device should first reconstruct both shares of the groups it currently belongs, and then recover K_{t+1} from these shares.

Obviously, computing K_{t+1} in this way is more complicated than in case of assigning a device to a single group – execution time is at least doubled. However, there is an interesting twist in the performance. In order to revoke a device it suffices to revoke it in *any* of these two groups. If reasonable secret sharing schemes are used, then one share bears no information on the value of K_{t+1}. Having this in mind, the broadcaster can perform revoking in a clever way. Namely, if z devices are to be revoked, then it suffices to choose for each revoked user exactly one group, where it becomes revoked. This gives the broadcaster some freedom and helps to avoid assigning too many devices for revocation to a single group.

Finding an optimal mapping of devices to be revoked into groups, where revocation should occur, might be a challenging combinatorial problem. However, there are very promising results for the following greedy procedure:

- the devices to be revoked are considered one by one, e.g. according to some ordering of their serial numbers,
- when a device d_i is considered, we assign it to the group, where there are less revoked devices already assigned. If both groups, where d_i belongs, have the same number of already assigned devices, then we use the group of a lower index.

It has been shown that such a procedure significantly reduces the difference between the highest number of assignments in a group and the average value. Namely, if there are μ groups and z devices to be revoked, then the highest number of revoked users assigned to one group is $z/\mu + O(\ln \ln \mu)$ if power of two choices paradigm is used (see [16]). Symmetry breaking procedure described above is borrowed from [18]. Note that the difference between the maximum load and the average one has been reduced from logarithmic to double logarithmic.

Note that not all possibilities have been explored yet. If finally too many to-be-revoked users are assigned to the same group, then the broadcaster can reconsider each of these users and re-assign it to a different group, if there is room there or at least surplus over η is lower. This process can be iterated, until all local peaks are eliminated or there is no improvement possibility via a single step.

Chains of secrets. Each PUF module may be attached a chain of secrets which is unique for this PUF and which is uncorrelated with such chains of different PUF modules. The construction of the next secret of the chain could depend on:

- the previous element from the chain,
- the group shares that the device should be aware of,
- a parameter revealed by the broadcaster separately for each round,

and should involve using device's PUF in a substantial way. Usage of PUF should guarantee that the chain can be computed only by the PUF card, usage of the parameter revealed by the broadcaster ensures that a device can compute only the secrets up to the current round and cannot derive any values in advance. Usage of shares guarantees that after failing at least once to get the current group share of the K_t, prevents a device to reconstruct any later secrets from the chain, unless the device gets some specific data from the broadcaster.

5.2   Sketch of the System

Below we sketch design of the system. We omit some details that should be obvious for the reader.

As the basic scheme from Sect. 2, each PUF-card can be used for a limited number T of rounds. Nevertheless, the system as the whole can run forever without restarting. After T rounds either the PUF module must be re-enabled by the broadcaster $\mathcal{B}$ – for this purpose physical presence of the module at the broadcaster is necessary. Alternatively, a user may obtain a new module (like for ATM cards, credit cards, . . .).

Setup of the system. First, $\mathcal{B}$ runs a setup phase during which

- $\mathcal{B}$ chooses at random the current broadcast key K_i for each period $i \leq T$.
- It splits each K_i into shares $K_{1,i}, \ldots K_{\mu,i}$, according to a threshold 2-out-of-μ scheme. Share $K_{j,i}$ is assigned to group j at round i.
- For each $i \leq T$ and $j \leq \mu$, broadcaster $\mathcal{B}$ chooses at random a polynomial $L_{j,i}$ of degree η such that $L_{j,i}(0) = K_{j,i}$.
- For each $i \leq T$, it chooses at random secret reconstruction parameters t_i and t_i'.

The setup procedure is continued during running the system: $\mathcal{B}$ appends new data for new periods so that there are always at least T periods with determined parameters.

Enabling a module. In order to enable a device u, broadcaster $\mathcal{B}$ performs the following steps for each round i:

- $\mathcal{B}$ determines to which groups device u belongs at round i. Namely, the groups $g_i(u)$ and $g_i'(u)$ are indicated by $\log \mu$ low significant bits of, respectively,

$$H(0, u, i, t_i) \text{ and } H(1, u, i, t_i) \tag{2}$$

  where H is a strong hash function.
  Note that assignment of a device to the groups at round i is known for $\mathcal{B}$, but remains hidden until t_i is revealed by $\mathcal{B}$. Therefore, the adversary cannot make any clever choice when purchasing devices so that the devices belong to the same group at the same time.
- The secrets $S_i(u)$, for $i \leq T$, are constructed iteratively as follows: $S_0(u)$ is chosen at random, and

$$S_{i+1}(u) = \text{PUFH}_u(t_{i+1}, S_i(u), K_{g_i(u),i}, K_{g_i'(u),i}) \tag{3}$$

  where $\text{PUFH}_u = H \circ P_u$ is a composition of a secure hash function H and PUF P_u of device u (H is used to compress the result if the output of PUF is too long).
  Again, notice that a device cannot derive its secrets in advance as it does not know the strings t_{i+1}. On the other hand, the broadcaster $\mathcal{B}$ must compute the chain of secrets while holding the module with the PUF P_u.
  If the application scenario assumes that a revoked device cannot be enabled again, the secrets $S_i(u)$ are stored only temporarily by $\mathcal{B}$ and after initializing the memory module of the PUF card u they may be erased. Otherwise, they are stored in a directory corresponding to device u.
- For each revocation period $i \leq T$ it is necessary to compute the values $x_{u,i}$ and $x_{u,i}'$ used as arguments of interpolation of, respectively, $L_{g_i(u),i}$ and $L_{g_i'(u),i}$. They are computed as follows:

$$x_{u,i} = \text{PUFH}(0, S_i(u), t_i), \quad x_{u,i}' = \text{PUFH}(1, S_i(u), t_i) \tag{4}$$

Then the broadcaster computes the y values:

$$y_{u,i} = L_{g_i(u),i}(x_{u,i}), \quad y_{u,i}' = L_{g_i'(u),i}(x_{u,i}')$$

and the blinding factors:

$$c_{u,i} = \text{PUFH}(0, S_i(u), t_i'), \quad c_{u,i}' = \text{PUFH}(1, S_i(u), t_i') \tag{5}$$

Then it computes the blinded y values

$$b_{u,i} = y_{u,i} + c_{u,i}, \quad b_{u,i}' = y_{u,i}' + c_{u,i}' \tag{6}$$

Finally, the following values are stored:
- the triples $i, b_{u,i}, b_{u,i}'$ for $i \leq T$ are stored in a memory module of device u,
- the triples $i, x_{u,i}, x_{u,i}'$ are stored by $\mathcal{B}$ for its own use during revocation.

Revocation and transmitting the new broadcast key. The first step in the revocation is to determine for each device from the revocation list which group should be used. For this purpose $\mathcal{B}$ uses the procedure sketched in Sect. 5.1. In particular, $\mathcal{B}$ determines which blocks correspond to a given device according to (2).

If any group contains more than η devices for revocation, then some of them are postponed to the next round – the devices from the waiting list are placed on top of the list for this round. On the other hand, it may happen that some groups still have not reached the maximal capacity of η for revocation. In this case $\mathcal{B}$ may decide to use it for performing revocation twice for any device that is assigned to such a group. (We shall see in the next subsection that this increases immunity to attacks based on reverse engineering many devices.)

Once for each group it is determined which devices should be revoked there. For each such device $\mathcal{B}$ retrieves the stored values $x = x_{u,i}$ or $x = x_{u,i}'$,, computes the values

$$y = y_{g_i(u),i} = L_{g_i(u),i}(x) \quad \text{or} \quad y = y_{g_i'(u),i}' = L_{g_i'(u),i}'(x) \, ,$$

and finally uses the pair (x, y) in the enabling block of the group (see Sect. 2.3).

Finally, $\mathcal{B}$ composes an enabling block that consists of t_i, t_i' and the enabling blocks of all groups.

Key recovery. A non-revoked device u performs the following steps:

- It uses the parameter t_i transmitted in the enabling block to compute its groups $g_i(u)$ and $g_i'(u)$ according to rule (2).
- It computes the secret $S_i(u)$ according to rule (3),
- It computes the arguments $x_{u,i}$ and $x_{u,i}'$ according to rule (4).
- It reads the corresponding values $b_{u,i}$ and $b_{u,i}'$ from the memory module, computes $c_{u,i}, c_{u,i}'$ according to rule (5), and then $y_{u,i}, y_{u,i}'$ according to rule (6).
- It uses Lagrangian interpolation in the groups $g_i(u)$ and $g_i'(u)$ to recover polynomials $L_{g_i(u),i}$ and $L_{g_i(u),i}'(x)$ and then their values at point 0, that is $K_{g_i(u),i}$, $K_{g_i'(u),i}$. For Lagrangian interpolations the device uses the pairs from the enabling block transmitted by $\mathcal{B}$ and the pairs $(x_{u,i}, y_{u,i})$, $(x_{u,i}', y_{u,i}')$.
- It reconstructs the broadcast key K_i from $K_{g_i(u),i}, K_{g_i'(u),i}$.
- The values $K_{g_i(u),i}, K_{g_i'(u),i}$ and $S_i(u)$ are retained by the device for the next round (and change of the chain secret).

5.3 Escaping Revocation via Collusion

The same properties as described in Sect. 4 hold. The crucial issue is whether the scheme proposed is immune against an adversary, who tries to break effectiveness of revoking by techniques such as mentioned in Sect. 5. Note that as before, an adversary may transmit the group share from a non-revoked device to a revoked one.

Assume now that $\mu = 1000$. If an adversary holds two devices (as before) then revocation is ineffective with probability 0.002, as with this probability the second device belongs to the group where the first device is revoked. Therefore revocation is effective with probability 99.8%, which might be enough from the business point of view. However, an adversary may use more devices. If he uses even $\mu/2$ devices, then there are about μ/e groups, to which none of these devices is assigned. Now assume that another device held by the adversary is revoked. The probability that the group where it is revoked is one of these μ/e groups is about $\frac{1}{e}$ – i.e. the adversary cannot stop revocation with probability about $\frac{1}{e}$. If $\frac{1}{e}$ is considered as too low, one can design a system in which each device is revoked k times. Then the probability of escaping revocation goes down to $(1 - \frac{1}{e})^k$ at the price of increasing the length of the enabling blocks k times.

6 Conclusions

As we have seen, construction of strong PUFs would open new opportunities of broadcast encryption. In particular we make advantage of the fact that it is unknown which arguments will be used for a PUF, and that due to the size of the argument space it is impossible to pre-compute answers for future challenges. We also believe that strong guarantees (as in case of signing algorithms) are not crucial for BE as the adversary has the choice over attacking the scheme (and e.g. cloning the devices) or just re-broadcasting the transmission. So it is a matter of convenience and scale of a possible attack rather than strong immunity.

References

1. Pappu, R.S., Recht, B., Taylor, J., Gershenfeld, N.: Physical one-way functions. Science 297, 2026–2030 (2002),
   http://web.media.mit.edu/~brecht/papers/02.PapEA.powf.pdf (cited on page 2) (cited on page 49.)
2. Gassend, B., Clarke, D.E., van Dijk, M., Devadas, S.: Silicon physical random functions. In: Atluri, V. (ed.) ACM Conference on Computer and Communications Security, pp. 148–160. ACM, New York (2002) (cited on page 2) (cited on page 49.)
3. Guajardo, J., Kumar, S.S., Schrijen, G.J., Tuyls, P.: Fpga intrinsic pufs and their use for ip protection. In: Paillier, P., Verbauwhede, I. (eds.) CHES 2007. LNCS, vol. 4727, pp. 63–80. Springer, Heidelberg (2007) (cited on page 2) (cited on page 49.)
4. Gassend, B.: Physical Random Functions. Master's thesis. MIT, USA (2003) (cited on page 2) (cited on page 49.)
5. Pappu, R.S.: Physical one-way functions. PhD thesis, Massachusetts Institute of Technology (2001), http://pubs.media.mit.edu/pubs/papers/01.03.pappuphd.powf.pdf (cited on page 2) (cited on page 49.)

6. Rührmair, U., Sehnke, F., Sölter, J., Dror, G., Devadas, S., Schmidhuber, J.: Modeling attacks on physical unclonable functions. In: Al-Shaer, E., Keromytis, A.D., Shmatikov, V. (eds.) ACM Conference on Computer and Communications Security, pp. 237–249. ACM, New York (2010) (cited on page 2) (cited on page 49.)

7. Tuyls, P., Škorić, B.: Strong authentication with physical unclonable functions. In: Security, Privacy, and Trust in Modern Data Management, pp. 133–148 (2007) (cited on page 2) (cited on page 49.)

8. Fiat, A., Naor, M.: Broadcast encryption. In: Stinson, D.R. (ed.) CRYPTO 1993. LNCS, vol. 773, pp. 480–491. Springer, Heidelberg (1994) (cited on page 3) (cited on page 50.)

9. Tzeng, W.-G., Tzeng, Z.-J.: A public-key traitor tracing scheme with revocation using dynamic shares. In: Kim, K. (ed.) PKC 2001. LNCS, vol. 1992, pp. 207–224. Springer, Heidelberg (2001) (cited on page 3) (cited on page 50.)

10. Dodis, Y., Fazio, N., Kiayias, A., Yung, M.: Scalable public-key tracing and revoking. In: PODC, pp. 190–199 (2003) (cited on page 3) (cited on page 50.)

11. Dodis, Y., Fazio, N.: Public key trace and revoke scheme secure against adaptive chosen ciphertext attack. In: Desmedt, Y.G. (ed.) PKC 2003. LNCS, vol. 2567, pp. 100–115. Springer, Heidelberg (2002) (cited on page 3) (cited on page 50.)

12. Kim, C.H., Hwang, Y.-H., Lee, P.J.: Practical pay-TV scheme using traitor tracing scheme for multiple channels. In: Lim, C.H., Yung, M. (eds.) WISA 2004. LNCS, vol. 3325, pp. 264–277. Springer, Heidelberg (2005) (cited on page 3) (cited on page 50.)

13. Cichoń, J., Krzywiecki, Ł., Kutyłowski, M., Wlaź, P.: Anonymous distribution of encryption keys in cellular broadcast systems. In: Burmester, M., Yasinsac, A. (eds.) MADNES 2005. LNCS, vol. 4074, pp. 96–109. Springer, Heidelberg (2006) (cited on page 3) (cited on page 50.)

14. Krzywiecki, Ł., Kubiak, P., Kutyłowski, M.: A revocation scheme preserving privacy. In: Lipmaa, H., Yung, M., Lin, D. (eds.) Inscrypt 2006. LNCS, vol. 4318, pp. 130–143. Springer, Heidelberg (2006) (cited on page 3) (cited on page 50.)

15. Barth, A., Boneh, D., Waters, B.: Privacy in encrypted content distribution using private broadcast encryption. In: Di Crescenzo, G., Rubin, A. (eds.) FC 2006. LNCS, vol. 4107, pp. 52–64. Springer, Heidelberg (2006) (cited on page 3) (cited on page 50.)

16. Azar, Y., Broder, A.Z., Karlin, A.R., Upfal, E.: Balanced allocations. SIAM J. Comput. 29(1), 180–200 (1999) (cited on pages 10 and 11) (cites on pages 57 and 58.)

17. Berenbrink, P., Czumaj, A., Steger, A., Vöcking, B.: Balanced allocations: The heavily loaded case. SIAM J. Comput. 35(6), 1350–1385 (2006) (cited on page 10) (cited on page 57.)

18. Vöcking, B.: How asymmetry helps load balancing. J. ACM 50(4), 568–589 (2003) (cited on page 11) (cited on page 58.)

A Practical Device Authentication Scheme Using SRAM PUFs

Patrick Koeberl, Jiangtao Li, Anand Rajan, Claire Vishik, and Wei Wu

Intel Corporation
{patrickx.koeberl,jiangtao.li,anand.rajan,claire.vishik,
wei.a.wu}@intel.com

Abstract. The contamination of electronic component supply chains by counterfeit hardware devices is a serious and growing risk in today's globalized marketplace. Current practice for detecting counterfeit semiconductors includes visual checking, electrical testing, and reliability testing which can require significant investments in expertise, equipment, and time. Additionally, best practices have been developed in industry worldwide to combat counterfeiting in many of its variants. Although the current approaches improve the situation significantly, they do not provide extensive technical means to detect counterfeiting. However, new approaches in this area are beginning to emerge.

Suh and Devadas recently proposed a low cost device authentication scheme which relies on Physically Unclonable Functions (PUFs) to implement a challenge-response authentication protocol. There are several constraints in their authentication scheme, e.g., their scheme requires a secure online database and relies on PUF constructions that exhibit a large number of challenge-response pairs. In this paper, we introduce a new device authentication scheme using PUFs for device anti-counterfeiting. Our scheme is simple and practical as it does not require any online databases and is not tied to any PUF implementations. For hardware devices which already have SRAM and non-volatile storage embedded, our scheme takes almost no additional cost.

1   Introduction

The contamination of electronic component supply chains by counterfeit hardware devices is a serious and growing risk in today's globalized marketplace. Remarked devices account for the bulk of counterfeits detected [13]. In a typical remarking attack a device's product markings are misrepresented by replacing the original markings with markings indicating a higher specification and hence more valuable part. Such a device, if embedded in an electronic system, may fail in the field when subjected to a different operational environment than the original part was designed for. The risk of counterfeit product entering the supply chain increases when devices suffer supply shortfalls or have production terminated by the manufacturer. In extreme cases, where the product life cycle includes a lengthy validation and certification phase, devices may be obsolete by

J.M. McCune et al. (Eds.): TRUST 2011, LNCS 6740, pp. 63–77, 2011.
© Springer-Verlag Berlin Heidelberg 2011

the time the product enters the field. In such cases purchasing managers may be forced to procure devices from non-certified sources. A number of high-profile instances of counterfeit product entering the supply chain have been reported, in one instance involving the US Air Force, microprocessors for its F-15 flight control computer were procured from a broker and found to have been remarked [11].

Current practice for detecting counterfeit semiconductors includes visual checking, electrical testing, and reliability testing which can require significant investments in expertise, equipment, and time. Additionally, best practices have been developed in industry worldwide to combat counterfeiting in many of its variants. Although the current approaches improve the situation significantly, they do not provide extensive technical means to detect counterfeiting. Such methods cannot guarantee the provenance or performance of a device and in many cases it may only be feasible to perform testing on a sample of devices, for example when tests are destructive. However, new approaches in this area are beginning to emerge. Since the introduction of SEMI T20-1109 in 2009 [15] standardised methods providing device traceability and authentication have been defined, however these are serialisation mechanisms based on the generation of unpredictable, random codes and are intended to be applied at the device package and higher levels. They also require on-line access to a secure manufacturer database which may constrain their deployment in production facilities.

Authentication mechanisms which operate at the silicon rather than packaging level are an attractive proposition, particularly if they utilise intrinsic characteristics of the silicon rather than a serialisation mechanism. Physically Unclonable Functions (PUFs), introduced by Pappu [12], enable a class of applications in which identifiers are inseparably bound to hardware instances. Silicon PUFs [7] take this concept further by focusing on the manufacturing variations of Integrated Circuits (ICs).

1.1   Related Work

Standard device authentication protocols rely on securely storing a cryptographic secret, typically in non-volatile on-chip memory such as EEPROM, flash or fuses. Devices using such schemes are open to attack if the secret can be extracted and replicated in another device. In a typical scheme each device is embedded with a unique public and private key pair. The hardware manufacturer certifies the device by issuing a digital certificate bound to the device public key. When the hardware device needs to be verified, it sends its device certificate to the verifier along with a signature signed with its private key. The verifier can then use the hardware manufacturer's public key to verify the device certificate and then use the device's public key in the certificate to verify the signature. This solution is secure, as long as the device can protect its private key; and it is reliable because only hardware devices made by the original manufacturer have valid device certificates. For example, the Trusted Platform Module (TPM) uses a similar solution for remote attestation [16], and each TPM can be embedded with an endorsement key and endorsement credential at the time of manufacture. Such an approach is good for remote device authentication or attestation, but may not be suitable for device authentication for many scenarios in the supply chain. This approach also requires protection of the device private key in non-volatile memory, a secure execution environment to protect the key during the signing operation and is not applicable to many types of hardware devices.

Suh and Devadas proposed a low cost authentication scheme leveraging PUFs to implement a challenge-response authentication protocol [14]. In their scheme, the manufacturer or a trusted third party applies a set of randomly chosen challenges to the device containing the PUF and records the responses in a secure database. The device then enters the untrusted supply chain. At a later date, in order to verify the authenticity of the device, the verifier selects a challenge from the database, applies it to the device to be authenticated and compares the stored response with that of the device. If they match the device is authentic. Challenges and responses can be sent in the clear, however, once used, a challenge must be removed from the database in order to prevent man-in-the-middle attacks.

The primary advantage of using a PUF-based scheme is that cryptographic secrets are no longer stored on the device in a digital form and extracting PUF-based secrets requires an increased effort on the part of the attacker. However, the low cost authentication scheme above places a number of constraints on the PUF type and the overall system for the following reasons. First, the deployed PUF must possess a large number of challenge-response pairs (CRPs). Second, authentications are on-line, placing availability constraints on the CRP database. Finally, if many authentications are expected per device and the device population is large, the CRP storage requirement may be prohibitive.

1.2 Our Contribution

In this paper we propose a PUF-based device authentication scheme targeted at manufacturing environments; increasingly manufacturers of electronic products require higher assurance that the semiconductor devices they integrate are genuine. Many PUF-based applications require additional on-chip functionality, such as error correction and supplementary cryptography [6,17], which increase cost as well as complicate security assumptions. The unique characteristics of manufacturing allow us to leverage PUFs for authentication, while keeping cost and additional requirements to a minimum. Our PUF based authentication scheme removes the need for authentication to be performed on-line, and for large and secure CRP databases to be maintained, both of which are impediments to adoption. We show that for reasonable cost in terms of on-chip storage and computational expense at the verifier, a level of security can be achieved which is sufficient to raise the effort for the attacker to uneconomic levels. Finally, we propose the ways for our scheme to be integrated into the manufacturing context by leveraging existing test methodologies and standards.

1.3 Organization of the Paper

The rest of this paper is organized as follows. We first give an overview of PUFs, introduce some state-of-art PUF constructions and propose a formal PUF definition in Section 2. We then present our PUF based off-line device authentication schemes in Section 3. We discuss the choice of parameters, perform a security analysis, and review some practical considerations of our scheme in Section 4. We conclude our paper and discuss the future work in Section 5.

2   Physically Unclonable Functions

A PUF can be informally described as a physical system which when measured or challenged provides unique, repeatable and unpredictable responses. Creating a physical copy of the PUF with an identical challenge-response behaviour is also hard, thus resulting in a structure which is unclonable even by the manufacturer. Gassend et al. introduced silicon PUFs in [7]. Silicon PUFs exploit the uncontrollable manufacturing variations which are a result of the IC fabrication process. Manufacturing variation of parameters such as dopant concentrations and line widths manifest themselves as differences in timing behaviour between instances of the same IC design. These timing differences can be measured using a suitable circuit.

The arbiter PUF [7] compares the relative delay of two delay paths using a series of configurable delay elements terminated by an arbiter. By using the PUF challenge as the delay element configuration vector, the circuit exhibits a challenge space which is exponential in the number of challenge bits, a feature which has been exploited in the lightweight authentication scheme of [14]. The ring oscillator PUF [7] compares the relative frequencies of self oscillating delay loops in order to generate PUF responses. A single response bit can thus be generated for a pair of oscillators.

In [8] a new PUF type was introduced based on the power-up state of uninitialised six-transistor SRAM cells. The structure of such a cell is shown in Figure 1. The storage mechanism in an SRAM cell consists of four cross-coupled transistors which assume one of two stable states after power-up. Which state the cell enters is largely determined by the relative characteristics of the transistors, any mismatch will cause the cell to have a bias to one of the states. The mismatch is fixed at manufacturing time, resulting in a cell that tends to power up in the same state. Experimental work in [8,9] shows that the power-up behaviour is random between cells, but robust for a single cell, resulting in a structure that is well suited for use as the basis of a PUF. The challenge in the case of an SRAM PUF can be considered to be a set of SRAM addresses, and the response the contents of those addresses post power-up. It is therefore useful to view the SRAM PUF as having a single challenge.

Definition of Single-Challenge PUF. A consistent view of what constitutes a PUF from the formal standpoint does not exist at this point in the literature, although there have been earlier attempts at formal definitions [12,7,8,3,2]. We now give a definition of single-challenge PUFs which builds on the PUF definitions of [3] and [2]. While our definition excludes PUFs with multiple challenges, most known silicon PUF constructions are of the single-challenge type with the exception of the arbiter PUF [7].

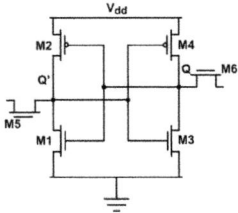

Fig. 1. Construction of an SRAM cell

Definition 1 (Single-Challenge PUFs). *A* (m, δ)-*family of single-challenge physically unclonable functions is a set of probabilistic algorithms with the following procedures:*

Instantiate. *The output of the* Instan *procedure is a* PUF *with a unique identity* $id_{\mathsf{PUF}} \in \{0, 1\}^m$.

Evaluate. *Given a physically unclonable function* PUF*, the* Eval *procedure on each query outputs a noisy identity* $id_{\mathsf{PUF}} \oplus e$ *where* $e \in \{0, 1\}^m$ *is a random noise vector with a Hamming distance of* δ *or less.*

For simplicity, we can set id_{PUF}, the unique identity of PUF, to be the initial evaluation result. We now define the unclonability property of single-challenge PUFs, the only security property of interest in our device authentication scheme.

Definition 2 (Unclonability). *We say that the PUF is unclonable if there exists no efficient clone procedure that gets n PUF devices $D_1, \ldots, D_n$ and builds another physical PUF device D' such that the Hamming distance between the identities id_{D_i} and $id_{D'}$ is less than 2δ for any $i = 1, \ldots, n$.*

3   Our Off-Line Authentication Scheme

In this section, we present our off-line device authentication schemes. We first present a basic authentication scheme using any single-challenge PUF and discuss the security properties of this scheme. We then describe a potential attack in the basic scheme and present a full-fledged device authentication scheme optimized for SRAM-PUF and mitigating against this attack.

3.1   Our Basic Scheme

Our off-line device authentication scheme makes use of a digital signature scheme (Sign, Verify) and a family of single-challenge PUFs (m, δ)-PUF. Let (mpk, msk) be the device manufacturer's public verification key and private signing key pair. Our scheme has two phases, an enrollment phase and an evaluation phase depicted in Figure 2. In the enrollment phase, each device is certified by the hardware manufacturer. In the evaluation phase, the hardware device is verified by a verifier who received the device from the supply chain.

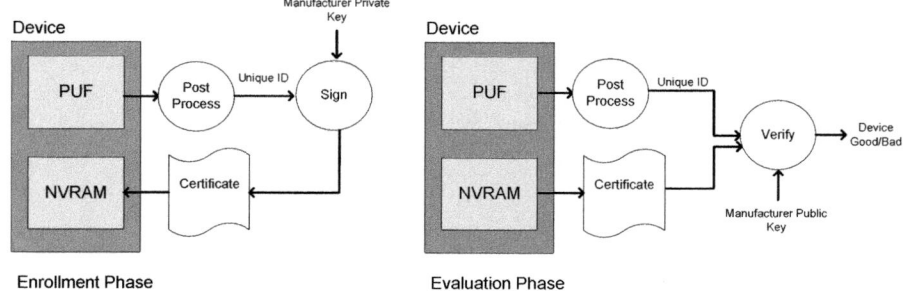

Fig. 2. Off-line device authentication flow

Enrollment Phase. A hardware device is certified by the manufacturer with the follow steps:

1. The manufacturer instantiates a PUF into the device.
2. The manufacturer runs the evaluation procedure Eval and obtains the unique identity id_{PUF}.
3. The manufacturer uses msk to sign id_{PUF} and creates a signature $\sigma = \mathsf{Sign}_{msk}(id_{\mathsf{PUF}})$.
4. The manufacturer sets the device certificate as $(id_{\mathsf{PUF}}, \sigma)$ and stores the certificate in the non-volatile memory (NVM) of the device.

Evaluation Phase. Once a verifier obtains a hardware device from the supply chain, he can verify the device with the following steps.

1. The verifier runs the evaluation procedure Eval of the PUF in the device and obtains id'.
2. The verifier reads the device certificate $(id_{\mathsf{PUF}}, \sigma)$ from the NVM of the device.
3. The verifier uses mpk to verify the signature σ on id_{PUF}. If the verification fails, the verifier rejects the device.
4. The verifier checks that the Hamming distance between id_{PUF} and id' is at most δ. If the Hamming distance is greater than δ, the verifier rejects the device.
5. The verifier accepts the device if all the above steps succeed.

Note that there is no post-processing function needed for the basic authentication scheme. It is reserved for the full device authentication scheme described in the rest of this section. One can choose the following parameters. Let $m = 256$, i.e., the output of PUF is 256-bit. Let (Sign, Verify) be the EC-DSA signature algorithm [5] on a 256-bit prime elliptic curve. The signature is only 512-bit in size. The size of the device certificate is 768-bit. The manufacturer can store the device certificate on device (e.g., in the flash or fuses of the device) without much overhead.

Our basic authentication scheme is very simple and cheap to implement. It does not require any online database access during the evaluation phase. The additional non-volatile storage required per device is small, thus it is cost-effective to implement in practice. Note that, unlike many PUF applications, the PUF queries and the device certificates in our scheme can be public and do not need to be protected. Also note that error correction or fuzzy extractors [4] are not needed in our scheme.

Theorem 1. *If the PUF in our scheme is unclonable and the signature scheme is unforgeable, and if the verifier indeed queries the PUF directly, then our device authentication scheme is secure, i.e., no efficient attacker can forge a device that can be successfully verified.*

Proof. Suppose an attacker breaks the device authentication scheme. In other words, the attacker forges a device D' without going through the enrollment phase and the device can be successfully verified in the evaluation phase. We can use this attacker to break either the signature scheme or the unclonability property of the PUF scheme. Suppose the manufacturer has produced n valid devices $D_1, \ldots, D_n$ during the enrollment phase. Let $(id_{D_1}, \sigma_1), \ldots, (id_{D_n}, \sigma_n)$ be the corresponding device certificates. Let (id', σ') be the device certificate in the forged device. Since the device D' can be successfully verified, σ' is a valid signature on id' and the evaluation result of PUF in D' must be close enough to the unique identity id' with Hamming distance no more than δ. We have the following two cases. First, if $(id', \sigma') \notin \{(id_{D_1}, \sigma_1), \ldots, (id_{D_n}, \sigma_n)\}$, then the attacker has successfully forged a signature on id'. We can use this attacker to break the digital signature scheme. Second, if $(id', \sigma') = (id_{D_i}, \sigma_i)$ for some index i, then the attacker successfully cloned a PUF in D' such that a PUF output of D' has Hamming distance less than δ from id_{D_i}. The attacker effectively breaks the unclonability property of PUF.

3.2 A PUF Simulation Attack on the Basic Authentication Scheme

Although our device authentication scheme is secure in theory, it may be vulnerable to the following PUF simulation attack. In this attack, the attacker obtains a valid device from the manufacturer and reads out the device certificate (id, σ). When the attacker counterfeits a new device, he copies the device certificate into the NVM of the new device. The attacker embeds a PUF simulator in the integrated circuit such that if a verifier queries the PUF of the new device, the simulator always outputs id instead of the result from the actual PUF. The counterfeit device can be successfully authenticated, if the verifier cannot distinguish whether the PUF evaluation comes from a real PUF or a PUF simulator.

It is interesting to consider the role that the PUF size plays in mitigating the above attack. Since such an attacker must be capable of re-engineering the device to include a PUF simulator at the silicon level, it is this technological barrier rather than the chosen PUF size that is likely to dissuade a device remarker, who is typically economically motivated. For attackers with other motivations, who are likely to be well-funded, the PUF size may not be a sufficient deterrent. Nevertheless, since SRAM is a common primitive in devices, we can use all or a portion of the SRAM as a PUF for supply chain authentication purposes.

For example, we can use the same basic authentication scheme as in Section 3.1 and set $m = 2^{18}$. In order to simulate the PUF the attacker must embed 256-kbit of information in the device. The main drawback of this approach is that the size of device certificate also becomes very large, thus the amount of non-volatile storage on the device required to store the certificate is also large. Of course, external storage could be used to store the device certificates, such as on hard disk or in an online database. These drawbacks reduce the appeal of our basic scheme.

3.3   Our Full Authentication Scheme Using SRAM PUF

We now present our full device authentication scheme mitigating against the hardware PUF simulation attack but not increasing the NVM requirement. The main idea of our scheme is as follows: we compress the m-bit identity of PUF (e.g., 256-kbit) into a k-bit device ID (e.g., 256-bit). The device ID and the corresponding signature together become the device certificate. In this way, the device certificate is small enough to fit into the non-volatile storage of the device. Note that the compression function (also denoted as the post-processing function in Figure 2) needs to be designed carefully to be noise preserving.

Before we present our device authentication scheme, we first define the SRAM PUF for the purpose of analyzing the quality of our post-processing functions. Our SRAM PUF definition builds on top of Definition 1 and [2].

Definition 3 (SRAM PUFs). *A (m, p)-family of Static Random Access Memory (SRAM) based PUFs is a set of probabilistic algorithms with the following two procedures:*

Instantiate. *The* Instan *process instantiates m physical SRAM cells $S_1, \ldots, S_m$, each storing an element from $\{0, 1\}$. The ideal noise-free power-up state s_i of the SRAM cell S_i is fixed for a specific instantiation, but independently and uniformly distributed over $\{0, 1\}$.*

Evaluate. *Given a PUF based on m SRAM cells, the* Eval *procedure on each query outputs a noisy power-up state $\tilde{s} = \tilde{s}_1 \cdots \tilde{s}_m$ where $\tilde{s}_i = s_i \oplus e$, with e a Bernoulli distributed random variable with probability p. Note that e is drawn independently for every SRAM cell at each evaluation.*

Note that given two evaluations $\tilde{s}$ and $\tilde{s}'$ on a single SRAM PUF device, the noise rate (bit error rate) between $\tilde{s}$ and $\tilde{s}'$ is larger than p in the above model. Let $\tilde{s} = \tilde{s}_1 \cdots \tilde{s}_m$ and $\tilde{s}' = \tilde{s}'_1 \cdots \tilde{s}'_m$, where $\tilde{s}_i = s_i \oplus e_i$ and $\tilde{s}'_i = s_i \oplus e'_i$ and e_i and e'_i are both independently Bernoulli distributed. We now have $\tilde{s}'_i = \tilde{s}_i \oplus e_i \oplus e'_i$, where $e_i \oplus e'_i$ is a Bernoulli distribution with probability $2p - p^2$. Therefore, if SRAM PUF has p bit error rate, the noise rate between two PUF evaluations on a single PUF device is $2p - p^2$. However, this analysis is based on the SRAM PUF definition above where the noise in the PUF evaluation is evenly distributed across all the SRAM cells. In practice, some SRAM cells are more stable than others. We expect the noise rate between two PUF evaluations to be close to p rather than $2p - p^2$.

Our full device authentication scheme makes use of a digital signature scheme (Sign, Verify) and a family of SRAM (m, p)-PUFs. Let (mpk, msk) be the device manufacturer's public verification key and private signing key pair. Let Extract : $\{0, 1\}^m \rightarrow \{0, 1\}^k$ be a post-processing function that extracts m-bit SRAM PUF evaluation result into a k-bit device ID. Our device authentication scheme is described as follows:

Enrollment Phase. A hardware device D is certified by the manufacturer with the following steps:

1. The manufacturer instantiates an SRAM PUF into the device.
2. The manufacturer runs the evaluation procedure Eval and obtains the unique identity $\tilde{s}$.
3. The manufacturer runs the post-processing function to compute the device ID $id_D = \mathsf{Extract}(\tilde{s})$. We provide the post-processing function at the end of this subsection.
4. The manufacturer uses msk to sign id_D and creates a signature $\sigma = \mathsf{Sign}_{msk}(id_D)$.
5. The manufacturer sets the device certificate as (id_D, σ) and stores the certificate in the NVM of the device.

Evaluation Phase. Once a verifier obtains a hardware device from the supply chain, he can verify the device with the following steps:

1. The verifier runs an evaluation of the SRAM PUF in the device using random access as follows:
   (a) It chooses a random permutation $(i_1, \ldots i_m)$ of $(1, \ldots, m)$.
   (b) It queries the SRAM cells using the following order $S_{i_1}, \ldots, S_{i_m}$ and obtains $\tilde{s}'_{i_1}, \ldots, \tilde{s}'_{i_m}$.
   (c) It outputs $\tilde{s}' = \tilde{s}'_1 \cdots \tilde{s}'_m$ as the PUF evaluation result.
2. The verifier computes $id'_D = \mathsf{Extract}(\tilde{s}')$.
3. The verifier reads (id_D, σ) from the NVM of the device.
4. The verifier uses mpk to verify the signature σ on id_D. If the verification fails, the verifier rejects the device.
5. The verifier checks that the Hamming distance between id_D and id'_D is at most δ, where δ is a security parameter. If the Hamming distance is greater than δ, the verifier rejects the device. We shall discuss how to choose the value of δ in Section 4.
6. The verifier accepts the device if all the above steps succeed.

We now present a post-processing function. The input to this function is an m-bit string $s = s_1 \cdots s_m$. The output is a k-bit string $t = t_1 \cdots t_k$. The idea is that we divide m bits of s into k different groups, and then for each group, we perform majority voting to output a single bit. The resulting k bits from k groups is the output of this post-processing function. The details of this function are given as follows:

1. Let ℓ be the largest odd number such that $k \cdot \ell \leq m$.
2. Divide the first $k \cdot \ell$ bits of string s into k groups $G_1, \ldots, G_k$, where each group has ℓ bits.

3. For each group G_i, where $1 \leq i \leq k$, compute $t_i = \text{Voting}(G_i)$, the majority voting result of bits in G_i. More specifically, let $G = \{b_1, \ldots, b_\ell\}$ where $b_1, \ldots, b_\ell \in \{0, 1\}$. The majority voting function $\text{Voting}(G)$ is defined as following: $\text{Voting}(G)$ outputs 1 if $b_1 + \cdots + b_\ell > \ell/2$ and outputs 0 otherwise.

Note that the random PUF evaluation in the device evaluation phase and the random mapping from bits to groups in the post-processing function are used to defend against a PUF simulation attack using less than m-bit storage. The mapping from bits to groups is random but fixed per function and is encoded in the algorithm. Also note that the mapping can be public. The security of our device authentication scheme does not rely on the secrecy of this function.

4   Discussion and Analysis

We first provide a security analysis of our device authentication scheme including choices of parameters, then discuss the practical aspects of our scheme.

4.1   Probability and Security Analysis

The full device authentication scheme relies on the post-processing function to compress the long m-bit PUF result into a shorter k-bit device ID, in order to mitigate against the hardware PUF simulation attack without increasing the NVM requirement. We first describe the capabilities of an attacker.

1. The attacker can access the post-processing function.
2. The attacker can capture n legitimate device certificates and put any one of the device certificates in the NVM of the forged device.
3. The attacker can put a new SRAM PUF in the forged device. Alternatively, he can simulate PUF in circuit with less than m-bit storage.

Theorem 2. *Given a legitimate device ID and certificate, it is impossible for an attacker to simulate a PUF with at most $(c \cdot k)$-bit storage and circuit size, where c is a small constant such that $c \cdot k$ is much smaller than m, such that a forged device with simulated PUF can be successfully verified.*

Due to space limitations, we will give the proof in the full paper. Since the PUF simulation attack is not possible for a storage-constrained attacker, we focus in the rest of this section to prove that if the attacker places a random SRAM PUF in the forged device, he has very little chance to win. We first define the following terms by borrowing terminologies from biometrics.

Definition 4 (False Rejection Rate). *If the manufacturer certifies a legitimate device in the enrollment phase, the False Rejection Rate (FRR) is the probability that the device fails to be verified in the evaluation phase.*

Definition 5 (False Acceptance Rate). *Assume the attacker has captured n legitimate device certificates, where n is a security parameter. The False Acceptance Rate (FAR) is the probability that an uncertified device with a random SRAM PUF embedded can be successfully verified in the evaluation, assuming the attacker can inject any one of the device certificates into the forged device.*

We now analyze how noise at the SRAM cell level propagates to the device ID and how to choose δ between the certified device ID and the one from evaluation procedure such that both FRR and FAR are sufficiently small.

Theorem 3. *If the SRAM PUF is modeled as in Definition 3, then the PUF evaluation result is random and unbiased.*

Proof. Recall that each PUF query outputs $\tilde{s} = \tilde{s}_1 \cdots \tilde{s}_m$ where $\tilde{s}_i = s_i \oplus e$. Since s_i is independently and uniformly distributed over $\{0,1\}$ and e is independently Bernoulli distributed. Thus $\tilde{s}_i$ is also uniformly distributed, and unbiased.

Let $\mathrm{FAR}(n)$ denote the false acceptance rate if the attacker has captured n legitimate device certificates.

Theorem 4. *In our device authentication scheme, $\mathrm{FAR}(n)$ is at most $n \cdot \mathrm{FAR}(1)$.*

We omit the proof and leave it in the full version of this paper. This theorem shows that the attacker can only linearly increase FAR by collecting more legitimate device certificates. In the rest of this section, we always use $\mathrm{FAR}(1)$ as the default false acceptance rate unless otherwise specified.

The Extract function given in Section 3 divides the m-bit PUF output string into k groups, each group has ℓ-bits. The majority voting result of each group is a corresponding bit in the device ID. We use P_0 and P_1 to denote the probability that a PUF bit in a PUF evaluation is equal to 0 and 1, respectively. By Theorem 3, we have $P_0 = P_1 = 0.5$. Let P_{cell} be the bit noise rate between two PUF evaluation results. Let p be the bit error rate defined in Definition 3. As we analyzed in Section 3.3, $P_{\text{cell}} = 2p - p^2$.

Let ℓ_0 be the total number of zeros in a voting group. Let x be the total number of bit flips in the voting group at the device evaluation phase, among them x_0 is the number of $0 \to 1$ flips and x_1 is for $1 \to 0$ flips, where $x_0 + x_1 = x$. The number of zeros in an evaluated result of the group equals to $\ell_0' = \ell_0 - x_0 + x_1$. PUF noise during evaluation may cause majority voting results to flip, this will be manifested as device ID bit noise. Let us define the event of a majority voting flipping as following:

$$\mathrm{Flip}(\ell, \ell_0, x_0, x_1) = ((\ell_0 > \lfloor \ell/2 \rfloor) \oplus (\ell_0 - x_0 + x_1) > \lfloor \ell/2 \rfloor) = \texttt{true})$$

We also define the three conditional probabilities for a single flipping event as:

1. The probability of having ℓ_0 zeros out of ℓ-bit voting group: $\mathbf{p_1}(\ell_0) = \binom{\ell}{\ell_0} \cdot (P_0)^{\ell_0} \cdot (1 - P_0)^{\ell - \ell_0}$
2. The probability of having x bit flips out of ℓ-bit voting group: $\mathbf{p_2}(x) = \binom{\ell}{x} \cdot (P_{\text{cell}})^x \cdot (1 - P_{\text{cell}})^{\ell - x}$
3. The probability of having x_0 out of x flips to be $0 \to 1$ flip: $\mathbf{p_3}(\ell_0, x, x_0) = \binom{\ell_0}{x_0} \binom{\ell - \ell_0}{x - x_0} / \binom{\ell}{x}$

Putting everything together, the device ID bit noise rate (P_{bit}), which is also the probability of a majority voting flipping is:

$$P_{\text{bit}} = \sum_{0 \leq \ell_0 \leq \ell} \sum_{0 \leq x \leq \ell} \sum_{0 \leq x_0 \leq x} \mathrm{Flip}(\ell, \ell_0, x_0, x - x_0) \cdot \mathbf{p_1}(\ell_0) \cdot \mathbf{p_2}(x) \cdot \mathbf{p_3}(\ell_0, x, x_0)$$

Figure 3 shows the P_{bit} under different voting group sizes and P_{cell}, which ranges from 0.25% to 10%. Since the PUF evaluation results are evenly distributed and the total numbers of 0 and 1 are balanced, a small disturbance may easily change the voting result. It is more likely to be flipped when the total number of flips is larger. The curves show the same trend. The larger P_{cell} leads to a larger P_{bit}. Also, when the size of voting group increases, the noise rates increase as well. More drastic increases are seen at small voting group sizes. As the size keeps increasing, the P_{bit} reaches a saturation level eventually.

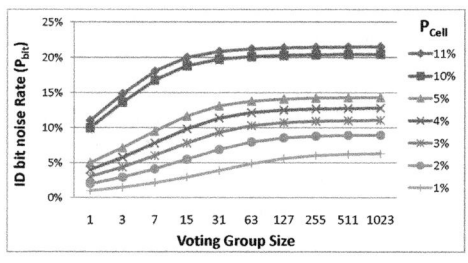

Fig. 3. The P_{bit} as a function of voting group size under different P_{cell}

There are two reasons for a device to fail verification during evaluation phase, one is due to the mismatched signature σ', the other is due to the Hamming distance between id_D and id'_D being greater than a predefined δ. For a legitimate device, the first case should never happen, then the FRR is essentially the probability of the second case. Figure 4 shows the FRR of a 256-bit device ID across a range of ID bit noise rates, from 1% to 20%. The y-axis is the FRR and x-axis is the Hamming distance. For a fixed bit noise rate in the device ID, when the Hamming distance increases the FRR reduces, as more devices are verified as valid. Among different bit noise rates, the lower rate can sustain the same FRR with a much smaller Hamming distance. For example, to achieve a FRR of 10^{-3}, a device with a noise rate of 1% requires a maximum Hamming distance δ of 9. However with a bit noise rate of 20%, it has to include all devices with δ up to 72. Reducing the FRR to 10^{-6}, a device with a noise rate 1% requires a δ of 13 instead of 9. Table 1 shows the Hamming distance values for both 256- and 512-bit device IDs under a fixed FRR of 10^{-3} and 10^{-6}.

Figure 5 shows the FAR(1) as a function of Hamming distance with two device ID lengths. Consider two PUF strings, assuming one from a legitimate device and the other from a forged device. The two device IDs are random and independent. Given a δ, the probability for the device ID extracted from a randomly instantiated PUF to be within the Hamming distance of a legitimate id ($\leq \delta$) is defined as FAR(1). Because $P_0 = 0.5$, on average, any random k-bit string can achieve a Hamming distance of $k/2$ when compared to a target id, therefore FAR(1) = 50% for $\delta = k/2$. For instance, this is the case for point(256, 0.5) on curve $k = 512$ and point(128, 0.5) on curve $k = 256$. However, when the Hamming distance δ becomes smaller, FAR(1) drops drastically. For $k = 256$, the FAR(1) reduces to 10^{-2} when δ is 109. Beyond the 10^{-2} point, the curve drops almost exponentially. The detailed values are listed in Table 2.

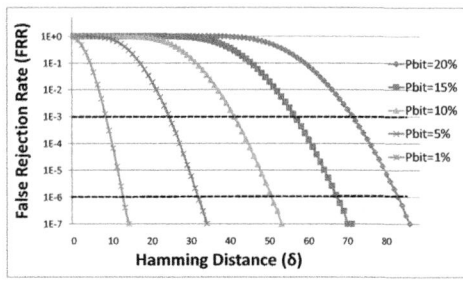

Fig. 4. FRR(k=256) for different P_{bit}

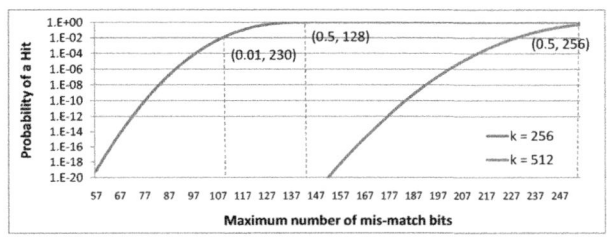

Fig. 5. FAR as a function of Hamming distance

Table 1. Max. Hamming Dist δ for FRR   **Table 2.** Min. Hamming Dist. for FAR(1)

	k=256	k=512				k=512	k=256	k=128
	FRR=10^{-3}	10^{-6}	10^{-3}	10^{-6}	FAR = 0.5	256	128	64
$P_{\text{bit}} = 1\%$	9	13	14	20	10^{-2}	230	108	51
5%	25	32	43	53	10^{-3}	221	104	46
10%	41	51	74	87	10^{-4}	214	99	42
12%	49	59	87	101	10^{-5}	208	95	39
15%	57	68	104	119	10^{-6}	202	91	36
20%	72	84	132	148	10^{-7}	198	88	34

We now give a sample set of parameters. Consider a PUF evaluation with $P_0 = 0.5$ and $P_{\text{cell}} = 4\%$. Results reported in [8] show that less than 4% of the SRAM cell population are noisy at room temperature. The following parameters are chosen: $k = 256$, $\ell = 1023$, and $m = k \cdot \ell = 261888$. From Figure 3, we estimate P_{bit} approximates to 12%. We choose $\delta = 60$. This value of δ is enough to keep both the FRR and FAR(1) values lower than 10^{-6}.

4.2 Practical Aspects of Our Scheme

We envisage our scheme to be deployed in an electronic manufacturing environment, where it may be used to authenticate populated devices from different manufacturers as part of a production-test regime. For devices already embedding SRAM and NVM, the cost imposed by our scheme can be low when standards such as the JTAG Test Access Port [1] are used for SRAM PUF and NVM access.

The storage requirements of the device certificate are relatively modest, on the order of 10^3 bits when augmenting data such as the device model number and speed grade are added. For devices already embedding NVM, this requirement might be met by spare capacity. In the case where no NVM is available for certificate storage, it may be possible to store the certificate on the device package. Matrix codes [10] are ideally suited here, although the IC package dimensions will in practice constrain how much data can be encoded.

Our scheme is motivated by the need to raise the effort level for device remarkers to uneconomic levels. A remarker wishing to clone the PUF must in effect re-engineer the device to include a PUF simulator at the silicon level; the cost of doing so is likely to outweigh the potential gain. We do not propose the scheme as a mitigation against well-funded and highly motivated attackers, whose motives are non-economic in nature.

5   Conclusion and Future Work

We presented a new authentication scheme using SRAM PUFs for device anti-counterfeiting. Our scheme is simple and practical and does not depend on an online database for authentication. The unique characteristics of manufacturing allow us to leverage PUFs for authentication, while keeping cost and additional requirements to a minimum. Our work is a first step toward an anti-counterfeiting method tailored to the manufacturing environment. Future work includes studying whether our device authentication scheme can be applied to other PUF constructions, such as those based D-type flip-flops [18] and prototyping our device authentication scheme in order to study the quality of our post-processing functions using experimental SRAM PUF data.

References

1. 1149.1-1990 - IEEE Standard Test Access Port and Boundary-Scan Architecture, http://standards.ieee.org/findstds/standard/1149.1-1990.html
2. Armknecht, F., Maes, R., Sadeghi, A.-R., Sunar, B., Tuyls, P.: PUF-PRFs: A new tamper-resilient cryptographic primitive. In: Advances in Cryptology – EURO-CRYPT 2009 Poster Session, pp. 96–102 (2000)
3. Armknecht, F., Maes, R., Sadeghi, A.-R., Sunar, B., Tuyls, P.: Memory leakage-resilient encryption based on physically unclonable functions. In: Matsui, M. (ed.) ASIACRYPT 2009. LNCS, vol. 5912, pp. 685–702. Springer, Heidelberg (2009)
4. Dodis, Y., Reyzin, L., Smith, A.: Fuzzy extractors: How to generate strong keys from biometrics and other noisy data. In: Cachin, C., Camenisch, J.L. (eds.) EU-ROCRYPT 2004. LNCS, vol. 3027, pp. 523–540. Springer, Heidelberg (2004)
5. Federal Information Processing Standard 186-3: Digital Signature Standard (DSS), http://csrc.nist.gov/publications/fips/fips186-3/fips_186-3.pdf
6. Gassend, B., Clarke, D., van Dijk, M., Devadas, S.: Controlled physical random functions. In: Proceedings of the 18th Annual Computer Security Conference (2002)
7. Gassend, B., Clarke, D., van Dijk, M., Devadas, S.: Silicon physical random functions. In: ACM Conference on Computer and Communications Security, pp. 148–160. ACM Press, New York (2002)

8. Guajardo, J., Kumar, S.S., Schrijen, G.-J., Tuyls, P.: FPGA intrinsic pUFs and their use for IP protection. In: Paillier, P., Verbauwhede, I. (eds.) CHES 2007. LNCS, vol. 4727, pp. 63–80. Springer, Heidelberg (2007)
9. Holcomb, D.E., Burleson, W.P., Fu, K.: Power-up sram state as an identifying fingerprint and source of true random numbers. IEEE Transactions on Computers 58(9), 1198–1210 (2009)
10. ISO/IEC16022:2006 Data Matrix bar code symbology specification, http://www.iso.org/iso/catalogue_detail.htm?csnumber=44230
11. U. S. G. A. Office. Defense supplier base: Dod should leverage ongoing initiatives in developing its program to mitigate risk of counterfeit parts. GAO-10-389 (March 2010)
12. Pappu, R.S.: Physical one-way functions. PhD thesis. Massachusetts Institute of Technology (March 2001)
13. Semiconductor Industry Association, http://www.sia-online.org/cs/anticounterfeiting
14. Suh, G.E., Devadas, S.: Physical unclonable functions for device authentication and secret key generation. In: Design Automation Conference, pp. 9–14. ACM Press, New York (2007)
15. S. T20-1109. Specification for authentication of semiconductors and related products (2009), http://www.semi.org/
16. Trusted Computing Group. TCG TPM specification 1.2 (2003), http://www.trustedcomputinggroup.org
17. Tuyls, P., Batina, L.: Rfid-tags for anti-counterfeiting. In: Pointcheval, D. (ed.) CT-RSA 2006. LNCS, vol. 3860, pp. 115–131. Springer, Heidelberg (2006)
18. van der Leest, V., Schrijen, G.-J., Handschuh, H., Tuyls, P.: Hardware intrinsic security from d flip-flops. In: Proceedings of the Fifth ACM Workshop on Scalable Trusted Computing, STC 2010, pp. 53–62. ACM, New York (2010)

Practical Property-Based Attestation on Mobile Devices

Kari Kostiainen, N. Asokan, and Jan-Erik Ekberg

Nokia Research Center
{kari.ti.kostiainen,n.asokan,jan-erik.ekberg}@nokia.com

Abstract. We address property-based attestation in the context of an in-vehicle communication system called Terminal Mode that allows mobile devices to "stream" services, such as navigation or music, to car head-units. In Terminal Mode, attestation of the mobile device is needed to enforce driver distraction regulations and traditional binary attestation is not applicable due to frequently needed measurement updates and limited connectivity of car head-units. We present a novel attestation scheme that bootstraps from existing application certification infrastructures available on mobile device platforms, and thus avoids the need to setup and maintain a new service that provides translation from software measurements to properties, and consequently makes realization of property-based attestation economically feasible.

1 Introduction

Embedded computers on modern car head-units are capable of running various applications such as navigation services or digital music libraries. By utilizing integrated displays, speakers and user input controls on cars usage of such applications is convenient even while driving. Like any other software system such applications benefit from frequent software updates (e.g., bug fixes and new features) and new content (e.g., updated map data or new music). On-demand software updates and content downloads to car head-units may be difficult to realize since cars typically have limited Internet connectivity. On the other hand, mobile devices, such as phones, are well-connected and frequent software and content updates are a matter of course. Additionally, a much wider range of applications is typically available for mobile devices than for car head-units. Thus, a natural approach is to let a mobile device provide, or "stream," application content to the car head-unit and to use the displays, speakers and user input mechanisms integrated to the cars for optimal user experience. Terminal Mode [6] is a recent industry standard that specifies such an in-vehicle communication system.

A system like Terminal Mode raises obvious driving safety concerns. Studies have shown that driver distraction due to usage of in-vehicle information systems is a major contributing factor to traffic accidents [5]. To limit driver distraction, regulatory authorities and automotive industry bodies have issued various regional recommendations and requirements for in-vehicle information

J.M. McCune et al. (Eds.): TRUST 2011, LNCS 6740, pp. 78–92, 2011.

systems [33]. While there is no single, globally accepted set of requirements that would be directly applicable to a system like Terminal Mode, representatives of the automotive industry required that the Terminal Mode system should address the following two issues: First, the car-head unit should present to the user only information that it has received from a device that has been authorized by the user. This requirement can be easily fulfilled by relying on secure pairing and first-connect mechanisms available on the most widely used short-range connections, e.g., Bluetooth Secure Simple Pairing [29] or WiFi Protected Setup [2]. Second, the car head-unit needs reliable means to learn the type of content streamed to it in order to enforce any applicable driver distraction regulation. For example, the head-unit might disallow video content while the vehicle is in motion. Thus, the head-unit needs to verify, or attest, the trustworthiness of the software component on the mobile device that provides such content type information.

During the past decade hardware-based "trusted execution environments" (TrEEs) have started to become widely available in commodity mobile devices. Many current mobile phones support integrated security architectures like M-Shield [30] and TrustZone [4] that augment the mobile device central processing unit with secure storage and isolated execution capabilities. The Trusted Computing Group (TCG) has specified a security element called the Trusted Platform Module (TPM) [32] that provides pre-defined hardware-based security operations. For mobile devices the equivalent is called Mobile Trusted Module (MTM) [13]. Whereas the TPM is always a separate security processor, the MTM interface can be implemented on top of a general-purpose TrEE, such as M-Shield or TrustZone.

The TCG standards include a mechanism called "remote attestation" [32] that allows an *attesting* device to prove the current (software) configuration of the attesting device to a remote *verifier*. In a typical remote attestation process, a trusted software component on the attesting device measures other software components that are executed on the same device and accumulates these measurements into so called Platform Configuration Registers (PCRs) of the TrEE. A signature calculated with a TrEE-resident key over the PCRs proves to the verifier the software configuration the attesting device is running.

Such "binary attestation" has well-known drawbacks. Modern computing devices consist of large number of software components that must be updated frequently. To be able to verify the trustworthiness of the attesting device the verifier must know the exact measurement of each trustworthy software component. For many use cases this assumption does not hold true. For example in the Terminal Mode system the mobile device might be manufactured after the car head-unit has been shipped, and the applications on the mobile device may be updated frequently, but deploying frequent software measurement updates to car-head units is not always practical due to the limited connectivity.

Another well-known drawback of binary attestation is loss of privacy. For example in Terminal Mode, the car-head unit only wants to guarantee that the content it receives has been assigned correct type information. Attesting exact software measurements of the mobile device leaks more information about the attesting mobile device than is necessary to ensure driving safety. (Since head-units typically have limited connectivity, such information leakage may not be considered harmful in this particular use case.)

To address these drawbacks of binary attestation, several researchers have proposed attestation of *high-level properties* instead of exact measurements [25], [23], [7], [19], [8], [17], [16]. In "property-based attestation" a trusted authority defines and maintains mappings from approved software component measurements to more high-level properties, e.g., in the form of signed property certificates. The attesting device, or another device acting as a trusted attestation proxy, can report these properties instead of exact measurements to the verifier based on the matching property certificates.

Despite many research papers, property-based attestation has not seen wide-scale deployment. We feel that the primary reason for this is that there has not been a concrete use case in which deployment of property-based attestation is both highly needed and practical to realize. All property-based attestation schemes are based on the assumption that there exists a trusted authority that defines and maintains mappings from acceptable software measurements to properties. Without a concrete use case it is unclear what the exact requirements for a property-based attestation scheme are, what exact properties should be attested, and most importantly, which entity would have the required business incentive to set up and maintain such a translation service, especially since due to the large number of software components and frequent software updates on current devices running such a translation service is a non-trivial task.

Another drawback of existing property-based attestation schemes is that attesting an unlimited number of properties with a limited number of registers requires that multiple properties are accumulated into a single register. For successful attestation verification all accumulated properties must be reported to the verifier which leaks more information about the attesting device than is necessary.

Contributions. The primary contributions of this paper are two-fold: First, we have identified a concrete use case, the Terminal Mode system, in which property-based attestation is needed to enforce driver distraction regulation. Binary attestation is not applicable to Terminal Mode because of frequent software updates on mobile devices and the difficulty to issue updated measurements to car head-units due to their limited connectivity. Second, we present a novel property-based attestation scheme that bootstraps from existing mobile application certification infrastructures, and thus eliminates the need for setting up and maintaining a *new* trusted authority that defines translation from exact software measurements to properties, and consequently makes deployment of property-based attestation feasible. We describe two variants of our attestation scheme: one for TrEEs that support secure execution of arbitrary code and a TCG-compliant variant for TrEEs that are limited to MTM functionality. Our scheme provides attestation of mobile applications and we show how application-specific content attestation can be built on top. We have implemented both of

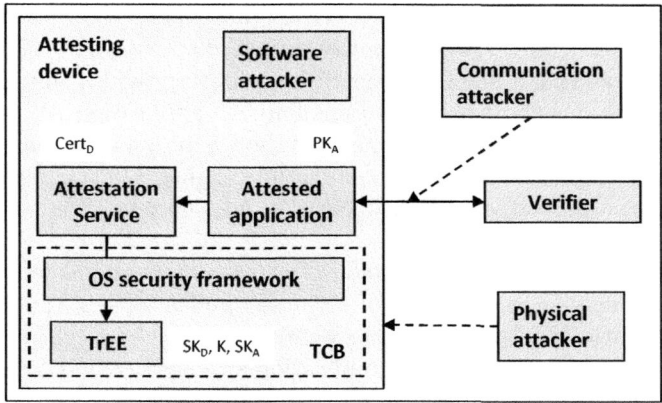

Fig. 1. Remote attestation scheme system model

these variants on mobile phones with M-Shield TrEE by taking advantage of the Symbian Signed application signing infrastructure and the platform security architecture available on Symbian OS devices. We also discuss how our attestation scheme can be implemented on other mobile platforms. The TCG-variant of our attestation scheme has been included as part of the recent Terminal Mode industry standard [6].

The secondary contribution of this paper is a simple register re-use technique that allows unlimited number of properties to be attested independently of each other with a single register, and thus preserves privacy of the attesting device, since only the property that the verifier is interested in must be reported to the verifier.

2 Assumptions and Objectives

Assumptions. The entities involved in the attestation process are shown in Figure 1. We assume that the attesting device has a hardware-based TrEE. The TrEE may either support secure execution of arbitrary manufacturer signed code or it may be limited to MTM functionality. The TrEE is equipped with a statistically unique asymmetric device key SK_D. The public part of this key PK_D has been issued a certificate $Cert_D$ by a trusted authority. The TrEE is also equipped with a symmetric key K that can be used for sealing (local authenticated encryption). For MTM TrEE, the asymmetric device key is called Attestation Identity Key (AIK) and the symmetric sealing key Storage Root Key (SRK).[1]

We assume that the attesting device has an operating system (OS) security framework with a permission-based security model in which access to system services can be limited either in terms of permission or application identifiers. The OS security framework enables the called system service to reliably determine the

---

[1] The TPM specifications define SRK as an asymmetric key. The MTM specifications allow implementation of SRK as a symmetric key, as well.

identity of the calling application. We assume that the application identities are assigned by a (central) trusted authority and verified with code signing during application installation. The OS security framework provides runtime isolation between applications and isolated storage for each application. We assume that the integrity of the OS security framework itself is protected with secure boot, i.e., the TrEE enforces that only manufacturer signed OS images are booted. For more information on security frameworks and secure boot on current mobile platforms see e.g. [18].

The attesting device has a trusted software component called Attestation Service. There may be any number of attested applications on the device. Each attested application has an application identity assigned by a central application signing infrastructure and its own application-specific key pair SK_A/PK_A. The private part of this key SK_A can be kept within the TrEE. We assume that the verifier device has a trust root for verifying the device certificate $Cert_D$ of the attesting device.

Threat model. The attacker may have any of the following capabilities:

- "Software attacker" can install any applications on the attesting device and reset the device.
- "Physical attacker" can read and modify any data persistently stored on the file system of the attesting device when the attesting device is turned off.
- "Communication attacker" can control all communication between the attesting device and the remote verifier according to the typical Dolev-Yao model [9].

On the attesting device, the trusted computing base (TCB) consists of the TrEE and the OS security framework. The attacker cannot read or modify secrets stored or alter any computation that takes place within the TrEE of the attesting device. The attacker cannot compromise the OS security framework of the attesting device at runtime either.

Objectives. The attestation scheme should enable the verifier to verify that the application that it is communicating with on the attesting device complies with a chosen property. In the context of Terminal Mode, this is needed so that the verifier may trust content type information provided by the attested application. More precisely, the attestation scheme should fulfill the following objectives:

- *Attestation trustworthiness*: The verifier should only accept attestations of application properties reported by a trusted Attestation Service, i.e., the attacker should not be able to report false properties.
- *Attestation freshness*: The attacker must not be able to replay old attestations.
- *Attestation binding*: The attestation of an application should be securely bound to the subsequent communication between the attested application and the verifier, i.e., the attacker must not be able to masquerade as a previously attested application.
- *Attestation independence*: Attesting one application property should not disclose information about other properties of the same or another application on the attesting device.

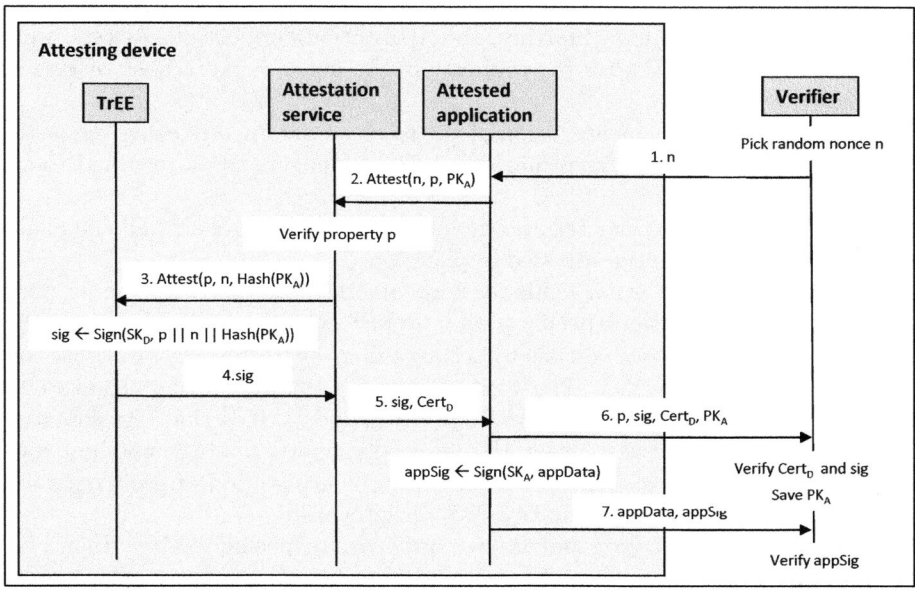

Fig. 2. Attestation protocol for TrEEs that support execution of arbitrary code

3   Attestation Scheme

Our attestation scheme bootstraps from existing application certification infrastructures. Instead of maintaining mappings from exact software measurements to properties, the trusted Attestation Service component on the attesting device maintains mappings from *application identifiers* issued by the application signing infrastructure to properties. The Attestation Service component determines the identity of the attested application using the underlying OS security framework. An application-specific key is appended to the reported property for attestation binding.

3.1   Attestation Protocol

Figure 2 shows the attestation protocol for TrEEs that support execution of arbitrary code.

1. The verifier picks a random nonce n, saves it for later verification, and sends the nonce to the attested application.
2. Each application may match multiple properties. The attested application picks the property p that should be attested and calls an attestation function Attest() from the Attestation Service with the nonce n, the property p and an application-specific public key PK_A as parameters.
3. The Attestation Service determines the identity of the calling attested application and checks if the requested property matches the application identity

in a translation table that contains list of properties for each application identity. If the property matches, the Attestation Service calls Attest() function from the TrEE with the property p, the nonce n and a hash of PK_A as parameters.

4. The TrEE signs a concatenation of the received parameters using the device private key SK_D. The resulting attestation signature sig is returned to the Attestation Service.

5. The Attestation Service returns the attestation signature sig and the device certificate $Cert_D$ to the attested application.

6. The attested application sends these parameters together with the property p and the application-specific public key PK_A to the verifier. The verifier checks that the device certificate $Cert_D$ validates with respect to a trust root available on the verifier. The verifier validates the attestation signature sig using the public key extracted from $Cert_D$ and verifies that the signature contains the expected nonce n, the received property p and a matching hash of PK_A. If this is true, the verifier accepts the attestation of property p and saves the application public key PK_A for later use.

7. The attested application may use the application-specific key to authenticate all subsequent communication with the verifier. One approach is to sign all sent application data appData with the private part of the application-specific key SK_A and append the resulting signature appSig to the message. Another alternative is to establish a client-authenticated TLS connection using the application-specific key.

3.2   Attestation Protocol for MTM TrEEs

Figure 3 shows the attestation protocol for MTM TrEEs. We assume that a fixed Platform Configuration Register (PCR) is reserved for application attestation on the TrEE of the attesting device. All attested properties are accumulated into that register, but instead of reporting all accumulated properties to the verifier, the PCR is extended with a random value for each attestation, and the random value is reposted together with the extended property to allow independent attestation of properties.

1. The verifier picks a random nonce n, saves it for later use, and sends the nonce n to the attested application.

2. The attested application picks the property p that should be attested and calls Attest() function from the Attestation Service with the nonce n, the property p and the application public key PK_A as the parameters. The Attestation Service checks the identity of the calling application and checks if the requested property matches the application identifier in its translation table.

3. The Attestation Service picks a random value r and extends the reserved PCR with r by calling TPM_Extend().

4. The TPM_Extend() command returns the current PCR value. The Attestation Service saves this value for later use as old.

5. The Attestation Service extends the same PCR by calling TPM_Extend() function. As a parameter, the Attestation Service uses a hash calculated

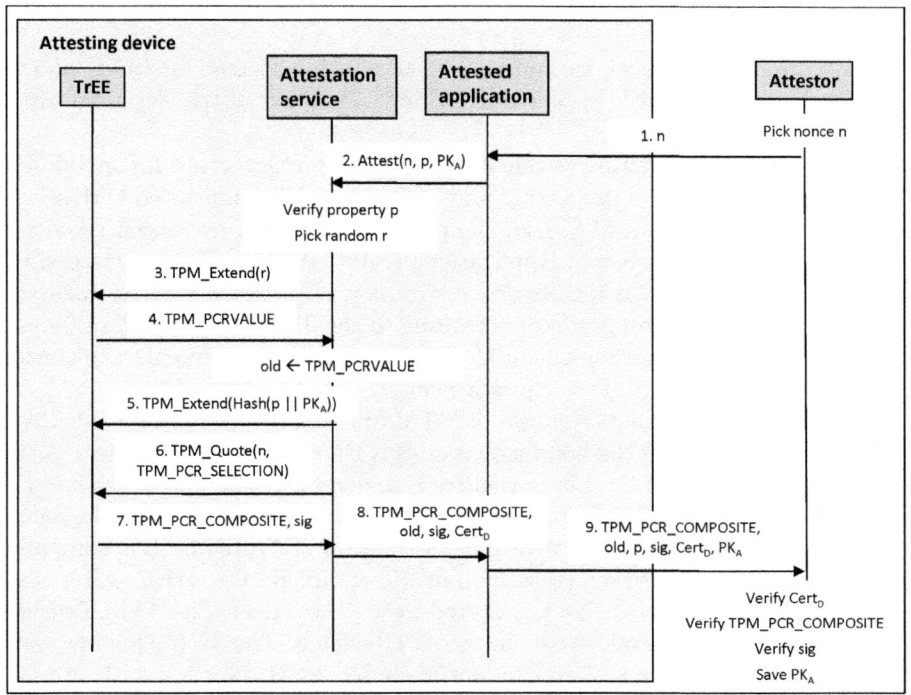

Fig. 3. Attestation protocol for MTM TrEEs

over the concatenation of property p and the public application key PK_A. The return value is ignored.

6. The Attestation Service signs this extended PCR value by calling TPM_Quote with the nonce n as parameter. Additional TPM_PCR_SELECTION parameter is used to define that the signature should be calculated over the reserved PCR.

7. The TrEE constructs a TPM_PCR_COMPOSITE structure and signs it using the SK_D (AIK). The composite structure and the resulting signature sig are returned to the Attestation Service.

8. The Attestation Service returns these parameters together with the saved PCR value old and the device certificate $Cert_D$ (AIK certificate) to the attested application.

9. The attested application sends these values, the property p, PK_A and $Cert_D$ to the verifier. First, the verifier validates the device certificate $Cert_D$. Then, the verifier checks that the received TPM_PCR_COMPOSITE structure matches a structure that would result when TPM_PCRVALUE old is extended with a hash calculated over p and PK_A. After that, the verifier validates the attestation signature sig. If all these conditions hold true, the verifier accepts the attestation of property p and saves PK_A for authentication of subsequent communication with the attested application.

4   Implementation

We have implemented both variants of our attestation scheme for Nokia phones running Symbian OS with M-Shield TrEE in the context of the Terminal Mode system.

TrEE implementation. M-Shield is a security architecture for mobile devices in which the central processing unit of the device is augmented with secure storage and execution. In M-Shield, the pieces of code that are executed within the TrEE are called Protected Applications (PAs). We have implemented three PAs. Our first PA creates the needed device key, seals it for local storage and runs a device certification protocol according to the TCG Privacy CA principles [32] with a CA we have implemented. The second PA implements attestation signatures for our first protocol variant using the sealed device key.

The third PA implements a subset of MTM functionality needed for the MTM protocol variant. During the first invocation this PA creates an MTM state structure within the TrEE. The state structure is sealed for persistent storage on the OS side and a hash of the state is saved inside the TrEE in volatile secure memory. During subsequent invocations of the same PA, this hash is compared to a loaded state to prevent state modifications outside the TrEE. After each operation an updated state hash is stored inside the TrEE. The TPM_Extend() operation updates the state with the new PCR value. The TPM_Quote() operation unseals the device key and signs the chosen PCR selection with it using formats defined in the TPM and MTM specifications. We use the Symbian OS security framework to enforce that only trusted operating system components, i.e. components with manufacturer vendor identity, are allowed to use these PAs.

Symbian implementation. We have implemented the Attestation Service as a Symbian server component. The Attestation Service has a translation table, in the form of a text file, that contains list of properties for pre-defined Symbian application identifiers. This table is stored in so called "private directory" of the Attestation Service component—Symbian security framework provides an isolated storage mechanism called private directory for each application and system server. The Attestation Service determines the identity of the attested applications using the Symbian inter-process communication (IPC) framework that allows the called server process to determine the application identifier of the calling application. The Attestation Service component itself has manufacturer vendor identity that allows it to access our PAs.

Terminal Mode integration. A straight-forward design choice would have been to directly attest each application on the mobile device that "streams" data to the car head-unit. The drawback of such an approach is that changes would have been needed to many applications, since each application would have had to implement the attestation protocol. For Terminal Mode deployment we wanted to re-use existing applications as much as possible, and thus we chose a hierarchical attestation approach in which the mobile device attests the Terminal Mode system core components using our attestation scheme, and these core components in turn attest, or *label*, the content sent through them by different applications. The content labeling must be integrity protected using keys bound during attestation.

The Terminal Mode system uses several widely used protocols for communication between mobile devices and car head-units. Universal Plug and Play (UPnP) [10] is used for service discovery and remote control of applications on the mobile device from the car head-unit. Virtual Network Computing (VNC) and Remote Framebuffer (RFB) protocol [24] are used for streaming application video and Real-time Transport Protocol (RTP) [27] is used for streaming application audio from the mobile device to the head-unit. In our implementation, the mobile device attests the in-device server processes that implement these protocols. Thus, the attested properties are names of Terminal Mode core components, such as TerminalMode:UPnP-Server and TerminalMode:VNC-Server. Each attested property is prefixed with a use case specific label to prevent collisions with attestations for use cases.

Each of these Terminal Mode core components maintains a list of known application identifiers and matching *application categories*, such as Navigation or Music. When an application sends data to the car head-unit, the mediating and already attested Terminal Mode core component labels the data accordingly. The identity of the active application is determined from IPC calls between applications and Terminal Mode core components.[2] In case of UPnP communication, the integrity of such content labeling is protected by signing the sent UPnP messages with the UPnP server specific key that was bound to the attestation of the UPnP server component. We use standard XML signatures. Transfer of frame buffers generates large amount of traffic and thus creating an asymmetric signature over each frame update causes an unacceptable performance overhead. Instead, the car head-unit picks a symmetric session key, encrypts that using the public key that was bound to the attestation of the VNC server, and sends the encrypted key to the VNC server which may then create symmetric signatures (HMAC-SHA-256) over frame buffer updates.

5   Analysis

Objective analysis. A noteworthy aspect of our attestation scheme is that the Attestation Service does not measure and report the entire OS, as is typically done in TCG-style attestation. Instead, we rely on availability of secure boot on the attesting device. The verification of the device certificate guarantees that the attested device originates from a trusted manufacturer and on such devices only trusted OS images are booted. Thus, it is sufficient to only measure and attest the application at hand.

Our first objective was attestation trustworthiness. The verifier should accept attestations of properties that have only been reported by a trusted Attestation

---

[2] Transfer of video content is an exception. The VNC server sends system frame buffer updates without communicating with the application directly. For content labeling, the the VNC server can determine the identity of currently active application with a Symbian OS system call that reports application currently holding the screen.

Service. In our scheme attestation signatures are made with a TrEE-based device key. The attacker does not have direct access to TrEE-resident secrets. We limit software-based access to these keys to software components that have manufacturer vendor identifier, and assume that other system components with the same identifier do not use the device key for signing arbitrary data that could be used as false attestations. The application identifiers used by the Attestation Service are provided by the OS security framework. For the integrity of this framework, we rely on secure boot.

The attestation trustworthiness also relies on the integrity of the Attestation Service itself, the integrity of the translation table maintained by it, and the integrity of the attested application code, i.e., the attacker must not be able to modify the attested application after successful attestation. The integrity of all of these is guaranteed by the OS level security framework against a software attacker. In our implementation platform, Symbian OS, the integrity of the translation table can be protected against offline attacks of a physical attacker by sealing it with a TrEE-resident key. The integrity of the Attestation Service itself can be enforced with TrEE-based secure boot.

Our second objective, attestation freshness, is easily fulfilled with the use of random nonce in both of the attestation protocols. To meet our third objective, attestation binding, we use a well-known technique to include a hash of application-specific public key to the measurement that is signed and reported (see e.g. [12,11] for more details on binding attestation to subsequent communication). The private part of the application-specific key must not leak to the attacker. Against software attackers it is sufficient to use the means provided by the OS security framework, i.e., in Symbian we can store the private key to the private directory of the application. To protect against physical attackers the key should be sealed in TrEE. If TrEE-based sealing is not available to applications, an alternative is to create an ephemeral application-specific key after each boot and discard it when the device is powered off.

In our implementation, we attest the Terminal Mode system core components that in turn attest or label application-specific data sent via them with matching application categories. Thus, the implementation must preserve integrity of the application category configuration files maintained by these Terminal Mode core components as well. Again, for software attackers we rely on application-specific storage provided by the OS security framework, for physical attackers TrEE-based sealing must be used.

Our last objective, attestation independence, is not an issue in our first protocol version. For the MTM protocol variant we apply simple PCR re-use technique. Instead of reporting all properties accumulated to the dedicated PCR, we extend the PCR with a random value and only report this random value and the property that has been extended to the PCR after that.

Deployment analysis. Traditional property-based attestation schemes are based on the assumption that there exists a trusted entity that maintains mappings from approved software measurements to properties. Maintaining such a translation service is a tedious task if the attested software components are updated frequently and originate from various sources, as is the case with most application level software on mobile devices today. Our approach bootstraps from existing application certification infrastructures, and thus in our attestation scheme we only need to maintain a translation table from application identifiers to properties. When mobile applications are updated, the applications identifiers remain unchanged, and consequently no changes to the translation table are needed.

In the Terminal Mode system the translation table maintained by the Attestation Service component is constant, since the set of attested properties, the Terminal Mode core components, is fixed. The attested software components maintain their own translation tables that contain identifiers of known applications and matching application categories. These tables need to be updated whenever a new application is added to or removed from the list. Such updates are expected to be considerably less frequent compared to software updates to the applications themselves.

The Terminal Mode system is an industry standard that should be applicable to all major mobile device platforms. The MTM-based variant of our attestation protocol can be implemented in variety of mobile devices, including devices with M-Shield or TrustZone TrEE, MTM TrEE, or even purely software-based implementations relying on OS level security and device authentication are possible. Naturally, purely software based implementations are not resistant against physical attackers.

Our implementation is based on Symbian application signing infrastructure and OS security framework, but the same protocol can be implemented for other mobile platforms as well. For example the MSSF security framework [15] used in MeeGo devices provides similar IPC mechanism that allows the called process to determine the identity of the calling process (assigned by a trusted authority). Also Windows Phone OS and iOS platforms are based on centralized application signing infrastructures. Although the internals of these platforms are not public, most likely similar attestation could be implemented on those platforms as well. Android platform is not based on centralized application signing infrastructure, instead most applications are self-signed. On Android devices, the Attestation Service would need to maintain mappings from signing key and application identity pairs to properties. The Attestation Service itself could be implemented as part of the virtual machine that runs the Android applications (similar to the designs reported in in [14] and [22]).

6   Related Work

Binary attestation. Using a trusted software entity to measure other, untrusted software components is by no means a new invention. The concept of software measurement based secure boot was introduced in the early 90's [20] and concrete bootstrapping architectures were built later in the same decade (see e.g. [3]). The Trusted Computing Group (TCG), and its predecessor the Trusted Computing Platform Alliance (TCPA), standardized the notion of software measurement based authenticated boot and binary attestation [32]. While the basic TCG-attestation is limited to measuring the booted operating system components, architectures exist for measuring loaded applications during system runtime as well [26], and binding application produced data to the attestation of applications [28]. The current PC processors allow security-critical parts of applications to be measured, executed in isolation, and attested to a remote verifier [21].

Property-based attestation. Attesting high-level properties of native software components based on TPM technology was first proposed in [25]. Based on this concept researchers have proposed various property-based attestation schemes for TPM-based platforms ranging from provably secure protocols [7] to schemes that do not require a trusted third party (the attesting device and the remote verifier agree on the attested properties directly) [8], utilize a trusted proxy [23], or bundle multiple attestation requests into a single signature operation for better scalability [31]. Implementation of an operating system boot loader that is enhanced with a translation table that provides mappings from measurements to properties is described in [19] and further developed in [17].

In the context of managed code running on virtual machines, property-based attestation, or "semantic attestation," was first proposed in [14]. In their approach a trusted virtual machine determines properties of applications based on byte code inspection and application runtime monitoring. Attestation based on static analysis and runtime monitoring has been proposed for native code as well [16]. Similar concepts are discussed also in [1].

The Mobile Trusted Module (MTM) specifications introduce a concept of Reference Integrity Metric (RIM) certificates [13]. A RIM certificate contains a software measurement reference value and a matching identifier, e.g. a property, that should be extended to an MTM register when such a software component is loaded. Thus, RIM certificates can be used to implement property-based attestation on mobile devices.

Attestation on mobile devices. Recently binary attestation has been implemented for Android devices [22]. In Android, applications run on top of Java-based Dalvik virtual machine (VM). Traditional TCG-style measurements are used to attest the trustworthiness of the VM which in turn measures either entire Android applications or individual Java classes that are loaded. The measurements are accumulated into a single PCR of a software-based minimal TPM implementation that is included to the kernel.

The primary difference between all of the above mentioned attestation approaches and our scheme is that we bootstrap from existing application certification infrastructures, and thus with our scheme it is sufficient to maintain a translation from application identities to properties. There are also noticeable difference in the amount of code that is attested. While in most the TPM-based approaches, e.g. [25,19,17], the entire OS is measured and attested, in our approach the integrity of the OS is guaranteed with secure boot, and thus it is sufficient to measure and attest only the application at hand. In that sense, our approach bears similarities to [14] in which a trusted virtual machine attest byte code applications.

7   Summary

In this paper we have presented a novel attestation scheme that bootstraps from existing application certification infrastructures, and thus makes deployment of property-based attestation practical to realize. This attestation mechanism has been included to the recent Terminal Mode industry standard and the deployment is currently on-going to mobile devices and car head-units from multiple manufacturers.

We acknowledge Jörg Brakensiek and Matthias Benesch for intoruducing us to the problem and for their feedback during the design.

References

1. Alam, M., et al.: Model-based behavioral attestation. In: Proc. 13th ACM Symposium on Access Control Models and Technologies (2008)
2. WiFi Alliance. WiFi protected setup specification v1.0 (2007)
3. Arbaugh, W., et al.: A secure and reliable bootstrap architecture. In: Proc. IEEE Symposium on Security and Privacy (1997)
4. ARM. Trustzone-enabled processor, http://www.arm.com/products/processors/technologies/trustzone.php
5. National Highway Safety Traffic Association. The impact of driver inattention on near-crash/crash risk: An analysis using the 100-car naturalistic driving study data (2006), http://www.nhtsa.gov/DOT/NHTSA/NRD/Multimedia/PDFs/Crash%20Avoidance/2006/DriverInattention.pdf
6. Brakensiek, J.: Terminal mode technical architecture (2010), http://www.nokia.com/terminalmode
7. Chen, L., et al.: A protocol for property-based attestation. In: Proc. First ACM Workshop on Scalable Trusted Computing (2006)
8. Chen, L., et al.: Property-based attestation without a trusted third party. In: Proc. 11th International Conference on Information Security (2008)
9. Dolev, D., Yao, A.: On the security of public key protocols. Technical report. Stanford University (1981)
10. UPnP Forum, http://upnp.org/sdcps-and-certification/standards/
11. Gasmi, Y., et al.: Beyond secure channels. In: Proc. 2nd ACM Workshop on Scalable Trusted (2007)
12. Goldman, K., et al.: Linking remote attestation to secure tunnel endpoints. In: Proc. 1st ACM Workshop on Scalable Trusted Computing (2006)
13. Trusted Computing Group. Mobile trusted module specification, version 1.0 (2008)
14. Haldar, V., et al.: Semantic remote attestation - virtual machine directed approach to trusted computing. In: Virtual Machine Research and Technology Symposium (2004)
15. Kasatkin, D.: Mobile simplified security framework. In: Proc. 12th Linux Symposium (2010)
16. Kil, C., et al.: Remote attestation to dynamic system properties: Towards providing complete system integrity evidence. In: Proc. International Conference on Dependable Systems and Networks (2009)
17. Korthaus, R., et al.: A practical property-based bootstrap architecture. In: Proc. 4th ACM Workshop on Scalable Trusted Computing (2009)

18. Kostiainen, K., et al.: Old, new, borrowed, blue: A perspective on the evolution of platform security architectures. In: Proc. 1st ACM Conference on Data and Application Security and Privacy (2011)
19. Kühn, U., et al.: Realizing property-based attestation and sealing with commonly available hard- and software. In: Proc. 2nd ACM Workshop on Scalable Trusted Computing (2007)
20. Lampson, B., et al.: Authentication in distributed systems: theory and practice. In: Proc. 13th ACM Symposium on Operating Systems Principles (1991)
21. McCune, J., et al.: Minimal TCB Code Execution (Extended Abstract). In: Proc. IEEE Symposium on Security and Privacy (2007)
22. Nauman, M., et al.: Beyond kernel-level integrity measurement: Enabling remote attestation for the android platform. In: Proc. International Conference on Trust and Trustworthy Computing (2010)
23. Poritz, J., et al.: Property attestation scalable and privacy-friendly security assessment of peer computers. Technical Report RZ3548, IBM Research (2004)
24. Richardson, T.: The rfb protocol (2010), http://www.realvnc.com/docs/rfbproto.pdf
25. Sadeghi, A.-R., Stüble, C.: Property-based attestation for computing platforms: caring about properties, not mechanisms. In: Proc. Workshop on New Security Paradigms (2004)
26. Sailer, R., et al.: Design and implementation of a tcg-based integrity measurement architecture. In: Proc. 13th USENIX Security Symposium (2004)
27. Schulzrinne, H., et al.: RTP: A transport protocol for real-time applications (2003)
28. Shi, E., et al.: Bind: A fine-grained attestation service for secure distributed systems. In: Proc. IEEE Symposium on Security and Privacy (2005)
29. Bluetooth SIG. Bluetooth specification version 2.1 + edr (2007)
30. Srage, J., Azema, J.: M-Shield mobile security technology (2005), TI White paper, http://focus.ti.com/pdfs/wtbu/ti_mshield_whitepaper.pdf
31. Stumpf, F., et al.: Improving the scalability of platform attestation. In: Proc. 3rd ACM Workshop on Scalable Trusted Computing (2008)
32. Trusted Platform Module (TPM) Specifications, https://www.trustedcomputinggroup.org/specs/TPM/
33. International Telecommunications Union. Decreasing driver distraction, itu-t technology watch report (August 2010), http://www.itu.int/dms_pub/itu-t/oth/23/01/T230100000F0001PDFE.pdf

Taming Information-Stealing Smartphone Applications (on Android)

Yajin Zhou[1], Xinwen Zhang[2], Xuxian Jiang[1], and Vincent W. Freeh[1]

[1] Department of Computer Science, NC State University
yajin_zhou@ncsu.edu, {jiang,vin}@cs.ncsu.edu
[2] Huawei America Research Center
xinwen.zhang@huawei.com

Abstract. Smartphones have been becoming ubiquitous and mobile users are increasingly relying on them to store and handle personal information. However, recent studies also reveal the disturbing fact that users' personal information is put at risk by (rogue) smartphone applications. Existing solutions exhibit limitations in their capabilities in taming these privacy-violating smartphone applications. In this paper, we argue for the need of a new *privacy mode* in smartphones. The privacy mode can empower users to flexibly control in a fine-grained manner what kinds of personal information will be accessible to an application. Also, the granted access can be dynamically adjusted at runtime in a fine-grained manner to better suit a user's needs in various scenarios (e.g., in a different time or location). We have developed a system called TISSA that implements such a privacy mode on Android. The evaluation with more than a dozen of information-leaking Android applications demonstrates its effectiveness and practicality. Furthermore, our evaluation shows that TISSA introduces negligible performance overhead.

Keywords: smartphone applications, Android, privacy mode.

1 Introduction

Mobile phones are increasingly ubiquitous. According to a recent Gartner report [2], in the third quarter of 2010, worldwide mobile phone sales to end users totaled 417 million units, a 35 percent increase from the third quarter of 2009. Among the variety of phones, smartphones in particular received incredible adoption. This trend is further propelled with the wide availability of feature-rich applications that can be downloaded and run on smartphones. For example, Google provides *Android Market* [1] that contains a large collection of Android applications (or apps for short). It is important to note that these app stores or marketplaces contain not only vendor-provided programs, but also third-party apps. For example, Android Market had an increase from about 15,000 third-party apps in November 2009 to about 150,000 in November 2010.

Given the increased sophistication, features, and convenience of these smartphones, users are increasingly relying on them to store and process personal

J.M. McCune et al. (Eds.): TRUST 2011, LNCS 6740, pp. 93–107, 2011.
© Springer-Verlag Berlin Heidelberg 2011

information. For example, inside the phone, we can find phone call log with information about placed and received calls, an address book that connects to the user's friends or family members, browsing history about visited URLs, as well as cached emails and photos taken with the built-in camera. As these are all private information, a natural concern is the safety of these data.

Unfortunately, recent studies [9,8,13,3] reveal that there are malicious apps that can be uploaded to the app stores and successfully advertised to users for installation on their smartphones. These malicious apps will leak private information without user authorization. For example, TaintDroid [9] shows that among 30 popular third-party Android apps, there are 68 instances of potential misuse of users' private information. In light of these privacy-violating threats, there is an imperative need to tame these information-stealing smartphone apps.

To fulfill the need, Android requires explicit permissions in an app so that the user is aware of the information or access rights that will be needed to run the app. By showing these permissions to the end user, Android delegates the task to the user for approval when the app is being installed. However, this permission mechanism is too coarse-grained for two main reasons. First, the Android permission mechanism requires that a user has to grant *all* the requested permissions of the app if he wants to use it. Otherwise the app cannot be installed. Second, if a user has granted the requested permissions to an app, there is no mechanism in place to later re-adjust the permission(s) or constrain the runtime app behavior.

To effectively protect user private information from malicious smartphone apps, in this paper, we argue for the need of a new *privacy mode* in smartphones. The privacy mode can be used to lock down (or fine tune) an app's access to various private information stored in the phone. More specifically, if a user wants to install an untrusted third-party app, he can control the app's access in a fine-grained manner to specify what types of private information (e.g., device ID, contracts, call log, and locations) are accessible to the app. Further, the user can flexibly (re)adjust at runtime the previously granted access (e.g., at install time).

As a demonstration, we have implemented a system called TISSA that implements such a privacy mode in Android. Our development experience indicates that though the privacy mode support requires modifying the Android framework, the modification however is minor with changes in less than 1K lines of code (LOC). We also have evaluated TISSA with more than a dozen of Android apps that are known to leak a variety of private information. Our results show that TISSA can effectively mediate their accesses and protect private information from being divulged. Also, the privacy setting for each app is re-adjustable at runtime without affecting its functionality.

The rest of this paper is organized as follows: Section 2 describes our system design for the privacy mode support in Android. Section 3 presents its detailed prototype. Section 4 presents evaluation results with a dozen of information-stealing Android apps as well as its performance overhead. Section 5 discusses the limitations of our approach and suggests future improvement. Finally, Section 6 describes related work, and Section 7 summarizes our conclusions.

2   Design of TISSA

2.1   Design Requirements and Threat Model

Design Requirements. Our goal is to effectively and efficiently prevent private information leakage by untrusted smartphone apps. Accordingly, to support the new privacy mode in smartphones, we follow several design requirements to balance privacy protection, system performance, user experience, and application compatibility.

Lightweight Protection: Smartphones are usually resource constrained, especially on CPU, memory, and energy. Therefore, it naturally requires that our security mechanism should be memory- and energy-efficient. Also, the performance overhead of the solution should not affect user experience.

Application Transparency: The privacy mode should also maintain the compatibility of existing Android apps. Accordingly, we may not change APIs currently provided by the default Android framework. Also, from the usability perspective, it is not a good design to partially grant permissions at install time or later revoke permissions at runtime. This is because when a permission is taken away or does not exist, the app may suddenly stop or even crash. As a result it could interfere with the normal execution of the app and hurt the user experience.

Small Footprint: Built on top of existing Android framework including its security mechanisms, the privacy mode support should minimize the changes necessary to the Android framework.

Threat and Trust Model. As our purpose is to prevent private information from being leaked by untrusted apps, we assume user downloaded third-party apps as untrusted. Note that although our scheme can be equally applicable to pre-installed apps on the device, we assume they are benign from privacy protection perspective and will not release private data of the device without authorizations. These pre-installed apps include those from device manufacturers or network operators.

In addition, we also trust the underlying OS kernel, system services, and the Android framework (including the Dalvik VM). Aiming to have a minimal modification to the Android code base, our system is designed to build on top of existing Android security mechanisms, which include the primitive sandbox functions and permission enforcement of Android [11,16]. Naturally, we assume that an untrusted app cannot access system resources (e.g., filesystem) or other apps' private data directly. Instead, they can only be accessed through the normal APIs provided by various content providers or service components in the Android framework.

2.2   System Design

In a nutshell, TISSA provides the desired privacy mode on Android by developing an extra permission specification and enforcement layer on the top of

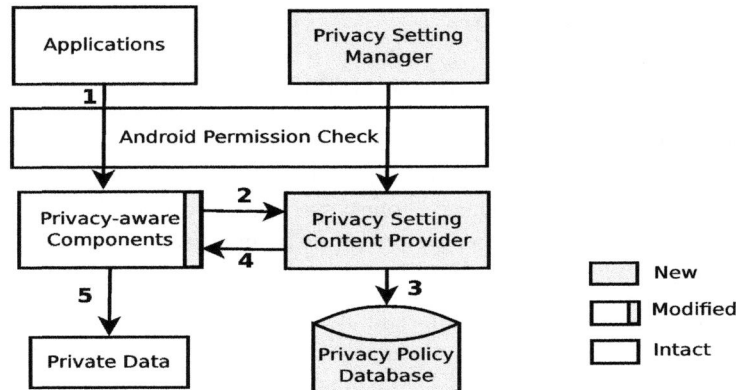

Fig. 1. The TISSA Architecture

existing Android permissions. As shown in Figure 1, TISSA consists of three main components. The first one is the *privacy setting content provider*, which is a privileged component to manage the privacy settings for untrusted apps. In the meantime, it also provides an API that can be used to query the current privacy setting for an installed app. If we consider TISSA as a reference monitor, the privacy setting content provider is the Policy Decision Point (PDP). The second component is the *privacy setting manager*, which is a privileged app that a mobile user can use to manage or update the privacy settings for installed apps. Therefore, it acts as the Policy Administration Point (PAP) in TISSA. The third component is *privacy-aware components*, including those content providers or services that are enhanced in a privacy-aware manner to regulate the access to a variety of user's personal information, including contacts, call log, locations, device identity. These privacy-aware components are designed to cooperate with the first component. In particular, once they receive requests from an app to access private data they manage, they will query the privacy settings, and response to the requests according to the current privacy settings for the app. In other words, they function as the Policy Enforcement Points (PEPs) in TISSA. As a result, there is only one instance of PDP and PAP while multiple PEPs exist and they are integrated with individual content providers or services in the Android framework.

To further elaborate how TISSA works, when an app tries to read a piece of private data, it sends a reading request (arrow 1 in Figure 1) to the corresponding content provider. The content provider is aware of the privacy requirement. Instead of serving this request directly, it holds the request and makes a query first to the privacy setting content provider (arrow 2) to check the current privacy settings for the app (regarding the particular reading operation). The privacy setting content provider in turn queries its internal policy database (arrow 3) that stores user specifications on privacy settings of all untrusted apps, and returns the query result back to the content provider (arrow 4). If this reading operation is permitted (stored in the policy database), the content serves the access request and returns normal results to the app (arrow 5). This may include querying its internal database managed by the content provider.

However, if the reading operation is not permitted, the privacy setting may indicate possible ways to handle it. In our current prototype, we support three options: empty, anonymized, and bogus. The *empty* option simply returns an empty result to the requesting app, indicating "non-presence" of the requested information. The *anonymized* option instead provides an anonymized version from the original (personal) information, which still allows the app to proceed but without necessarily leaking user information. The *bogus* option on the other hand provides a fake result of the requested information. Note these three options may be further specialized for different types of personal information and be interpreted differently for different apps. Accordingly, the apps will likely behave differently based on the returned results. As a result, mobile users need to be aware of the differences from the same app under different privacy settings and exercise different levels of trust.

Through TISSA, we currently provide three levels of granularity for privacy policy specifications. In the first level, a policy defines whether a particular app can be completely trusted. If yes, it is given all requested accesses through the normal Android permission mechanisms. If not, TISSA provides the second level of policy specification, where one particular setting can be specified for each type of personal information the mobile user wants to protect. Note that it is possible that one app may access one type of personal information for its legitimate functionalities, but should be denied to access other types of information. For example, the *Yellow Pages* app (Section 4) may be normally allowed to access the current location but the access to phone identity or contacts should be prevented. Also, for the non-trusted access to other personal information, the third level of policy specification specifies the above empty, anonymized, and bogus options to meet different needs. For example, for a call log backup app, we do not want to give the plain-text access to the call log content, but an anonymized version. For a *Coupon app* (Section 4), we can simply return a bogus phone identity.

3   Implementation

We have implemented a proof-of-concept TISSA system based on Android version 2.1-update1 and successfully run it on Google Nexus One. In our current prototype, we choose to protect four types of personal information: phone identity, location, contacts, and call log. Our system has a small footprint and is extensible to add the support of other personal information. In the following, we explain in more details about the system implementation.

3.1   Privacy Setting Content Provider

The privacy setting content provider is tasked to manage a local SQLite database that contains the current privacy settings for untrusted apps on the phone. It also provides an interface through which a privacy-aware component (e.g., a location manager) can query the current privacy settings for an untrusted app. More specifically, in our current prototype, the privacy-aware component will provide as the input the package name of the requesting app and the type of private information it is trying to acquire. Once received, the privacy setting content provider will use the package name to query the current settings from the database. The query result will be an app-specific privacy setting regarding the type of information being requested.

There are some design alternatives regarding the default privacy settings. For example, in a restrictive approach, any untrusted app will not be given the access to any personal information. That is, we simply apply the empty or even bogus options for all types of personal information that may be requested by the app – even though the user approves all requested permissions when the app is being installed. On the contrary, a permissive approach may fall back to the current Android permission model and determine the app's access based on the granted permissions. To provide the compatibility and transparency to current apps, our current prototype uses the permissive approach.

Beside the API interface used to query the privacy settings for a given app, there exists another API interface (in the privacy setting content provider) through which the privacy setting manager can use to initialize or adjust privacy settings in the policy database. Similarly, the input of this interface includes the package name of a target app and its privacy settings. The output will be the confirmation to the requested initialization or adjustment.

Because our policy database stores actual privacy settings for untrusted apps, the security itself is critical. In our prototype, we leverage the existing Android sandbox and permission mechanisms to protect its integrity. Specifically, the database file is a private data file of the privacy setting content provider (thus with the same UID in filesystem). Other apps have different UIDs and will be denied to access it directly. To further restrict the update capability of the database via corresponding API, we declare a dedicated Android permission (in the privacy setting content provider) with the protection level of `signature`. This means that the permission will only be granted to apps signed with the same certificate as the privacy setting content provider. In our prototype, the privacy setting manager is the only one that is signed by the same certificate.

In total there were 330 LOC in the privacy setting content provider implementation.

3.2   Privacy Setting Manager

The privacy setting manager is a standalone Android app that is signed with the same certificate as the privacy setting content provider. As mentioned earlier, by doing so, the manager will be given the exclusive access to the privacy setting database. In addition, the manager provides the visual user interface and allows the user to specify the privacy settings for untrusted apps. We stress that the privacy setting here is orthogonal to the permissions that the user has granted at the app install time; that is, the privacy setting manager provides a separate setting for the privacy mode.

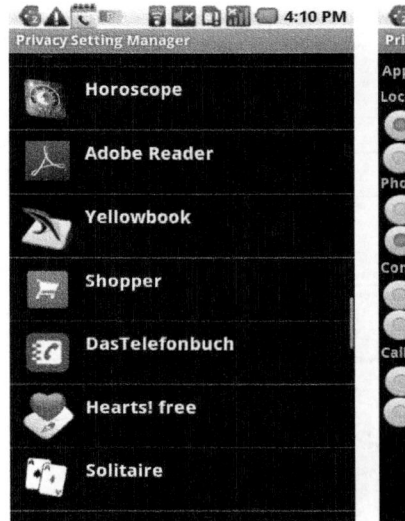 

(a) A list of installed apps   (b) The privacy settings for the *YellowPages* app

Fig. 2. The Privacy Setting Manager

In particular, the manager app includes two activity components. The default one is `PrivacySettingManagerActivity`, which when activated displays a list of installed apps. The phone user can then browser the list and click an app icon, which starts another activity called `AppPrivacySettingActivity` and passes the app's package name. When the new activity is created, it queries the privacy setting content provider for the current privacy settings and displays the results to the user. It also has radio buttons to let user customize or adjust the current settings. Any change of the settings will be immediately updated to the policy database via the privacy setting content provider. In Figure 2, we show the screenshots of the manager app, which show the list of installed app (Figure 2(a)) and the privacy setting for the *Yellow Pages* app (Figure 2(b)).

In total there were 452 LOC in the privacy setting manager implementation.

3.3   Privacy-Aware Components

The third component in our prototype is those privacy-aware Android components, including the contacts content provider, the location manager, and the telephony manager. These Android components are enhanced for the privacy mode support.

Contacts and Call Logs: Figure 3 shows the flowchart for the contact information that is being accessed. Specifically, when an app makes a query to the contacts content provider, the request is received by the content resolver, which checks whether the app has the permission (based on existing Android permissions). If not, a security exception is thrown to the app and the access stops. Otherwise, it dispatches the request to the contacts content provider, which in the privacy

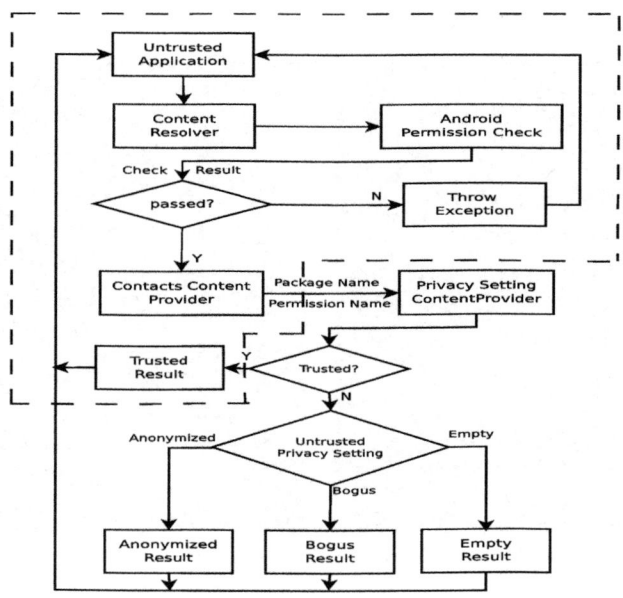

Fig. 3. Protecting Contacts in TISSA

Table 1. Detailed Breakdown of Android Modification in TISSA

Component Name	LOC
Privacy Setting Provider	330
Application Management Program	452
LocationManager & LocationManagerService	97
TelephonyManager	61
ContactsProvider (Contacts&Call Log)	48
Total	988

mode in turn queries the privacy setting content provider to check if the requesting app can access the contacts data. If the app is allowed, the contacts content provider then queries its own database and returns back authentic contacts to the app. The dotted line in Figure 3 encloses those components that also exist in the original Android. The rest components (outside the dotted area) show the additional components we added for the privacy mode support in Android.

From the privacy setting database, if the app is not trusted to access the requested data, the contacts content provider will respond differently: an *empty* setting returns an empty contact record; an *anonymized* settings returns an anonymized version of the contact records; and an *bogus* setting simply returns fake contact information. By doing so, we can protect the authentic contacts information from being leaked by this untrusted app. In the meantime, as the app is given different results, the mobile user should expect different app behavior and exercise different levels of trust when interacting with the app.

Phone Identity: Mobile phones have unique device identifier. For example, the IMEI and MEID numbers are unique identities of GSM and CDMA phones, respectively. An Android app can use the functions provided by telephony service to obtain these numbers. As a result, we hook these functions and return a device ID based on the current privacy setting for the requesting app. For example, in the case of the *Yellow Pages* app (Figure 2(b)), we simply return a bogus phone identity number.

Location: There are several location content providers in Android to provide either coarse-grained or fine-grained information (e.g., based on different devices such as GPS and Wifi). However, for an app to obtain the location, there are two main ways: First, it can obtain the information from the related devices through the `LocationManager`; Second, an app can also register a listener to receive location updates from these devices. When there is a location change, the registered listener will receive the updated location information. Accordingly, in our current prototype, we hook related functions to intercept incoming requests. To handle each request, we query the privacy setting for the initiating apps and then respond accordingly. Using the same *Yellow Pages* app example, our current setting (Figure 2(b)) returns the authentic location information.

Our TISSA development experience indicates that the privacy mode support in Android involves no more than 1K LOC implementation. As a result, we believe our approach has a small footprint – satisfying our third design requirement (Section 2). The detailed breakdown of revised components in Android is shown in Table 1.

4   Evaluation

We use a number of Android apps as well as standard benchmarks to test the effectiveness and performance impact of our system. Some of the selected Android apps have been known to leak private information [9]. Our testing platform is Google Nexus One that runs the Android version 2.1-update1 enhanced with the TISSA privacy mode.

4.1   Effectiveness

To evaluate the TISSA effectiveness in preventing private information leakage by untrusted apps, we choose 24 free apps from the Android Market at the end of November 2010. (The complete list of tested apps is in Table 2.) Among these 24 apps, 13 of them (marked with † in the table) are known to be leaking private information as reported from the TaintDroid system [9]. The remaining 11 apps are randomly selected and downloaded from the Android Market. Most of these apps require the permissions for locations (`ACCESS_COARSE_LOCATION` or `ACCESS_FINE_LOCATION`) and phone identity (`READ_PHONE_STATE`). Also, one third of them require the access of contacts and call log (`READ_CONTACTS`).

In our experiments, we divide these apps into two sets. The first set has the 13 apps that are known to be leaking private information and the second set has the

Table 2. Example Apps for TISSA Effectiveness Evaluation

Third-party Apps (24 in total)	Location	Phone Identity	Contacts	Call Log
The Weather Channel[†]; Movies[†]; Horoscope[†]; Layar[†]; Coupons[†]; Trapster[†]; Alchemy; Paper Toss; Disney Puzzle; Find It; (10)	×	×		
Wertago[†]; Yellow Pages[†]; DasTelefonbuch[†]; RingTones[†]; Knocking[†]; (5)	×	×	×	×
Wisdom Quotes Lite[†]; Classic Simon Free; Wordfeud FREE; Moron Test:Section 1; Bubble Burst Free; (5)		×		
Astrid Tasks[†]; (1)	×			
CallLog; Last Call Widget; Contact Analyzer; (3)		×	×	×

remaining 11 apps. While both sets are used to verify the transparency of TISSA to run apps, we use the first set to evaluate the effectiveness of TISSA. In the second set, we use TISSA to capture suspicious access requests from these apps and then verify possible information leakage with the TaintDroid system. Before running the experiments, we turn on restrictive privacy policy as the default one, i.e., not trusting any of these apps in accessing any personal information. If a particular app requires the user registration, we will simply create a user account and then log in with the app.

Our results with the first set of information-leaking apps show that TISSA is able to effectively capture the access requests from these untrusted apps to private data and prevent them from being leaked. As a demonstration, we show in Figure 4 two experiments with the same app named *Wisdom Quotes Lite*: one without the TISSA protection (Figure 4(a)) and another with TISSA protection (Figure 4(b)). Note that this app has declared the permission to access the phone identity, but this information will be leaked to a remote data server. The evidence is collected by TaintDroid and shown in Figure 4(a). In particular, it shows that the app is sending out the IMEI number to a remote server. From the log, we can see that the data sent out is tainted with the taint tag 0x400, which indicates the IMEI source. The destination IP address is xxx.59.187.65, a server that belongs to the company that developed this app. The leaked IMEI number (354957034053382) of our test phone is in the query string of HTTP GET request to the remote server. After confirming this leakage, we use the privacy setting manager to adjust the phone identity privacy for this app to be bogus. Then we run this app again. This time we can find (Figure 4(b)) that although the app is sending an IMEI number out, the value sent out is the bogus one, instead of the real IMEI number – this is consistent with our privacy setting for this app.

As another example, an app named *Horoscope* requested the permission of reading current locations. However this app's functionality does not justify such need. In our experiments, we find that phone location information is leaked by this app (confirmed with TaintDroid and the leaked information was sent to a remote server xxx.109.247.8). Then we use the privacy setting manager to adjust the location privacy to be empty, which means the location service neither

```
  dalvikvm  W  TaintLog: OSNetworkSystem.sendStream(209.59.187.65) received data wi
th tag 0x400 data=[GET /ad/ad.php?width=480&height=75&platform=andro
id&name=wisdom_quotes_lite&version=1.2.0&hid=354957034053382 HTTP/1.
1
```

(a) The leaked IMEI number without TISSA

```
  dalvikvm  W  TaintLog: OSNetworkSystem.sendStream(209.59.187.65) received data wi
th tag 0x400 data=[GET /ad/ad.php?width=480&height=75&platform=andro
id&name=wisdom_quotes_lite&version=1.2.0&hid=821291666911081 HTTP/1.
1
```

(b) The leaked IMEI number with TISSA

Fig. 4. Experimenting with an Android App *Wisdom Quotes Lite*

returns the last known location nor updates the new location to this app. We then re-run this app and do not find the true location information leaked.

In the experiments with the second set of apps, we use the default restrictive privacy policy and enable the bogus option for the phone identity. Interestingly, we observe that among these 11 apps, seven of them accessed the phone identity information. We then re-run them in TaintDroid and our results successfully confirm the information leakage among all these 11 apps. From the same set, we also confirmed that two of them leak location information. As a result, among the two sets of total 24 apps, 14 of them leak location information and 13 of them send out the IMEI number. Six of them leak both location and IMEI information. With TISSA, users can select the proper privacy setting and effectively prevent these private information from being leaked.

We point out that although no app in our study leaks the contacts and call log information, they can be similarly protected. Specifically, we can simply adjust the privacy setting of an app which has the READ_CONTACTS permission to be *empty*, then any query from the app for contacts will be returned with an empty contact list. Also, our experiments with these 24 apps indicate that they can smoothly run and no security exceptions have been thrown to affect the functionalities of these apps, which satisfies our second design requirement (Section 2).

4.2 Performance

To measure the performance overhead, we use a JAVA benchmark – Caffeine-Mark 3.0 – to gauge Android app performance and the resulting scores from the benchmark are shown in Figure 5. Note that the benchmark contains a set of programs to measure the app runtime (in particular the Dalvik VM) overhead. From the figure, we can see that there is no observable performance overhead, which is expected as our system only made minor changes to the framework and the Dalvik VM itself was not affected by our system.

In summary, our measurement results on performance indicate that TISSA is lightweight in successfully supporting the privacy mode on Android, which meets our first design requirement.

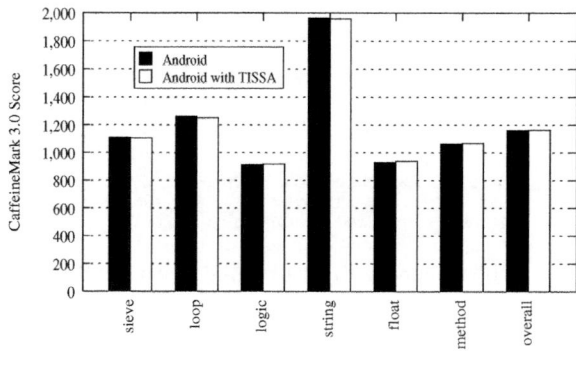

CaffeineMark 3.0 Benchmark

Fig. 5. The Result of CaffeineMark 3.0 Benchmark

5   Discussion

We observe that giving bogus private information could be problematic for some apps. For example the *Weather Channel* app needs to access the device location information to provide the weather forecast of a particular area. If the user chooses the bogus option for its access to this information, it will certainly not work as intended (even though the program does not crash and still functions). One possible enhancement is to provide accurate, but low-fidelity data. With the same app example, it can work equally well with an approximate location. In fact, a simple approximation option could return a random location within a radius (say 10 or 100 miles) of the current location. This indicates that our system can be readily extended to support much finer-grained access than currently demonstrated in this paper. Also, for efficiency, TISSA only uses one single privacy setting for one type of private information. This can be further extended to provide finer access to user data. An example will be to release some personal information, an option between empty and anonymous.

From another perspective, current application development can be improved to provide more contextual information to better help users to make the decision. Though the risk is still on the mobile user side, a privacy-aware app developer can offer alternative mechanisms to obtain private information, such as by providing a UI with necessary context information to justify the need for the access and asking the user to provide the required input (e..g, a ZIP code).

We also note that TISSA is not a panacea for privacy protection. For an app that backs up user contact data to a remote server, the user usually grants the access to the app. However, there is no assurance that the data will not be transferred to elsewhere or be stolen. Our solution does provide an *anonymized* option for lightweight protection. Specifically, when an app reads the contacts data, based on the anonymized setting, the privacy-aware component can return an encrypted version with a key specified by the user or derived from a password.

Therefore, even if data are leaked during transfer or at the server side, the clear-text information is not released. However, due to the resource constraints on mobile phones, the encryption for anonymization cannot be sufficiently strong as desired.

With TISSA enabled, a mobile user can specify privacy settings for installed apps at anytime. Furthermore, the privacy setting can be integrated with the application installer of Android, i.e., the privacy setting manager can be activated by the installer whenever a new app is installed. However, we note that TISSA fundamentally does not provide mechanisms or solutions to help user understand and reason about permission requirements for individual apps. To further improve the usability of TISSA, several approaches can explored. For example, as our future research directions, we can include additional contextual or guiding information to facilitate the privacy setting. Also, we can provide privacy-setting templates to reduce the burden on mobile users. This can be done by applying certain heuristics with the consideration of a device's location [5] or an app's category.

6   Related Work

Privacy issues on smartphones have recently attracted considerable attention. A number of research efforts have been conducted to identify private data leaking by mobile apps. TaintDroid [9] and PiOS [8] are two representatives that target Android and iOS platforms, respectively. Specifically, TaintDroid [9] uses dynamic taint analysis to track privacy data flow on Android. It first taints data from privacy information sources, and then integrates four granularities of taint propagation (i.e., variable-, method-, message-, and file-levels). When the data leaves the system via a network interface, TaintDroid raises an alert (Figure 4) with log information about the taint source, the app that sends out the tainted data, and the destination. PiOS [8] instead applies static analysis on iOS apps to detect possible privacy leak. In particular, it first constructs the control flow graph of an iOS app, and then aims to find whether there is an execution path from the nodes that access privacy source to the nodes of network operations. If such path exists, it considers a potential information leak.

From another perspective, Avik [6] presents a formal language to describe Android apps and uses it to formally reason about data flow properties. An automatic security certification tool called ScanDroid [12] has been developed to extract security specifications from manifests that accompany Android apps, and then check whether data flows through those apps are consistent with those specifications. Note that these systems are helpful to confirm whether a particular app actually leaks out private information. However, they are not designed to protect user private information from being leaked, which is the main goal of our system.

On the defensive side, Kirin [10] is a framework for Android which extracts the permissions from an app's manifest file at install time, and checks whether these permissions are breaking certain security rules. The security rules are manually defined to detect undesired combination of Android permissions, which may be insecure and misused by malicious programs. As a result, Kirin aims to enforce security check at install time, while our system provides a lightweight runtime protection (after an app is installed).

As with our research, Apex [14] utilizes the Android permission model to constrain runtime app behavior. However, there are three key differences. First, they share different design goals. The main objective of Apex is to restrict the usage of phone resources (e.g., when and how many MMS messages can be sent within a day), instead of the exclusive focus on personal information leakage prevention in our system. Second, by design, Apex limits itself to current available permissions but allows for selectively granting permissions at install time or possibly revoking some permissions at runtime. In comparison, our privacy settings is completely orthogonal to current Android permissions. Third, as mentioned earlier, one undesirable consequence of Apex in only partially granting requested permissions is that it may throw security exceptions to a running app, causing it terminate unexpectedly, which violates our second design requirement and is not user-friendly.

Saint [15] is another recent work that allows an app developer to provide a security policy that will be enforced (by the enhanced Android framework) to regulate install-time Android permission assignment and their run-time use. Security-by-Contract [7] similarly allows an app to be bound to a contract, which describes the upper-bound of what the app can do. Notice that these security policies or contracts need to be provided during application development, *not* by mobile users. As a result, it is unclear on how they can be applied by mobile users to customize the privacy protection. MockDroid [4] allows users to mock the access from an untrusted app to particular resources at runtime (by reporting either empty or unavailable). The mocked access can be naturally integrated into TISSA as another privacy setting option on smartphones.

7   Conclusion

In this paper, we argue for the need of a privacy mode in existing smartphones. The need comes from the disturbing facts that (rogue) smartphone apps will intentionally leak users' private information. As a solution, we present the design, implementation and evaluation of TISSA, a privacy-mode implementation in Android. TISSA empowers mobile users the fine-grained control and runtime re-adjustment capability to specify what kinds of user information can be accessible (and in what way) to untrusted apps. Orthogonal to current Android permissions, these privacy settings can be adjusted without necessarily affecting the normal functionalities of apps. Our experiments demonstrate its effectiveness and practicality. The performance measurements show that our system has a low performance overhead.

References

1. Android Market, http://www.android.com/market/
2. Gartner November Report, http://www.gartner.com/it/page.jsp?id=1466313

3. IPhone and Android Apps Breach Privacy, http://online.wsj.com/article/SB10001424052748704694004576020083703574602.html
4. Beresford, A.R., Rice, A., Skehin, N., Sohan, R.: MockDroid: Trading Privacy for Application Functionality on Smartphones. In: 12th Workshop on Mobile Computing Systems and Applications (2011)
5. Bernheim Brush, A.J., Krumm, J., Scott, J.: Exploring End User Preferences for Location Obfuscation, Location-Based Services, and the Value of Location. In: 12th ACM International Conference on Ubiquitous Computing (2010)
6. Chaudhuri, A.: Language-Based Security on Android. In: 4th ACM SIGPLAN Workshop on Programming Languages and Analysis for Security (2009)
7. Desmet, L., Joosen, W., Massacci, F., Philippaerts, P., Piessens, F., Siahaan, I., Vanoverberghe, D.: Security by Contract on the.NET Platform. Information Security Technical Report 13(1), 25–32 (2008)
8. Egele, M., Kruegel, C., Kirda, E., Vigna, G.: PiOS: Detecting Privacy Leaks in iOS Applications. In: 18th Annual Network and Distributed System Security Symposium (2011)
9. Enck, W., Gilbert, P., Chun, B.-G., Cox, L.P., Jung, J., McDaniel, P., Sheth, A.N.: TaintDroid: An Information-Flow Tracking System for Realtime Privacy Monitoring on Smartphones. In: 9th USENIX Symposium on Operating Systems Design and Implementation (2010)
10. Enck, W., Ongtang, M., McDaniel, P.: On Lightweight Mobile Phone Application Certification. In: 16th ACM Conference on Computer and Communications Security (2009)
11. Enck, W., Ongtang, M., McDaniel, P.: Understanding Android Security. IEEE Security & Privacy 7(1), 50–57 (2009)
12. Fuchs, A.P., Chaudhuri, A., Foster, J.S.: SCanDroid: Automated Security Certification of Android Applications (2009), http://www.cs.umd.edu/~avik/papers/scandroidascaa.pdf
13. Mahaffey, K., Hering, J.: App Attack: Surviving the Explosive Growth of Mobile Apps (2010)
14. Nauman, M., Khan, S., Zhang, X.: Apex: Extending Android Permission Model and Enforcement with User-Defined Runtime Constraints. In: 5th ACM Symposium on Information, Computer and Communications Security (2010)
15. Ongtang, M., McLaughlin, S.E., Enck, W., McDaniel, P.D.: Semantically Rich Application-Centric Security in Android. In: 25th Annual Computer Security Applications Conference (2009)
16. Shabtai, A., Fledel, Y., Kanonov, U., Elovici, Y., Dolev, S., Glezer, C.: Google Android: A Comprehensive Security Assessment. IEEE Security & Privacy 8(2), 35–44 (2010)

Towards Permission-Based Attestation for the Android Platform

(Short Paper)

Ingo Bente[1], Gabi Dreo[3], Bastian Hellmann[1], Stephan Heuser[2], Joerg Vieweg[1], Josef von Helden[1], and Johannes Westhuis[1]

[1] Trust@FHH Research Group, Fachhochschule Hannover - University of Applied Sciences and Arts in Hannover
{ingo.bente,bastian.hellmann,joerg.vieweg,josef.vonhelden,
johannes.westhuis}@fh-hannover.de
[2] Fraunhofer SIT, Darmstadt
stephan.heuser@sit.fraunhofer.de
[3] Universitaet der Bundeswehr Muenchen
gabi.dreo@unibw.de

Abstract. We propose a new attestation approach for the Android platform that integrates Trusted Computing concepts and Android's permission-based access control features. Recent research in the field of mobile security has shown that malware is a real threat. Trusted Computing in general and especially the concept of remote attestation can be leveraged to counter both the dissemination and the potential impact of such malware. However, current attestation approaches are not well suited for mobile platforms and crucial Trusted Computing components are still missing for them. Our approach introduces the necessary Trusted Computing building blocks for the Android platform. Furthermore, we detail how the permissions that are used by an Android phone's installed apps can be attested to a remote party at runtime. Additionally, we highlight areas that are subject of future work.

1 Introduction

Today's smartphones provide an impressive amount of features that are desired by users: manifold connectivity and communication abilities, a certain amount of computing power, built-in sensors for sophisticated, context aware applications and full-fledged operating systems are some of them. Furthermore, all important mobile platforms (Apple iOS, RIM Blackberry OS, Windows Phone, Symbian and Google Android) support an app-based architecture. Users can download and install apps on-demand from online market stores for various purposes in order to suit their smartphone for their needs. Doing an ordinary phone call seems to be a pretty boring feature of a modern smartphones compared to the versatility of the available apps. Instead, those handhelds are used for gaming, for surfing the internet or for doing online banking. Even in enterprise environments, smartphones can be used to improve established workflows [9]. Usage scenarios include location based services for outdoor staff and the tracking of goods in a warehouse.

J.M. McCune et al. (Eds.): TRUST 2011, LNCS 6740, pp. 108–115, 2011.

Unfortunately, the large set of features, the versatility of smartphones and the fact that they are also used for processing sensitive data introduces new security issues that one has to face. Recent research has shown that mobile malware, especially sensory malware which tries to snoop for sensitive data by using a smartphone's built-in sensors, is a real threat[1,4,10]. Other malware examples send SMS messages to premium service numbers [8] or try to steal the user's credentials [7]. An efficient way to spread mobile malware is to leverage the capabilities of the online market stores and to fool users to install apps with hidden, malicious functionality. Researchers also noted a trend in the evolution of mobile malware which is comparable to the evolution of PC malware: the proof-of-concept implementations that perform simple destructive, denial of service attacks are replaced by more sophisticated malware implementations that spy for valuable user information on a device or even aim to establish a mobile botnet [2].

Trusted Computing as proposed by the Trusted Computing Group (TCG) and its applications such as remote attestation can be leveraged in order to increase the security of computing platforms and especially to counter the dissemination and the impact of malware. However, current attestation approaches lack of an adaptation for the specific characteristics of modern smartphones and have known issues, especially in terms of scalability. The concept of property-based attestation [3] introduced by Sadeghi et al. aims to mitigate some of these general drawbacks, however, no attestation approach that addresses the specific characteristics of mobile platforms has been developed so far. A (hardware) security anchor for mobile phones, the Mobile Trusted Module, was proposed but has to date never been widely deployed. The TCG's Mobile Phone Work Group addresses the still insufficient adoption of Trusted Computing concepts for mobile phones. They have recently published a revisited version of the MTM specification [6].

In order to address the missing adaptation of Trusted Computing concepts, we propose a new attestation scheme that is specifically tailored for the Android platform: permission-based attestation (PeBA). In contrast to the classical binary attestation that is known from commodity computing platforms, we do not solely measure and attest the binary part of the application code. Instead, we follow a hybrid approach that combines classical binary attestation with our new PeBA concept. A special PeBA app (PeBAA) is responsible to measure and to attest the set of permissions that are used by an Android phone's installed apps at runtime. The PeBA app itself plus further components that form our trusted computing base are measured and attested by leveraging binary attestation. Thus, a remote party can reason about the security status of an Android phone based on the set of permissions that are granted to the installed applications. Our approach is lightweight and mitigates the scalability issues that are known from approaches that solely rely on binary attestation.

2 Android

Android, which is developed by Google as open-source, is both an operating system and application framework designed for mobile devices such as smartphones or tablets. It is possible to extend an Android system by installing third party applications (apps). These apps can be downloaded, usually from the so called Android market, and installed by the user. To develop such apps, one can use the Android SDK, which is also provided by Google.

Architecture. The architecture of an Android system consists of different layers: A Linux kernel based on the version 2.6 builds the bottom layer and is responsible for handling the hardware resources. The layer above the kernel layer supplies some native C and C++ libraries like SSL or WebKit, as well as the Android runtime. This runtime environment consists of a set of Java libraries and the Dalvik virtual machine (DalvikVM), which launches and runs the applications for Android. The virtual machine launches an instance for every application that is started on the system. The next layer is called the application framework and provides high level services in Java, like a window manager or services to access the file system and transfer data between applications. On top lies the application layer, which holds Java applications that use the underlying libraries and services to provide functions to the user like phone, contacts or applications that use the build-in sensors, like GPS or accelerometers. Third party apps also reside within this layer.

Permission-based Security Model. The security model of Android consists of two main concepts. First, every application that runs gets its own process ID and its own user at installation time. Combined with an exclusive directory in the file system, every application is run in a sandbox and cannot act malicious to other apps. The communication between apps is done by specific functions of the supported libraries.

Secondly, the system works with permissions to grant an application access to vital parts of the system. Such a permission could be sending of SMS or starting a phone call. By default, an app has no permissions at all. To get access to vital services, it has to define these services via the corresponding permissions it wants to use in its Manifest file. When an application is installed, all needed permissions are shown to the user who has to make a decision whether he accepts or declines the use of these services. When running the application, every usage of a service that is not registered by a permission in its Manifest will throw an exception. Also, usage of services the user has declined at installation time will be blocked.

3   Permission-Based Attestation

In the following, we present the concept of permission-based attestation. Considering the architecture of the Android platform as described in section 2, an easy approach to perform remote attestation could be to simply binary attest all components of a device, including all installed (third party) apps. While this simplistic approach works well in theory hence it leverages the existing concepts in the field of Trusted Computing (that is, measure before load anything), it also conserves the known drawbacks of binary attestation, especially in terms of scalability. In order to avoid these drawbacks and to leverage the characteristics of the Android platform, we propose the concept of permission-based attestation (PeBA).

PeBA is a hybrid approach that consists of two conceptual parts: (1) a Static Chain of Trust (SCoT) that covers the components of our trusted computing base and which can be binary attested and (2) an agent which is part of the SCoT that performs secure measurement and attestation of all permissions that are granted to apps installed on the respective device. The combination of those two parts allows a remote party to reason about the security status of the Android phone.

3.1   Architecture Overview

In the following, we will detail the conceptual Trusted Computing components that are needed by our permission-based attestation approach and furthermore describe how they can be implemented with minor modifications and extensions to the Android platform. The extended architecture is depicted in figure 1.

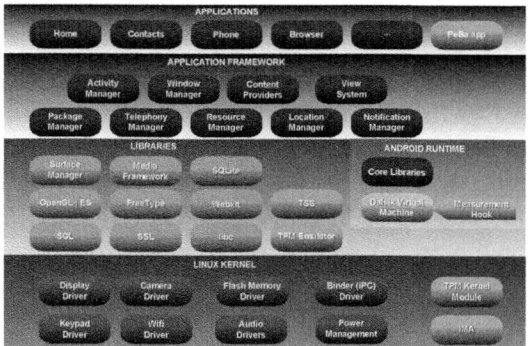

Fig. 1. PeBA-extended Android architecture

In total, there are four Trusted Computing building blocks that provide the necessary functionality for PeBA: (1) a Root of Trust for Measurement (RTM), (2) Roots of Trust for Storage and Reporting (RTS/RTR), (3) a Static Chain of Trust (SCoT) and (4) a permission measurement and attestation agent. The SCoT encapsulates all components of the Android platform that have been executed prior to the execution of the measurement agent. From there on, it is the agent's responsibility to measure the permissions of the installed applications. However, none of the mentioned building blocks is available on a commodity Android phone by default. In order to implement the required functionality, the following components need to be extended or added: the bootloader that starts the Android platform on a device, the Android Linux kernel, the Android native library layer, the DalvikVM and an Android app that implements the permission measurement and attestation agent.

Bootloader. Among the above mentioned components, the bootloader is a special case. In the absence of a BIOS on Android phones, the bootloader would be the hook to implement a RTM. However, the implementation of bootloaders is vendor-specific and not part of the Android platform itself. Thus, we ignore the bootloader for our further explanation and consider the Android Linux kernel as the RTM. That is, building block (1) is mapped on to the kernel itself.

Android Linux Kernel. To perform measurements and to actually bootstrap the establishment of a Static Chain of Trust, the Android Linux kernel is enhanced with the Integrity Measurement Architecture (IMA)[1]. IMA ensures that any executable, library or kernel module is measured before it is executed. Furthermore, IMA can be triggered in order to measure further files as needed. In the absence of a hardware TPM or MTM for Android phones, both the RTR and the RTS have to be implemented in software as well. For this purpose, we leverage a software based TPM/MTM emulator [5], thus mapping building block (2). The TPM functions are provided as a user space service and are thus not part of the kernel itself. However, the emulator also includes a kernel module in order to provide a TPM character device. Therefore, applications that normally communicate with a TPM through such a character device will also work with the software-emulated TPM.

Android Native Library Layer. This layer implements the actual functionality of the emulated TPM as a system service, which maps building block (2). Furthermore, we add a TSS service in order to expose the TPM capabilities to the application layer. The TSS provides features in order to realize the SCoT, thus mapping building block (3).

DalvikVM. The SCoT which is building block (3) must include any components of our trusted computing base. In addition to the components that are measured by IMA, this also includes code that is executed by the Android runtime environment. Thus, we extend the DalvikVM with appropriate measurement hooks. This way we ensure that the whole, Java based Android framework as well as the permission measurement app, that is responsible for the measurement of the permissions, are part of the Static Chain of Trust. The measurements are done by triggering the IMA extended Android kernel.

PeBA app. While we do not measure any other app with the DalvikVM extension, our approach demands that the permission measurement app (PeBa app) takes care of measuring the installed apps and their respective permissions (building block (4)). Note that the PeBA app will not measure the actual code of the installed apps.

All taken measurements are extended to the emulated TPM's PCRs. The history of all taken measurements, whether they are binary or permission-based, is encapsulated in appropriate log files. The binary measurements undertaken by IMA are rendered to a classical Stored Measurement Log (SML). A second log file, the Permission Measurement Log (PML), stores the permission measurements that are performed by the PeBA app. Each PML entry consists of the

---

[1] http://linux-ima.sourceforge.net/

PCR number where the permission measurements have been extended to, the SHA-1 hash of the concatenated permission strings, the name of the application and the actual permissions that are used by the corresponding app. During the attestation process, the SML, the PML and the quoted PCR values enable the verifier to recalculate the permissions and to check them against a policy.

3.2   Steps to Perform Permission-Based Attestation

The permission-based attestation process consists of several steps, which are conceptual divided into three parts. The first steps establish a Static Chain of Trust starting from the kernel to the PeBA app. In the second part, the PeBA app measures the permissions granted to the installed apps on the device. Finally, the third part includes the challenge response protocol between the attestor and the verifier. Figure 2 gives an overview of the whole process.

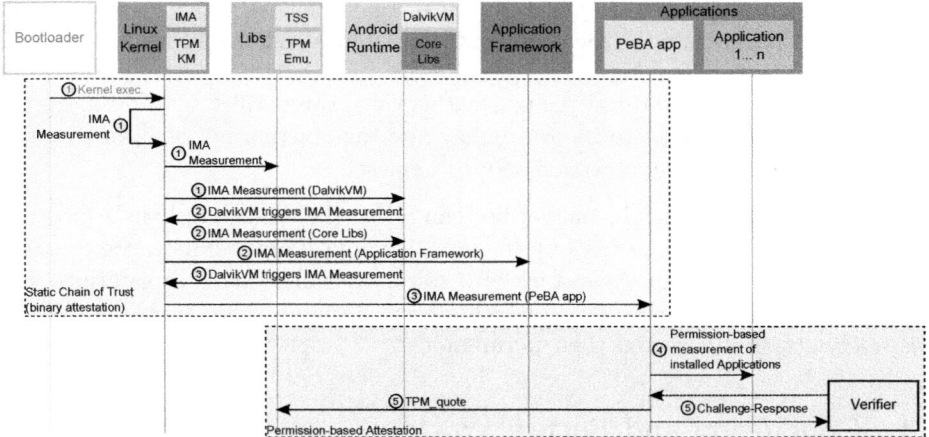

Fig. 2. PeBA flow of operations

In the following, we detail each step in the process. When we refer to *taking a measurement* this includes the actual measurement (whether binary-based or permission-based), the extend Operation that updates the TPM's PCRs as well as updating the corresponding log file (SML and PML).

1. Since we consider the bootloader to be out of scope, the first step is the execution of the Android Linux kernel. The IMA extension of the kernel measures all crucial system components which are not Java-based (executables, kernel modules, shared libraries). This also includes the software-based TPM emulator, the TSS service and the DalvikVM.
2. The next measurements are performed by the modified DalvikVM. It leverages IMA to measure any Java-based part of the Android runtime and application framework.

3. Next, the DalvikVM binary measures the PeBA app prior to its execution. At this point, the Static Chain of Trust for the binary attestation part is complete. It allows to verify the integrity of the PeBA app, which in turn can perform any further, permission-based measurements.

4. When executed, the PeBA app measures all installed apps and their permissions on the device. For each installed app, the list of requested permissions is obtained. These permissions, which are basically Java strings, are concatenated and a SHA-1 hash of the resulting string is calculated. The result is then extended to a PCR of the TPM: $PCR_n = SHA1(PCR_n \oplus SHA1(Permission_0 \oplus Permission_1 \oplus ... \oplus Permission_c))$, with c being the number of permissions for the respective app. Furthermore, the PML is updated with the corresponding values.

5. After receiving an appropriate challenge from a verifier, the PeBA app now performs a TPM_Quote that covers the PCRs for the Static Chain of Trust as well as the one that includes the permission measurements. The quote, the SML and the PML are sent back to the verifier.

6. Based upon the TPM_Quote, the SML and the PML, the verifier is now able to recalculate the measurements. If the logs and the TPM_Quote result match, the verifier knows the set of apps and their respective permissions of the attestors Android phone. In this case, the verifier may compare the granted permissions to its own policy and take further actions (for example allowing or denying a certain service request).

By using this approach, the verifier can check the Android phone's integrity state and the permissions used by the installed apps. Only a minor, pretty static part of the device's software stack is verified by using binary attestation. The more dynamic part of the device (which are the actual installed third party apps) is solely attested based on their permissions.

4   Conclusion and Future Work

In this paper, we have introduced the concept of permission-based attestation (PeBA) for the Android platform. PeBA enables to attest the set of installed third party apps and the permissions that they use to a remote party. It follows a hybrid approach that integrates binary attestation for verifying the integrity of the trusted computing base and our new permission-based attestation to reason about the security state of installed third-party apps. As we already have implemented PeBA as a proof-of-concept, our next short term step will be an evaluation of the practicability based on this implementation.

PeBA is just the first approach for a more sophisticated attestation model for mobile devices. The fact that classical binary attestation has not been widely adopted in the last decade should motivate future work in this field. Considering PeBA, we will work on extending our approach in numerous directions: 1) we aim to include context-awareness in our attestation model, 2) further aspects of the app's security configuration (for example `intent-filters`) could be considered as well and 3) we will investigate options to detect mobile Malware that uses covert channels to bypass Android's permission-based security model (like Soundminer [4]).

References

1. Cai, L., Machiraju, S., Chen, H.: Defending against sensor-sniffing attacks on mobile phones. In: Proceedings of the 1st ACM Workshop on Networking, systems, and Applications for Mobile Handhelds - MobiHeld 2009, p. 31 (2009), http://portal.acm.org/citation.cfm?doid=1592606.1592614
2. Enck, W., Ongtang, M., McDaniel, P.: On lightweight mobile phone application certification. In: Proceedings of the 16th ACM Conference on Computer and Communications Security, CCS 2009, pp. 235–245. ACM, New York (2009)
3. Sadeghi, A.-R., Stüble, C.: Property-based attestation for computing platforms: caring about properties, not mechanisms. In: Proceedings of the 2004 Workshop on New Security Paradigms, NSPW 2004, pp. 67–77. ACM, New York (2004)
4. Schlegel, R., Zhang, K., Zhou, X., Intwala, M., Kapadia, A., Wang, X.: Soundminer: A Stealthy and Context-Aware Sound Trojan for Smartphones. In: Proceedings of the 18th Annual Network and Distributed System Security Symposium (NDSS), pp. 17–33 (Febraury 2011)
5. Strasser, M., Stamer, H.: A software-based trusted platform module emulator. In: Lipp, P., Sadeghi, A.-R., Koch, K.-M. (eds.) Trust 2008. LNCS, vol. 4968, pp. 33–47. Springer, Heidelberg (2008)
6. TCG Mobile Phone Work Group: Mobile Trusted Module Specification, Version 1.0 Revision 7.02 (April 2010), http://www.trustedcomputinggroup.org/resources/mobile_phone_work_group_mobile_trusted_module_specification
7. The H Security: Android app steals bank login details (January 2010), http://www.h-online.com/security/news/item/Android-app-steals-bank-login-details-901895.html(accessed on February 27, 2011)
8. The H Security: First SMS trojan for Android detected (August 2010), http://www.h-online.com/security/news/item/First-SMS-trojan-for-Android-detected-1053466.html(accessed on February 27, 2011)
9. Thumher, B.: The impact of mobile technology on business processes results from 5 case studies. In: 2nd IEEE/IFIP International Workshop on Business-Driven IT Management, BDIM 2007, (21-21 2007), pp. 108–109 (2007)
10. Xu, N., Zhang, F., Luo, Y., Jia, W., Xuan, D., Teng, J.: Stealthy video capturer: a new video-based spyware in 3g smartphones. In: Proceedings of the Second ACM Conference on Wireless Network Security, WiSec 2009, pp. 69–78. ACM, New York (2009)

Trusting to Learn: Trust and Privacy Issues in Serious Games

Miguel Malheiros, Charlene Jennett, Will Seager, and M. Angela Sasse

Dept. of Computer Science, University College London (UCL), Gower Street,
WC1E 6BT, UK
{m.malheiros,c.jennett,w.seager,a.sasse}@cs.ucl.ac.uk

Abstract. Organizations are increasingly investing in technology-enhanced learning systems to improve their employees' skills. Serious games are one example; the competitive and fun nature of games is supposed to motivate employee participation. But any system that records employee data raises issues of privacy and trust. In this paper, we present a study on privacy and trust implications of serious games in an organizational context. We present findings from 32 interviews with potential end-users of a serious games platform called TARGET. A qualitative analysis of the interviews reveals that participants anticipate privacy risks for the data generated in game playing, and their decision to trust their fellow employees and managers depends on the presence of specific trust signals. Failure to minimize privacy risks and maximize trust will affect the acceptance of the system and the learning experience – thus undermining the primary purpose for which it was deployed. Game designers are advised to provide mechanisms for selective disclosure of data by players, andorganizations should not use gaming data for appraisal or selection purposes, and clearly communicate this to employees.

Keywords: trust, privacy, serious games, technology-enhanced learning.

Introduction

Organizations are increasingly turning to e-learning solutions to save time and travel costs associated with traditional training through outside courses [1]. *Serious games –* which facilitate learning whilst simultaneously entertaining and engaging learners – are emerging as a promising e-learning solution.The simulation of real-world experience is thought to improve transfer of learning to applied contexts [2],[3].Also, the competitive element of serious games is a source of motivation for players; thus serious games have already been deployedas part of some corporate learning programmes.

To develop competencies, serious games deployed in organizations need to collect and store personal data. Research suggests that privacy and trust can be important factors influencing user acceptance and the effectiveness of specific systems [4], [5], [6]. When these concerns are not addressed, the potential consequences of workplace monitoring include – low employee morale, chilling effects, deterioration of work relationships, reduced commitment to the organization, lower productivity and economic loss [7], [8], [9], [10].

J.M. McCune et al. (Eds.): TRUST 2011, LNCS 6740, pp. 116–130, 2011.

Although some research has been carried out on the impact of privacy issues on technology-enhanced learning (TEL) [11], [12], [13], it has focused on types of data assumed to be sensitive, and how generic privacy technologies could be used to protect it. There is currently a gap in the literature regarding the specific privacy and trust issues of learning systems: (1) how learner-users perceive and react to different data practices and interactions with other stakeholders, and; (2) what impact this can have on system acceptance and effectiveness. There is also a lack of methods to help TEL developers incorporate privacy and trust considerations into the design of their systems.

In this paper, we describe an investigation of privacy and trust issues in TARGET, a platform for developing serious games. The aim of our research was to understand how the design and configuration of TARGET-based games might impact privacy and trust perception among employees, and to develop guidelines for designing and operating such games in organizational contexts. The first game being developed aims to support the rapid development of competence in project management skills. Thirty-two interviews were conducted with potential end-users of TARGET – 16 focused on privacy and 16 on trust – and analyzed using Grounded Theory. The results show that participants' perceptions of privacy risks depends on the validity of the data collected, the extent to which it is linked to an individual, and the data receiver, among other factors; while their level of trust in other players and management depends on the presence of trust signals, such as the existence of a code of conduct for players' behavior in the game, or a clear statement of purpose for the game. Based on these results, a joint framework of privacy and trust was created where the perception of privacy risks is related to having trusted relationships with other stakeholders.

In Section 2, we describe TARGET and review related research on privacy and trust. In Sections 3-5, we present our research aims, methodology and findings. In Section 6, we present our conclusions and several recommendations for practitioners.

Background

TARGET

TARGET (Transformative, Adaptive, Responsive and enGaging Environment) is a collaborative project funded by the European Community under the Seventh Framework Programme. The main aim of TARGET is to research, analyze, and develop a new genre of TEL environment to support the rapid competence development of project managers. TARGET adopts a serious games approach to competence development. Learners encounter realistic game scenarios that simulate project management experiences that characterize the real-world [14]. TARGET also aims to foster the development of communities of practice [15], [16] and promote social learning, enabling players to interact with each other via multi-player gaming and other social tools. TARGET is intended for use within enterprise environments, academic environments and interest-focused communities.

Privacy in TEL and Multimedia Systems

Research on TEL has identified privacy as an important issue in the field – in particular, *linkability* of data, *observability* of data, *identity disclosure* and *data disclosure* [11], [12], [13]. These views reflect a "data-centric perspective" that assumes that specific data items are sensitive; it does not take the contextual nature of users' privacy perceptions into account. Privacy is *"individually subjective and socially situated"* [17]– there is no specific type of information which is considered personal in all situations, and no situation which is seen as a privacy violation by all persons [18]. It is, therefore, necessary to understand which factors influence the way individuals perceive different data practices.

According to Adams [4], technology users' privacy perceptions depend on: (1) sensitivity of the information being broadcasted; (2) the information receiver, and; (3) usage of the information[1]. Users evaluate the sensitivity of the information they are broadcasting not in a binary way – sensitive vs. non-sensitive – but according to a *"scale of sensitivity"*; depending on how "personally defining" the information is deemed to be and how the user predicts others will interpret the information. If individuals think that the information being disclosed *"will be used to draw reliable and valid inferences about them"* and is relevant for the interaction they will consider it less privacy invasive [19].

The level of trust and the type of relationship with the information receiver also determines how an individual sees the privacy implications of a disclosure[19]. Data that can portray the user in a negative way is more sensitive if seen by someone she has a close relationship with –e.g. friend or colleague– than by a stranger[4]; for this reason, both current and future information flows should be clarified so that users know who will see their data [20].

Information usage is assessed by looking at the way the information is being used in the current moment and can be used in the future [4]. When data is recorded, for example, it gives more control to the data receiver. The receiver can then edit it or broadcast the data at a later date, which can cause it to lose contextual cues, increasing its sensitivity [4]. Although it is true that users evaluate the situation more negatively when they perceive a loss of control [19], they will make the trade-off if they think that the benefits of a specific current data usage outweigh the risks of a harmful future usage [4].

All the above factors are influenced by the context in which the interaction takes place. Trust in the organization deploying the system will affect how risky from a privacy point of view users think the technology is [4]. Auser's past experiences, knowledge and preconceptions of the technology, and the level of interaction s/he will have with it, will also have an influence on his/her perceptions [4], [18], [21].

Privacy has been addressed in TEL literature in a generic way, which does not take into account the context in which the learning technology is deployed, or the users' views of specific privacy issues with it. Since our research aim is to understand how privacy and trust influence user acceptance,a user-centered model – i.e. Adams' privacy model [4] –provides a suitable starting point forexamining how privacy is perceived in serious games in organizational contexts.

Trust in Technology-Mediated Interactions

Riegelsberger et al. [6] argue that trust and the conditions that affect it must become a core concern of systems development. *Trust* is defined as *"an attitude of positive*

---

[1] Adams' privacy model [4] is the result of empirical studies in multimedia communications but comprehensive enough to be applicable to other technologies.

expectation that one's vulnerabilities will not be exploited" [6], [22], [23], [24], [25]. In their framework, Riegelsberger et al. identify contextual and intrinsic trust-warranting properties that designers should provide to encourage trustworthy behavior and enable well-placed trust (also see [26]). Contextual properties are the most relevant for our purposes.

Contextual properties are attributes of the context that provide motivation for trustworthy behavior. There are three types: temporal, social and institutional [27]. A trustee's motivation to fulfill will increase if the trustee believes that they will interact again with a particular trustor (*temporal embeddedness*). *Stable identities* and *information about the likelihood of future encounters* will influence this property. *Reputation* information – e.g. honesty, reliability, dependability – provides an incentive to fulfill for trustors who are socially embedded, because of the trustee's interest in future interactions with trustors who may gain access to this reputation information (*social embeddedness*). Factors that influence the effect of reputation are: identifiability, the traceability of trustee actions, the social connectedness of the trustor, the topology of the social network, the cost of capturing and disseminating reliable past information, and the degree to which such information itself can be trusted to be truthful. Institutions can support trustworthy actions by providing incentives and sanctions (*institutional embeddedness*), but to have an effect on a trustee's behavior, his or her actions must be traceable, and the cost of investigation and sanctioning must be low compared to the cost of non-fulfillment.

Applying their framework to the context of voice-enabled online gaming, Riegelberger et al. [6] make a number of suggestions for how online games can support well-placed trust and trustworthy behaviors: stable identities, block lists, reputation scores, enforcement bodies, player-formed groups/organizations, profiles containing personal information, buddy lists (with presence indicators) and communication tools such as email and chat. Such features could also support trust in the TARGET platform – however, being a serious game for use in an organizational setting, it is possible that other factors would also be at play.

Research Aims

The frameworks of Adams [4] and Riegelsberger et al. [6] have revealed a number of factors for creating and sustaining privacy and trust in computer-mediated interactions. However, it is uncertain whether the same privacy and trust issues would be identified for serious games in an organizational context. Although Adams [4] does mention that trust in the information receiver (trustee)affects users' (trustors')decisions (see section 0) there is no elaboration of how which factors influence that trust decision, and in turn privacy. The current research aimed to extend upon the previous literature by answering the following questions:

1. What are the specific privacy risks that players associate with TARGET?
2. How do players expect their data to be used by key stakeholders, such as managers and other employees (trust dynamics)?
3. How do privacy and trust interact in this specific context?
4. What design recommendations can be made to support privacy and trust in TARGET and other learning platforms in organizations?

Interviews were conducted with 32 individuals (16 on privacy, 16 on trust) whose profile matched that of potential TARGET users. The data was then combined to explore the interplay between privacy and trust. It is a challenge to anticipate the privacy risks of a system before that system is fully developed. This study relied on: (1) a demo of a TARGET game to help participants envision the system, and how they would interact with it; and (2) scenarios of potential uses of player's data to contextualize the questions and elicit more realistic reactions from participants. (Scenarios are commonly used in privacy research – see [5])

1 Methodology

1.1 Participants

Participants had to have at least 1 year of work experience in large (more than 100 employees) organizations. 27 were recruited online and the remaining 5 through personal contacts. 17 were female, 15 were male. Ages ranged from 20-59, the median age being 26 years. 18 participants worked in the commercial sector, 11 in the public sector and 3 selected "other". The median sizeof participants' organizations was 800 employees. 25 participants had experience of playing digital games.

1.2 TARGET Demo Video

The demo video introduced participants to the TARGET platform. They were told that learners interact with other characters – real people represented by avatars or computer-based characters – within in a 3D virtual environment. The system provides several stories that the learner can play to develop skills such as leadership, communication, or conflict resolution. Within each story, the learner can develop multiple competencies. The system also provides a 'lounge' – a social space, where learners can interact with each other. Several types of data can be generated and/or stored by the system. These data types are explored in the scenarios.

1.3 Scenarios

Several scenarios and interview questions were created to elicit responses to privacy and trust. The scenarios were based on: (1) a workshop with TARGET developers, (2) focus groups conducted with prospective learner-participants, and (3) Adams' privacy model [4].The privacy scenarios portray situations with different data receivers, types of data, and data usages; with an emphasis on performance data:

1.   displaying performance data as a score on a public scoreboard and alternatives to that option;
2.   use of aggregated performance data to guide training decisions;
3.   the use of performance data to guide internal recruitment decisions;
4.   playing a scenario with other players with everyone using pseudonyms;
5.   the player profile, the information it contains, and other players' access to it;
6.   interaction with other players in the game scenarios and lounge.

Riegelsberger et al. [6] advocate not only designing to support well-placed trust, but to incentivize trustworthy behavior. The trust scenarios explore: (1) trust in TARGET, and (2) trust in other players of TARGET. The scenarios topics were:

1. implementation of TARGET in an organizational setting;
2. data access;
3. use of data, e.g. score boards, recruitment, identification of training needs;
4. initial contact with other players;
5. maintaining/limiting contact with other players;
6. realvs. pseudonymous identities.

1.4 Procedure

Interviews were semi-structured and conducted in a lab setting. Each participant was shown a 3 minute demo of TARGET and was briefed on the main features of the system. They were asked to imagine several scenarios related to the game and how they would respond if it happened at their organization. Privacy interviews lasted 60-90 minutes, and participants were paid £15. Trust interviews lasted 30-60 minutes and participants were paid £10. All interviews were audio-recorded.

Transcripts were coded using a qualitative methodology known as grounded theory [28]. Using open coding, axial coding and selective coding, two researchers created separate grounded theories for privacy and trust. The codes were pooled and underwent a further round of selective coding to create a joint framework, wherein privacy refers to vulnerabilities associated with game data, and trust refers to specific vulnerabilities associated with information receivers.

2 Findings

The framework shown in Figure 1 will be explained in three parts:

— Players'interaction with the system (1)
— Players' interaction with other stakeholders: player-manager interaction (2) and player-player interaction (3).

When numbers are given in support of codes, the number of participants from the privacy and trust interviews will be followed by P and T respectively.

2.1 Players' Interaction with the System

Players interact with the system through two game areas: game scenarios and lounge. When playing game scenarios, the performance of the player will be analyzed and transformed into a performance assessment. The time spent playing and the different game scenarios played can also be recorded. When players interact with other players in the lounge (by text or voice), the conversations could – from a technical point of view – be stored. Demographic and job-related data could be aggregated into a profile that would identify the player when interacting with others.

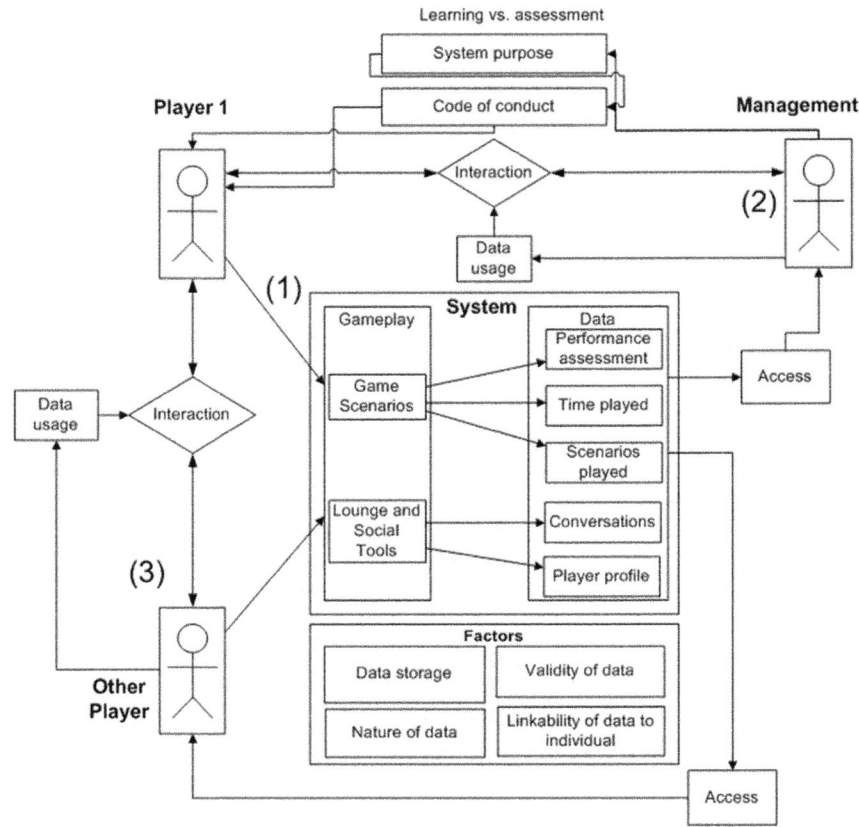

Fig. 1. Stakeholder interactions

Participants' privacy concerns centered around: (1) data storage (2) nature of the data; (3) validity of the data; and (4) linkability of the data to the player.5(3P, 2T) participants wanted to know where game data would be stored, and what kind of *security measures* would be deployed. One perceived risk was that the management of the data might be outsourced to another company, or even sent outside the country or the E.U. Another risk was that there could be a security breach that resulted in unauthorized people getting access to a player's personal data.

The *impression of the player* that the data projected to others was a major concern. If the data showed the player in a good light,s/he might not mind sharing it. If the data revealed weaknesses or shortcomings, the player would prefer it not to be public. 15 (7P, 8T) participants mentioned that a poor performance assessment could make other people in the organization think the player was not good enough to perform his job. Time spent playing and game scenarios played were also considered sensitive: by seeing which scenarios another player had played, it might be possible to infer his/her weaknesses. If a player had played the game for much longer or much less than what was expected in the organization, this could be perceived negatively.

25(13P, 12T) participants questioned the *validity of performance assessment*– i.e. the system's ability to correctly gauge real job-related competencies. One concern was that the game scenario might not be a realistic portrayal of the actual task because communication within the game occurs through a computer. Also, the game might not cover enough relevant aspects of the job domain; if this was the case, it was thought to be unfair to assess an employee based on their performance in the game.

5(3P, 2T) participants said they would prefer human assessment to an automatic one, because a human assessor can probe and ask questions, while a computer cannot. Another (1P) participant argued that an automatic assessment is fairer because it does not rely on the subjective judgment of a manager.

A further issue was external factors that couldhamper a player's performance: experience with computer games and computers in general; technical problems (e.g. the system crashing), and personal issues (e.g. returning from maternity leave, a recent family bereavement, or having a bad day). Participants proposed that player's overall personal context should be considered when assessing his performance, and that there should be a way for players to correct or erase erroneous data.

The extent to which game data is *linked to an individual*also affected players' perceptions. 13 (4P, 9T) participants mentioned that the use of pseudonyms instead of real names would have a positive effect on how they perceived the system. The use of pseudonyms couldallow a player to interact more freely with the system, feel less embarrassed, pressured, andthreatened.On the other hand, the use of pseudonyms could also make a player lose interest in the game – if a player's performance cannot be traced back to him/her, there is less incentive to take the game seriously (1P).

Regarding aggregationof performance data, 7 (7P) participants said that they would view this as less threatening than displaying individual data. This would make itmore difficult to identify individual players who did notperformwell. Players would feel free to experiment and choose riskier options. 3(3P) participants even argued that – since in most organizations work is usually done in teams – aggregation on a work group or team basis would be more appropriate.

A possible limitation of aggregation was the risk of "tarring everyone with the same brush" – e.g. one player could be given unnecessary training because s/he was part of team that had not performed well on a specific task (6P). If there is no way of knowing which individual had not performed well, some players might work less (3P).It was viewed as important to provide feedback at the individual level, so that the player would know what s/he had done wrong and whatto do to improve (4P).

2.2 Interactions with Other Stakeholders

Different *roles in the organization* should have different levels of access to their game data; but there was no consensusabout what those access levels should be for each role. Participants distinguished between *colleagues and management*. 19 (9P, 10T) participants said that management should have access to their game data, but not colleagues. 6 (3P, 3T) participants had the opposite view, arguing that it was precisely from people who *had power over them* that they would want to protect data from. One factor was whether the potential receiver had a*legitimate purpose* for accessing the data. Other factors included the personal and work *relationship* they had with that individual, how much they *trusted* him/her, and the department s/he belonged to (3P).

In the remainder of this section we will provide more detail regarding participants' perceptions of potential issues that can result from a player's game-supported interactions with management or other players.

2.3 Player-Manager Interaction

Managers would have an interest in players' game data because it provides an easy way of checking their employees' performance and assessing their skills. However, our interviews revealed that, if not handled in an appropriate way, such data use could be perceived as a major threat by employees. Participants were receptive to positive uses of game data that led to constructive criticism on their performance, or new job opportunities, but they were apprehensive about the use of game data for making decisions about promotions or redundancy. There were two perceived risks: (1) unfair assessment, and (2) negative perceptions of game play.

Regarding unfair assessment, one concern was that managers'*data use*would not be transparent. 18 (7P, 11T) participants worried that – if game data that for training purposes was subsequently used for assessment – they might be perceived negatively. While *training*was associated with exploration and trying out new approaches to problems, *assessment*meantemployeeshad to try their best. A player under the impression that the game's purpose was training might not perform optimally.

Another concern was that managers would *over-rely* on the performance assessment data to identify skill levels. Related to the *validity* of the performance assessment (see Section 5.1), participants did not want their data to be taken out of context. A distinction was made between *new recruits* and *current employees* (4T)– game scenarios might be too simple for senior employees. Also, whereas managers have little knowledge about the competencies of new recruits, they should already have knowledge of their current employees.

Negative assumptions can also be made about other game data(see Section 5.1). To overcome this perceived risk, participants wanted management to provide clear guidance in terms of *how much time* they would be expected to play the game, and *when* they should play it. For example, can they play the game anytime during work, or only during set hours? Can the game be played at one's desk, or only in a separate training environment away outside of the office?The possibility of conversations being *monitored* in the lounge or game scenarios was another concern. Monitoring was viewed as an invasion of privacy, and would put participants off networking.

2.4 Player-Player Interaction

Players are interested in interacting with each other because it can add to the fun of the game–socializing with colleagues and developing skills together. Butthere were two perceived risks of interacting with other players: (1) unpleasant interactions; and (2) negative use of information gained during game play.

Firstly, other players might act in an inappropriate manner during game play (e.g. swearing, abusive language). Participants wanted management to provide *clear guidelines* as to what behavior is and is not acceptable within the game environment. If the workplace made it clear that there would be reprimands for misuse of the game, participants believed that this would encourage trustworthy behavior from users.

Real-life consequences for good performance in the game would be further motivation for good behavior.

Secondly, information gained during the game interaction might be used against the player. Participants were worried that if they played against a senior colleague or manager and performed poorly, then *negative assumptions* might be made about their competence in real-life (3P, 8T).Bad performance in game scenarios could also be used by a player's peers to *humiliate*him/her (4P, 10T)–in the form of gossip, ridicule or bullying. Career-oriented colleagues might try to use that information to *gain leverage* on the player – if, for example, they were both competing for the same job or were in conflict (6P, 8T).

The use of pseudonyms was viewed as a way of protecting employees from the repercussions of low performance, by reducing the *linkability* of the data (see Section 5.1). Pseudonyms might prevent real-life biases and prejudices from contaminating in-game interactions and affecting performance. This could improve learning as players might interact in a more neutral way by starting from a "clean slate".

A perceived limitation of pseudonyms, was that it could have a negative impact on *socialization*. Players feeling less accountable for their actions might behave less responsibly.They might disclose more personal information if real identities were not known. Such behavior could have repercussions for their relationships in real-life, if their pseudonym identity was found out. 14 (8P, 6T) participants said that they would be reluctant to interact with other players if they did not know who they were; they would be wary of other players acting in an inappropriate manner, and find it difficult to determine the potential benefits of the interaction.

3 Discussion

The findings identified a number privacy risks that players associate with TARGET – data storage, nature of the data, validity and linkability. With managers, the risks are related to negative career consequences – being viewed as incompetent, or being made redundant.With other players, the risks are related to negative social effects – unpleasant interactions and humiliation.

Players want to keep a certain degree of separation between their real-world job and the game interactions. They did not want data that could show them in a negative light to transfer from the game to the real-world, or vice-versa. However, to achieve this, game playing would become a fairly insulated experience. Not only would this reduce the level of constructive feedback that players can get from their managers or other employees, but it could also work against organizational interests –such as integrating game experiences with social networking or communities of practice. Furthermore, in order to realize the benefits of serious games – where part of the motivation comes from the competitive element – it is important to allow players to compare their performances to each other while assuring that the data collected for that purpose won't be applied outside the learning context.One possible way forward is to allow selective disclosure of data by players and creating a trustworthy environment where they are not afraid to share data.

The actual purpose of the system, and the way the purpose is communicated to users, will have an impact on acceptance. The system described in this study is a learning tool, with the primary focus of developing project management skills. But it could also be used for assessment– this makes gaming appear more risky to users, and undermines the primary purpose – learning.If assessment is used, there should be distinct modes for learning and assessment.

Whether the evaluation of players is human or automatic will also impact acceptance. There is a dilemma –human assessors are expensive, andmay have biases; but they allow players to explainand contextualize their performance. Purely automatic assessment would make it difficult for a player to explain his or her results. One possible way to address this issue is to have automatic assessment, but allow players to correct or erase erroneous data.

In some game situations, there could be a trade-off between trust and privacy. While the use of stable identities associated to avatars contributes to trustworthy behavior(by providing temporal, social and institutional embeddedness) and builds relationships between players [6], it can work against players if management use performance data to make decisions that have a negative impact for players' careers. Moreover, the game experience could be affected if real-life biases and prejudices transferred into the game. The use of pseudonyms can provide stable identities to increase embeddedness without reducing privacy.

A joint framework was created based on our analysis of the interaction between privacy and trust in the context of this system (see Figure 2). *Privacy risks* represent the possibility of the player's privacy being invaded, with consequences varying in severity. Whether these risks are perceived depends on the value of the factors described above (see Section 0)–e.g. high linkability or low validity of data might increase risk perception. If users think that the potential risks of using a system

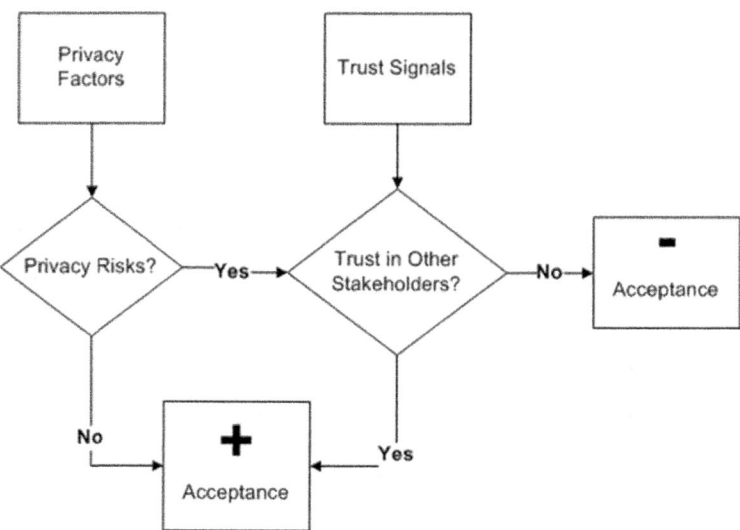

Fig. 2. Trust-privacy interaction

outweigh its benefits, they are likely to reject the technology [4]. But if players trust other stakeholders – colleagues or managers – not to exploit the vulnerabilities the player has identified, then the player will be more willing to engage with the system. Trust – in the context of this system – is assessed by looking at the contextual features identified by [6]. If the purpose of the system is clarified in the start, and there is regulation and sanctions to the organization in case of abuse, this is a trust signal for the player. A code of conduct for the interaction between players, sanctions and stable identities are signals for trusting other players. If players do not even recognize privacy risks in the first place, then there is no need for trust, and they will engage with the system. Previous research [4], [29], [30] found that people were more receptive to monitoring technologies if they trusted the people operating the system.

4   Conclusions and Recommendations

We have identified a number of factors that influence privacy and trust perceptions in TARGET, and propose a framework for how these factors affect the interactions between the player, the system, and other stakeholders. Our findings link the frameworks by Riegelsberger et al. [6] and Adams [4] by clarifying the relationship between trust and privacy –in the context of a TEL system deployed in an organizational context. The contextual properties of Riegelsberger's trust framework were present in our findings: stable identities; accountability and reputation; and institutional code of conductwere mentioned as promoters of a trustworthy environment. Also, the three main factors of Adams' privacy model were present: information receiver; information usage; and information sensitivity. The main take-away point resulting from the trust-privacy interaction is that if a serious-game is perceived by users to have privacy invasive features and is introduced in a low-trust organizational environment the acceptance will be low, while in a high-trust environment the privacy risks will have a smaller impact on acceptance. This phenomenon is not specific to serious-games but the work presented in this paper supports this conclusion in the context of serious-games.

Consistent with workplace privacy literature, our findings identifiedperceived risks associated with monitoring and the resulting employee evaluation[7], [8], [9], [10], [31]. Whereas past literature has focused on the employee-employer relationship, our research also acknowledges the potential risks associated with colleagues seeing data of fellow employees, which can damage reputation or lead to humiliation.

In addition to the factors mentioned in TEL literature –linkabilityand disclosure of data [11], [12], [13]– our research found that nature of the data and its validity also influence privacy perceptions of potential users.Our research also considered the organizational environment in which the technology is deployed and the tensions between theinterests of different stakeholders.

We now present several recommendations for practitioners –game designers and employers / management:

1. Game designers should emphasize the benefits of the system to the organization and give them guidance on how to incorporate the game into the working week. Managers must be on board, as they are the ones who will be implementing the system and deciding which employees should be given which game scenarios;

2. Management should inform employees of the purpose of deploying the system: assessment or learning.
3. Employees should be made aware of any consequences for their careers – negative or positive – resulting from playing the game;
4. Management should inform employees what data is being collected by the system, where the data is going to be stored and the security measures being used to keep it safe;
5. Players should have control over the disclosure of game data to other stakeholders; particularly, performance data, time playedand scenarios played;
6. Players should be provided with channels to challenge or justify their performances and correct or erase incorrect data. The performance assessment process should take into consideration the player's overall personal context;
7. Interactions that take place in the loungeshould not be monitored and/or recorded because there is an expectation of privacy in that area;
8. Developers should include game features that encourage trustworthy behavior – e.g. block lists, rating systems.
9. Managers should develop a code of conduct that is enforced by the workplace to remind players to act in a professional manner;
10. Real names are preferable for socializing in the lounge; in the game scenarios, however, the enforcement of pseudonyms could have a positive effect on the player's performance and learning experience.

The findings from our study were fed back to the TARGET developers and partner organizations planning to deploy it. To our knowledge, scenarios have not been employed before to aid the development of a privacy sensitive system – only in understanding its privacy issues.

In future studies, we plan to interview other stakeholders to obtain their perceptions of privacy and trust: managers in companies deploying TARGET and– once the platform is completely developed– actual players.

References

1. Clark, R.C., Mayer, R.E.: E-learning and the science of instruction: Proven guidelines for consumers and designers of multimedia learning, 2nd edn. Jossey-Bass/Pfeiffer, San Francisco (2007)
2. Van Eck, R.: Digital Game-Based Learning: It's Not Just the Digital Natives Who Are Restless. EDUCAUSE Review 41 (2006)
3. Fletcher, J. D., Tobias, S.: Using Computer Games and Simulations for Instruction: A Research Review. Society for Applied Learning Technology Meeting, New Learning Technologies, SALT, Orlando, FL (2006)
4. Adams, A.: Users' Perceptions of Privacy In Multimedia Communications. PhD. University College London (2001)
5. Iachello, G., Hong, J.: End-user privacy in human-computer interaction. Found. Trends Hum.-Comput. Interact. 1(1), 1–137 (2007)
6. Riegelsberger, J., Sasse, M.A., McCarthy, J.D.: The Mechanics of Trust: A Framework for Research and Design. Int. Journal of Human-Computer Studies 62(3), 381–422 (2005)

7. Fairweather, N.B.: Surveillance in Employment: The Case of Teleworking. Journal of Business Ethics 22, 39–49 (1999)
8. Ariss, S.S.: Computer monitoring: benefits and pitfalls facing management. Information & Management 39(7), 553–558 (2002)
9. Snyder, J.L.: E-Mail Privacy in the Workplace. Journal of Business Communication 47(3), 266–294 (2010)
10. Chen, R., Sanders, G.L.: Electronic Monitoring in Workplace: Synthesis and Theorizing. In: Proceedings of AMCIS (2007)
11. Anwar, M.M., Greer, J., Brooks, C.A.: Privacy enhanced personalization in e-learning. In: Proceedings of the 2006 International Conference on Privacy, Security and Trust: Bridge the Gap Between PST Technologies and Business Services, pp. 1–4. ACM, Markham (2006)
12. Jerman-Blazic, B., Klobucar, T.: Privacy provision in e-learning standardized systems: status and improvements. Computer Standards & Interfaces 27(6), 561–578 (2005)
13. Nejdl, W., Wolpers, M.: European E-Learning: Important Research Issues and Application Scenarios. In: Proceedings of ED-MEDIA 2004, World Conference on Educational Multimedia, Hypermedia & Telecommunications. Lugano, Switzerland: Association for the Advancement of Computing in Education, AACE (2004)
14. Andersen, B., Fradinho, M., Lefrere, P., Niitamo, V.: The Coming Revolution in Competence Development: Using Serious Games to Improve Cross-Cultural Skills. In: Online Communities and Social Computing, pp. 413–422 (2009)
15. Lave, J., Wenger, E.: Situated Learning. In: Legitimate Peripheral Participation. Cambridge University Press, Cambridge (1991)
16. Wenger, E.: Communities of Practice: Learning, Meaning, and Identity. University Press Cambridge, Cambridge (1998)
17. Ackerman, M.S., Mainwaring, S.D.: Privacy Issues and Human-Computer Interaction. In: Security and Usability: Designing Secure Systems That People Can Use, pp. 381–399. O'Reilly, Sebastopol (2005)
18. Hine, C., Eve, J.: Privacy in the Marketplace. The Information Society 14, 253–262 (1998)
19. Culnan, M.J.: How Did They Get My Name?: An Exploratory Investigation of Consumer Attitudes toward Secondary Information Use. MIS Quarterly 17(3), 341–363 (1993)
20. Lederer, S., Hong, I., Dey, K., Landay, A.: Personal privacy through understanding and action: five pitfalls for designers. Personal Ubiquitous Comput. 8(6), 440–454 (2004)
21. Stone, E.F., Stone, D.L.: Privacy in organizations: Theoretical issues, research find- ings, and protection mechanisms. Research in Personnel and Human Resource Management 8, 349–411 (1990)
22. Corritore, C.L., Kracher, B., Wiedenbeck, S.: On-line trust: concepts, evolvingthemes, a model. International Journal of Human Computer Studies 58(6), 737–758 (2003)
23. Rousseau, D.M., Sitkin, S.B., Burt, R.S., Camerer, C.: Not so different after all: A cross-discipline view of trust. Academy of Management Review 23(3), 393–404 (1998)
24. Mayer, R.C., Davis, J.H., Schoorman, F.D.: An Integrative Model of Organizational Trust. Academy of Management Review 20(3), 709–734 (1995)
25. McAllister, D.J.: Affect- and Cognition-based Trust as Foundations for Interpersonal Cooperation in Organizations. Academy of Management Journal 38(1), 24–59 (1995)
26. Bacharach, M., Gambetta, D.: Trust as Type Detection. In: Castelfranchi, C., Tan, Y. (eds.) Trust and Deception in Virtual Societies, pp. 1–26. Kluwer, Dordrecht (2001)
27. Raub, W., Weesie, J.: The Management of Matches: A Research Program on Solidarity in Durable Social Relations. Netherland's Journal of Social Sciences 36, 71–88 (2000)

28. Strauss, A., Corbin, J.: Basics of Qualitative Research: Techniques and Procedures for Developing Grounded Theory. SAGE publications, London (1998)
29. Melenhorst, A., Fisk, A.D., Mynatt, E.D., Rogers, W.A.: Potential Intrusiveness of Aware Home Technology: Perceptions of Older Adults. In: Proceedings Of The Human Factors And Ergonomics Society 48th Annual Meeting, pp. 266–270 (2004)
30. Alder, G.S., Noel, T.W., Ambrose, M.L.: Clarifying the effects of Internet monitoring on job attitudes: The mediating role of employee trust. Information & Management 43(7), 894–903 (2006)
31. George, J.F.: Computer-Based Monitoring: Common Perceptions and Empirical Results. MIS Quarterly 20(4), 459–480 (1996)

Modifying Trust Dynamics through Cooperation and Defection in Evolving Social Networks

Luca Allodi, Luca Chiodi, and Marco Cremonini

University of Milan
Via Bramante 65, 26013 Crema (CR), Italy

Abstract. We present a model of social network that shows a dynamic emergent behavior simulating actors that exchange knowledge based on their preferences, expertise and friendship relations. The network presents a stochastic interaction behavior that tends to create communities, driven by the assortative mixing and triadic closures. Our first research goal is to investigate the features driving the formation of communities and their characteristics under different configurations of the network. In particular we focus on trust which we analyze qualitatively as dependent on the frequency and pattern of interactions. To this aim, we ran simulations of different network configurations and analyzed the resulting statistics. The second research goal is to study the effects of node deception and cooperation on the social network behavior; our primary metric is trust and we evaluated how, under specific conditions, it is possible to manipulate trust in some non trivial ways.

1 Introduction

The properties of networked systems have been studied since long in various scientific fields, like sociology, biology, economics, physics and informatics. Researchers have modeled and analyzed different kinds of networks, focusing on common properties that emerge from their structure and dynamic behavior [17,21,1,11,12]. Social networks, in particular, exhibit peculiar characteristics with respect to non-social networks, the most notable of which are related to degree correlations of adjacent nodes and to clustering [7,13,16]. Degree correlations in non-social networks are typically negatively correlated (this property is also called "disassortativity"), that is, nodes of high degree tend to be connected to others of low degree and *vice versa*. Disassortative networks are extremely common, in biology, epidemiology and in computer networks too, e.g., Internet topology has been observed to match this condition [14]. On the contrary, social networks are typically *assortative*, meaning that the degree correlations of adjacent nodes is positive, i.e., nodes of high degree tend, on average, to be connected with other nodes of high degree. This observation has fostered some relevant studies about the special structure and behavior of social networks, which distinguish them from other non-social networks. The second peculiar characteristic, *clustering*, has been extensively studied and contribute to explain

J.M. McCune et al. (Eds.): TRUST 2011, LNCS 6740, pp. 131–145, 2011.

the assortativity of social networks. Clustering has been defined in term of network transitivity, that is, given an edge between a pair of nodes A and B and another edge between nodes A and C, a network is said to be high transitive if it is likely that there will also be a connection between nodes B and C [13]. For social networks, it has been observed how the clustering coefficient is typically greater, possibly orders of magnitude greater, than in the corresponding random graph [21,12,8]. The clustering effect of social networks has been observed since long by sociologists, which have called it "triadic closure bias", i.e., the tendency that individuals have of meeting a friend of a friend rather than maintaining relations with reciprocally disconnected friends or meeting strangers [5]. The clustering effect is key to the study of social networks and consequently for the work we are presenting in this paper, because it implies that the network's dynamic behavior is nonrandom and that communication of a node with new nodes is mainly driven by information made available by already known "friends" or "acquaintances". This effect forms the basis for the definition of trust we adopted in this work, which depends on a self-declared attribute of nodes representing their expertise in a specific topic and on the frequency of interactions between two nodes.

With this background of interdisciplinary research on social networks, our work has three main goals:

- The definition of a social network model exhibiting both interaction and behavioral dynamics;
- The study of the stochastic behavior and emergent properties of the model through simulation;
- The study of the effects of deception and cooperation on trust in the social network behavior.

More precisely, our social network model includes the selection of partners and the action choice, mimicking the diffusion of knowledge between actors, in the form of questions and answers. Each actor knows a variable number of topics, each one characterized by a degree of knowledge and a degree of interest in knowing more. As a result, some not trivial, recurrent behaviors have been observed and analyzed. Trust manipulations have been modeled as shocks happening during the evolution of the social network: during the simulation some nodes are forced to modify their behaviors and trust related attributes, so as to cooperate when previously they were not interacting or to defect when previously they were collaborating. The presence of shocks that modify the system behavior has been assumed in other studies on social networks [16]. Typically, though, they are random exogenous shocks, which are external events that may happen with a given probability and whose effects are to force a modification either in the environment or in some actors behavior. In our work, instead, shocks are nonrandom and intentional. The goal is to study how intentional actions taken by some nodes when the social network reaches some characteristic configurations could deliberately change the otherwise stochastic evolution of the social network.

2   Related Work

Recent research has dealt with models of social networks more complex than the ones studied in the past, which were mostly concerned with studying the fundamental mechanisms of social network growth. More recent studies have, instead, focused on advanced features like trust, recommendation, cooperation and information exchange, as we did in this work.

Walter *et al* presented the work most closely related to ours, although different in the research goal [20]. They considered a model of trust-based recommendation system on a social network, which assumed the transitivity of trust along a chain of relationships connecting agents, while the trust dynamics is restricted to neighbors only. Similarly, in our work trust is local because a node maintains trust relationships with friends only but, differently to them, we admit only a limited degree of trust transitivity (which is restricted to the best friend-of-friends) and did not model trust chains. However, in many other aspects the two models have similar features, such as the correlation between trust and node similarity, node's preferences heterogeneity, and the dependence on knowledge sparseness.

Hanaki *et al.* provided relevant observations with regard to the emergent cooperative behavior in social networks [5]. In particular, they examined the correlation between the strength of ties and the level of cooperation of the network. With respect to our work, the interaction dynamics driving the evolution of the network are based on different assumptions and rules for the node selection. We have verified their findings in our context and found a confirmation under certain configurations of the simulated social network.

Santos *et al.* analyzed the way cooperation prevails on defection when actors are constrained to interact with few others along the edges of a sparse graph [15]. This analysis is relevant for our work, because it highlights an important outcome of our simulations based on defections, that is, under certain conditions, cooperation prevails and is enhanced even when a critical node defects.

Important for the analysis of mixing patterns and community structures in networks is the work by Newman and Girvan [10]. This research analyzed most of the characteristics that our model of social network presents and that we have tested and discussed in this work, from the assortative mixing to the formation of communities, from the relevance of friend-of-friend relationships to the dynamics of the growing network.

The work by Holme *et al.* studied the effects of attacks on nodes and edges on a complex network [6]. While not strictly related with social networks, it analyzed the way different type of networks react to the removal of nodes or edges. Our work is not explicitly focused on malicious actions carried out to impair the network performance, but rather we followed a more general approach by considering cooperation and defection as events able to alter the stochastic behavior of the network. Nevertheless some observations they made, in particular concerning the relation between node degree and betweenness, provided relevant insights.

3   Model Description

We consider a set of N nodes, $n_1, n_2, ..., n_N$ each one characterized by a *Personal state* PS_{n_i} and a *Friend state* FS_{n_i}.

Personal State. The Personal state PS represents: which topics a node knows, how well it knows them, and how much interested it is in each one of them. In the model these information are described as tuples having the form $(topic, quality, interest)$. We consider a set of topics T representing all distinct topics that the population of nodes knows; each node n_i knows a variable subset of them, $T_i \subseteq T$. Therefore each node n_i has a Personal state having the form $PS_{n_i} = (\bigcup_{j \in T_i} (topic_j, quality_{i,j}, interest_{i,j}))$.

Friend State. The Friend state FS represents connections a node has with other nodes (i.e., "friends"). A connection is a reciprocal relation between two nodes and is established when a question is asked by one and a valid answer is provided by the other (details about the interaction mechanics will be described in the following). When the first interaction between two nodes occurs, both nodes update their Friend states by adding a new pair composed by the friend's identifier n_i and a counter *answers* keeping track of the answers received by another node: friendship is considered reciprocal in our work. On the contrary, trust, which in our model is a function of the number of answers received, is directed, therefore the parameter *answers* is increased only by the receiver node when an interaction takes place. More formally, each node n_i has $N_i \subset N$ friends, and a Friend state having the form $FS_{n_i} = (\bigcup_{j \in N_i} (n_j, answers_{i,j}))$.

3.1   Node Setup

The Personal and the Friend state of nodes are initialized as follows:

Topics. A random set T_i of topics is defined for each node. The maximum number of topics assigned to the nodes can be limited by setting the maximum rate $\lambda_T \in (0, 1]$, so that $|T_i| \leq \lambda_T \cdot |T|$.

Quality and Interest. The quality associated to each topic of a node's Personal state is set to a random value in $[1, 100]$. For the interest, the initial value is equally distributed among all topics, and is calculated as $100/|T_i|$.

Topic 0. A dummy topic called $topic_0$ is always present. It represents the mechanism that allows a node to ask to another node for a topic that does not belong to its Personal state and therefore about which it knows nothing. Forcing its presence in the Personal state means that each node has always a chance of requesting an unknown topic. It acts as a noise term in the dynamics of a node. The *quality* associated to $topic_0$ is always zero, while the *interest* is calculated as for the other standard topics during the network evolution.

Friends. All nodes have no friends at setup, making the evolution of the network fully stochastic. As for the topics, a maximum number of friends per node can be configured by setting a maximum rate $\lambda_N \in (0, 1]$, so that $|N_i| \leq \lambda_N \cdot |N|$.

3.2   Node Choice

Intuitively, in our model, interactions between nodes represent a flow of knowledge, with nodes knowing less about a topic that ask to those knowing more and with the answers that increase the topic's knowledge of the requesters. The node's choice is restricted to nodes already belonging to the requester's Friend state and to "*best friends-of-friends*".

"Best friend-of-friend" node. A "best friend-of-friend" node is a node belonging to a friend's Friend state, showing a selected topic in its Personal state (i.e., "a friend of a friend who knows about the topic that is requested") and having the higher value of the *answer* attribute ("the most reliable friend of a friend"). It is worth noting that the inclusion of "best friends-of-friends" among the nodes that could be chosen fosters network transitivity and the triadic closure bias. More specifically, a node chooses another node as follows:

1. For a given node $n_{i'}$, a topic ($topic_{j*} \in T_{i'}$) is selected among those in the node's personal state $PS_{n_{i'}}$. The selection is made by chance, with the chances being determined by the relative weights, i.e., the value of the interest associated to the topic ($interest_{i',j*}$).
2. The node $n_{i''}$ to interact with is chosen based on the quality associated to the selected topic. Node $n_{i''}$ is the one owning $topic_{j*}$ and having the maximum $quality_{i'',j*}$ among node $n_{i'}$'s friends and "best friends-of-friends".
3. Node $n_{i''}$ must know more than node $n_{i'}$ about $topic_{j*}$, that is $quality_{i'',j*} > quality_{i',j*}$, otherwise the selection of a counterpart for node $n_{i'}$ is made randomly over the entire population T.

3.3   Personal State Update

The update of the Personal state after a successful interaction is the key mechanism of our model. The Personal state is updated by the requestor only, because an assumption of our model is that the behavioral dynamics of the nodes is driven by the new knowledge that a requestor node gains when an interaction is completed. The idea is that the new knowledge depends on the difference between the *quality* associated to the *topic* known by the responding node and the quality associated to the same topic known by the requestor. That difference increases both the requestor's topic quality ("the node learns something about that topic") and its interest in that topic ("the node wants to learn more about it"). In this way, the interaction between nodes based on a topic that both know enhances the similarity of connected nodes, which tends to form clusters as a consequence of the triadic closure bias.

Quality Increase. More formally, we call $n_{i'}$ the requestor node, $n_{i''}$ the respondent node, and $topic_{j*}$ the topic for which the interaction takes place. The *quality gain* obtained by $n_{i'}$ is calculated as $\Delta quality_{j*} = \lceil \gamma(quality_{i'',j*} - quality_{i',j*}) \rceil$, with $\gamma \in (0, 1]$ the *learning coefficient*, which we tune for simulating a system that learns with different ability. For $\gamma = 1$, the requester reaches the same quality level of the respondents in a single interaction, while for $\gamma \to 0$ there is virtually no learning. Therefore, assuming that the interaction happens at time t_k, the updating rule for the quality associated to a topic after a successful interaction is:

$$quality_{i',j*}(t_k) = quality_{i',j*}(t_{k-1}) + \lceil \gamma(quality_{i'',j*}(t_{k-1}) - quality_{i',j*}(t_{k-1})) \rceil \tag{1}$$

Interest Increase and Reduction. The dynamics of the interest of a topic could be either positive (*interest gain*) or negative (*interest reduction*).

The interest associated to the topic that a node requested *increases* when the interaction successfully completes, otherwise it remains unmodified. The new interest depends on the quality calculated in (1). The function to calculate a new value of the interest has the exponential form:

$$interest_{i',j*} = \alpha(1 - e^{-\frac{quality_{i',j*}}{\beta}}) \tag{2}$$

with $\alpha > 1$ and $\beta > 1$ the two parameters we use to control, respectively, the scale and the slope of the function. This function has $\frac{\partial interest}{\partial quality} > 0$ and $\frac{\partial^2 interest}{\partial quality^2} < 0$, meaning that the interest is increasing, but with diminishing marginal gains. This way nodes tend to exhibit preferences among the topics of their Personal state, but the polarization is mitigated and the emergent behavior is not trivial. During simulations we have consistently seen heterogeneous behaviors among nodes, with some strictly polarized, while others not showing strong preferences.

Parameter β is important, because changing the slope of the interest growth modifies the tendency of interests to polarize. Nodes strongly polarized on few topics (i.e., high interest values) tend to acquire knowledge more quickly and so be more likely to act as respondents in following iterations. In general, the result is a tendency to form isolated communities connected with strong ties. With interests less polarized, instead, nodes tend to choose a wider range of topics, then forming larger communities connected with weaker ties.

As a result of a successful interaction and the increase of the chosen topic's interest, a proportional *interest reduction* is applied to all the other topic's interests belonging to the node's Personal state. The reason for decreasing interests associated to topics known by a node except the one chosen, intuitively, is that it seemed to us not reasonable to model actors of a social network as having an always increasing total amount of interest. On the contrary, interests in different topics should balance each other, within certain limits. There is another reason for this choice, more related with the mechanisms driving the nodes behavior. Interest values are bounded by the parameter α of equation (2), therefore, without a compensation mechanism between interests or other solutions like, for example, a progressive degradation of interests as time passes, nodes would always tend to an equilibrium state with interest, for all topics, with value α.

For these reasons, when an interaction completes successfully, all topics known by node $n_{i'}$, except $topic_{j*}$, have their corresponding interest[1] decreased by $\Delta interest_{i',j \neq j*}(t_k, t_{k-1}) = \Delta interest_{i',j*}(t_k, t_{k-1})/(|T_{i'}| - 1)$.

---

[1] The interest reduction applies to $topic_0$ as well, which is included in the total number $|T_i|$ of topics known by node $n_{i'}$.

3.4   Trust

In our model, the meaning of trust is *"an expectation of technically competent role performance"*, as for Barber's subtypes of trust [2,18]. Although relatively general, this definition reflects the dynamics of nodes in our social network. A node interacts with another based on the expectation of increasing its knowledge by establishing a relationship with a more competent counterpart. Trust tends to be local in our model, because a node interacts with unknown ones only when neither a friend nor a best friend-of-friends nodes can answer to its question.

More specifically, in our model, the notion of trust is key to the behavior of a node in two different actions: the choice of the peer node to interact with and the knowledge it gains from the selected peer. In other words, a node trusts another one when it decides to interact with and when subsequently it learns from it. Operationally, the two attributes that control these actions are the *quality* associated to the topic for which an interaction takes place and the *answers* recording the past history of interactions between the two nodes. In particular:

- Attribute *quality* is used for node selection among friends and best friend-of-friends and attribute *answers* for selecting the best friend-of-friends.
- The difference between values of attribute *quality* owned by the respondent and the requester node represents the amount of learning of the latter node.

In general, there should be a time dependency of trust; typically, a repetition of interaction within a time period could reinforce trust, while the absence of interaction could reduce trust [3]. Such dependency could affect the interaction of nodes in our model in two ways, at least: *(i)* Answers could be discounted, that is recent interactions would weight more than older ones in selecting the best friend-of-friends; *(ii)* The quality gain could be discounted too, that is recent friendships (those with low values of *answers*) would result in smaller gains (with respect to the difference of quality between the respondent node and the requester) with respect to older friendships. These time dependencies identify two dynamics associated to trust, both based on the history of interactions, one affecting the selection of the peer and the other controlling the learning.

In this work, we have not yet included and simulated these time dependencies and therefore we give a simplified, operational definition of trust expressed as the number of interactions (i.e. attribute *answers*) between nodes. As for Burt [3], this assumption could be seen as the "baseline hypothesis" for trust setting the benchmark for future improvements and, by analyzing the dynamics of interactions, some interesting, qualitative insights could be derived about the dynamics of trust in the evolution of a relatively complex social network and under certain peculiar conditions as those we have tested.

3.5   Metrics

For the analysis of the network's dynamics, we consider some relevant metrics, which provide useful information about global properties and relations of the emergent behavior. They are the *Clustering Coefficient*, the *Communication Efficiency*, and the *Similarity*, which we describe in the following.

Clustering Coefficient. For the Clustering Coefficient we adopted the definition introduced by Watts and Strogatz: the Clustering Coefficient in social networks measures the cliquishness of a typical friend circle [21].

Communication Efficiency. With Communication Efficiency (CE) we want to measure how often nodes are able to successfully interact, i.e. to receive an answer to a request, with respect to the number of requests they made during a simulation. The number of requests made by the population of nodes equals the number of ticks of the simulation, shown as Γ, because for each tick a node is selected and a request is produced. Formally, we define it as: $CE = \frac{Total\ No.\ of\ Answers}{Total\ No.\ of\ Requests} = \frac{\sum_{i=1}^{N} \sum_{j \in N_i} answers_{i,j}}{\Gamma}$.

The meaning is that if $CE = 0$, then the network stagnates, because there is no communication; if $CE = 1$, then there is perfect communication, because every interaction attempt is successful.

Similarity. With the Similarity index we want to measure the rate of topics known by nodes belonging to a cluster that are associated to a sufficiently high interest value. Intuitively, that set of shared topics for which nodes have high interest represents the characteristic knowledge of that cluster, for which most communications are established. In this sense, nodes are "similar" when share common knowledge and interests. Operationally, the Similarity index is calculated by setting a threshold rate $\theta \in (0, 1]$. For each node n_i, a subset of the Personal state $\widehat{PS_{n_i}}$ is derived by selecting the characteristic topics only, i.e. those whose associated interest is greater than θ multiplied the highest interest of node n_i. Then, considering the union $\bigcup_{n_i \in Cluster} \widehat{PS_{n_i}}$ of all characteristic topics of cluster's nodes, we count the number of different topics $T_{cluster}$ and the number of topics that appear at least twice $T_{cluster}^{duplicated}$. Then the Similarity index is calculated as the rate of these two values: $Similarity = \frac{T_{cluster}^{duplicated}}{T_{cluster}}$.

The meaning is that if $Similarity = 0$, then there are no nodes in the cluster sharing a topic associated to a sufficiently high interest value; if $Similarity = 1$ then all characteristic topics of cluster's nodes are shared among them.

4   Network Simulations

All simulations have been run with the same basic configuration:

- Number of nodes $N = 150$;
- No limitation to the number of friends (out-degree);
- Duration of the simulation/No. of ticks $\Gamma = 150000$.

Number of friends. The first result regards the number of friends, which is a critical attribute because it represents the average outdegree of the network. It

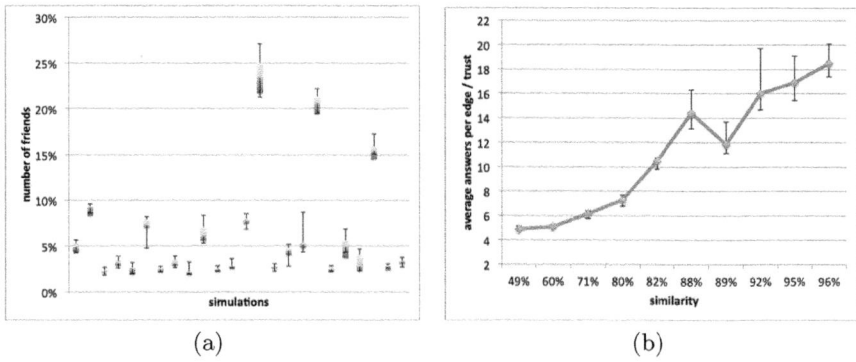

Fig. 1. (*a*) Boxplot of the average rate of friends over the entire population. (*b*) Relation between the Similarity index and the average number of answers per friend of a cluster.

influences the topology and, as already mentioned, in social network it should be limited. In our simulations we have observed that the limited outdegree is an emergent behavior and does not need to be limited by design. Figure 1(a) shows the average rate of friends in 24 simulations in which the relevant model's parameters have been varied. In particular, simulations were run for these settings: $\beta \in \{50,500\}$; $\gamma \in \{0.25,0.05\}$; *# of topics* $\in \{20,50,100\}$; *% of topics per node* $\in \{10,100\}$.

Due to the stochastic nature of our model, each of these simulations has been run 10 times in order to obtain a more significative analysis. In 21 cases the rate was between 2% and 10% of the node population, and in the remaining cases it was higher (i.e. 15%-25%). These outliers were obtained with very particular and unlikely configurations of the model, in which the rate at which the interest per topic increases is very low ($\beta = 500$, $\gamma = 0.05$), and with very few topics per node.

Similarity and trust. Then we tested another important characteristic of social networks, that is the positive correlation between trust and similarity. As described by Golbeck [4] and by Walter *et al.* [20], trust within a community is high if the members are similar among them. This observation matches with results of our simulations, as shown in Figure 1(b), in which a positive correlation between trust and similarity is clearly pictured.

Learning coefficient γ. Another set of results from our simulations are aimed at studying the dynamics of the network when some characteristic parameters are varied, in particular: the learning coefficient γ defined in equation (1), which determines the quality increase after a successful interaction; the average number of topics per node and the total number of topics in the population. In Figure 2, we show how by modifying the learning coefficient γ we obtain very different behaviors. In particular, with respect to CE and the average number of answers per friend, there is a negative correlation. This means that low values of γ let the nodes communicate frequently and successfully. Intuitively, this effect is due to the fact that knowledge flowing in small chunks (i.e. small increments of

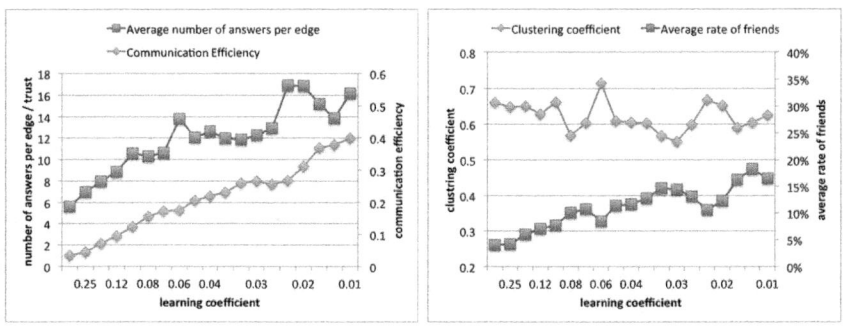

Fig. 2. Influence of the the learning coefficient γ on network dynamics

the quality) enhances the tendency of nodes to have multiple interactions with a counterpart and do not strongly polarize their interests on few topics only. On the contrary, high values of γ make the network stagnate. A similar trend is showed by observing the average number of friends, which is also negatively correlated to the learning coefficient γ. Differently, the clustering coefficient does not exhibit any evident correlation with the learning coefficient.

Number of topics. An important set of results depends on the total number of topics in the network and on the number of topics per node. These are global values that, given a fixed number of nodes, have strong influence on the network dynamics. In Figure 3 we present the variations of the main attributes and metrics when the number of topics in the network changes. With respect to the Clustering coefficient, the CE and the average rate of answers per edge, the dynamics exhibits a positive correlation. This trade-off is visible in the relation between the CE and the total number of topics, which first decreases (Number of topics=100), then presents a increasing trend until a threshold value (Number of topics=350), when the lower probability of finding a counterpart becomes dominant. A different dynamic, instead, is showed by the average number of friends, which is not increasing but remains in the range we have observed before in Figure 1(a). A notable exception in this analysis is represented by the first tested value: Number of topics=50. In that case, the topology of the network presents a giant component that is not present (or less relevant) for the following values. The giant component has the effects showed: a high outdegree represented by the high number of friends; a small Clustering coefficient, because it is extremely dense in the core of the giant component but sparse in the periphery; and a small average number of answers per friend because nodes, on average, own few topics.

5   Node Cooperation and Defection

In this section, we discuss how localized perturbations could change in a relevant way the subsequent growth of the network or provoke a temporary modification and be absorbed later. The analysis presents the initial results: we have not yet

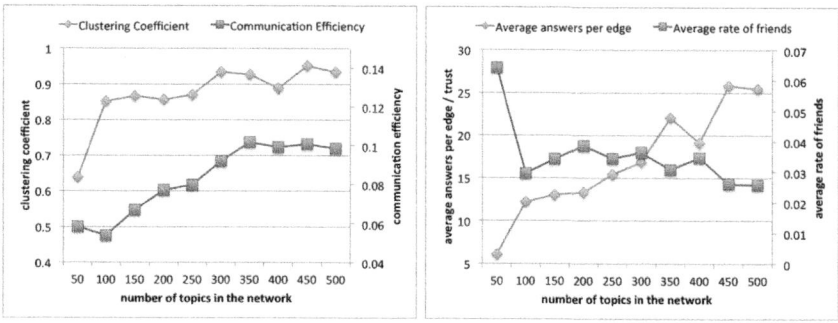

Fig. 3. Network dynamics varying the number of topics in the network

fully explored the many reference cases that could be identified and the case of nodes playing complex strategies with the aim of perturbing the whole evolution of the network. However, the cases discussed are two of the most fundamental.

Case Study 1: The expert defection. The simulation for Case Study 1 was run with $N = 150$, $T = 100$, $\alpha = \beta = 500$, and $\gamma = 0.1$. Figure 4(b) shows the network configuration stopped at 30000 ticks, when the network topology assumed a stable state with most connection confined within established clusters, and the *expert* node of the small cluster we considered.

With the simulation suspended, we manually dropped to zero the value of the *quality* attribute, for all topics owned by the *expert* node, and activated an additional feature that blocks the node activity. This way, we simulated a complete defection of the *expert* node, which autonomously modifies its Personal state and changes its cooperative behavior. Both actions are intended to produce effects on trust other cluster's nodes had with respect to the *expert* one. From this localized perturbation, the goal is to study how an isolated defection of a critical node in a cluster could influence the propagation of trust both inside and outside the same cluster by producing new connections and friendships.

After the modification, the simulation was resumed and Figure 4(c) (*left*) shows the network configuration at about 32000 ticks. What happened was that friends of the *expert* node tried to further communicate with it, because its defection did not modified the Friend state of its peers. However, finding the *expert*'s quality associated to the selected topic dropped to zero, peers turned to the best friend-of-friends, which was one of the cluster's peers in this particular case study of an isolated cluster.

Some of them could have found a sufficient quality in a peer to produce an answer, but for others, no peer was selected. Therefore, these nodes unable to find a selectable peer in their friend circle turned to the random choice of a node to query. When the first peer found by chance a node in the foreign cluster that was selectable, it established a communication and updated its Friend state; this way, the first tie between the two clusters was established. Starting from that first weak tie, with the least possible associated trust, the triadic closure bias represented by the best friend-of-friends mechanism fostered new ties to

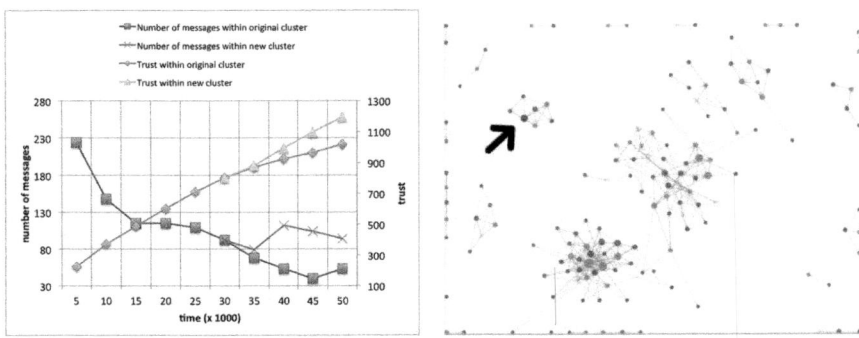

(a) Trends before and after the *expert* (b) The expert node and the network each time period and cluster's trust.
node deception for messages produced in configuration at 30000 ticks.

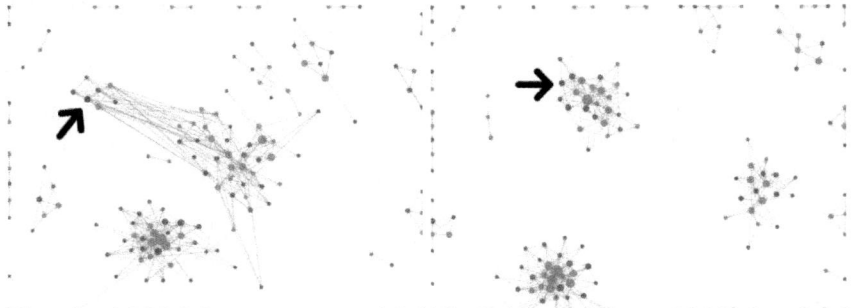

(c) (*left*) The expert node and its original cluster's peers establish new connections with a foreign cluster. (*right*) A new cluster is formed.

Fig. 4. Case study 1

be established, trust increased and a cascade effect merged the two clusters, as showed in Figure 4(c) (*right*), which is a snapshot of the network configuration at about 36000 ticks. Analyzing the dynamics of answers before and after the *expert* node deception, we have observed how the nodes of the original cluster, i.e. the *expert* node and its peers, behaved. Figure 4(a) presents two trends. The first is the trend of the number of messages produced starting from the beginning of the simulation (*time* = 0) and referred to time periods of 5000 ticks each. The trend is decreasing, because at the beginning the network grows fast, so from *time* = 0 to *time* = 5000 the messages exchanged by the nodes are more than 200, then the rate of messages decreases because the cluster tends to stabilize. At *time* = 30000, the number of messages is around 100, when we induce the deception of the *expert* node. From that point on, we see the effects of the formation of the new cluster. Messages exchanged among the nodes of the original cluster drop to about 40, while messages that the same nodes start exchanging with foreign nodes of the new cluster raise to about 120. The second trend is the total number of interactions of the nodes of the cluster, which gives a qualitative measure of the cluster's trust in our model. It's an increasing trend

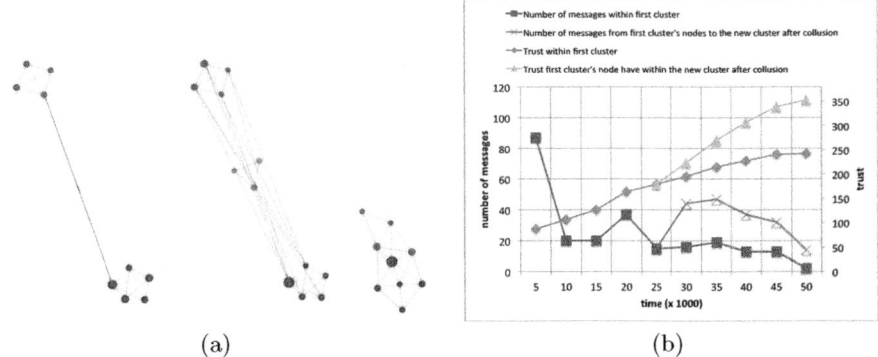

Fig. 5. (a)(*left*) The two nodes of distinct clusters cooperate by forcing a reciprocal friendship, which leads to establish the first tie. (*center*) Friendship propagates to the other cluster's peers (i.e. the triangle of three nodes crossed by the edges is not involved in the interactions). (*right*) A new cluster is formed.(b)Trends before and after the cooperation between the two nodes. Effects on the first cluster.

with diminishing marginal increments. At $time = 30000$ it is visible the effect on trust of the *expert* node deception. Rather than producing a negative effect, the trust referred to the nodes of the original cluster increases. Although the definition of trust we have assumed is simplified, qualitatively the result is not trivial, meaning that under certain conditions, *the deception of a key node of a community could increase the activity of the members and then their global trust towards their peers.*

Case Study 2: Cooperation between nodes. Parameters for the simulation of Case Study 2 were the same of the first case study. This time, the goal was to study the effects of a cooperation between two nodes belonging to distinct clusters. Like in the previous case study, we were particularly interested in analyzing the dynamics of answers produced and trust for the two clusters. To induce the cooperation, we operated as in the previous case. The simulation was suspended at $time = 25000$, then we manually modified the Friend states of the two nodes by adding the identifier of the counterpart. Finally, the simulation was resumed. Figure 5(a) shows the snapshots of the two clusters taken when the cooperation started (*left*), then the cascade effect of the triadic closure that spread friendship to the nodes of the two clusters (*center*), and the formation of the new cluster (*right*). We analyzed the dynamics and the trust associated to the two clusters involved. In Figure 5(b) we present the results for the first cluster (the one on top composed by four nodes in Figure 5(a) (*left*)). Before the cooperation, at $time = 25000$, the dynamics of answers produced in each distinct period and of cluster's trust is similar to the previous case. When the cooperation starts propagating friendships, the effect it produces is remarkable, with an increase in the number of answers of up to 300% (in period from $time = 30000$ to $time = 35000$) and a pronounced increase of the slope of the trust function. The results for the second cluster (the one at the bottom composed by five nodes in Figure 5(a)(*left*)) are not showed, since qualitatively the trend is similar to the first cluster, with a notable difference in scale, which, in proportion, is clearly smaller. Qualitatively, we observed that the cooperation of two nodes, under certain conditions, could trigger a cascade effect that produces the formation of a new cluster. While in this case the increase of the trust was expected, given the intentionality of the cooperation between two foreign nodes, the different scale of that gain exhibited by the two clusters seems not trivial. In particular, the first cluster obtains a greater advantage from the cooperation than the second one in terms of communication and trust. From this we extrapolate the indication that *intentionally merging communities could be not equally convenient for both clusters in terms of trust and communication*, which provides interesting insights for future works.

6   Conclusions

The research on evolving social networks has explored different kinds of emergent behavior, for example introducing noise or discounting the past [16]. Differently, our research is to investigate a form of noise, which, to date, has received little attention: the effects on the stochastic evolution of the network of specific nodes that autonomously change their characteristics or their behavior. Our goal is to explore how localized intentional perturbations in the interaction dynamics could drive a different evolution of large parts of the network. In this work, we have presented our first results as two case studies that, in simple contexts, showed some not trivial effects produced by the deception of a key node of a cluster and the cooperation of two nodes. There are some extensions that should be done. One of the most important is to improve the modeling of trust, explicitly including the time dependency and the relation with the *quality* attribute. Another important future work will be to test our cases of node cooperation and defection and confront our theoretical results with the corresponding rich dynamics of a real-life case. In the literature, there exist many works that have applied models of social networks to real case studies. The exchange of the emails in a community of people, for instance, represents a relevant case study [19], as well as the dynamics showed by individuals joining and leaving groups of interests, which may stem from leisure (e.g. the case of online games) to scientific research or corporate projects [9]. In those works, however, the goal was to provide an interpretation of a real dynamics through a model of social network. To the best of our knowledge, our research goal of simulating a real-life dynamics and then introducing intentional perturbation to analyze different evolutionary paths or as a means to self-organize a network to obtain some global behavior is still unaddresed. Nevertheless, the interaction dynamics in presence of nodes that intentionally change their behavior does appear as a promising and interesting research direction and worthy of further development.

References

1. Albert, R., Barabasi, A.L.: Statistical mechanics of complex networks. Rev. Mod. Phys. 74(1), 47–97 (2002)
2. Barber, B.: The Logic and Limits of Trust. New Rutgers University Press (1983)
3. Burt, R.S.: Bandwidth and echo: Trust, information, and gossip in social networks. In: Casella, A., Rauch, J.E. (eds.) Networks and Markets: Contributions from Economics and Sociology. Russell Sage Foundation, Thousand Oaks (2001)
4. Golbeck, J.: Trust and nuanced profile similarity in online social networks. ACM Trans. Web, 3:12:1–12:33 (September 2009)
5. Hanaki, N., Peterhansl, A., Dodds, P., Watts, D.: Cooperation in evolving social networks. Management Science 53(7), 1036–1050 (2007)
6. Holme, P., Beom, J.K., Chang, N.Y., Seung, K.H.: Attack vulnerability of complex networks. Physical Review E 65(056109) (2002)
7. Jin, E.M., Girvan, M., Newman, M.E.J.: Structure of growing social networks. Physical Review E 64(4), 046132+ (2001)
8. Newman, M.E.J.: The structure of scientific collaboration networks. Proceedings of the National Academy of Sciences of the United States of America 98(2), 404–409 (2001)
9. Newman, M.E.J.: Coauthorship networks and patterns of scientific collaboration. Proceedings of the National Academy of Sciences, 5200–5205 (2004)
10. Newman, M.E.J., Girvan, M.: Mixing patterns and community structure in networks. In: Pastor-Satorras, R., Rubi, M., Diaz-Guilera, A. (eds.) Statistical Mechanics of Complex Networks. Lecture Notes in Physics, vol. 625, pp. 66–87. Springer, Heidelberg (2003)
11. Newman, M., Barabasi, A.L., Watts, D.J.: The Structure and Dynamics of Networks. Princeton University Press, Princeton (2006)
12. Newman, M.E.J.: The structure and function of complex networks. SIAM Review 45(2), 167–256 (2003)
13. Newman, M.E.J., Park, J.: Why social networks are different from other types of networks. Physical Review E 68(3) (2003)
14. Pastor-Satorras, R., Vazquez, A., Vespignani, A.: Dynamical and correlation properties of the internet. Phis. Rev. Lett. 87(258701) (2001)
15. Santos, F.C., Pacheco, J.M., Lenaerts, T.: Cooperation prevails when individuals adjust their social ties. PLoS Comput. Biol. 2(10), e140 (2006)
16. Skyrms, B., Pemantle, R.: A dynamic model of social network formation. Proc. Natl. Acad. Sci. U. S. A. 97(16), 9340–9346 (2000)
17. Strogatz, S.H.: Exploring complex networks. Nature 410, 268–276 (2001)
18. Thomborson, C.: Axiomatic and behavioural trust. In: Acquisti, A., Smith, S.W., Sadeghi, A.-R. (eds.) TRUST 2010. LNCS, vol. 6101, pp. 352–366. Springer, Heidelberg (2010)
19. Tyler, J.R., Wilkinson, D.M., Huberman, B.A.: Email as spectroscopy: automated discovery of community structure within organizations, pp. 81–96. Kluwer, B.V., The Netherlands (2003)
20. Walter, F.E., Battiston, S., Schweitzer, F.: A model of a trust-based recommendation system on a social network. Auton. Agent Multi-Agent Syst. 16(1), 57–74 (2008)
21. Watts, D.J., Strogatz, S.H.: Collective dynamics of 'small-world' networks. Nature 393, 440–442 (1998)

Who Is Concerned about What?
A Study of American, Chinese and Indian Users'
Privacy Concerns on Social Network Sites

(Short Paper)

Yang Wang, Gregory Norcie, and Lorrie Faith Cranor

School of Computer Science,
Carnegie Mellon University, U.S.A.
{wang,ganorcie,lorrie}@cs.cmu.edu

Abstract. We present a study that investigates American, Chinese, and Indian social networking site (SNS) users' privacy attitudes and practices. We conducted an online survey of users of three popular SNSs in these countries. Based on 924 valid responses from the three countries, we found that generally American respondents were the most privacy concerned, followed by the Chinese and Indians. However, the US sample exhibited the lowest level of desire to restrict the visibility of their SNS information to certain people (e.g., co-workers). The Chinese respondents showed significantly higher concerns about identity issues on SNS such as fake names and impersonation.

Keywords: Social Networking Site, Privacy, Trust, Culture, Survey.

1 Introduction

Social networking services (SNSs) have become a global phenomenon. For instance 70% of Facebooks 500 million users are located outside the United States [8]. Other SNS sites tend to dominate various parts of the world, such as CyWorld in Korea, and Orkut in Brazil. Meanwhile, privacy issues in SNS have been hotly discussed in public media, particularly about Facebook in the US media [9]. Despite the steady rise of SNS worldwide, there is still little understanding of SNS privacy in other countries, especially non-Western developing countries.

Several studies have shown that general online privacy concerns [3], SNS usage patterns [12], and even privacy policies of SNS platforms [4] vary across different countries. We hypothesize that cultural differences may affect how SNS users perceive and make privacy-sensitive decisions. While we recognize that culture is fluid, dynamic, and often difficult to define, we chose to take Hofstede's approach [10] in using country as a proxy for culture in our study. This is because users from the same country usually use the same SNS. We conducted a multi-national survey to investigate SNS users' privacy attitudes and practices in three countries: China, India, and the US. To the best of our knowledge, this is the first empirical study that investigates users' attitudes about SNS privacy across countries.

J.M. McCune et al. (Eds.): TRUST 2011, LNCS 6740, pp. 146–153, 2011.

2   Survey

2.1   SNS Sites and Respondents

We chose three SNSs for this study: Facebook, Renren, and Kaixin001. According to Alexa (as of August 3, 2010), Facebook has the highest traffic among SNS sites in both the US and India, while Renren.com and Kaixin001.com (two domestic Chinese SNS sites) are the top two SNS sites in China [2]. Since they were very close in terms of traffic, we decided to include both Chinese sites in our study. The three selected sites share several common features such as profiles, walls, photo sharing, shared links, and games. Also the sites are primarily geared towards personal or leisure use; and they support third-party application development on their platforms.

We recruited Facebook users who reside in the US or India, and Kaixin001 and Renren users who reside in China. We recruited only users who were 18 years or older.

2.2   Survey Design

The survey was designed to gain a better understanding of SNS users' demographics and SNS usage patterns, to elicit their attitudes towards sharing information on the Internet and on SNS, and to investigate their privacy-related experience and behavior on SNS. The survey has 10 questions covering demographic information and SNS usage patterns, 2 multiple-choice questions, 8 open-ended questions, and 69 Likert-scale questions covering privacy-related attitudes and practices with SNS.

2.3   Survey Administration

The survey was developed in an English master version. The master version was then translated to Simplified Chinese. We deployed three versions: an English version for American and Indian Facebook users, and two Simplified Chinese versions for Kaixin001 and Renren users. All three versions were hosted on SurveyGizmo for about two weeks in July 2010. We recruited our participants from crowd sourcing sites. American and Indian participants were recruited from Amazon's Mechanical Turk (MTurk). An accepted valid response received 50 US cents. Since the survey would take about 10-15 minutes to finish, our compensation rate was about $2-3 per hour, which is on a par with the normal hourly pay on MTurk. Similarly, we recruited our Chinese participants from a Chinese crowd sourcing site zhubijie.com (ZBJ) and each accepted valid response received 3 RMB (roughly 50 cents).

We acknowledge that this methodology is subject to self-selection bias and any bias that may reside in the recruiting sites. Therefore, we cannot make claims about whether our sample is a representative sample of the SNS users in the three countries.

2.4   Data Cleaning and Analysis

By July 27, 2010, we received 343, 354, and 355 complete responses from China, India, and the US, respectively. We used a combination of measures to help determine whether our participants from these crowdsourcing sites were taking their tasks seriously. We paid attention to unusually short completion time (two standard deviation from the mean), inconsistent answers (we asked the same underlying question with slightly different wordings), and verbatim repetition or nonsense free-response answers. After manually checking the answers and filtering out suspect participants, we were left with 321 valid responses from the US, 312 from India, and 291 from China. Our Chinese sample consists of 138 Kaixin001 users and 153 Renren users.

We analyzed the data using a series of Analysis of Covariance (ANCOVA) with country as the independent variable. The dependent variables were the answers to the 69 privacy-related Likert scale questions. Age, gender, educational level, computer/IT career experience, the SNS site used, and the frequency of visiting the SNS site were used as covariates. ANCOVA was used because our dependent variables are intervals (Likert scales) and we have both categorical (e.g., country, gender) as well as continuous independent variable or covariates (e.g., age).

3   Survey Results

Overall, participants from the three countries exhibited very different privacy attitudes, concerns, and behaviors on SNS. Since the three country samples also differed significantly in terms of their demographics, we controlled for individual characteristics such as age and gender. On nearly every question, the results differed significantly by the country variable. In general, US users tend to be the most privacy concerned among all, followed by Chinese users. Indian users were the least privacy concerned. Compared with the US and Indian samples, the two Chinese sub-samples (Kaixin001 and Renren users) were more similar than different for most measures. Therefore, we do not report their results separately, but instead report them collectively as the Chinese sample. Since we had a relatively large sample and many measures exhibited statistically significant difference by country, we paid most attention to measures where the results were particularly interesting, results diverted from the general pattern (US > China > India), or measures where country was not the most important predictor of the results. More detailed results of this survey can be found in [13].

3.1   Demographics

Valid answers from 924 respondents were used for the analysis. Table 1 presents the demographic make-up of our sample.

3.2   Privacy Attitudes of Personal Content on SNS

We asked how comfortable participants would be with everyone on the Internet seeing content from their SNS profiles such as their walls and status updates (on a 7-point likert scale). Figure 1 shows the percentages of respondents who had each level of comfort with everyone seeing these types of content for our three country samples. Content types listed from top to bottom in the figure generally followed an increasing order of privacy sensitivity. We can observe that the three country samples largely agreed on the privacy sensitivity ranking of different types of content. For nearly all items, US repondents were the most privacy concerned, followed by the Chinese and the Indian

Table 1. Demographics of our study participants:

		China	India	US
Sample size		291	312	321
Gender ***	Men	56.4%	60.9%	36.4%
	Women	43.6%	39.1%	63.6%
Age ***	Mean	23.5	27.1	31.4
	SD	3.8	6.7	11.0
IT education or career ***	IT	41.6%	65.7%	12.1%
	Non-IT	58.4%	34.3%	87.9%
At least some college education		88.3%	90.7%	86.0%

Note: *, **, *** statistical significance at p<.05, .001, .0001

repondents, and we found statistically significant differences (at least p<.001) among the three countries (US > China > India). Phone number, residence street address, email address, photo, employer were considered as privacy sensitive by more than half of both the US and Chinese respondents. However, only phone number was considered privacy sensitive by more than half of the Indian respondents. The list of privacy sensitive items considered by our US sample is similar to prior research [1].

We tested the inter-item reliability of the 16 content items using Cronbach's alpha [7]. The alpha value indicates to what extent questions measure the same underlying concept (or how they correlate with each other). Usually a scale is considered consistent or reliable if the alpha value is above .7. The alpha value of these 16 items is .94, indicating they are reliable in measuring the sensitivity of various content. We then computed a privacy sensitivity score for each respondent by averaging his or her answers to these 16 questions. The higher the score, the more privacy sensitive this person is with regard to the information she posts on the SNS. As Table 2 shows, the privacy sensitivity scores of the American sample (mean=4.7, sd=1.5) were significantly higher (ANCOVA, p<.0001) than that of the Indian sample (mean=3.3, sd=1.1) and Chinese sample (mean=4.2, sd=1.1). Notably, technical knowledge, gender, age and frequency of visit (in decreasing order of significance) were also statistically significant predictors. Although not universally, users without technical knowledge, female users, older users, and less frequent users are less likely to be comfortable with anyone seeing their data than their counterparts. For instance, we found that older users tend to be more uncomfortable if anyone can see their religious views.

3.3   Privacy Concerns on SNS

The privacy sensitivity dimension models how users control or decide what to post on SNS sites. To assess respondents' privacy concerns about what others can do with their data on SNS sites, we asked 15 questions such as whether the site has too much information about you, whether you are concerned that the site shares your information with third parties, and whether your data on the site is secure. Again, we tested the inter-item reliability of the 15 questions using Cronbach's alpha, and the alpha value

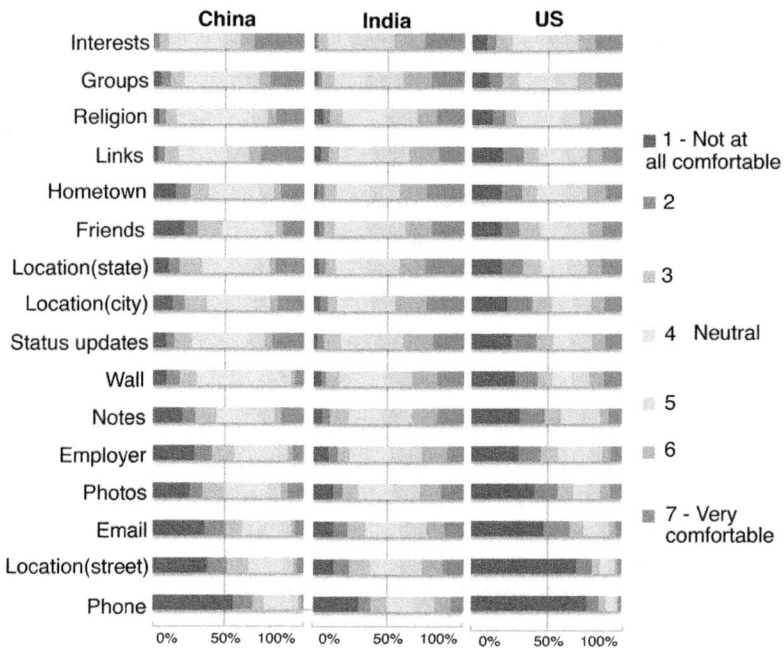

Fig. 1. Privacy Attitudes of Personal Content on the SNS (7-point likert scale)

is .87 indicating they are consistent. We then computed a privacy concern score for each respondent by averaging his or her answers to these 15 questions. The higher the score, the more privacy concerned this person is with regard to SNS. As Table 2 shows, the privacy concern scores of the American sample (mean=5.0, sd=1.0) were significantly higher (ANCOVA, p<.001) than that of the Indian sample (mean=4.6, sd=0.9) and Chinese sample (mean=4.8, sd=0.9). While the same pattern seemed to apply to SNS privacy concerns (US > China > India), the Indian respondents were more worried about what others can do with their data (e.g., other people posting false information about the user) on the SNS than their own postings (i.e., having everyone on the Internet seeing their information) on the SNS.

3.4   Trust in SNS System or Operator

We examined to what extent SNS users trust the SNS system and operator. We asked four questions such as whether the particpant trusts the SNS with their personal information, and whether the participant feels the SNS employs trustworthy staff. We tested the inter-item reliability of the four questions using Cronbach's alpha, and the alpha value is .75 indicating they are consistent. We then computed a lack-of-trust score for each respondent by averaging his or her answers to these four questions. The higher the score, the less trust this person has with regard to the SNS system and operator. As Table 2 shows, American sample had the highest lack-of-trust score (mean=4.5, sd=1.2) in the SNS system and operator, followed by the Chinese sample (mean=3.4, sd=1.0) and

Table 2. Dimensions of SNS Privacy Attitudes (7-point likert scale)

		China	India	US
Privacy sensitivity score ***	Mean	4.2	3.3	4.7
	SD	1.1	1.1	1.5
Privacy concern score ***	Mean	4.8	4.6	5.0
	SD	0.9	0.9	1.0
Lack-of-trust score ***	Mean	3.4	3.2	4.5
	SD	1.0	1.0	1.2
Desire-to-restrict score *	Mean	4.8	4.6	4.2
	SD	1.2	1.2	1.4

Note: *, **, *** statistical significance at p<.05, .001, .0001

Indian sample (mean=3.2, sd=1.0). The differences in this score were strongly statistically significant (p<.0001) among the three country samples (US > China > India).

3.5 Desire to Restrict Information on SNS

To gauge user's desire to control the visibility of their information on SNS, we asked respondents five questions about whether they want to restrict some of their information so that certain people (parents, family, or co-workers) cannot see it or only certain people can see it. We tested the inter-item reliability of the five questions using Cronbach's alpha, and the alpha value is .77 indicating they are consistent. We then computed a desire-to-restrict score for each respondent by averaging his or her answers to these five questions. The higher the score, the more desire this person has to restrict the visibility of her information on the SNS site. Interestingly, we observed a different pattern (China > India > US) than from previous privacy measures. As Table 2 shows, the Chinese sample had the highest desire-to-restrict score (mean=4.8, sd=1.2), followed by the Indian sample (mean=4.6, sd=1.2) and American sample (mean=4.2, sd=1.4). The differences in this score were statistically significant (p<.05) among the three countries.

3.6 Fake Names and Impersonation

One of our research team members uses Kaixin001 and Renren, and has noticed that some friends use fake names. To investigate whether this is common in the Chinese SNS sites, we asked about instances of fake names and concern about impersonation.

Table 3. Fake Names and Impersonation

	China	India	US
Have friends use fake names ***	45.7%	39.3%	18.5%
Concerned about impersonation ***	36.3%	19.4%	28.6%

Note: *, **, *** statistical significance at p<.05, .001, .0001

Table 3 shows that the Chinese sample had the highest percentage of respondents that have friends who use fake names, followed by the Indian and US samples. Similarly, the Chinese sample had the highest percentage of respondents who were concerned about impersonation, followed by that of the US and Indian samples. Both differences were statistically significant (chi-square tests).

4   Discussion

Our American, Chinese, and Indian SNS respondents had significant differences in their privacy-related attitudes and behaviors. We observed a recurring pattern - the US sample was the most privacy concerned, followed by the Chinese and Indian samples. According to Hofstede's measurement on individualism almost three decades ago, the US is more of an individualistic society and thus values more personal privacy, whereas China is more of a collective society and India is somewhere in between [10]. While these individualism scores may help explain why American respondents were more privacy concerned than the Chinese respondents, they alone cannot explain why Indian respondents were the least privacy concerned. We also suspect that the recent intensive media focus on Facebook privacy raised American users' awareness of these issues and their concerns, but we could not measure this effect in the current study.

We observed this pattern (US > China > India) in many privacy aspects such as how comfortable respondents were with everyone on the Internet seeing their different types of information on SNS (privacy sensitivity score), how concerned they are about what other people can do about their SNS data (privacy concern score), and how much they trust the SNS system and operator (lack-of-trust score). However, this pattern was reversed when it comes to users' desires to restrict their information on SNS so that either certain people (friends, family, coworkers) cannot see or only certain people can see (desire-to-restrict score). Somewhat surprisingly, the Chinese sample had the highest level of desire, while the US sample had the lowest. One possible explanation is that American users may be more privacy concerned with regard to the site operator and businesses than with their interpersonal relationships. Another possible explanation is that American users post less sensitive information and therefore have less need for restrictions.Further work is needed to investigate these possibilities.

Prior research on Chinese SNS users suggests that they use SNS as a venue for meeting new people and for entertainment [5,6]. This may explain why they are generally not very privacy concerned. However, our results show that they were particularly concerned about identity issues on SNS such as fake names and impersonation. We suspect this may be due to strict government regulations and monitoring and thus they tend to use anonymous or pseudonymous identities online. This in turn makes establishing online trust challenging. Our results with the Indian SNS users were largely similar to a previous study [11] that shows that Indian users are less privacy concerned than American users.

Our results suggests that different users may have varying priority or emphasis with regard to their privacy because of their cultural background and individual characteristics. Designers of privacy management tools need to take into account these factors. Personalized privacy tools that learn a user's cultural background, characteristics and routine patterns of privacy decisions over time seem to be a promising direction.

References

1. Ackerman, M.S., Cranor, L.F., Reagle, J.: Privacy in e-commerce: examining user scenarios and privacy preferences. In: Proceedings of the 1st ACM Conference on Electronic Commerce, pp. 1–8. ACM, Denver (1999)
2. Alexa: Alexa: Top sites on the web (August 2010), http://www.alexa.com/topsites/
3. Bellman, S., Johnson, E., Kobrin, S., Lohse, G.: International differences in information privacy concerns: A global survey of consumers. The Information Society 20, 313–324 (2004)
4. Bonneau, J., Preibusch, S.: The privacy jungle: On the market for data protection in social networks. In: the 8th Workshop on the Economics of Information Security, WEIS (2009), http://citeseer.ist.psu.edu/viewdoc/summary?doi=10.1.1.153.7796
5. China Internet Network Information Center: Survey report on Chinese SNS users. Tech. rep. (2009), http://www.cnnic.net.cn/uploadfiles/doc/2009/11/11/142713.doc
6. China Internet Network Information Center: Statistical survey report on Internet development in China. Tech. rep. (January 2010), http://www.cnnic.net.cn/uploadfiles/pdf/2010/3/15/142705.pdf
7. Cronbach, L.: Coefficient alpha and the internal structure of tests. Psychometrika 16, 297–334 (1951)
8. Facebook: Facebook statistics (August 2010), http://www.facebook.com/press/info.php?statistics
9. Gates, G.: Facebook Privacy: A Bewildering Tangle of Options. The New York Times (May 2010), http://www.nytimes.com/interactive/2010/05/12/business/facebook-privacy.html
10. Hofstede, G.H.: Culture's consequences: international differences in work-related values. Sage, Thousand Oaks (1980)
11. Kumaraguru, P., Cranor, L.F.: Privacy in india: Attitudes and awareness. In: Danezis, G., Martin, D. (eds.) PET 2005. LNCS, vol. 3856, pp. 243–258. Springer, Heidelberg (2006)
12. Vasalou, A., Joinson, A.N., Courvoisier, D.: Cultural differences, experience with social networks and the nature of "true commitment" in facebook. International Journal of Human-Computer Studies 68(10), 719–728 (2010), http://www.sciencedirect.com/science/article/B6WGR-508K86F-1/2/c92ba5dbed69ed22b02e92f45f88511d
13. Wang, Y., Norcie, G., Cranor, L.F.: Who is Concerned about What? A Multi-National Study of Users' Privacy Concerns on Social Networking Sites. CyLab Technical Report CMU-CyLab-11-006 (2011), http://www.cylab.cmu.edu/files/pdfs/tech_reports/CMUCyLab11006.pdf

Systematic Security Assessment at an Early Processor Design Stage

Ruirui Huang[1], David Grawrock[2], David C. Doughty[2], and G. Edward Suh[1]

[1] Cornell University, Ithaca, NY 14853, USA
{huang,suh}@csl.cornell.edu
[2] Intel, Hillsboro, OR 97124, USA
{david.grawrock,david.c.doughty}@intel.com

Abstract. One critical aspect of a secure hardware design is the ability to measure a design's security. In this paper, we propose a hardware security assessment scheme that provides a systematic way of measuring and categorizing a hardware feature's security concern at an early design stage. The proposed scheme is developed to measure security exposure and risk of a design. The scheme takes a two level questionnaire format and scores a feature based on the answers to the questions. Based on the security score, a feature is then categorized into no, low, medium or high security concern. We discuss several representative questions in detail and evaluate a number of current and future processor features using the scheme. Overall, the assessments from our scheme concur with the security evaluation results by industry security experts, providing an effective security measurement for hardware designs.

1 Introduction

As we place more responsibilities into computing devices, making sure the devices have a secure design becomes critical. Unfortunately, it is quite often the case that the actual engineers who design and implement hardware devices are not necessarily security experts. Thus, the overall security of a hardware design needs to be evaluated by separate security specialists, which adds an extra layer of indirection in terms of designing secure hardware. Evaluating security by separate specialists is also not scalable in practice. The number of security specialists is often limited and can be a bottleneck in the overall design process. In order to make the cooperation between the hardware design engineers and security evaluators as productive and smooth as possible, we need a systematic and scalable way of assessing security of hardware designs.

However, how to measure a hardware design's security impact remains to be an open question [17]. Previous efforts [10, 3, 1, 4, 14] to measure security focus on evaluating security of a fully implemented system or a shipped product, and require full implementation details of a system. In practice, it is also desirable to have an effective security assessment at an early design stage so that a design can be changed if necessary before implementation. One of the main challenges to measure security properties of a hardware design at the early design stage

J.M. McCune et al. (Eds.): TRUST 2011, LNCS 6740, pp. 154–171, 2011.
© Springer-Verlag Berlin Heidelberg 2011

is the limited amount of available information. This is because a design would only be proposed but not yet implemented at this stage. A hardware such as a processor is generally designed by a number of design teams at a fine granularity, therefore full system information is also not available at the early design stage.

We propose a hardware security assessment scheme that provides systematic security assessment at the early design stage. The scheme focuses on evaluating a processor design at a "hardware feature" granularity. A feature level granularity for our assessment scheme does not require its users to have full system level information, which is not available at the early design stage. The scheme targets the hardware designers as the intended users since they have the best knowledge of features at the early design stage, thus allowing a more accurate and consistent security assessment. Having the hardware designers as users also helps offloading the work from a limited number of security experts.

The security assessment scheme combines both quantitative scores and coarse-grain categorization for security measurement. In our scheme, the quantitative measurements are used to categorize designs into various levels of security concern. We believe that coarse categorization of security measurements is sufficient in practice, especially at the early design stage where the main goal is to categorize hardware features into different levels of security concern rather than having accurate numeric security measurements. At Intel, our scheme has received initial success with numerous processor features, and is currently being evaluated for broader deployment for multiple product lines.

By learning from past experiences and intuitions of various security experts at Intel, we have found that security experts in practice typically focus on assessing exposure (i.e. likelihood of having a vulnerability) and risk (i.e. potential impact when being compromised) of a hardware feature. We have developed a list of questions that covers both security exposure and risk. Each question has a preset list of answers to provide a more systematic measurement.

There are many benefits in using the security assessment scheme. The designers and the security experts can identify designs with high security concern thus allowing both parties to focus on features that need more rigorous security evaluation and validation. The scheme would also allow designers to understand the potential security impacts of the decisions made at an architectural level. Such understanding can lead the designers to a more secure design.

In order to evaluate the effectiveness of our scheme, we have used it to assess various hardware features from Intel's current and future processor families. Overall, we found that the scheme is efficient and effective at accurately identifying features with security concern and subsequently placing each feature in an appropriate category. The results from our scheme also concur with real-world security evaluation results from security experts at Intel.

The main contributions of this paper are:

– *Systematic security assessment scheme*: We introduce a scheme that provides a systematic measurement of security concern for hardware features at an early design stage. Features can be categorized into various levels of security concern so that additional security review decisions can be made based on the categorization.

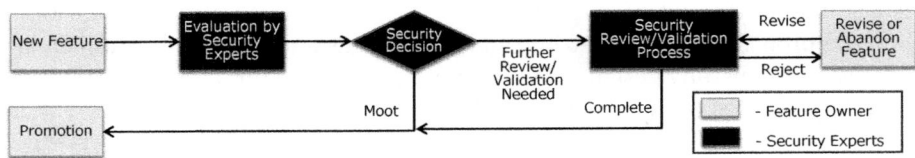

Fig. 1. Today's security review process at the early design stage. A feature owner is responsible for the green (light color) blocks and a security expert is responsible for the blue (dark color) blocks.

- *Demonstate the effectiveness of security categorization*: In general, quantifying security is widely known to be difficult. We demonstrate that quantitative scores can be effectively used when the goal is coarse-grained categorization. Particularly, we have shown that the categorization results from our scheme matches closely with Intel's internal security experts' evaluation decisions.
- *Real-world lessons of security measurement*: We present the underlying principles and approaches of developing the security assessment scheme. We also discuss a number of representative questions that were used for the scheme, which provide insights into security measurements in the industry.

The rest of the paper is organized as follows. In Section 2, we discuss a current processor design process which can benefit from our scheme. In Section 3, we present the overall structure of the assessment scheme. In Section 4, we discuss the representative questions used in the scheme in detail. In Section 5, we evaluate the overall assessment results of a broad range of processor features. Then, we discuss the related work and conclude the paper.

2   Processor Design and Security Review Process

Here, we discuss the current processor design and its security review process based on field experiences from Intel. We further make observations on the limitations of the current process due to the lack of a systematic security assessment in place. Our discussion is focused on an early design stage in the processor development cycle. Within the scope of our paper, the early design stage is defined as a design stage where a feature owner/designer would have finished high level architectural designs but have not yet started implementing the design (i.e. at the RTL level, etc.). In general, the earlier a hardware feature with high security concern can be identified the better.

2.1   Today's Process

Today, the processor design process employs a "divide and conquer" design methodology. Namely a new processor design is divided into various hardware features. A hardware feature can be viewed as a new or improved capability or characteristic that is being added to the new processor. For example, a hardware feature can be an improved branch predictor, a new cache replacement policy, or an additional data access port, etc. Each hardware feature is usually proposed by one or more engineers from a product team. An engineer or architect personnel, often the original proposer, is then identified as the "feature owner".

Once a hardware feature is proposed, the feature owner is responsible for a series of functional reviews and validations. Such reviews include functional review on the high level architectural design, pre and post silicon functional validations, various code reviews, etc.

The design of the hardware feature needs to go through various security reviews and validations as well. Security experts are responsible to review all of the proposed features at their early design stage. In general, one security expert is enough to evaluate each proposed feature, and the security expert is usually from outside of the feature's design team and act as a consultant to the feature owner. As shown in Figure 1, based on the high level architectural design documents and communications with the feature owner, a security expert decides to either require the feature to go through a further review and validation process or identify the feature as a security moot feature. Based on experiences from previous and currently under development Intel processor products, roughly 10% of the proposed features require an additional security review and validation process. The rest of the features are evaluated to be security moot features.

2.2   Limitations of Today's Security Review Process

Unfortunately, there are some limitations in the current security review process due to the lack of a systematic security assessment scheme in place. Today's security review process employs an ad hoc and inconsistent approach among limited number of security experts available. The process is also wasteful when security experts are assigned to evaluate features with no security concern.

In the current security review process, security experts are generally from outside of the design team. As a result, additional engineering time is required for necessary learning and communication between the design team and the security expert. Such engineering time is particularly wasteful for features that are identified to be security moot after the evaluation. Also, the number of security experts are limited and become a bottleneck in the design process.

As security experts are assigned to features in an ad hoc fashion, there is inconsistency in the security evaluation process. Currently, the evaluations are largely based on intuitions and past experiences of individual security experts. Since no two security experts would have the exact same intuition and past experience, their evaluations may not be consistent. Such inconsistency could also negatively impact the quality of communication between the security experts and the feature owners, especially when the same designer works with different security experts who have different security evaluation intuitions and focuses.

Finally, the security review process is currently limited to a passive feedback model. Namely, the feature owner would propose and design a new feature, and passively wait for the security expert to evaluate the new feature. Any feedback from the security expert happens only after the design is finished rather then during the design process. Such passive and delayed feedbacks is counter-productive.

There are times when an entire design needs to go back to the scratch pad due to high security concern. In fact, many features are rejected because there is security concern in the designs that need to be addressed and there is simply not enough time to meet the production schedule.

3   Security Assessment Scheme

In this section, we present our security assessment scheme that is targeted to be used at an early design stage in the processor development cycle. We discuss the goal of the scheme, and the approach that we used in developing the scheme. We also present the overall structure of the scheme and provide reasons behind the design choices that we have made. Finally, we discuss how the proposed security assessment scheme can be incorporated into today's security review process.

3.1   Goals

With the limitations of today's security review process in mind, our security assessment scheme has the following design goals. First, the scheme should provide an effective and consistent security assessment at the early design stage of a feature. The scheme needs to be systematic so that every feature can be evaluated consistently. Second, the scheme should target the feature owners as the intended users. The limited number of security experts can be a bottleneck to the entire security review process. We would like to alleviate the problem by having a distributed process that allow feature owners to be a part of the security review process. Finally, the scheme should provide effective security measurements which would allow categorization of features in terms of security concern. In our scheme, features are quantitatively scored and then categorized into no, low, medium, or high security concern. Such categorization can be used to decide whether additional security reviews are needed.

3.2   Development Approach

We have learned from past experiences of various security experts to develop our scheme. In the current security review process, the security evaluation at an early design stage is largely based on the security expert's experiences and intuitions. Because only a high level architectural design description is available, code review and formal verification of the RTL design are generally not possible. Our approach here is to extract the intuitions and past experiences out of security experts and make them into a more systematic and consistent measurement. After interviewing and discussing with a large number (15+) of security experts at Intel, we were able to identify and develop a list of security assessment questions that the reviewers typically ask.

In a high level, we found the security experts typically try to measure the security exposure and risk of a feature. In this paper, exposure is defined as the likelihood of the feature containing a vulnerability, and risk is defined as the potential impact (i.e. cost) when the feature is compromised. If we can measure how likely a feature contains a vulnerability and the impact of a feature being compromised, the feature's security concern can be thoroughly understood.

We have further fine-tuned the list of questions with the help of security experts and feature owners through piloting and experimenting the questions on a number of real product features. More specifically, for features that were promoted past the early design stage, the feature owners and associated security experts were asked to evaluate those features using our scheme. The evaluation results were then compared with the actual security review decisions to determine the effectiveness of the questions.

Overall, the list of questions reflects the experiences and intuitions that security experts use to evaluate hardware features. We have made the proposed scheme in a questionnaire format, and the list of questions is used for every feature's evaluation thereby providing a more consistent security measurement. The list of questions also allows feature owners to evaluate the security of their design directly, which was not possible before without security expertise.

3.3   Overall Structure

We have further divided the questions in our proposed security assessment scheme into two levels. The first level questions, which are called "Tripwire Questions", are used to filter out security moot features to eliminate wasted time for designer and security expert. The second level questions, which are called "Detailed Questions", are used to provide detailed evaluation scoring for those features with security concern. We have divided the second level questions into four categories, namely Complexity, Risk, Confidentiality, Integrity and Availability (CIA), and Side Channel. As discussed previously, the proposed scheme measures the exposure and risk of a feature. Here, complexity, CIA, and side channel questions are three sub-categories of questions that are used to measure the exposure of a feature. Overall, there are 7 tripwire questions and 36 detailed questions. The representative questions of the two-level scheme and their associated scoring are discussed in the next section.

Tripwire Questions: Based on previous experiences on Intel products, roughly 90% of all hardware features proposed for a processor do not need any additional security reviews. The tripwire questions are developed to filter out features that have no security concern. The tripwire questions have strict "yes" or "no" answers. If any of the tripwire questions are answered "yes", a feature then must go through the detailed questions.

Detailed Questions: The detailed questions cover various security aspects in order to provide a security assessment score of a feature. Each of the detailed question comes with a preset list of answers, and each answer is associated with a security score value. With a few exceptions, most of the detailed questions have an integer score from 0 to 5.

The detailed questions are divided into four categories, namely complexity, risk, CIA, and side channel questions. The complexity questions measure the general exposure of a feature to possible security exploits. The risk questions measure the potential impact when a feature is compromised. The CIA questions focus on

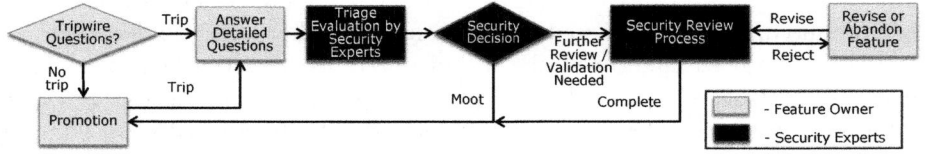

Fig. 2. Security review process with the proposed security assessment scheme

measuring the potential exposure of a feature in confidentiality, integrity, and availability. The side channel questions focus on measuring the potential exposure of a feature to side channel attacks. The CIA and side channel questions measure the exposure just as the complexity questions do. However, the CIA and side channel questions cover specific and known areas of security exploits and vulnerabilities while the complexity questions are much more general in nature. Separating the CIA and side channel questions from the general ones provides insights on where a feature design has the highest security concern.

Upon completion of answering all of the applicable detailed questions, the overall score is used to put features into one of the three categories, namely low, medium, and high security concern. The overall security score is out of 180. Through piloting our scheme among feature owners and security experts, we have found that in practice the highest security score a feature can achieve is around 100. We have mapped low, medium, and high categories to less than 30, 30 to 60, and greater than 60 respectively.

3.4   Security Review Process with the Proposed Scheme

In this section, we present how the proposed security assessment scheme can improve the current security review process. As shown in Figure 2, the security assessment scheme changes the front end of the security evaluation process. A new feature is first evaluated against tripwire questions. If all of the tripwire questions are answered "no", the feature is then categorized as one with no security concern. Otherwise, the feature needs to go through detailed questions. Upon answering the detailed questions, the feature is then triaged into one of the three categories, namely low, medium, and high security concern. The security experts would use the categorizing information to decide whether any additional security review/validation is needed. If the new feature is identified to have no security concern, the feature is ready to move beyond the early design stage and into implementation stages upon finishing a promotion review meeting. In order to prevent false negative cases, the tripwire questions must be reviewed thoroughly by all of the security experts present during the promotion review meeting for those features that answered "no" to all of the tripwire questions. If the feature is found to actually trip any of the tripwire questions, it is then bounced back to answer the detailed questions.

Table 1. Selected questions from the proposed security assessment scheme

Category		Question	Answer (Score)
Tripwire	T1	Does this feature make a security claim, create or modify any security, cryptographic, or fuse functionality, or create or modify a protection mechanism?	Yes/No
	T2	Does this feature use any data that may be kept secret?	Yes/No
	T3	Does the feature store or transfer any architectural state to a shared memory or unsecured storage location?	Yes/No
	T4	Does this feature involve a large number of states/modes?	Yes/No
	T5	Does this feature create or change a component with high security impact?	Yes/No
	T6	Does this feature (including DFx) have any capabilities to bypass the protections or safeguards of any other functionality?	Yes/No
	T7	Can this feature's operation (including DFx) circumvent the normal interface of another feature, thus enabling it to read or modify the input, output, or operation of the other feature?	Yes/No
Complexity	C1	Is there any mode/state (i.e. a fault, exception, power management state change, mode change) that is unexpected or not recommended?	Yes (5)/No (0)
		a) How many modes/states (both expected and unexpected) are not identified clearly in the specification document?	10+ (5); 5+ (3); 1 (1)
	C2	How many components that this feature needs to coordinate with?	6+ (5); 3-4 (3); 1 (1)
	C3	What is the operational granularity of this feature (Choose the highest level if multiple ones exist)?	Per-platform (5); Per-package (4); Per-core (2); Per-thread (1)
Risk	R1	Which processor component would the feature have an impact/change on (choose the component with the highest privilege level)?	Refer to Figure 3 (1-8)
	R2	What method can we use to undo any change done by this feature?	HW Arch.(5); uCode patch (3); Defeature (2) SW/BIOS (1)
CIA	Q1	If an encryption (i.e. AES, etc.) or an integrity (i.e. Hash/MAC, etc.) scheme is used, is an industry proved standard scheme used?	Yes (0) /No (Review needed)
	Q2	Could sensitive data (i.e. keys, decrypted data/code, generated random number, etc.), be left in a cache, register, memory or any other place where a different feature/user/program could find it?	Yes (5)/No (0)
	Q3	Is there a mode or setting that enables or disables the entire feature or a subset of the feature?	Yes (5)/No (0)
Side Channel	S1	Are hardware resources in this feature being shared across multiple threads?	Yes (5)/No (0)
	S2	Can this feature disable any side-channel protections?	Yes (5)/No (0)

4 Representative Questions

Here, our discussion covers all of the tripwire questions and representative detailed questions. We do not discuss all of the detailed questions mainly due to the limited space. However, we believe that the questions covered in this section provide a good overview of the proposed scheme with sufficient insight into the development and the usage of the scheme. It is important to note that since the intended audience of the proposed scheme is not security experts, we intentionally word the questions using as little security specific terms as we can.

4.1   Tripwire Questions

There are 7 tripwire questions in our scheme as shown in Table 1. The tripwire questions are also included in the detailed questions in a similar format. T1 basically asks whether a feature has any security claims or functionality. Specifically, the cryptographic functionality includes encryption, decryption, digital signature, MAC/hash, etc. Fuse functionality includes adding or changing hardware fuses, modifying the way hardware examine/blow the fuses, etc. A feature can also create or modify a protection mechanism, such as the memory range protection mechanism, etc.

T2 and T3 cover CIA concerns. T2 covers data confidentiality. Here, the word "secret" is defined as anything that must not be shared with any other feature or hardware component. T3 covers data integrity. We have limited T3 to architectural state since we do not want to force a large number of non-security features that save data in system memory to go through the detailed questions.

T4 and T5 cover security complexity. In T4, "state" refers to hardware state in a state machine and "mode" refers to execution or privilege mode. In general, the number of states/modes in a feature is a good indicator of how complex a feature is. T5 asks if a feature changes or impacts sensitive components. In this question, components that either have had serious vulnerabilities in the past (i.e. exposure) or would have relatively high impact (i.e. risk) once compromised are considered. For example, system management mode (SMM), virtual management mode (VMM), memory range protection, translation look-aside buffer (TLB), boot flow and reset component, and any debugging features (DFx) are all considered sensitive components.

T6 and T7 cover security risk. In T6, protections and safeguards of other functionality refer to existing protection schemes such as segmentation protection, memory range protection, etc. For example, DFx features such as setting an encryption key to a default value, etc. are covered by this question. In T7, we are targeting features that can bypass the normal interfaces to other features and affect the operations of others. Note that this question is different from T6 because T6 focuses on bypassing specific protection mechanisms where as T7 focuses on bypassing normal interfaces from non-protection features. The phrase "normal interface" refers to a interface that is a part of a feature's normal operation, such as taking input values from parenting components. The normal interface of another feature may be circumvented under specific conditions. A good example is a feature that changes a control register's value on a cold boot sequence, which bypasses the normal interface that changes the register value.

There are certain redundancies that exist in the 7 tripwire questions above. For example, a feature that makes security claims (T1) would normally also either create or change a sensitive component with high security impact (T5). A DFx feature would likely answer "yes" to both T6 and T7 in many cases. Such redundancies are included by design. The goal of the tripwire questions is to filter out features with no security concern. However, such filtering could potentially result in false negative cases. The redundancies in tripwire questions help reduce the false negative rate. A user who answered incorrectly to one question would have another chance to answer correctly to another question with redundant coverage. There is also a review process to help address the false negative concern as discussed in Section 3.4.

4.2   Detailed Questions

There are 36 detailed questions in our scheme, which are separated into four categories: complexity, risk, CIA, and side channel questions. Here, we discuss several detailed questions that are representative to each of the four categories.

Complexity Questions: The complexity questions focus on the general exposure of a feature to potential security exploits and vulnerabilities. The more complex a feature is, the more areas would be exposed to potential security attacks or bugs for that feature. The total complexity score is out of 48.

C1 asks whether there is any unexpected mode or state in the feature's design, which could be a security vulnerability. The second part of C1 focuses on whether all the modes and states are defined clearly in the specification. Clear identification of all modes and states is critical for a correct implementation and a thorough security validation of the feature. In C2, the number of coordinations is an indicator of a feature's complexity. C3 is used to determine the operation scope's complexity level. For example, a feature that operates on a per-thread basis is generally less complex than a feature that needs to be implemented in multiple packages (i.e. per-platform).

Risk Questions: The security risk questions focus on the potential impact of a compromised feature. We design the risk questions by assuming a feature is exploitable at first, then try to evaluate the potential damage of such an exploit. The total risk score is out of 52.

In R1, we have arranged the major components in a processor in a stack diagram as shown in Figure 3. The order of the stack diagram is arranged according to the privilege level of the component. The higher privilege level a feature has, the higher risk there is if the feature is compromised. In R2, we evaluate the potential risk by how difficult it is to reverse any effect of a feature. The difficulty level is evaluated based on the potential efforts needed to deploy such a reverse change in a timely manner.

CIA Questions: The total CIA score is out of 55. Q1 is a question that guides the designers to always use industry standard schemes that have been proven to be secure in real world practice. In fact, if a designer would like to use a scheme that is developed in-house without the proper industry certification, the designer should go through a series of rigorous security reviews in order to justify such a design choice. Q2 implies that the protected data must not be left behind in common storage areas where potential adversaries could access it. In other words, proper clean-up is a must in a feature. Q3 focuses on the availability of the feature. If there exists a mode or setting that could either unlock some premium functionality of the feature or disable some of the feature's functionality, the exposure of such a feature to potential attacks would increase because the attackers could try to compromise the availability of the feature.

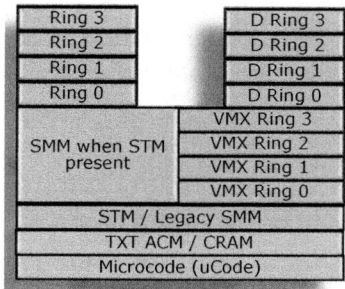

Fig. 3. Stack diagram for major components in a processor design. The diagram is arranged by the privilege level, from low to high in a top down order.

A hardware fuse or e-fuse that either unlock or restrict a feature's functionalities is a good example for this question.

Side Channel Questions: There are many well studied side channel attacks that can be used to compromise the security of a computer system [9, 20]. Due to space constraints, we only discuss two side channel questions from our scheme that focus on the design choices. Our scheme also includes additional questions that cover well-known side channel attacks such as timing, power, temperature, and fault injection differential analysis. The total side channel score is 25.

S1 asks if hardware resources in a feature are being shared across multiple threads. If so, it is possible for an offending thread (i.e. controlled by an adversary) to affect the legitimate threads' operations and/or extract sensitive information through the shared resources. For example, an offending thread can obtain confidential information from other legitimate threads through a shared cache. It is possible for a feature to have side-channel protections but also have controls to disable such protections for validation, debugging, or performance purposes. S2 asks if the side-channel protection may be by-passed.

5   Case Studies

In this section, we evaluate the effectiveness of the proposed scheme through a range of processor features with various levels of security concern. We have included two sets of feature samples. One set is based on the current Intel Nehalem processor family, and the other set is based on a next generation Intel processor family that is scheduled to be released in 2013. Overall, the security assessment scheme has shown to be an effective tool for both current and future processor products.

5.1   Nehalem

The five features from the Nehalem processor family [6, 7, 8] are Execution Disable (XD) bit, page protection, segment protection, SMM, and TXT. Overall, the security experts at Intel agreed with our assessment results. As shown in

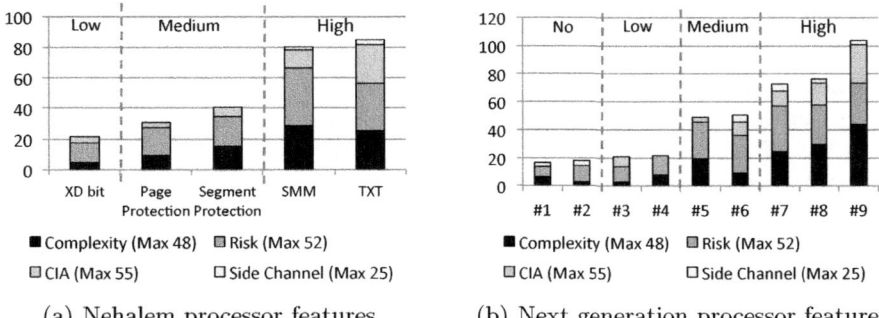

(a) Nehalem processor features   (b) Next generation processor features

Fig. 4. Security assessment scores for processor features

Table 2. Intel's SMM and TXT security assessment scores (scores include additional questions that are not discussed in this paper)

Questions	SMM		TXT	
	Answer	Score	Answer	Score
Tripwire	T1 and T3-7 - Yes		T1-5 and T7 - Yes	
Complexity	C1 - Yes (5); C1.a - 3; C2 - 3; C3 - Per Package (4)	29	C1 - No (0); C1.a - 0; C2 - 5; C3 - Per Platform (5)	26
Risk	R1 - SMM (3); R2 - uCode/Patch (3)	38	R1 - TXT (6); R2 - uCode/Patch (3)	37
CIA	Q1 - N/A (0); Q2 - No (0); Q3 - No (0)	12	Q1 - N/A (0); Q2 - No (0); Q3 - Yes (5)	25
Side Channel	S1 - No (0); S2 - No (0)	2	S1 - No (0); S2 - No (0)	3
Score Sum		81 - High		91 - High

Figure 4(a), the XD bit scores the lowest among the five features, and it is categorized as having low security concern. The XD bit is a technology that marks a certain region of the system memory as non-executable, therefore refusing any execution requests for code residing in the non-executable memory region. Overall, the XD bit feature scores low in complexity and CIA questions because it is not very complex to implement and only requires integrity of the XD bits. The XD bit feature scores slightly higher in risk questions because once compromised it can be used to enable execution of malicious codes. The page protection and segment protection features have medium level scores. Overall, these two protection features are somewhat more complex compared to the XD bit. For both page and segment protection features, they have specific modes where the page or segment protection can be bypassed, which result in a higher risk score than the XD bit. The segment protection has higher complexity and CIA scores than page protection because there are a larger number of privilege modes used in the segment protection feature, and each privilege mode requires a data integrity protection. It is also possible to use the segment and page protection features to prevent proper memory accesses, thus affecting the availability of the system.

The Intel's SMM feature is an operating mode that is executed under a high privilege mode for firmware or debugger software routines (normally specified by motherboard manufacturers) while all other normal system executions are suspended [8]. The SMM feature's privilege mode is sometimes described as "ring -2" since it provides an even higher privilege than the hypervisors (VT) (i.e. "ring -1") [19]., Specifically, the processor executes high privileged software routines, which are used as System Management Interrupt (SMI) handlers. The SMM routines are stored in a specially protected system memory region called SMRAM. The SMRAM is configured in such a way that no access from outside the SMM is possible, even from a hypervisor or OS kernel.

Table 2 shows security assessment result for SMM. SMM has tripped almost all of the tripwire questions except T2 since it does not involve any data that must be kept secret. SMM has a high complexity score due to undefined states and a number of components to coordinate with. For example, the response of a processor when using SMIs to recover from shutdown states is not well defined [8]. The SMM feature also has an above average number of components to coordinate with, including the Virtual Machine Monitor (VMM), various motherboard hardware or chipset components that generates SMIs, and memory components for SMRAM usage, etc. SMM operates on a per-package span as each processor in a multi-processor setup needs its own SMRAM space.

The SMM feature also scores high for risk due to its high privilege level. Once an adversary compromises the SMM, even the OS kernel or hypervisor code cannot interrupt the SMM operations. Recently two groups of researchers [19, 2] independently found exploits (which were subsequently fixed by Intel) to the SMM feature through SMRAM cache poisoning, and were able to cause serious consequences such as SMM rootkits, hypervisor compromises, etc.

The SMM feature has low CIA and side channel scores. The CIA concern mainly rises from the fact that the SMRAM requires data integrity protection. The SMM only operates in a single privilege mode, and it does not have an option that would disable the feature or limit the feature to a subset of its functionalities. The SMM feature has almost no side channel concern. The only side channel concern is that it might be feasible to use either time or power analysis to deduce some implementation details of the SMM feature.

The Intel's Trusted Execution Technology (TXT), formerly known as the LaGrande technology, provides a trusted way of loading and executing system software such as OS kernel or VMM [5, 6]. The purpose of the TXT is to allow a potentially compromised system to securely load a clean OS kernel or VMM while preventing further infection in the system. It provides launch time protection to ensure that the system starts with a clean slate. AMD also has its own version of the TXT, namely the AMD Presidio technology [16].

As shown in Table 2, the TXT feature has tripped almost all of the tripwire questions except for T6 as it does not have the capability to bypass any protection mechanisms. The TXT feature has a large number of states/modes, namely 5 locality modes, Authenticated Code Module (ACM) mode, BIOS/ACM call modes, etc. The TXT also has a large number of components to coordinate with, including Trusted Platform Module (TPM), chipset, BIOS, CMOS, VMM, etc. Overall the TXT has a comparable complexity score when compared with the SMM feature, though the two features scored differently on particular questions.

Table 3. Next generation processor features' assessment results compared with real world security expert's decisions

Features	Assessment	Expert's Decision	Match
#1	No trip - moot	Moot	Yes
#2	No trip - moot	Moot	Yes
#3	Low	Only test needed	Yes
#4	Low	Only test needed	Yes
#5	Medium	Part of additional reviews	Yes
#6	Medium	Part of additional reviews	Yes
#7	High	Part of additional reviews	**Yes***
#8	High	Complete additional reviews	Yes
#9	High	Complete additional reviews	Yes

The TXT feature has a relatively high risk score. The TXT feature has a higher privilege level than the SMM feature as shown in Figure 3. However, we did not identify any DFx capability that would allow the TXT feature to bypass security or protection of any other component. Recently, an attack to the TXT mode has been published which uses infected SMM handler to compromise the just-securely-loaded code at the supposedly secure boot process [18]. This particular attack shows that a feature with high security concern (i.e. SMM) may affect other features (i.e. TXT) once compromised.

Unlike SMM, the TXT feature has a relatively high CIA score. The TXT feature uses a secret signing key for the ACM signing certificate. TXT also has hardware fuses that allow the feature to operate in either debug or production mode. The TXT feature has a very low side channel score. The only side channel concern is that it might be feasible in theory to deduce some implementation details and the secret key of the feature.

5.2   Next Generation Processor

In order to evaluate future generation processor features, we used a next generation Intel processor product that is scheduled to be released in 2013. As the future processor product was still under development at the time we proposed the assessment scheme, we were able to obtain the security review decisions from Intel for various features. We have picked nine features that cover a broad range of security review decisions in order to evaluate our scheme thoroughly. Due to corporate trade secret concern, these features can only be numerically numbered instead of named in detail. Feature 3 to 9 have tripped at least one tripwire question, and they were subsequently scored using the detailed questions. Feature 1 and 2 did not trip any of the tripwire questions, however, we still scored these two features using the detailed questions. The results confirm that they have little to no security concern. As shown in Figure 4(b), Feature 3 and 4 are of low security concern, Feature 5 and 6 are of medium security concern, Feature 7, 8 and 9 are of high security concern. Additionally, after security reviews, Feature 9 was rejected largely because the new capability of Feature 9 was deemed to be not good enough to justify the potential security cost.

Table 3 compares our scheme's assessment results with real world security review decisions at Intel. As discussed in Section 2.1, currently security experts are responsible for reviewing new features at their early design stage. The security experts then decide whether an additional testing or review process is needed. Namely, a feature may be security moot, only need additional security validation tests, need to go through a part of additional review processes, or need to go through a complete review processes (4 stages of reviews). The four decision types match well with the four levels of security concern in our scheme. As shown in the table, all nine features' assessment results match with the expert's decisions, showing that the proposed scheme provides an effective security assessment. Note, Feature 7 was only required to go through a part of the additional reviews by a security expert while it scored high in our scheme and should have required complete reviews. However, Feature 7 is a feature that is built on top of a previous generation feature's architecture and it is thought to be well understood and thoroughly tested previously. This is why the expert's decision for Feature 7 was to skip the architectural part of the additional review processes. The security experts at Intel agree with the high level of security concern that Feature 7 has, and would have required the complete review processes had the feature not built on top of a thoroughly tested and validated architecture.

5.3   Strengths and Limitations

The security assessment scheme has a number of strengths. First, the scheme provides systematic security assessment at the hardware feature granularity, which can be easily incorporated into the current hardware design and security review process. Second, the scheme focuses on measuring security at the early design stage, which allows identifying security concern as early as possible. Third, the scheme effectively filters out security moot features to prevent wasting resources. Finally, the scheme targets the feature owners as users. Such distributed user base can alleviate the bottleneck of having limited number of security experts.

The proposed scheme has a couple of limitations. First, the scheme is focused on and mainly useful at the early processor design stage. The scheme is in no way intended to replace the necessary pre and post silicon security validation and review processes. However, we believe that the proposed scheme can identify features with high security concern, thus allowing better resource allocation and management for the additional security validation and review processes. Second, the scheme's detailed scoring should only be used as a categorizing indicator. Specifically, if two features scored to be in the same category, the actual scores should not be used for direct comparisons between features.

6   Related Work

This section summarizes previous work on security metric and measurement schemes for computer systems. There exists a large body of work on security metric and measurements in various domains. Due to the space limit, we discuss the most closely related work that either provides general coverage or has similarities in the approach.

In general, our scheme differs from prior work in three key aspects. First, our work focuses on measuring security at an early design stage while the previous techniques [10, 3, 1, 4] take measurements on finished products. Second, our work measures security at a finer grain of hardware features while the previous approaches [11, 3, 1, 14], focus on measuring the entire system as a whole. Third, our work targets the hardware designers, not the security specialists, to be the users. The intended users of our scheme is different from all of the previous proposals that we have come across.

General Framework: Lie and Satyanarayanan have proposed a general framework for quantifying the strength of security systems by utilizing third-party security certifications [10]. Compared to their work, our work focuses specifically on the hardware design space. Our work also focuses on security assessment at the early design stage rather than on finished products. Sibert et. al. have presented an analysis of the early 80x86 processor families and identified architectural properties that may have unexpected security implications [15]. Their work studies a particular architecture while our scheme assesses security concern for general processor features.

Security Measurement: Manadhata et al. proposed a formal model for evaluating a system's attack surface [11], which is similar to our approach of measuring security exposure. However, their work focuses on providing practical software security metrics while ours focuses on the hardware design space. Our scheme also provides additional security coverage on the overall risk of the system. The Common Vulnerability Scoring System (CVSS) is an industry standard process for assessing the potential impact and severity of vulnerabilities [4]. The CVSS approach of using both quantitative and qualitative metrics is similar to our work. However, unlike our work which focuses on security assessment at the early design stage, the CVSS is designed to assess known security vulnerabilities on shipping products. The CVSS is also designed for software and network vulnerabilities, not hardware.

Economic Scale Measurement: There are attempts at measuring security using economic units, such as dollars [12, 13] and using economic models [14]. In particular, Stuart proposed to measure the overall security risk as the likelihood of security breach and the cost of security breach, which is similar to our approach [14]. However, our work measures security in terms of severity of security concern instead of economic units. It is also very difficult to predict the economic impact of a feature's security concern at the early design stage. In general, Stuart's studies focus on the software attack domain, and presented general framework rather than concrete measurement scheme.

7   Conclusion

This paper proposes a hardware security assessment scheme that provides a systematic way of measuring and categorizing security concern of hardware features. The proposed scheme focuses on security measurements at the early design stage by utilizing experiences of the security experts and design knowledge of the feature owners. The assessment scheme employs a two level questionnaire format that scores and categorizes security measurements. By targeting the feature owners as the intended users, our proposed scheme alleviates the potential bottleneck of having limited number of security experts , thus making the overall security review process more scalable. The case studies show that the real world security experts' decisions concur with the assessment of our proposed scheme.

Acknowledgment

We thank anonymous reviewers, Kevin Gotze, and other coworkers from Intel for their feedback. This work was performed as part of an Intel internship with the Security Center of Excellence. This work was partially supported by the Air Force Office of Scientific Research under Grant FA9550-09-1-0131 and an equipment donation from Intel Corporation.

References

[1] Common Criterial Portal. Common criteria for information technology security evaluation part 1: introduction and general model (July 2009)

[2] Duflot, L., Grumelard, O., Levillain, O., Morin, B.: Getting into the SMRAM: SMM reloaded. In: Proceedings of the 10th CanSecWest Conference (2009)

[3] Ferraiolo, K.: The systems security engineering capability maturity model (SSE-CMM) (June 2003), http://www.sse-cmm.org/model/

[4] Forum of Incident Response and Security Teams (FIRST). CVSS, http://www.first.org/cvss/

[5] Grawrock, D.: The Intel safer computing initiative: building blocks for trusted computing (computer system design) (2006)

[6] Intel Corp. Intel® trusted execution technology software development guide (2009)

[7] Intel Corp. Intel® 64 and IA-32 architectures software developer manual (#253668) (2010)

[8] Intel Corp. Intel® 64 and IA-32 architectures software developer manual (#253669) (2010)

[9] Kelsey, J., Schneier, B., Wagner, D., Hall, C.: Side channel cryptanalysis of product ciphers. Journal of Computer Security 8(2,3), 141–158 (2000)

[10] Lie, D., Satyanarayanan, M.: Quantifying the strength of security systems. In: Proceedings of the 2nd USENIX Workshop on Hot Topics in Security (2007)

[11] Manadhata, P.K., Kaynar, D.K., Wing, J.M.: A formal model for a system's attack surface (2007)

[12] Schechter, S.E.: How to buy better testing: using competition to get the most security and robustness for your dollar. In: Infrastructure Security Conference (2002)

[13] Schechter, S.E.: Quantitatively differentiating system security. In: The First Workshop on Economics and Information Security (2002)

[14] Schechter, S.E.: Toward econometric models of the security risk from remote attack. IEEE Security and Privacy 3, 40–44 (2005)

[15] Sibert, O., Porras, P.A., Lindell, R.: An analysis of the Intel 80x86 security architecture and implementations. IEEE Transactions on Software Engineering 22, 283–293 (1996)
[16] Strongin, G.: Trusted computer using AMD "Pacifica" and "Presidio" secure virtual machine technology (2005)
[17] Jansen, W.: Directions in security metrics research (April 2009)
[18] Wojtczuk, R., Rutkowska, J.: Attacking Intel® trusted execution technology (2008), Invisible Things Lab
[19] Wojtczuk, R., Rutkowska, J.: Attacking SMM memory via Intel® CPU cache poisoning (2009), Invisible Things Lab
[20] Zhou, Y., Feng, D.: Side-channel attacks: ten years after its publication and the mpacts on cryptographic module security testing. Cryptology ePrint Archive, Report 2005/388 (2005)

CPU Support for Secure Executables

Peter Williams[1] and Rick Boivie[2]

[1] Stony Brook University
petertw@cs.stonybrook.edu
[2] IBM Research
rhboivie@us.ibm.com

Abstract. Vulnerabilities in complex software are a major threat to the security of today's computer systems, with the alarming prevalence of malware and rootkits making it difficult to guarantee security in a networked environment. Due to the widespread application of information technology to all aspects of society, these vulnerabilities threaten virtually all aspects of modern life.

To protect software and data against these threats, we describe simple extensions to the Power Architecture for running Secure Executables. By using a combination of cryptographic techniques and context labeling in the CPU, these Secure Executables are protected on disk, in memory, and through all stages of execution against malicious or compromised software, and other hardware. Moreover, we show that this can be done efficiently, without significant performance penalty. Secure Executables can run simultaneously with unprotected executables; existing applications can be transformed directly into Secure Executables without changes to the source code.

1 Introduction

The Internet is a powerful tool that has transformed the world. But as this tool becomes increasingly integrated into society, the real-world implications of software vulnerabilities become severe. Almost every week, we hear of incidents in which systems are compromised and sensitive information is stolen in an Internet-based attack, with victims suffering significant financial harm. A selection of recent startling examples includes [2,3,8,12].

An entire security industry has been built around protecting this information, with a variety of approaches to prevent these kinds of attacks. The techniques range from network devices limiting access to target machines, to analysis tools reducing the number of vulnerabilities in software, to malware scanners attempting to identify malware before information is compromised. But as the defenses increase in sophistication, the attackers follow suit, and the situation worsens.

While we do not believe a single solution can solve the entire problem, part of the comprehensive approach required is to focus on protecting the sensitive information itself. This protection should come in the form of a simple, robust barrier against potential attackers. Moreover, we believe that to be broadly applicable to today's software industry, such a solution needs to work transparently

J.M. McCune et al. (Eds.): TRUST 2011, LNCS 6740, pp. 172–187, 2011.

with existing software, given the prevalence of legacy software and the expense of developing new software.

Given the evident difficulty in creating bug-free operating systems that reliably protect software, hardware support should be employed to minimize the trusted code base. In particular, to achieve a meaningful protection boundary around the sensitive information, the Operating System must be outside the trusted base. On the other hand, we believe a small set of architecture extensions is acceptable if they realize guarantees of software protection while avoiding significant performance penalty. Existing work (described below) has looked into this approach; we will identify and attempt to solve the set of issues that are still preventing these approaches from revolutionizing the security industry.

In summary, a dire need exists for systems and methods that can help prevent the theft of information from a computer system in an Internet-based attack. In particular, this includes the need to protect sensitive data and software on a computer system from other software, including software that an attacker may be able to introduce into a targeted computer system. We take a fresh look at hardware-based isolation techniques in this paper, providing a developer-transparent solution for achieving strong protection of sensitive software.

Overview

We provide a trusted execution environment for individual applications, protecting an application from other software, including privileged software such as the operating system and malware that manages to obtain root privileges. The set of hardware changes described below provides this strong isolation in a way that is nearly transparent. In particular, we can run Secure Executables side-by-side with unprotected software, with only a small performance impact to the Secure Executable, and no performance impact while running unprotected software. The software source code requires no changes to build a Secure Executable; we simply link with a new startup library and system call handlers.

We describe the required hardware changes, showing they are limited in scope, and convenient for integration into mainstream CPUs. We begin with a summary to provide the intuition behind how sensitive applications are protected at all stages—on disk, in memory, in cache lines, and in registers. A "Secure Executable" is an executable file, encrypted (aside from a cleartext loader) so that only a specific target Secure-Executable-enabled CPU can access it. The cleartext loader attached sets up the memory space and enters secure mode, enabling the CPU to decrypt the rest of the executable. Confidentiality and integrity of the encrypted portion of the secure executable in memory are protected by keys that are not available to software. Cache lines are stored in cleartext, but associated with a Secure Executable ID that limits access of a line to the Secure Executable that loaded the line. Thus, reads and writes to locations in the CPU cache incur no new overhead (aside from verifying the cache label). Finally, on interrupts, the contents of the registers are protected from the Operating System by moving them to protected memory.

Related Work

There is a long history of using hardware features to isolate software from a compromised Operating System. Figure 1 summarizes related work.

	SCPU (IBM 4764)	Flicker	SP Secret-Protecting Architecture	XOM	Aegis	Overshadow	Secure Executables
Requirements							
Works without Hardware Changes	N	✓	N	N	N	✓	N
No OS in Trusted Code Base	Card OS in TCB	✓	✓	✓	✓	Host OS in TCB	✓
Works without OS Support	N	✓	N	N	N	✓	N
Transparent to Developers	N	N	N	N	N	✓	✓
Protection							
Code privacy (transparently)	✓	N	N	N	✓	N	✓
Resilient to Memory Replay Attacks	✓	✓	N	N	✓	✓	✓
Protection from Physical Attacks	✓	N	✓	✓	✓	N	✓
Features							
Multiple Simultaneous Instances	✓	N	N	✓	✓	✓	✓
Multi-threading / Multi-core support	✓	N	N	N	N	✓	✓
Support Shared Memory Regions	✓	N	N	N	N	N	✓
Virtualization Support	N	N	N	N	N	✓	✓

Fig. 1. Comparison with existing work

XOM. XOM [10] is a set of architecture changes that extends the notion of program isolation and separate memory spaces to provide separation from the OS as well. They introduce "secure load" and "secure store" instructions, which tell the CPU to perform integrity verification on the values loaded and stored. For this reason, the *application transparency* is limited: developers must tailor a particular application to this architecture.

Aegis. Aegis [13] fixes an attack in XOM by providing protection against replay attacks. This requires introducing an integrity tree to protect memory. The authors also offer optimizations specific to hash trees in this environment that greatly reduce the resulting performance overhead. These optimizations include batching multiple operations together for verification, and delaying the verification until the time where the values affect external state. Again, the approach is not transparent to developers. This is because the set of protected loads and stores must be specified by the developer.

Secret-Protecting Architecture. Secret-Protecting Architecture [9] provides a mechanism to run code in a tamper-protected environment. The authors design in [5] a mechanism extending a root of trust to supporting devices. However, this technique does not have the transparency of other techniques. For example, there can be only one Secret-Protected application installed and running at a given point in time. The ability of protected applications to make use of system calls is likewise limited.

Cell. The Cell Broadband Engine Architecture [7] provides a POWER-based secure execution environment isolating applications from the rest of the system. Each chip contains multiple "Synergistic Processing Elements" running simultaneously, each with a fixed amount of on-chip protected memory for use by the application. Due to the strict memory limitations and lack of support of interrupts, applications must be designed specifically for this architecture.

TPMs. The Trusted Platform Module, widely deployed on existing consumer machines, can be used to provide guarantees that the operating system has not been tampered with. It does not exclude the operating system from the trusted code base, however. Instead, the TPM signs the current memory and register state, and it is up to other parties to decide if this signed value constitutes a valid operating system state. There are other ways this hardware can be employed to protect software. Flicker, in particular, makes use of the TPM's late launch feature to protect software from a compromised operating system.

Flicker. Flicker [11] provides a hardware-based protection model that functions on existing, commonly deployed hardware (using mechanisms available in the TPM). As with other solutions, this incurs only minimal performance overhead. It provides a protected execution environment without requiring new hardware. The trade-off is that software has to be redesigned to run within this environment. The protected environment is created by locking down the CPU using TPM late-load capabilities, so that the protected software is guaranteed to be the only software running at this point. System calls and multi-threading in particular do not work for this reason. Moreover, hardware interrupts are disabled, so the OS is suspended while the protected software is running. Thus, software targeted for Flicker must be written to spend only short durations inside the protected environment. The advantage of Flicker is the reduced hardware requirements: it is supported by existing TPM-capable processors.

Overshadow. Overshadow [4] provides guarantees of integrity and privacy protection similar to AEGIS, but implemented in a virtual machine monitor instead of in hardware. This approach has several other advantages as well; making the implementation transparent to software developers—for example, software shims are added to protected processes to handle system calls seamlessly. This means, however, that there is no protection provided against a malicious host OS or against physical attacks. Nonetheless, the authors provide an updated approach using techniques that we can adapt to our hardware-based-protection model. One example is the use of system call wrappers, which transparently manage system calls from a secured application, otherwise unmodified.

New contributions

We detail several novel contributions in this paper, addressing components missing from much of the related work. Moreover, we believe these features need to be provided by any secured architecture that will achieve widespread adoption. See Figure 1 for a comparison with existing work.

- minimal size of trusted computing base (TCB). In the Secure Executables architecture, the TCB consists of just the secured application and the hardware.

Relying on the security of any other components makes it much more difficult to obtain reasonable security guarantees.

- minimal changes to hardware and software, including minimal changes to OS. Instead of defining a new hardware architecture altogether, we provide a small set of changes that can be applied to existing architectures, without affecting other software running on the system.
- transparency to applications. Developers do not need to design programs any differently in order to make Secure Executables. An existing program can quickly and easily be rebuilt into a Secure Executable (not even requiring recompilation from source code).
- transparency with respect to build tools. There are no language changes required to take advantage of Secure Executables, and we are compatible with existing compilers and link editors. We do introduce a new linking step that links system call wrapper code in with an existing application, and a final step to encrypt the application and enable Secure Mode.
- protecting confidentiality and integrity of sensitive information. We encrypt the Secure Executable binary, so sensitive information is protected even in the file system before execution. The architecture establishes a root of trust guaranteeing the integrity of a Secure Executable, ensuring its sensitive information is readable only by the target CPU, and only during execution of that Secure Executable.
- shared memory. We provide a mechanism allowing seamless sharing of memory regions between Secure Executables. Furthermore, as long as values stay in the cache, this sharing avoids expensive cryptographic operations.
- multi-threading. We support multiple threads (again, seamlessly) for a single Secure Executable. This is a critical feature if the architecture is to be used by modern day applications.
- virtual machine support. Our architecture is compatible with both type-1 "bare metal" and type-2 "hosted" virtual machines monitors, and can be used to establish a root of trust all the way up to the physical CPU.

2   Model

We employ standard cryptographic constructions, using hashes, symmetric encryption, and public-key encryption. We do not specify the particular constructions to use at this point; however, candidates include AES and RSA with 1024 bit keys. Our model assumes the adversaries are unable to defeat the employed cryptographic encryption primitives.

We consider an attacker who has full control of the software running on the system, aside from the Secure Executable. We do not protect the Secure Executable from itself: vulnerabilities in the Secure Executable will remain exploitable. However we significantly reduce the size of the trusted code base—instead of trusting the entire OS, developers merely have to trust the code that they have control over. We believe a Secure Executable can be much smaller, and consequently more easily verifiable, than an entire operating system.

The attacker may also have physical access to the system, and we protect against attacks to this memory, disk, buses, and devices. However, we assume that it is beyond the abilities of the attacker to successfully penetrate the CPU boundary. That is, the gates and registers inside the CPU are not considered subject to tampering or leak. We believe this is a reasonable assumption for most scenarios and adversaries. However, in situations where it is not, there are existing physical protection techniques, such as those employed on the IBM 4764 [1] that can be used to increase the cost of physical attacks against the CPU. These techniques typically result in increased CPU cost and/or decreased performance due to limited heat transfer capacity.

It is beyond the scope of this paper to consider side channel attacks. We note, for example, that the addresses of the accessed memory locations are revealed to the Operating System, which is necessary to allow it to service page faults. There are existing techniques which can hide the access patterns such as Oblivious RAM [6]. However, existing access-pattern-hiding techniques are slow, and our goal here is to provide an inexpensive, broadly applicable solution.

The mechanism we provide consists of a set of changes to a CPU architecture (in this paper we address the POWER architecture specifically, but the techniques can be adapted to most modern CPU architectures). A few new instructions enable an application to enter Secure Mode, under which decryption and execution of the protected code is possible, while outside tampering or snooping is simultaneously prevented.

3 Approach

In our design, sensitive information is cryptographically protected whenever it is outside the CPU chip. It is available in cleartext inside the chip but only by the software that "owns" the sensitive information. This information is decrypted as it moves from external memory into the chip and encrypted as it moves from the chip into external memory. Integrity values are also checked when information moves into the chip and updated when information moves back out.

A public/private key pair is installed in the CPU at manufacture time, with the public portion signed by the factory. This establishes the root of trust, allowing Secure Executable binaries to be encrypted so that only a target CPU can access the embedded code and data.

Due to space constraints, many of the technical details are omitted. This should be considered an abbreviated version of the full paper.

New Hardware Logic

Memory encryption. Encryption/decryption is performed between cache and main memory. That is, cache lines corresponding to the protected region are decrypted as they are brought into the cache, and encrypted as they are evicted.

Integrity tree verification/update. A cache line is verified using the integrity tree when data is brought into the cache. This may require performing additional fetches to make sure enough of the tree is present to perform this verification. When lines are evicted from the cache, the corresponding parts of the integrity tree are updated.

Cache line label. On loads from a protected region, the ID of the Secure Executable associated with that cache line is compared to the current Secure Executable ID. If there is a mismatch, the access is treated as a cache miss. On stores, the cache line Secure Executable ID is updated to match the currently running Secure Executable.

Register protection. The CPU ensures that application registers are not visible, or undetectably modified while the Secure Executable is suspended. Two obvious approaches are to encrypt the registers before giving control to the OS interrupt handler, or to store the registers on chip while the Secure Executable is suspended. Both approaches have drawbacks. Encryption takes time, and is potentially vulnerable to replay attacks unless a hash is stored on chip; storing a copy of the registers on chip uses valuable space and severely limits the number of simultaneous suspended Secure Executables that can be supported.

We choose instead to store the register set in protected memory corresponding to each Secure Executable. The registers end up protected in the cache (and ultimately by the Secure Executable root hash value, if these values get evicted from the cache). Only the Secure Executable root hash value, plus the meta-data required to use this hash value, are stored on-chip. This eliminates the performance penalty of the crypto operations, while avoiding the need for the bulk of the expensive on-chip dedicated storage.

Software Changes

At run time, when the Secure Executable is to be launched, the OS executes the Secure Executable binary, as a normal ELF (Executable and Linkable Format) file. The ELF file consists of a protected region and a cleartext region. The confidentiality of the protected region is protected using a symmetric encryption algorithm; the integrity of the protected region is protected by an integrity tree in the cleartext region. The cleartext region also includes loader code and an ESM instruction. The loader code copies the initial integrity tree into memory. It then issues the ESM instruction, which enables decryption of protected regions, and jumps to the entry point (identified in the ESM operand). Integrity and confidentiality protection of memory accesses is also enabled at this point.

4   Integrity Tree

The integrity tree is the construction protecting information in external memory. It consists of a set of encrypted hash values of memory locations, with these hashes themselves protected by parent hashes. The branching factor of this tree is the number of hashes that fit in a cache line. For 128-byte cache lines, and 128-bit hash values, for example, each node of the tree protects 8 nodes below.

The initial value of the integrity root is signed, then loaded with the Enter Secure Mode (ESM) instruction, which is used to start the Secure Executable. This root ensures that the CPU will only use an intact version of the code; the CPU provides the guarantee that only integrity-verified words are visible to the application in regions of the protected address space.

Ancestors of a dirty cache line are pinned in the cache to avoid updating the tree all the way to the top on each write. Evicting a node from the cache requires updating its parent, which might require evicting another node. Pinning all ancestors in the cache ensures that the parent of any dirty node is always present. Thus, every dirty line in the cache has all the ancestors pinned in with a reference counter.

This requires considering the case in which a parent cannot be brought in, because all the lines where it could go are already pinned. In this case, the tree computation is performed immediately, as far up the tree as necessary (until a line whose ancestors all fit is found). The procedure to perform a store from a Secure Executable context is as follows. First, bring ancestors in, starting at top (if they're not already there). Lock each parent when one of its children comes in, by incrementing its reference counter. If a child cannot be brought in, compute the path up to this point, reading and writing all the children directly to/from memory. Then the parent is updated to reflect the new value, and marked as dirty in the cache.

This approach has the property that the CPU can evict a cache line with a zero reference count at any time, with one hash operation, requiring no additional loads or stores. Lines representing instructions or data can always be evicted, as can nodes of the integrity tree whose protected lines are no longer in the cache. Flushing the cache requires starting with all the lines with a zero reference count, evicting these, and repeating as many times as necessary (which can be up to the tree height). On each iteration one level of the integrity tree is evicted.

Due to cache locking conflicts, we can't guarantee that a write requires only updating the parent; it could require up to $\lg(n)$ loads/stores. But this stalls only the current running Secure Executable, and it can be paused and resumed later. This case should be rare, with high enough cache associativity.

This integrity tree needs to be correct over the whole protected address space, even those parts of the address space that have not yet been allocated. Moreover, the parts of the tree covering these unallocated regions should not require initialization, since the protected memory region is potentially much larger than the portion ever accessed. We introduce the notion of a "sparse" integrity tree: one that correctly protects the whole memory region, but is zero everywhere that it protects unallocated memory. In this sparse integrity tree, these zeroes protecting unallocated memory are implicit. Memory is not allocated for these integrity values until they are accessed, at which point they are initialized (by the OS) to zero. Implementing this sparse integrity tree requires a property of the integrity hash function: the hash of an empty region must be zero.

A second requirement for this property of integrity tree correctness over uninitialized data is that the *cleartext* corresponding to uninitialized memory is also zero. To achieve this, we consider all memory locations protected by a hash value of zero to be zero themselves.

Overcommit

Since we target a 64-bit architecture, the size of protected memory regions can be large. For this reason, we need a simple way to dynamically grow the integrity tree. The Linux overcommit mechanism allows us to reserve room in the address space corresponding to a tree protecting large memory regions, while delaying the physical memory allocation until each page is accessed. In overcommit mode, available in recent Linux kernels, application memory allocations always succeed, even if there is not enough physical memory or swap space to support the entire allocation. Thus, pages are not mapped to physical memory until they are accessed.

Since the hash tree is maintained implicitly by the CPU, instead of the software, any solution must involve the CPU as little as possible; the CPU in particular should not be involved in memory management, and should not issue memory allocation requests. Overcommit provides a convenient solution: the Secure Executable loader can allocate a portion of the virtual address space large enough to contain a hash tree over the rest of the address space. With overcommit enabled, this can be much larger than the available physical memory plus swap space. When the CPU attempts to access an address in this range, a page fault is generated, since this address has not yet been assigned to physical memory. Since the virtual address has been reserved by the secure executable process (with the mmap syscall), the OS handles this fault transparently by assigning a physical page to this location. This provides exactly the behavior we desire, with no changes to the OS (aside from enabling overcommit).

Drawbacks to using overcommit. When overcommit is enabled, processes run the risk of running out of physical memory at any time—and being targeted by the kernel's Out-of-memory killer. A potential workaround described here prevents this from occurring. That is, when the machine is out of memory, only new malloc's will fail, rather than leaving the potential for any process at all to be killed. Our workaround is to implement a new mode of memory allocation for integrity trees, with OS support. Processes are still allowed to allocate the large integrity tree, but the OS is now aware that the total space used by this integrity tree will stay within a fraction of the rest of the process's used memory. Thus, instead of over-committing to the entire allocation, the OS is only committing to the normally allocated memory plus a constant fraction.

5   System Calls

Since we prevent any other process from reading values in our Secure Executable's registers or address space, we naturally need a new mechanism to support passing data in system calls. Nevertheless, we support system calls transparently to both the secure executable and the operating system. We describe two mechanisms here to support system calls transparently. To make both approaches transparent to the operating system, the CPU leaves the general purpose registers alone on a system call interrupt, so that these registers can still be used to pass parameters to the OS system call handler. Recall that on all other interrupts, the registers are hidden before control is giving to the interrupt handler. For this reason, both approaches move the application registers to protected memory before invoking the system call.

Approach: System call wrappers

We use this approach in our proof of concept implementation. The application is linked with a custom version of libc, that replaces system calls with wrappers. These wrappers copy the system call parameters from the protected memory region to the unprotected, OS-readable region.

On invocation, each wrapper performs the appropriate copy, depending on the parameter types. Note that in order to correctly copy the system call parameters, the wrappers have to be aware of each system-call. The wrapper then copies the general purpose registers to the stack, and zeros them, aside from the ones being used as parameters in the system call. Each wrapper then invokes the appropriate system call, and copies the result back into the protected region. Finally, it restores the registers from the stack.

Naturally we must consider the privacy and integrity of the parameters while they are in unprotected memory. We necessarily give the OS the ability to read the parameters and choose arbitrary return values. There is nothing we can do to ensure the OS is correctly handling these system calls; thus we leave it to the Secure Executable application code to make the appropriate decisions about the information it passes to the system call. For example, we do not prevent the secure executable from printing out sensitive information if that is what it is programmed to do.

New approach: New system call instruction

This approach allows for full application transparency, by avoiding the requirement for a modified version of libc (and thus, now supporting executables that are not even linked with libc). We still add a layer to the system call invocation, but rather than adding this layer as a set of wrappers sitting before the system call invocation, we add the layer after the invocation.

To do this we employ two system call instructions, illustrated in Figure 2. The first, existing POWER sc (System Call) instruction behaves as today (passing control to the OS system call handler), unless we are in Secure Mode. If we are in Secure Mode, this instruction instead returns control to a previously registered location within the application. A new POWER instruction, sesc (Secure Executable System Call) gives control to the OS system call handler, *regardless of whether we are in Secure Mode.*

Now, the Secure Executable registers a system call wrapper to the CPU, so that when sc is issued, the system call wrapper gets control. The system call wrapper performs the equivalent memory copies / register cleanup as the previous approach, then invokes the new system call instruction sesc to give control to the Operating System.

The advantage of the second approach is that we do not have to modify libc (thus eliminating part of the complexity of turning a conventional binary into a Secure Executable). The system call wrapper still needs to be located somewhere in the application address space, and registered by the Secure Executable loader as a parameter to the ESM operand. This address space modification is more application-agnostic than modifying the libc being linked with. For example,

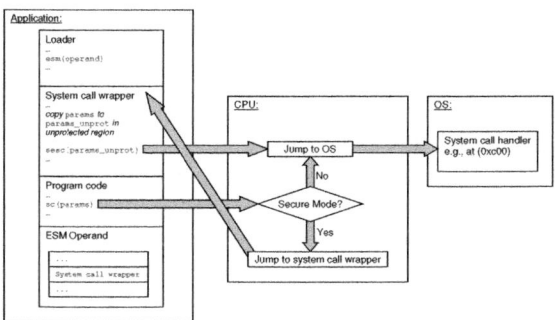

Fig. 2. sesc (Secure Executable System call) handling

this transformation can be performed directly on a statically compiled binary. Moreover, this modification to the address space and entry point are already performed anyway in other steps as part of the Secure Executable build process.

The majority of system calls are handled in the straightforward manner described above—the only change required is moving the parameters to and return values from the unprotected region to enable communication with the OS. However, system calls that modify the application memory or registers require special handling. Due to space constraints, these cases are not detailed here.

6   Other Considerations

Shared Memory and Multi-threading

We exclude the details in this version of the paper, but we provide hardware support for these semantics to enable full application transparency. In brief, shared memory requires a many-to-many mapping of Secure Executables to protected memory regions. Multi-threading requires tracking multiple thread restore points (instead of just one). The interesting challenge in both cases is providing an efficient, transparent hardware implementation.

Shared Libraries and Dynamic Linking

Our current implementation builds a statically linked binary, since it is unsafe to allow the host machine to load untrusted code into our memory space at runtime. Static linking allows all code to be verified at compile time, on the build machine. There are downsides to statically linked executables. First, they require extra storage space, since common libraries used by multiple applications cannot be consolidated. Second, the libraries cannot be updated once the secure executable has been deployed—in particular, bugs in these libraries cannot be fixed without rebuilding the secure executable.

Another potential solution is to use signed libraries, that are loaded and verified at runtime. A Secure Executable library loader, in protected memory, verifies the integrity of the library as it loads it in protected memory, and provides dynamic linking. That is, a module can be linked at build time with the Secure Executable that will load external libraries of unresolved symbols. These external libraries will only be accepted if there is a certificate chain, with the root signed by a party trusted by the developer, attesting to the trustworthiness of the library code. This mechanism provides integrity guarantees of the shared library, while allowing the library to be patched or replaced in the future. However, it is not as simple as merely dynamically linking to the host libc, since the matching certificate must be generated and transmitted to the host.

Virtual Machines

We consider support for two types of virtual machines monitors (VMMs) here. By "hardware" virtual machine monitors we refer to VMMs that do not require software assistance in executing non-privileged instructions (e.g., "Type 1", or "bare-metal" VMMs). Non-privileged instructions in the guest are run directly on hardware. By "software" virtual machine monitors, we refer to VMMs that have a software hypervisor to assist in executing instructions (e.g., "Type 2", or most "hosted" VMMs).

While our Secure Executable model can be applied to both virtualization scenarios, we consider hardware virtual machines to be the more relevant case for the high-performance server market. In a hardware virtual machine model, a Domain 0 OS typically controls switching between domains. The guest OS remains outside the TCB; Secure Executables operate as in the non-virtualized case. The Domain 0 OS is also outside the TCB, since hypervisor interrupts are treated as regular interrupts with respect to hiding the register contents. We simply require the Domain 0 OS to save and restore the SEIDSR register along with the rest of the registers during domain switching. The trick is that the Domain 0 interrupt handler needs to invoke the RestoreContext instruction to return to a Secure Executable, if one was running (the SE-ID register is set) during the hypervisor interrupt.

Software virtual machines require a different approach, since the software hypervisor needs access to the sensitive application in order to process its code and data. Thus, we wrap the VMM inside the secure executable boundary. This is illustrated in Figure 3. Note that any VMM that emulates instructions in software must be included in the trusted code base, since the instructions and data are considered sensitive.

In neither scenario is the host OS part of the TCB. The interesting question is whether, in software VMMs, the guest OS must be part of the TCB. We show it does not. Building the software VMM as a Secure Executable offers an environment where the VMM is protected from the host OS. With support from the software VMM, constructing virtual Secure Executables protects guest applications from both the host OS *and* the guest OS. Compare this to Overshadow, which protects guest applications in software VMMs from the guest OS but not the host OS. The TCB in our case is just the guest application plus the VMM.

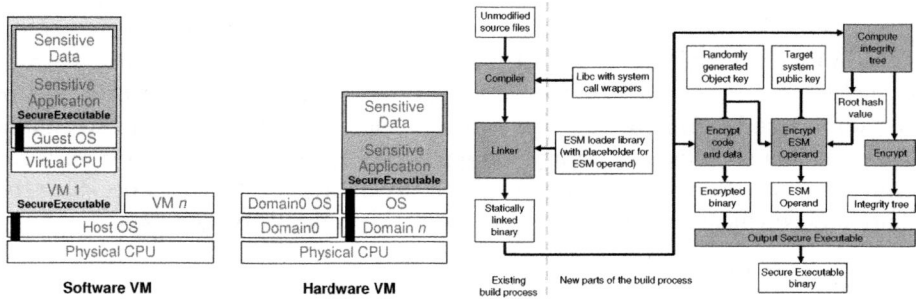

Fig. 3. Virtual Machine Configurations   **Fig. 4.** Build Process

Hardware-targetted binaries

We use a separate binary for every target machine. This does not require re-compilation, merely re-encryption. If we consider a Distribution Server to be the party that encrypts the code for each target CPU, the developer must trust the Distribution Server with the code and static data. This is necessary since this server decides who can read the code (and attached data). We thus assume this Distribution Server is part of the trusted build environment; however, this may not always be a reasonable assumption.

7   Implementation

Build process

The encryption key protecting this Secure Executable is generated by the build machine. This is used to encrypt the static code and data, and to compute the integrity tree. System call wrappers are linked in. The unencrypted loader code that initializes the integrity tree and issues the ESM instruction is linked in, and the ELF entry point is set to match. This process is illustrated in Figure 4.

Finally, all sections of the ELF that overlap the protected region are encrypted with the newly generated static key (the "Object key"). The operand for the ESM (Enter Secure Mode) instruction is constructed by concatenating the various parameters, encrypting with the Object key, then encrypting the Object key with the target system key and attaching to the binary.

Performance analysis

It is beyond the scope of this project to obtain performance results from a full CPU simulation. Future work includes both extending a POWER architecture system simulation to provide cycle-accurate timing results, and expanding the system wrapper library to the point where we support existing of-the-shelf software. Ideally, performance measurements will look at real software.

Instead, we built a cache simulation to validate the memory protection model. This simulation shows that it is practical to implement the integrity trees as described in this paper. Even though verifying a memory location potentially requires verifying several locations, up to the memory root, we see that with normal cache hit rates, the overhead due to the integrity trees is very reasonable.

Figure 5 (a) shows the new overhead per load, as a function of the measured cache hit rate. A sequence of 10^6 addresses sampled from an exponential distribution is chosen to simulate an application's access pattern. As the exponential distribution is varied, the hit rate and number of RAM accesses is measured. The cache is first put through a warm-up phase of 10^6 accesses before we begin measuring, to avoid being affected by the cold-start cache misses.

A fixed cache size (4096 rows with 8 associative columns of 32 words each) is used for all simulations. For a normal application (not a Secure Executable), the RAM accesses counted matches the number of load instructions when the cache hit rate is near 0. As the cache hit rate increases, the number of RAM accesses decreases linearly (which follows from the definition). The simulation was repeated, with the same address distribution parameter, for a secure executable. We then vary the exponential parameter to obtain different cache hit rates. The Secure Executable cache hit rate are slightly lower than the normal application hit rate since cache lines are occupied with integrity tree values in the Secure Executable case. To measure the performance penalty of this aspect, the values are plotted against the normal application hit rate corresponding to this distribution.

Figure 5 (b) repeats this simulation, measuring stores instead of loads. While the cache logic is significantly different in the Secure Executable case, we see the measured performance exhibits similar behavior to the loads test. Note that in both figures, the integrity tree lookups dominate at low cache hit rates. Even so, the bulk of the integrity tree levels remain in cache, such that only a few locations at the lower level need to be brought in. For cache hits, the integrity tree does not even need to be consulted. This is reflected in the better performance at high cache hit rates.

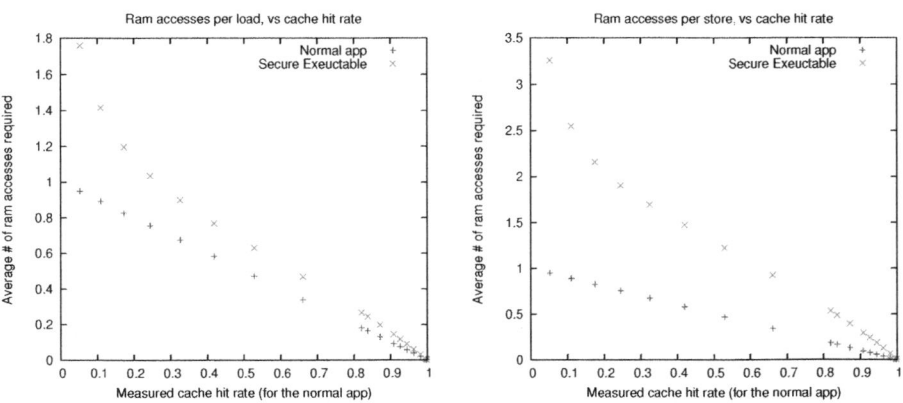

Fig. 5. (a) Left: RAM accesses per load. (b) Right: RAM access per store.

These figures do not address cryptographic performance. Since the number of cryptographic operations is equivalent to the number of RAM accesses, these graphs can be trivially adjusted to reflect this performance penalty by scaling the Y axis to the ratio of the latency of a hardware cryptographic operation vs. a RAM access.

8   Conclusion

This paper outlines a comprehensive set of hardware changes that together enforce the software isolation guarantees the Operating System is expected to provide, as well as protecting from physical attacks, malicious Operating Systems, and malware. Notably, we achieve this in a manner mostly transparent to the application developers, and compatible with existing software. By providing a convenient way to achieve fundamental guarantees about the security of a software execution environment, the adoption of such an architecture will address some of the most pressing security issues today.

References

1. IBM 4764 PCI-X Cryptographic Coprocessor (PCIXCC) (2006),
   http://www-03.ibm.com/security/cryptocards/pcixcc/overview.shtml
2. Bates, D.: Eight million people at risk of ID fraud after credit card details are stolen by hotel chain hackers. (UK) Daily Mail (August 25, 2008)
3. Blakely, R., Richards, J., Rossiter, J., Beeston, R.: Britain's MI5: Chinese cyber-attacks target top companies. The Times of London (December 3, 2007)
4. Chen, X., Garfinkel, T., Lewis, E.C., Subrahmanyam, P., Waldspurger, C.A., Boneh, D., Dwoskin, J., Ports, D.R.K.: Overshadow: A virtualization-based approach to retrofitting protection in commodity operating systems. In: Proc. of the 13th Conference on Architectural Support for Programming Languages and Operating Systems, ASPLOS (2008)
5. Dwoskin, J.S., Lee, R.B.: Hardware-rooted trust for secure key management and transient trust. In: Proceedings of the 14th ACM Conference on Computer and Communications Security, CCS 2007, pp. 389–400. ACM, New York (2007)
6. Goldreich, O., Ostrovsky, R.: Software protection and simulation on Oblivious RAM. Journal of the ACM 43(3), 431–473 (1996)
7. Gschwind, M., Hofstee, H.P., Flachs, B., Hopkins, M., Watanabe, Y., Yamazaki, T.: Synergistic processing in cell's multicore architecture. IEEE Micro. 26, 10–24 (2006)
8. Harkavy, J.: Illicit software blamed for massive data breach: Unauthorized computer programs, secretly installed on servers in Hannaford Brothers supermarkets compromised up to 4.2 million debit and credit cards. AP (March 28, 2008)
9. Lee, R.B., Kwan, P.C.S., McGregor, J.P., Dwoskin, J., Wang, Z.: Architecture for protecting critical secrets in microprocessors. In: Proceedings of the 32nd Annual International Symposium on Computer Architecture, ISCA 2005, pp. 2–13. IEEE Computer Society, Washington, DC (2005)
10. Lie, D.J.: Architectural support for copy and tamper-resistant software. PhD thesis, Stanford, CA, USA. Adviser-Horowitz, Mark (2004)

11. McCune, J.M., Parno, B., Perrig, A., Reiter, M.K., Isozaki, H.: Flicker: An execution infrastructure for TCB minimization. In: Proceedings of the ACM European Conference on Computer Systems(EUROSYS) (2008)
12. Stempel, J.: Bank of NY Mellon data breach now affects 12.5 million. Reuters (August 28, 2008)
13. Edward Suh, G., Clarke, D., Gassend, B., van Dijk, M., Devadas, S.: Aegis: Architecture for tamper-evident and tamper-resistant processing, pp. 160–171. ACM Press, New York (2003)

Extracting Device Fingerprints from Flash Memory by Exploiting Physical Variations

Pravin Prabhu[1], Ameen Akel[1], Laura M. Grupp[1], Wing-Kei S. Yu[2],
G. Edward Suh[2], Edwin Kan[2], and Steven Swanson[1]

[1] UC San Diego, La Jolla CA 92093
[2] Cornell University, Ithaca NY 14853

Abstract. We evaluate seven techniques for extracting unique signatures from NAND flash devices based on observable effects of process variation. Four of the techniques yield usable signatures that represent different trade-offs between speed, robustness, randomness, and wear imposed on the flash device. We describe how to use the signatures to prevent counterfeiting and uniquely identify and/or authenticate electronic devices.

1 Introduction

Many computing applications require the ability to uniquely identify a particular electronic device. Personalized services, digital rights management, and authentication schemes can all leverage per-device identifiers that are difficult (or impossible) to forge.

At the same time, the growing economic importance and popularity of electronic devices has provided criminals with incentives to sell counterfeit items. Counterfeit phones [1], music players [4], and solid state drives [6] abound for sale on the Internet and in cut-rate electronics boutiques around the world. Counterfeiters may surreptitiously insert fake devices into the supply chain or sell fabricated, look-alike models directly to consumers. The result is substandard or non-functioning products, dissatisfied users, and economic losses.

Due to the widespread use of flash memory, an identification or authentication scheme based on flash memory would be widely applicable. Flash memory suffers from idiosyncrasies such as unpredictable access latencies and a range of reliability problems. The variation that gives rise to these idiosyncrasies is due in part to random process variation, so the same variability can serve as the basis for extracting unique signatures from flash devices.

This paper examines seven techniques for extracting unique signatures from individual flash devices. These signatures depend on random changes in flash device behavior that arise from manufacturing variation and are detectable through the devices' normal electrical interface. The variation occurs between chips and between the blocks and pages that make up the flash storage array. This means that a single signature generation technique can, in most cases, extract thousands of different signatures from different portions of a chip. The signatures are instances of the physically unclonable functions (PUFs) [17] that previous researchers have proposed for IC authentication and hardware-based cryptographic key generation. Similarly, our flash-based PUFs (FPUFs)

J.M. McCune et al. (Eds.): TRUST 2011, LNCS 6740, pp. 188–201, 2011.
© Springer-Verlag Berlin Heidelberg 2011

can extract signatures to authenticate a chip and generate unpredictable numbers to generate cryptographic keys. Unlike most of other PUF circuits, however, FPUFs do not require any custom hardware circuits and work witwithh unmodified flash chips today.

We consider several usage models for FPUFs. For instance, to identify counterfeit flash chips, the device manufacturer would extract the signature from each flash device and permanently mark it with a unique serial number (e.g., by using an write-once, anti-fuse memory). To check the authenticity of the device, the purchaser provides the device serial number to the manufacturer who responds with a challenge in the form of an array address. The purchaser uses the FPUF to extract the signature for that address and transmits the result back to the manufacturer, who checks for a match. In a consumer device the flash controller would use the FPUF to extract a unique identifier for the device to bind media content to the device or authenticate the device when it attaches to a provider's network.

In order to be useful, FPUFs must meet four criteria: They should be fast, not cause significant damage to the flash device, have a low false-positive rate, and should make it intractable for a counterfeiter to forge the generated signatures.

We evaluate our seven FPUFs according the above criteria across fourteen flash devices. Our results examine the trade-offs between different FPUFs, and show that it is tractable to generate useful signatures in a few seconds. We also discuss usage scenarios that either use FPUFs directly or as part of a larger system to provide useful identification or authentication services.

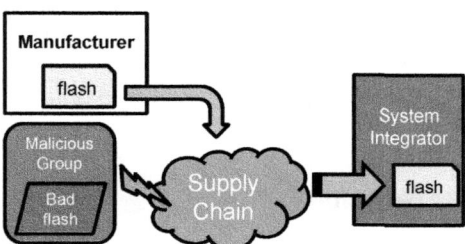

Fig. 1. Threat model for counterfeit detection

Section 2 describes usage scenarios for FPUFs. Section 3 gives a brief overview of the details of flash memory operation relevant to our study. Section 4 presents our FPUFs, analyzing the trade-offs and effectiveness of each. Section 5 describes related work and Section 6 concludes.

2   Applications

FPUFs have a wide range of applications because they require no special hardware and flash devices are ubiquitous. Below we describe three applications for the FPUFs we describe in this paper.

2.1   Counterfeit Detection

Figure 1 illustrates the threat model for chip counterfeiting that we assume in this paper. In the model, a trusted manufacturer makes flash chips and a trusted consumer purchases the chips through an untrusted supply chain. The consumer in this case is assumed to be a system integrator that purchases individual flash chips, not the end-user. The system integrator would have direct access to the flash chips and be able to perform low-level flash operations such as read, write, and erase operations at will. An adversary attempts to inject their own counterfeit or malicious chips into the supply chain, masquerading them as brand-name chips in order to make a profit at the expense of the manufacturer and/or deliver a malicious payload to the end-user. We assume the adversary has access to the supply chain but not the chip manufacturing process or the system integrator's facilities.

Our technique focuses on preventing the adversary from injecting fake or bad chips into the supply chain. Non-working chips are easy to detect and remove from the supply chain. We assume the adversaries do not have their own fabrication facilities, as this is prohibitively expensive. Under this threat model, a unique physical signature for each flash chip can be used to detect counterfeit devices by having the manufacturer and the system integrator measure and compare signatures.

2.2 Device Identification

Many modern computing devices contain a flash memory IC for non-volatile storage. Therefore, the proposed authentication technique is useful as a way to provide a secure hardware-based identifier for a device. If a device provides a low-level interface to a flash chip with direct access to read/write/erase operations, the FPUF signatures of the flash can be obtained externally and used to uniquely identify or possibly authenticate a device. As an example, such a capability can provide a way to authenticate mobile devices in a way that cannot be bypassed by malicious software even without adding any new hardware module.

2.3 Random Number Generation

The effects that our FPUFs exploit are probabilistic and vary both due manufacturing-induced variations and from operation-to-operation. Therefore, variation in device behavior can potentially be used to provide physical randomness in a random number generator.

3 Flash Memory

The FPUFs we describe in Section 4 rely on details of flash cells and how flash chips organize them into memory arrays. This section summarizes the characteristics of flash memory that we rely on for this study.

3.1 Flash Cells

Flash memory uses a single floating gate transistor to store one or more bits. The transistor includes an electrically isolated floating gate between the channel and the gate. To maximize density, NAND flash arranges between 32 and 64 floating gate transistors in series as a flash chain.

Charge on the floating gate affects the threshold voltage of the transistor, so the chip can read one cell in a chain by turning on all the transistors in the chain other than the target. By applying a voltage to the control gate and measuring current flow through the target cell, the chip can effectively measure its threshold voltage.

Changing the value of a cell requires moving electrons on or off of the cell's floating gate. The "program" operation moves electrons onto the gate and changes a cells value from a logical '1' to a logical '0'. Programming uses a process called Fowler-Nordheim tunneling that draws electrons onto the floating gate by applying a large voltage between the gate and channel. An "erase" operation removes electrons from the gate by applying an opposite voltage between the gate and channel. Unlike the program operation, the erase operation affects the entire chain at once.

Some flash devices can store n bits per transistor by programming and measuring 2^n voltage levels on the floating gate. These multi-level cell (MLC) devices offer increased density, but also reduced reliability and performance than single-level cell (SLC) devices.

3.2 Array Organization

Flash chips organize thousands of flash chains into a memory array that support high-bandwidth access by reading, writing, and programming many flash cells in parallel.

The basic unit in a flash array is a "block" comprised of between 16 and 32 thousand parallel flash chains. Each cell in a chain belongs to a different "page," so the nth cells across the chains comprise the nth page in the block. A single word line connects the gates on all the transistors in a page. In MLC devices, each bit in a single cell resides in a different page to prevent correlated errors between consecutive bits in a single page. Read and program operations apply to individual pages, while erase operations apply to an entire block. An entire chip contains thousands of independent blocks.

Due to this organization, it is possible for two bits in separate pages to electrically influence each other. During a program or read operation, unselected word lines experience an intermediate gate voltage, allowing current to flow to the target cell. This intermediate voltage exerts an electromagnetic stress on the oxide layer of each bit, resulting in a mild programming force. After many operations, these program and read disturb effects can cause bit errors. For program operations, the effect is especially strong for cells physically adjacent to the programmed page. This is due to capacitive coupling between the selected word line and the physically adjacent flash cells.

3.3 Variation Mechanisms

Flash cells are packed as closely together as possible to maximize density, so small variations in feature geometry or oxide thicknesses can have a measurable impact on both individual cell behavior and inter-cell effects (e.g., capacitive coupling between cells). For instance, some cells may be more or less susceptible to program disturb, read disturb, or program/erase-induced wear.

The variation also affects how difficult it is to program or erase pages and blocks. Both operations are iterative in flash memories: The chip partially programs or erases the cells, checks their value, and program or erases them again as needed. The result is that operation latency varies between pages and between blocks.

Since the physical effects underlying these variations are random (e.g., shot noise in dopant ion distributions), we can expect the pattern of variation between pages, blocks, and chips to be uncorrelated. Since the variation is random, FPUFs based on detailed measurements operation latency and unreliability should be unique across flash devices.

4 Techniques

Process technology-induced variation provides the basis for extracting signatures from flash devices, but the details of how we extract variation information will determine the FPUFs' effectiveness. This section describes our approach to extracting and using raw variation information to create signatures that can differentiate between individual chips. First, we discuss qualities desirable in a flash chip signature. We then describe the FPUFs and evaluate them according to those criteria.

4.1 Data Collection Hardware

To extract signatures from the flash devices, we use a testing board that contains two flash chip test sockets. This board connects to a Xilinx XUP board running Linux. The system accesses the flash memory via a custom-built flash controller running on the FPGA. It allows us to send program, read, and erase operations to the device at will. The FPGA on the XUP board implements a custom flash controller that supports timing measurements with 10 ns resolution.

We evaluate FPUFs with a set of chips of varied geometry. Table 1 summarizes the flash chips we use in this study.

Table 1. Parameters for the 27 flash devices we studied in this work

Name	Manufacturer	Cap. (GBit)	Tech. Node (nm)	Pg Size (B)	Pgs/Blk
A-MLC16-$\{1,2\}$	A	16		4096	128
A-SLC8	A	8		2048	64
A-SLC2-$\{1,2\}$	A	2		2048	64
A-SLC4	A	4		2048	64
B-SLC4-$\{1...5\}$	B	4	72	2048	64
B-MLC8-$\{1...5\}$	B	8	72	2048	128
B-MLC32-$\{1,2,3\}$	B	32	34	4096	128
B-MLC128	B	128		4096	256
B-MLC2	B	2		2048	64
C-MLC64	C	64		8192	128
D-MLC32	D	32		4096	128
E-SLC8	E	8		2048	64
E-MLC8	E	8		4096	128
H-MLC16-$\{1,2\}$	H	16	41	4096	128

4.2   Evaluating FPUFs

FPUFs differ along several axes and trade-offs across these axes will determine whether a particular FPUF is a good fit for a given application. In this work, we consider four criteria for evaluating FPUFs.

First, an FPUF should be able to differentiate between different chips with very high confidence. That is, the signatures from two different devices (or portions of a device) should vary randomly and widely from one another. At the same time, the signatures must be robust in that repeatedly extracting a signature from the same device should give very similar, if not identical, results.

Second, FPUFs should be fast. Some applications require extracting a signature from every flash chip coming off an assembly line. If an FPUF takes many hours, it will not be practical to apply it at large scales.

Third, it should be difficult to forge the results of an FPUF for a chip. If FPUFs are going to be useful in authentication applications, it must be infeasible or impossible for the counterfeiter to forge the signature. In particular, it should not be possible to store the signature on the chip and "replay" it when the chip detects that an FPUF is being applied.

Finally, applying an FPUF should not significantly damage the flash chip. Modern, high-density flash blocks can tolerate as few as 3000 program/erase cycles before becoming unreliable. If an FPUF renders part of the chip unusable, the FPUF will be less useful.

4.3   Program Disturb

The first FPUF measures variation in how cells respond to the program disturb effects described in Section 3. To create the signature, we erase a block and then repeatedly program one page in the block. Between each program, we read physically adjacent pages for program disturb-induced errors. For each bit in the adjacent page, we record the number of programs required to cause the first bit error. Those values comprise the signature. If program disturb never affects the bit, then the value for that position is set to 0. Algorithm 1 contains pseudocode for this process.

The resulting signature is noisy: Extracting the signature from a single page repeatedly will yield different signatures. Signatures for the same page are highly correlated, however. Figure 2(a) is a scatter plot of two signatures from one block on B-MLC8-1. (Table 1 summarizes the flash chips we use in this study).

Figure 2(b) shows the same plot for pages in two different devices, and shows that the two signatures are not strongly correlated. The noise in the correlations are due to the probabilistic nature of program disturb. Since each program operation is iterative, the number of programming pulses that act on the disturbed cells will vary from trial to trial.

We use a formal correlation metric (the Pearson correlation) to measure the robustness of the signatures and their ability to uniquely identify individual flash devices. To measure the correlation between two signatures, we form a pair, (X, Y) for each bit position in a flash page. The pair contains the number of program disturbs required to flip that bit in each of the two extracted signatures. We then compute the Pearson correlation as

Algorithm 1. Extracting program disturb-based signatures ProbePage and Observed-Page are physically adjacent in TheBlock.

```
EraseBlock(TheBlock)
for Cycle = 0 . . . 10000 do
    ProgramAllZeroes(ProbePage)
    bits = ReadPage(ObservedPage)
    for b = 1 . . . BitsPerPage do
        if bits[b] then
            Signature[b] = Cycle
        end if
    end for
end for
```

$$P(X,Y) = \frac{E[(X - \mu_X)(Y - \mu_Y)]}{\sigma_X \sigma_Y}. \tag{1}$$

The nearer $P(X,Y)$ is to 1, the more similar to the two signatures are. If $P(X,Y)$ is near zero, the signatures are very dissimilar.

Our measurements of the correlation between signatures from the same pages and between signatures from different pages show that the program disturb-based signatures can reliably distinguish between flash devices. For instance, the correlation between the two signatures from the same page in Figure 2(a) is 0.94, while the two signatures in Figure 2(b) have a correlation of just 0.012.

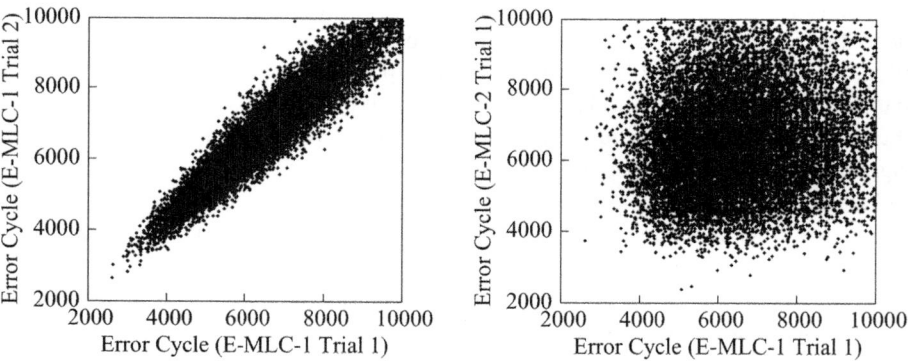

Fig. 2. Program disturb signature correlation. Extracting a program disturb signature from the same page twice gives highly correlated signatures (a). Signatures from different pages are uncorrelated (b).

Figure 3 extends this analysis to a larger population of devices. It illustrates the selectivity of our program disturb-based signature. We extracted signatures from one block from each of 10 chips (B-MLC8-1...5 and B-SLC4-1...5). The histogram shows the distribution of statistical correlations across all pairs of signatures, including signatures from the same block pair with each other. The white bars measure the correlation

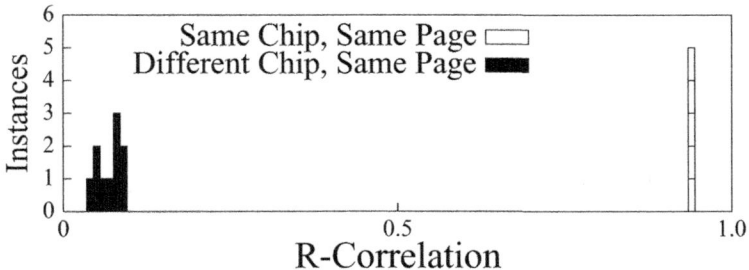

Fig. 3. Selectivity of the program disturb-based FPUF. The black and white bars are histograms of correlations between signatures from different pages and signatures from the same page, respectively. The large gap between the distributions shows program disturb signatures can reliably differentiate between different chips.

of signatures from the same block. The black bars are pairings of two different chips. The distributions of both sets are very tight and there is a large gap between the two groups, demonstrating that the likelihood of false positives (i.e., of two different blocks producing signatures that would appear to be the same) is very low.

Since this FPUF relies on per-cell variation in disturb sensitivity, it can extract a signature from each of the thousands of pages in a flash device. While this number is large, it is still linear in the size of the flash devices. As a result, this FPUF (like all the FPUFs we describe) is "weak" in that it cannot respond to an exponential number of challenges.

Extracting a single program disturb-based signature takes between 1 and 5 minutes, since it takes several thousand program operations to disturb a significant fraction of bits. We can reduce this latency and sacrifice some of the signature's power by limiting the number of program operations, k. Figure 4 shows the effect of varying k on the gap between signatures from the same chip and signatures from different chips. Each line in the graph represents a different pair of signatures from B-MLC8-1...5. The dashed lines are pairs of signatures from the same page. The solid lines are mismatched pairs. The vertical axis measures the correlation between the two. The data show that for $k <$ 4500, the signatures do not reliably distinguish between devices, but that by 5000 they can do so reliably. Limiting signature extraction to 5000 programs reduces extraction time to just 50 seconds.

In order to forge a chip's signature, the counterfeiter would need to store the signature information inside the flash chip, detect attempts to extract the signature, and replay the signature back in response. Extracting a program disturb signature requires a unusual and easy-to-detect access pattern, so replaying the signature is a definite danger.

To make forging signatures infeasible, the manufacturer can collect a signature for a random subset of the pages. In response, the counterfeiter would need to store the signatures for all the pages. Whether this is feasible or not depends on the information content of the signatures. Ideally, a signature would extract more than one bit of signature information for each bit in the page or block it targets. This would imply that storing the signatures for the chip would require more capacity than the chip can provide.

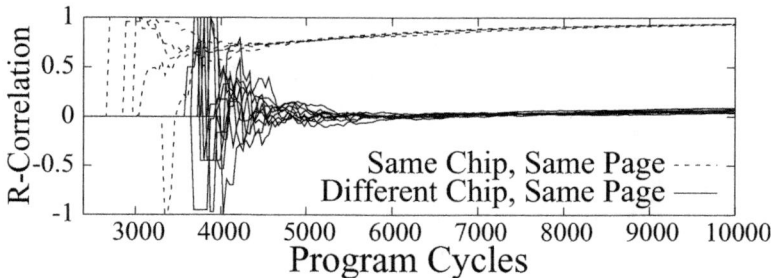

Fig. 4. Sacrificing accuracy for speed. Program disturb signatures can more reliably distinguish between different chips if the number of disturb operations is larger. The dotted lines measure correlation for signatures for the same page. Solid lines are pairs of different pages. Using more than 5000 program operations does not provide significant benefit.

The data in Figure 2 show that the values in the signature fall between 3000 and 10,000. Representing each value in a signature precisely would require about 10 bits per flash cell, making it impossible to store signatures for every cell in the flash device itself. However, because the signatures are noisy, the counterfeiter would only need to store an approximation of the signature, which would require fewer bits. For instance, the counterfeiter could store quantized signatures, restricting cycle counts to a few values in the forged signature.

We evaluated this forgery technique by quantizing signatures and measuring their correlation with the original. We found that quantizing the signature into four values would still provide correlations over 0.8. Storing the quantized signature would require two bits of signature data per flash bit. We measured the entropy of the quantized signatures as

$$H = - \sum_{i=0...3} p_i \ln p_i \qquad (2)$$

where p_i probability that a bit had value i in the quantized signature. The entropies were close to two, suggesting that the signatures are not significantly compressible. As a result, forging signatures by storing even compressed quantized signatures in the chip is not feasible, requiring a larger amount of storage than the authentic device.

The final concern is that extracting the program disturb signature will cause irreparable damage to the page. Extracting a signature requires one erase operation and many program operations. We have measured the reliability of the flash cells after repeated programming and found that the programs do not significantly affect reliability.

4.4 Read Disturb

The second FPUF uses read disturb instead of program disturb to extract signatures. We first erased the entire block and then program it with random data. Next, we read from each page in the block several million times to induce read disturb. After every 1000 read iterations, we checked each page in the block for errors. If we observed an error on a page, we recorded the bit, page, and cycle of the error. We repeated this process 10 million times. We use the read cycle counts for all the bits in the block as the signature.

Read-disturb signatures are less noisy than program disturb signatures, with correlations between multiple signatures from the same block averaging 0.98. Correlations between signatures from different blocks were extremely low: 0.0 for tests chip of B-MLC8-1 through B-MLC8-5.

The main disadvantage of this technique is that it is slow. It takes about 6 hours to extract a useful signature from MLC chips. SLC chips are less susceptible to read disturb, so we were not able to extract useful signatures from any SLC chips.

Finally, this technique is less resistant to counterfeiters than the program disturb technique. Quantizing the signatures to just a single bit provides correlations in excess of 0.98. Furthermore, the signatures we can extract in six hours have only between 3 and 7 disturbed bits. Storing this data for a single block would require fewer than 70 bits, suggesting that it might be possible to store all of a forged chip's signatures in the chip.

Extracting this kind of signature is, however, non-destructive, since the read operation does not move charge on or off of the floating gate.

4.5   Program Operation Latency

The next two FPUFs use per-bit variation in program latency to create a signature. The FPUF programs one bit at a time in a page, and records the latency for each operation.

We tested two variations of the write latency signature: single-page and multi-page. Each variation requires erasing the block, first. The single-page version programs each bit in a single page within a block: the first program operations programs a single '0' followed by ones, the second program operation programs two '0's followed by ones, and so on. In the multi-page version, we program just the nth bit in page n, so the programs are spread across all the pages in the block. After every n programs, we erase the entire block to make sure that each program goeas to an empty page. Each cell contributes a single measurement to the string of latency values, resulting in the desired signature.

We extracted signature pages in two SLC and two MLC chips: H-MLC16-1, H-MLC16-2, A-SLC2-1 and A-SLC2-2. Both versions of the technique had similar selectivity: Correlations between signatures from the same page was between 0.83 and 0.84,

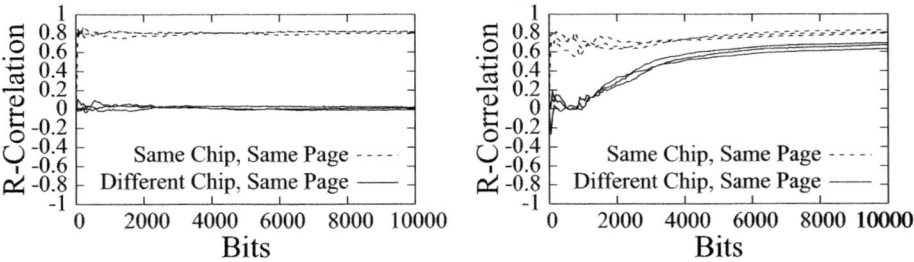

Fig. 5. Single page write latency selectivity. For SLC devices (a) just 100 per-bit program latency measurements give correlations over 0.8 and provide good selectivity. For MLC devices (b) 100 measurements also give good results, and selectivity actually decreases as the number of measurements rises (see text).

between different pages it was between 0.02 and 0.03. While this range is not as wide as it was for the program-disturb based signatures, the gap between correlations for the same pages vs. different pages is still very large.

Extracting a program latency signature from a block requires thousands of program operations and takes over 5 seconds per block. Figure 5 shows the effect of truncating the signatures. For both SLC and MLC chips just 100 measurements is sufficient to give high selectivity. In fact, for MLC chips using more than 1000 measurements reduces selectivity as all signatures from different chips become correlated. This effect is due to systematic variations in program latency that are a product of the chip's memory array architecture rather than process variation. We can account for this systematic variation by measuring latencies across many pages and subtracting the average per-bit latency from the measured latency for page we are targeting. The resulting signatures reduce correlation between mismatched full-length multi-page MLC signatures from 0.7 to 0.5. This is an improvement, but still suggests that smaller signatures are superior in this case.

The main drawback of this technique is that the information content of the signatures is low. Our latency measurements take on $\sim$20 discrete values[1], so storing each takes just a few bits. Since smaller signatures are preferable for this technique, forging these signatures will be even easier.

Signature generation is, however, very quick and causes almost no wear on the device: It takes between 1 and 3 seconds to generate a 1000 measurement signature, and the process takes a single program/erase cycle to extract a signature from a block.

4.6   Other Potential Signatures

We have not explored all of the potential sources for flash chip signatures, but we did examine several additional techniques that turned out not to be useful.

Erase latency. We measured the erase latency for each block in a device and used the resulting sequence of values to form a signature. This signatures was ineffective because erase latency times showed little variation and were inconsistent for individual blocks.

Read latency. Per-page read latency also varies little between devices, so it makes a poor signature. In fact, the read latency of the entire device is constant for SLC chips.

Whole-page program latency. In addition to the per-bit measurements described above, we tried whole page program latency as a signature. It was ineffective due to lack of variation.

Program/erased wear. We have measured the susceptibility of individual cells to program/erase-induced wear, but extracting such a signature takes at several hours and renders the target block unusable. Furthermore, as the work in [8] demonstrates, it would be easy to identify which blocks the manufacture had extracted signatures from by measuring wear-induced changes in program and erase latency. It would be easy, therefore, for a forger to determine which signatures to store and play back.

---

[1] The discrete values are a result of the iterative process of flash programming. Each program operation comprises a series of programming "pulses" under control of the flash chip's internal state machine.

4.7 Summary

Table 2 summarizes the results for all the FPUFs we studied. It contains the range of values we measured for the gap in correlation values comparing signatures from the same chip and those from different chips, the time required to extract a signature, the number of bits (as measured via the entropy calculation given above) per signature, and the number of program and erase cycles extracting a signature requires.

The results show that FPUFs based on program disturb rate and program latency are the most useful.

The program disturb FPUF does the best job of distinguishing between different chips, but this comes at the price of increased extraction time – it has the second longest extraction time of the useful techniques. The signatures it generates are also the most information-dense, making it the best choice for applications where latency is less important.

The program latency FPUF is the fastest of the useful FPUFs, and its signatures still contain about 20Kbits of information. For performance-critical applications (e.g., for extracting signatures from every flash chip produced by a large manufacturer), it is the obvious choice.

5 Related Work

Traditional techniques to authenticate hardware devices rely on a secret key and cryptographic operations. For example, a trusted hardware module such as a smartcard contains a private key in internal storage and generates a cryptographic signature to prove its authenticity. While cryptographic solutions are widely used, they require significant computing resources as well as key management procedures. As a result, traditional digital signatures are not well-suited for low-cost device authentication.

More recently, researchers have proposed to use inherent hardware fingerprints based on unique physical characteristics for identification and authentication. For example, it is widely known that significant process variations exist in an IC fabrication process, which make analog characteristics different from instance to instance even for a single design [2,3,12]. These process variations have previously been used to identify ICs

Table 2. FPUF summary Three of the seven FPUFs we tested provided useful signatures in a few minutes. Read disturb also provide useful signatures but it is too slow to be practical.

FPUF	Correlation Gap (SLC)	(MLC)	speed (s)	bits sig.	program cycles	erase cycles	points used
Program disturb	0.80-0.95	0.85-0.90	100	160k	10000	1	1 page
Read disturb	n/a	0.98-1.00	86400	1.1k	1/page	1	1 page
Single-page bit prog. latency	0.65-0.85	0.40-0.90	15	20k	10000	1	10k
Multi-page bit prog. latency	0.70-0.85	0.00-0.10	20	20k	10000	1	10k
Erase latency	0.00	0.25-0.90	300	6k	0	1/blk	blks/chip
Read latency	1.00	0.00	300	0	0	0	pgs/chip
Page program latency	0.65-0.75	0.00	300	78k	1/blk	1/blk	pgs/blk

by exploiting fluctuations in drain currents [11] or initial states of bi-stable elements such as latches [16]. While useful for circuit identification, these circuits are not suitable for security applications because they only provide a single number. An intelligent adversary can easily read out an ID and create a duplicate.

For security applications, a notion of Physical Unclonable Functions (PUFs) has been proposed to extract many signatures from inherent analog properties of physical systems. Conceptually, a PUF is a function that maps challenges to responses using an intractably complex physical system. For example, the initial idea of Pappu [13] proposed to use light scattering patterns of optically transparent tokens. This construction is often called an optical PUF and can generate an extremely large number of patterns can be generated depending on how a light source is setup.

For silicon devices, researchers have shown that silicon PUFs can be constructed to produce unique responses for each IC instance, exploiting random manufacturing variations. For example, silicon PUFs may extract unique delay characteristics using ring oscillators [7] or race conditions between two identical delay paths [10]. Alternatively, recent studies showed that initial states of bit-stable elements such as SRAM cells are also unique for each IC instance [5]. The silicon PUFs can be implemented as either custom circuits or reconfigurable logic on an FPGA [15,9,14]. PUF responses can be directly used as fingerprints to identify each IC instance or combined with error correction techniques to generate a cryptographic secret key [17].

The proposed flash fingerprints can be seen as a new type of PUF as one can generate many fingerprints by changing the part of a flash chip that is used. While the overall idea of exploiting manufacturing variations for device fingerprinting is similar to other PUFs, the proposed FPUF is the first to exploit unique physical characteristics of flash memory. Moreover, the proposed approach does not require any change to today's commercial flash ICs while most of other silicon PUFs require carefully designed custom circuits.

6 Conclusion

This paper has described seven different FPUFs that can extract unique signatures from flash memory devices. We described a set of desirable characteristics for FPUFs and experimentally evaluated them using thirteen different flash memory devices. Our results show that four of the FPUFs produce reliable signatures, but that they vary in terms of speed, selectivity, the amount of damage they do to the flash devices, and the ease with which a counterfeiter could forge them. We conclude that flash-based FPUFs can provide a reliable means of uniquely identifying individual flash devices and, by extension, can aid in identifying and authenticating electronic devices.

References

1. Barboza, D.: In china, knockoff cellphones are a hit. The New York Times (April 2009)
2. Boning, D.S., Chung, J.E.: Statistical metrology: Understanding spatial variation in semiconductor manufacturing. In: Proceedings of SPIE 1996 Symposium on Microelectronic Manufacturing (1996)

3. Bowman, K.A., Duvall, S.G., Meindl, J.D.: Impact of die-to-die and within die parameter fluctuations on the maximum clock frequency distribution for gigascale integration. Journal of Solid-State Circuits 37(2), 183–190 (2002)
4. Cheng, J.: Beware of counterfeit ipods! Ars Technica (April 2006), http://arstechnica.com/apple/news/2006/04/3651.ars
5. Daniel, W.P.B., Holcomb, E., Fu, K.: Initial SRAM state as a fingerprint and source of true random numbers for RFID tags. In: Proceedings of the Conference on RFID Security
6. http://sosfakeflash.wordpress.com/
7. Gassend, B., Clarke, D., van Dijk, M., Devadas, S.: Silicon Physical Random Functions. In: Proceedings of the Computer and Communication Security Conference. ACM, New York (2002)
8. Grupp, L., Caulfield, A., Coburn, J., Swanson, S., Yaakobi, E., Siegel, P., Wolf, J.: Characterizing flash memory: Anomalies, observations, and applications. In: MICRO-42: 42nd Annual IEEE/ACM International Symposium on Microarchitecture, pp. 24–33 (December 2009)
9. Guajardo, J., Kumar, S.S., Schrijen, G.-J., Tuyls, P.: FPGA intrinsic pUFs and their use for IP protection. In: Paillier, P., Verbauwhede, I. (eds.) CHES 2007. LNCS, vol. 4727, pp. 63–80. Springer, Heidelberg (2007)
10. Lee, J.W., Lim, D., Gassend, B., Suh, G.E., van Dijk, M., Devadas, S.: A technique to build a secret key in integrated circuits for identification and authentication application. In: Proceedings of the Symposium on VLSI Circuits, pp. 176–179 (2004)
11. Lofstrom, K., Daasch, W.R., Taylor, D.: IC Identification Circuit Using Device Mismatch. In: Proceedings of ISSCC 2000, pp. 372–373 (February 2000)
12. Nassif, S.R.: Modeling and forecasting of manufacturing variations. In: Proceedings of ASP-DAC 2001, Asia and South Pacific Design Automation Conference 2001. ACM, New York (2001)
13. Pappu, R.: Physical One-Way Functions. PhD thesis, Massachusetts Institute of Technology (2001)
14. Morozov, P.S.S., Maiti, A.: A comparative analysis of delay based PUF implementations on FPGA. In: Proceedings of the 6th International Symposium on Applied Reconfigurable Computing (2010)
15. Kumar, R.M.G.S.S.S., Guajardo, J., Tuyls, P.: The butterfly PUF protecting IP on every FPGA. In: Proceedings of IEEE International Workshop on Hardware-Oriented Security and Trust (2008)
16. Su, Y., Holleman, J., Otis, B.: A 1.6pj/bit 96% stable chip-ID generating circuit using process variations. In: Proceedings of the IEEE International Solid-State Circuits Conference (ISSCC) (2007)
17. Suh, G.E., Devadas, S.: Physical Unclonable Functions for Device Authentication and Secret Key Generation. In: Proceedings of the 44th Conference on Design Automation (2007)

Enforcing Executing-Implies-Verified with the Integrity-Aware Processor

Michael LeMay and Carl A. Gunter

University of Illinois, Urbana IL 61801, USA

Abstract. Malware often injects and executes new code to infect hypervisors, OSs and applications. Such malware infections can be prevented by checking all code against a whitelist before permitting it to execute. The *eXecuting Implies Verified Enforcer (XIVE)* is a distributed system in which a kernel on each target system consults a server called the *approver* to verify code on-demand. We propose a new hardware mechanism to isolate the XIVE kernel from the target host. The *Integrity-Aware Processor (IAP)* that embodies this mechanism is based on a SPARC soft-core for an FPGA and provides high performance, high compatibility with target systems and flexible invocation options to ensure visibility into the target system. This facilitates the development of a very small trusted computing base.

1 Introduction

Hypervisors, OSs, and applications continue to be infected by malware [11]. One common result of compromise is the execution of foreign code on the target system. Foreign code can be injected directly into a process as a result of a memory corruption bug, or it can be a separate program that is downloaded and installed on the machine as a part of the attack. Eliminating this foreign code would severely limit a successful attack.

One way to prevent foreign code from running on a system is to whitelist the code in legitimate applications and refuse to run any code that is not on this whitelist, thus enforcing the *eXecuting → Verified* property on all code. This conceptually straightforward approach has been difficult to implement in practice. It is challenging both to identify legitimate applications and to enforce the resultant whitelist. We assume that legitimate applications are known in advance and focus on enforcement in this paper. Past efforts exhibit deficiencies in some combination of the following requirements: *1) Isolation*, making the integrity enforcer vulnerable to compromise; *2) Visibility*, reducing their capability to detect compromises in the target system; *3) Performance*, making them impractical for some applications; *4) Compatibility*, necessitating that the target be substantially modified.

Patagonix manipulates *Memory Management Unit (MMU)* page tables to cause a trap to the Xen hypervisor whenever an unverified page in a *Virtual Machine (VM)* is about to be executed [13]. Xen provides many features, but has a correspondingly large *Trusted Computing Base (TCB)* ($\sim$ 230K lines of

J.M. McCune et al. (Eds.): TRUST 2011, LNCS 6740, pp. 202–216, 2011.

code [4]) that may be unable to enforce isolation. Even target systems that can use minimalistic, security-oriented hypervisors, like SecVisor [18], may suffer from virtualization-related performance degradation. Furthermore, some virtualization approaches require substantial changes in the target system's code to make it compatible with the hypervisor.

Intel *System Management Mode (SMM)* can be used to overcome some of these limitations, since it provides hardware separate from the MMU to set up an isolated execution environment [4, 20]. However, the confidentiality and integrity of SMM handlers can be tricky to guarantee due to the complex interactions between the various system components involved in implementing SMM [9]. Furthermore, some system state is invisible in SMM, and SMM can only be triggered by an electrical signal at one of the processor's pins or by writes to a control register. Code has been observed to execute about two orders of magnitude more slowly in SMM compared to protected mode [4].

We propose a new hardware mechanism that addresses the limits of other approaches. The *Integrity-Aware Processor (IAP)* is an extended SPARC processor that provides an isolated execution environment for an *integrity kernel* that can enforce eXecuting → Verified or provide other functionality. Although the integrity kernel shares many processor resources with the target, IAP stores the integrity kernel in a completely separate address space from the target and does not permit the target to initiate any data transfers between the two spaces. On the other hand, the integrity kernel has full visibility into the target. IAP stores the entire integrity kernel on-chip to minimize access latency. Thus, integrity kernel code runs at least as fast as code in the target system, and it can be invoked with the same overhead as a native trap handler. IAP also incorporates hardware accelerators for essential cryptographic primitives.

IAP transfers control to the integrity kernel in response to several configurable conditions, including attempts by the processor to execute code that has not been verified by the integrity kernel. It includes hardware structures to track code that has been verified and to detect attempts to modify it after it has been initially verified, subsequently causing it to be re-verified before it is re-executed. IAP monitors individual pages of memory in the virtual address space of each process, or the physical address space when the MMU is disabled. These features permit the integrity kernel to enforce eXecuting → Verified without relying on the configuration of the MMU page tables, further simplifying the TCB.

We developed the *eXecuting → Verified Enforcer (XIVE)* to demonstrate the extent to which IAP can reduce the TCB of the integrity kernel. The XIVE whitelist is located on a centralized *approver* connected to the network, to minimize the complexity of the XIVE kernel and to simplify whitelist updates. We implemented XIVE for an FPGA-based IAP end node, the approver on a commodity Linux host, and connected the two using 100Mbps Ethernet. The XIVE kernel comprises 859 instructions, and successfully protects a Linux target system that has been slightly modified so that it is efficient to monitor and so that it tolerates sharing its physical network interface with the XIVE kernel.

The rest of this paper is organized as follows. §2 contains the rationale for our design decisions. §3 discusses implications and limitations of the design, including potential future directions. §4 evaluates our implementation. §5 explains the relationship of this paper to related work. §6 concludes the paper.

2   Design

2.1   Threat Model

We adopt the Dolev-Yao model for attacks on the LAN hosting XIVE [8]. The attacker is permitted to use *Direct Memory Access (DMA)* to modify memory. We disallow physical attacks.

2.2   Hardware

IAP is based on the LEON3 SPARCv8 soft core by Gaisler Research. We based our design on an instantiation of the LEON3 that implements a 7-stage pipeline, separate data and instruction caches *(D-cache* and *I-cache,* respectively*)*, an MMU with a split *Translation Lookaside Buffer (TLB) (D-TLB* and *I-TLB)* and a hardware page table walker, and an AMBA 2.0 AHB system bus. SPARC processors support several distinct address spaces. Some of the address spaces refer to main memory and peripherals, and others are used to configure the processor or access special features. Our changes to the LEON3 are mostly concentrated in the pipeline, cache, and MMU subsystems. IAP partially relies on the SPARC coprocessor interface to interact with the pipeline.

Figure 1 illustrates the internal connectivity of the major components in IAP, each of which will be discussed below. The central addition to the processor is a region of on-chip RAM (called the *integrity kernel RAM*) that is only accessible in integrity kernel mode, which is analogous to supervisor mode and possesses strictly greater access privileges. Integrity kernel RAM can be accessed by the I-cache and the D-cache, through a dedicated port for each. Integrity kernel RAM occupies a dedicated address space. Accesses to integrity kernel RAM are not mediated by the MMU since the entire integrity kernel is trusted. IAP contains a ROM from which the integrity kernel is loaded into integrity kernel RAM immediately after the processor is reset. Control is then transferred to the first instruction in the integrity kernel.

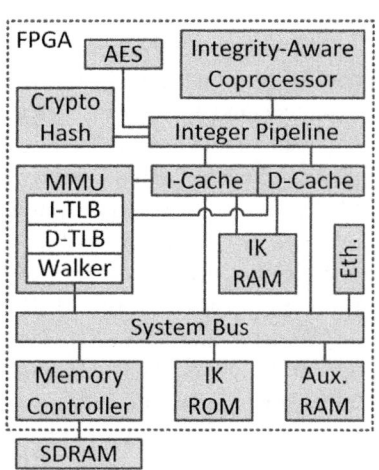

Fig. 1. Internal connectivity of IAP components

Attempts to execute unverified instructions are detected within the I-TLB and the I-cache. Each I-TLB entry contains a *V bit* (for "Verified") that is cleared whenever the entry is inserted into the I-TLB or the memory region that it encompasses is written. However, TLBs are only consulted when the MMU is enabled, so IAP also includes a separate set of *non-MMU V bits* that each map to a portion of the physical address space. V bits allow an integrity kernel to ensure that specific regions of virtual memory (in this context the physical address space constitutes a separate virtual space) have been verified before any of their contents are executed as instructions. The specific type of verification to be performed must be implemented by each integrity kernel. IAP provides facilities so that the integrity kernel can selectively and efficiently set or clear any number of V bits associated with a specific physical or virtual address region in constant time.

XIVE minimally requires hardware support for detecting and handling two types of events. Additional types of events could be supported by future versions of IAP to support other types of integrity kernels. The process for handling each event in hardware is described in Listing 1. Certain aspects of the event handling warrant further explanation, which we now provide. Native SPARC traps automatically allocate an empty register window for the handler by adjusting the register window pointer. However, integrity kernel traps may be invoked within a native trap, so they do not adjust the SPARC register window pointer. Thus, storing the current and next program counter values in local registers as usual would overwrite program data. In this case, IAP stores those values in shadow registers instead. Their contents shadow the corresponding normal registers for "long jump" and "return from trap" instructions. By only shadowing the registers for those instructions, we ensure that the registers can otherwise be used normally by the integrity kernel. Neither of the new *Processor State Register (PSR)* bits defined in Listing 1 is visible outside the integrity kernel.

The circuitry that fetches instructions for the pipeline is complex, and it is not immediately obvious that IAP correctly requires all instructions to be verified before being executed by the pipeline. We do not have space in this paper to provide a complete argument that it does so, but we note that it uses the D-cache bus snooping circuitry to detect write accesses by all bus masters to memory and appropriately update the affected V bits. It also contains circuitry to handle the corner cases that arise when bus masters write to memory that is currently being accessed by the I-cache in its various modes of operation.

IAP implements two cryptographic algorithms in hardware, since they are heavily used by XIVE and relatively expensive to implement in software. First, we selected the BLAKE hash routine for its open source VHDL implementation, status as a SHA-3 finalist, and good performance [19]. The implementation is sufficiently fast that hashing does not stall the pipeline, except during finalization. Second, IAP supports 128-bit AES. The AES implementation can cause pipeline stalls. However, it mostly operates in parallel with the pipeline, so stalls can be avoided by inserting sufficient instructions between the point at which each AES operation is initiated and the point at which its output is used.

The Ethernet interface in IAP has been modified to support dual MAC addresses, which permits the integrity kernel to receive packets without forcing the

Listing 1. Hardware handling of individual events

```
procedure HANDLEEVENT
    ε ← DETECTEVENT
    α ← PRESCRIBERESPONSE(ε)
    if α = ⟨Trap, τ, δ⟩ then
        TRAP(τ, δ)
    end if
end procedure
function DETECTEVENT
    if attempting to execute instruction from page with unset V bit then
        return ⟨HitVBit, ψ⟩                          ▷ ψ is the page information.
    else if PC ∈ Breakpoints then        ▷ Integrity kernel can modify breakpoints.
        return ⟨HitBreakpoint, None⟩
    else
        return None
    end if
end function
function PRESCRIBERESPONSE(ε)        ▷ Determine how to respond to the event.
    if ε = ⟨τ, δ⟩ then
        return ⟨Trap, τ, δ⟩  ▷ Other types of responses could be supported in future
versions of IAP.
    else
        return None
    end if
end function
procedure TRAP(τ, δ)                              ▷ Trap to the integrity kernel.
    ShadowPC ← PC
    ShadowNextPC ← NextPC
    PSR.IntegrityKernelMode ← True  ▷ Controls access to processor resources and
causes the I-cache to fetch trap handler code from integrity kernel RAM.
    PSR.TrapsPreviouslyEnabled ← PSR.TrapsEnabled            ▷ Used to restore
PSR.TrapsEnabled when exiting integrity kernel mode.
    (Continue invoking trap handler similarly to native trap handler.)
end procedure
```

interface into promiscuous mode or switching between MAC addresses. It places packets for both MAC addresses into a single DMA buffer.

2.3   Networking

There are three requirements that the network communications protocol between the integrity kernel and the approver must satisfy: *1) Security*, to prevent eavesdropping and to detect attempts to modify packets. *2) Low latency*, to minimize the amount of time that the end node is blocked waiting for a response from the approver. *3) Simplicity*, since it must be implemented in the integrity kernel, which has a very small codebase.

We constrain the approver to occupy the same local area network as the end node to minimize latency. This permits us to define a link layer protocol, called the *XIVE Network Protocol (XNP)*. Each XNP packet is 96 bytes long (excluding the 14 byte Ethernet header and four byte Ethernet CRC), and can be represented formally as a tuple $\langle \nu, \tau, \varsigma, \phi, \mu \rangle$ (excluding the Ethernet header). To prevent replay attacks, both approver and kernel nonces ν are drawn from a single, strictly increasing sequence. The packet type $\tau \in \{boot, verify, exit\} \times \{request, response\}$. The sequence number ς is used to match responses to requests. The composition of the payload ϕ is specific to each type of exchange described below. EAX mode is used to encrypt and authenticate $\langle \nu, \tau, \varsigma, \phi \rangle$ with AES, and the resultant MAC value μ is then appended [5]. The XIVE kernel implements logic to resend packets after some timeout until a response is received. We now discuss specific XNP exchanges between the XIVE kernel $\mathcal{K}$ and the approver $\mathcal{A}$. Only the payload ϕ is depicted (when non-empty), but each transfer actually involves a complete packet.

The approver resets its internal representation of an end node's state, which we discuss later, whenever it receives a boot request from that node.

The XIVE kernel issues a page verification request whenever it detects an attempt to execute instructions from a page with an unset V bit: $\mathcal{K} \xrightarrow{\langle \tau_p, \gamma, \beta, \theta \rangle} \mathcal{A}$, where the page type τ_p is derived from the size of the page, the state of the MMU (enabled/disabled), and the processor mode (supervisor/user), γ is a unique identifier for the currently-executing process, β is the virtual base address of the page, and θ is the result of hashing the entire page using BLAKE. The XIVE kernel blocks the execution of the processor until it receives a response from the approver: $\mathcal{K} \xleftarrow{\langle \alpha \rangle} \mathcal{A}$, where α specifies what action the XIVE kernel must take next, which can be either to terminate the process or to resume its execution.

The XIVE kernel issues an exit request when it detects that a process context is about to be destroyed: $\mathcal{K} \xrightarrow{\langle \gamma \rangle} \mathcal{A}$, where γ is the same process identifier used in the page verification requests. This permits the process identifier to subsequently be reused. Note that this does introduce a certain level of trust in the target OS to achieve the full assurances possible with XIVE, since an OS that causes XIVE to issue an exit request without actually destroying the appropriate context can then potentially be permitted by XIVE to execute programs that contain unapproved combinations of pages. However, all code that is executed must still be recognized and approved.

Approver. The approver's roles include generating and maintaining a whitelist, a database of pre-shared AES keys, and a representation of the internal state of each active end node on the network. Our initial prototype is simplified in that it only communicates with a single end node.

To maintain a partial representation of the internal state of each end node, the approver creates an empty state when it receives an XNP boot request packet and updates that state when each new page verification request or process exit request packet is received. The current state of each node n can be represented as a function $\sigma : \Gamma \to 2^{\Pi}$ generated in response to a set of "current" page request packets ρ received from n, where Γ is the set of all context numbers that are contained in ρ and Π is the set of all approved programs:

$$\sigma(\gamma) = \bigcap_{\langle \tau_p, \gamma, \beta, \theta \rangle \in \rho} \left\{ \pi \in \Pi \;\middle|\; \langle \tau_p, \beta, \theta \rangle \in \pi \right\}$$

where $\langle \tau_p, \beta, \theta \rangle \in \pi$ iff the page with the specified characteristics is contained within program π. When $\sigma(\gamma) = P$, it means that the process identified by γ has only previously executed code that is contained in all programs in P. P may contain many programs, since different programs can contain pages of code with identical characteristics. A page request packet $\langle \tau_p, \gamma, \beta, \theta \rangle$ loses currency and is removed from ρ when the approver receives a process exit request packet $\langle \gamma \rangle$. We say that n has entered an unapproved state as soon as $\exists \gamma. \; \sigma(\gamma) = \emptyset$, meaning that the process identified by γ is not a recognized program.

To generate a whitelist, the approver can be operated in learning mode, in which it approves all pages of code and outputs a database representing all programs that were executed by n.

The approver software is implemented as a multi-threaded C++ program. One thread performs administrative functions, another receives, decrypts, and verifies packets, a third processes the received packets with respect to the system state database, and the final thread encrypts, authenticates, and transmits newly-generated packets.

2.4   XIVE Kernel

The kernel was coded entirely in assembly language and is described in Listing 2. It contains 859 instructions and uses 488 bytes of integrity kernel RAM and 2952 bytes of auxiliary RAM. Each trap handler saves all of the local registers, which on the SPARC are eight registers in the current register window, and the processor state register to integrity kernel RAM upon entry, which permits the handlers to freely use the local registers as well as instructions modifying the condition codes in the processor state register. Some trap handlers require more than eight registers. Thus, blocks of integrity kernel RAM are reserved to implement a pseudo-stack for register swapping, although this is not described here. The prototype kernel does not implement an actual stack, because it is simpler to directly address the reserved memory in the few instances that it is required.

Physical pages of the target's kernel code and shared libraries are mapped into multiple virtual address spaces for different processes, so XIVE by default hashes and verifies them in each address space. To reduce this unnecessary overhead, we implemented an optional hash caching mechanism that stores the hash for each I-TLB entry at the time that it is calculated, and re-uses that hash during subsequent attempts to verify the same physical page, as long as it has not been modified. Our prototype uses 2304 bytes of auxiliary RAM for the hash cache, although this is in fact vulnerable to manipulation by the target OS. A deployable implementation would place the hash cache in integrity kernel RAM.

Listing 2. XIVE kernel

procedure BOOT   ▷ Obtains control immediately after every processor reset.
  η_{dc} ← ADDRESSOF(`destroy_context`)
  INITBP(η_{dc})   ▷ Initialize breakpoint to detect process context destruction.
  INITAES(κ)   ▷ Initialize AES using key shared with the approver.
  XNPBOOT   ▷ Perform XNP boot exchange.
  η_{to} ← ADDRESSOF(*target OS*)
  JUMP(η_{to})   ▷ Transfer control to target OS.
end procedure
procedure HANDLEBREAKPOINT
  SAVELOCALREGISTERS
  XNPPROCESSEXIT(γ)   ▷ Perform XNP process exit exchange.
  RESTORELOCALREGISTERS
end procedure
procedure HANDLEUNSETVBIT(ψ)   ▷ ψ is the page information.
  SAVELOCALREGISTERS
  SETVBIT(ψ, *True*)   ▷ Doing this first ensures that any DMA
accesses that occur during the subsequent verification operations are detected when
the processor resumes normal execution.
  θ ← BLAKEHASH(ψ)   ▷ Hash entire page.
  α ← XNPVERIFYPAGE(ψ, θ)   ▷ Perform XNP page verification exchange.
  if $\alpha = $ *resume* **then**
    RESTORELOCALREGISTERS
    (Resume process execution.)
  else
    HALTPROCESSOR   ▷ Our prototype
simply halts the target when it enters an unapproved state, rather than attempting
to selectively terminate the unapproved program.
  end if
end procedure

The integrity kernel shares the Ethernet incoming DMA buffers with the target OS whenever the target OS has enabled the Ethernet interface. This makes it possible for packets intended for the target that arrive while the integrity kernel is active to eventually be received by the target. Otherwise, the integrity kernel uses a total of 512 bytes of auxiliary RAM for incoming DMA buffers. The integrity kernel always uses 136 bytes of auxiliary RAM as outgoing DMA buffers.

3   Discussion

Deployment and Management. In any XIVE-protected environment, the following elements must be deployed: *1)* IAPs to operate all programmable portions of the end nodes, *2)* At least one co-located approver server that is statically configured to be resistant to attacks, since it is unable to rely on XIVE protection itself, *3)* An integrity kernel ROM image for each IAP, and *4)* Pre-shared keys to permit authenticated, encrypted communication between each end node and the approvers. A variety of protocols can be devised to install keys and ROM images in end nodes, and may resemble the protocols that have previously been developed to securely configure sensor nodes, such as SCUBA [17].

Limitations. XIVE currently exhibits several limitations, which we now discuss in conjunction with likely remediation strategies. Since XIVE relies on network communications to approve the forward progress of each end node, attackers can deny service to legitimate users of those nodes by interfering with XNP. However, XNP only operates on the LAN, which reduces the ability of attackers outside of the LAN to launch denial-of-service attacks.

Control flow attacks can succeed without injecting new code into the target system [7]. Thus, XIVE does not prevent them. However, some types of control flow attacks, such as return-oriented-programming, can be prevented using address space layout randomization [6]. Each XIVE whitelist is specific to a particular address space layout. However, XIVE could potentially be adapted to work with randomized address spaces by causing the approver to issue a seed to control the randomization process on an end node. That seed could then be used by the approver to translate page verification requests.

Bytecode is never directly executed, but is instead processed by an interpreter or a *Just-In-Time (JIT)* compiler, the output of which is ultimately executed. Currently, XIVE would simply verify instructions executed within an interpreter, a JIT, and the output from the JIT. Certainly, it is desirable to verify interpreters and JITs, but it is likely to be infeasible to whitelist JIT outputs, since the JIT may dynamically generate various instruction streams. This can be handled by monitoring data reads and writes by recognized JITs, so that bytecode inputs can be verified and the output instruction streams intended to be executed in the future can be excluded from verification. Patagonix includes some elements of this approach [13].

One potential strategy for adapting XIVE to a multicore environment is to replicate most of its functionality on each core, designate one instance as the leader, and create local communication channels that connect all instances. Then, whenever an instance needed to communicate with the approver, it could route the communication through the leader, which would be the sole instance with access to the Ethernet interface.

Alternate Usage Models. It would be a simple matter to adapt the approver to approve rather than deny by default, and thus enforce a blacklist of known malware, permitting all other software to execute.

Alternately, by simply approving all software that is measured by the end node on the approver rather than preventing the execution of non-whitelisted software, the approver could then field remote attestation requests on the behalf of the end node. Some advantages of this approach over conventional remote attestation, such as that implemented by the *Linux Integrity Measurement Architecture (Linux-IMA)* [16], are that audit logs are maintained in a central location further reducing the TCB on end nodes, cumulative attestation can easily be provided [12], it conclusively reveals the presence of malware on infected target systems since malware is unable to block attestation requests, and the use of *Public-Key Cryptography (PKC)* is centralized so that fewer nodes must be upgraded if it is eventually broken.

4   Evaluation

Implementation. We synthesized IAP to run on the Digilent XUPv5 development board. We also ported general performance enhancements in IAP (selective I-TLB and I-cache flushing) to a reference version of the LEON3, which we used as the basis for a series of benchmarks. Both versions of the processor configure their I-cache with four sets of 32KiB each, a line size of eight words, and an I-TLB with 64 entries. Each of the TLB and cache structures in both processors implements a *Least Recently Used (LRU)* replacement policy. We synthesized both processors at a clock frequency of 50MHz using the *Xilinx Synthesis Tool (XST)* v.13.1. The reference utilizes 52% of the FPGA slices and 33% of the BlockRAMs and FIFOs. IAP utilizes 71% of the slices and 40% of the BlockRAMs and FIFOs. The prototype includes various debugging features that weaken its security, but these would be removed from a deployable implementation.

Linux 2.6.36 serves as the target OS in our prototype, hosting a Buildroot userspace environment. It was necessary to modify the Linux kernel to allocate smaller pages of memory containing kernel code and data (256KiB versus 16MiB), to reduce the size of the whitelist and the number of re-verification operations. We optimized the context switching mechanism to cause the processor to switch back to a dedicated kernel context upon entering the kernel. The I-TLB and I-cache include the context number in their entries' tags, so this reduces pressure on those structures.

Userspace programs and libraries also presented challenges for XIVE, because they mixed code and data pages, and the dynamic linkage process incrementally modified an executable region in each program. These issues caused the overhead from XIVE to increase to the point of infeasibility. We modified the linker scripts to re-align the program sections and thus avoid the first issue. We configured all programs at link-time to preemptively complete the dynamic linkage process when they are first launched to resolve the second issue.

For the purposes of our experiments, the Linux kernel and the userspace root filesystem are merged into a monolithic memory image that is loaded before the system boots. To permit the construction of a whitelist, we cause the image to fill a whole 16MiB page, as initially used by the kernel, and zero-fill all unused space within the image.

TCB Size. XIVE was constructed to demonstrate that a very small integrity kernel is capable of enforcing eXecuting → Verified on IAP. We compare the size of XIVE against that of other systems with similar objectives in Table 1. All are discussed in §5. XIVE is clearly much smaller than Patagonix, due to the fact that Patagonix is incorporated into the full-featured Xen hypervisor. Like XIVE, SecVisor was developed with the specific objective of minimizing its size, so it is much closer. To be fair, we calculated the code size of SecVisor from the breakdown of code they provided, excluding their SHA-1 and module relocation implementations since XIVE does not contain analogous software functionality. SecVisor must use page tables to detect the execution of unverified code and to protect itself, which introduces additional complexity compared to XIVE. We thank the authors of [4] for furnishing us with the relevant line count in Table 1, which includes comments and debugging code, and could perhaps be reduced by future optimizations.

Performance Methodology. We evaluated the performance implications of XIVE using a series of benchmarks. The whole series of tests was run in sequence ten times for each processor configuration. The version of Linux running on the reference system retains a network driver receive buffer handling adaptation that introduces substantial overhead in network pro-

Table 1. Comparison of the TCB sizes of various systems

System	Lines of Code
XIVE	932
Patagonix	3544 + ~230K (Xen)
SecVisor	2682
HyperSentry	~3400

cessing, since we want to highlight the overhead introduced by XIVE's network traffic itself. The driver checks the whole DMA buffer for received messages during each poll operation, since XIVE can introduce "holes" in the buffer by removing messages that it receives. It may be possible to optimize the network driver in the future to reduce its overhead.

Figure 2a shows results from testing XIVE in two configurations. The one labeled "Hash Cache" includes the full functionality of the XIVE kernel as described in §2.4. The one labeled "No Hash Cache" disables the hash caching functionality, since it is not obvious a priori which configuration imposes less overhead.

Additionally, to demonstrate the overhead inherent in software-based approaches, we modified the Linux kernel to use page table manipulations to trap attempts to execute unverified code. The kernel does not actually hash or verify the code, so most of the overhead is generated by the page table manipulations and associated traps themselves. We compared the results of benchmarks running that configuration on the reference hardware, labeled "Page Tables," against a third configuration of XIVE that does not perform any hashing or network communication, labeled "Trap Only," in Fig. 2b.

Each of the configurations just discussed was used to run a series of five tests: *1) Create Processes:* A microbenchmark that demonstrates process creation overhead in an adverse case. It executes the ls command in an empty directory 10 times in succession. Since ls is a lightweight command that performs little work in this case, it demonstrates the time that XIVE requires to verify code during process creation and destruction. *2) Boot Kernel:* This tests the time it takes the Linux kernel to boot. We considered the kernel to be fully booted when we detected that the init process had been launched. *3) Download HTTP:* This demonstrates that XIVE is capable of sharing the Ethernet interface with the target OS. The end node downloaded a 2MiB file containing random data using

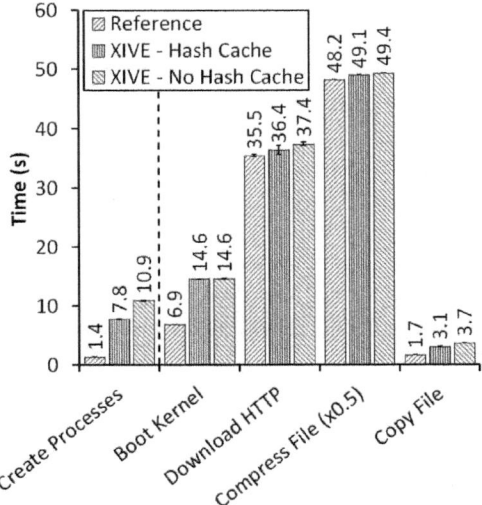
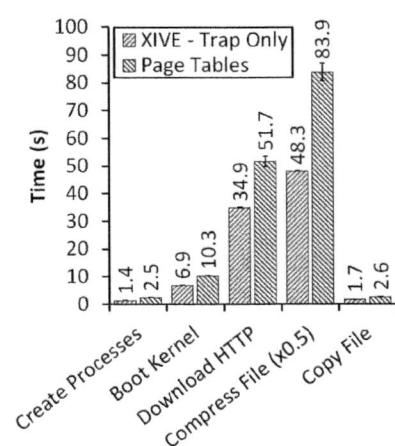

(a) Reference configuration and enforcing configurations of XIVE. The test to the left of the
dashed line is a microbenchmark, designed to
demonstrate process creation and destruction
overhead in an adverse case.

(b) Trap-only configuration of XIVE
and page table-based software implementation.

Fig. 2. Mean time required to perform benchmarks, including bars to show the standard error

the wget command from the LigHTTPD server running on the approver machine.
4) Compress File: This demonstrates the effect of XIVE on a computationally-
expensive process by compressing the previously-downloaded file using GZip.
GZip ordinarily involves a mixture of IO and computational operations, but the
entire filesystem of our prototype is hosted in RAM, so IO is relatively fast.
This fact can also be derived by noting the time difference between this test and
the next one showing the cost to copy the same file (*5: Copy File*). We scaled
all results from the compression test by a factor of 0.5 to prevent them from
dominating the chart.

The FPGA was directly connected with an Ethernet cable to the machine
running the approver. That machine was a Thinkpad T61 with a 2GHz Core 2
Duo processor and 2GiB of RAM running Ubuntu 10.10 64-bit desktop edition.

Performance Results. In general, the benchmark results in Fig. 2a demonstrate
that XIVE imposes low overhead for important types of tasks. However, we
present a detailed explanation of the "Create Processes" microbenchmark results
as well as those of the "Boot Kernel" benchmark below.

We hypothesized that the repeated verification of shared kernel code and
userspace libraries was partially responsible for the order of magnitude performance degradation observed between the reference and the "No Hash Cache"

configuration, which is what prompted us to develop the hash caching scheme. It is apparent from the results generated by the "Hash Cache" configuration that caching hashes for resident pages of memory dramatically reduces process creation and destruction overhead. It is also apparent that the overall effect of hash caching on the large-scale benchmarks is often positive.

Booting the kernel involves verifying a large quantity of code, including several verifications of the entire 16MiB system image prior to setting up fine-grained page tables, so boot time suffers a substantial slowdown. It is possible to modify the non-MMU V bits to operate with a finer granularity or to use a more sophisticated mapping structure to reduce this overhead, but that increases hardware complexity and seems unwarranted given the fact that this is a one-time cost per system reset.

We used the "Hash Cache" configuration to determine that XIVE generated an average of 3.7MiB of verification-related network traffic with a standard error of 7KiB as a result of running each series of tests and associated administrative commands.

5   Related Work

SecVisor seeks to ensure that all kernel code ever executed is approved according to a user-defined policy [18]. The prototype uses a whitelist of hashes as the policy. SecVisor uses a variety of mechanisms to enforce the policy, all based on an underlying hypervisor. XIVE monitors all code executed on the target system, including userspace.

Several projects have used Xen to isolate an integrity service from a target VM that is monitored. Lares allows the integrity service to insert hooks at arbitrary locations within the monitored VM that transfer control to the integrity service. *Hypervisor-Based Integrity Measurement Agent (HIMA)* enforces the integrity of user programs running in target VMs by intercepting security-relevant events such as system calls leading to process creation in the target and by permitting only measured pages to execute [3]. Patagonix also ensures that only measured pages can execute [13]. These approaches all have large TCBs, due to their reliance on Xen. Lares and HIMA also have the challenge of determining the proper locations for hooks and the proper types of intercepts, respectively, to achieve comprehensive protection.

HyperSentry and HyperCheck both use SMM to isolate an integrity service while it monitors the integrity of a hypervisor [4, 20]. HyperCheck also offloads a significant amount of functionality to a DMA-capable PCI *Network Interface Card (NIC)* [20]. Both exhibit *Time-Of-Check-To-Time-Of-Use* vulnerabilities, due to their periodic nature, and also depend on comprehensively identifying security-critical code and structures. However, they do have the advantage of measuring program data as well as instructions.

ARM TrustZone includes a collection of hardware isolation features that could be used to protect an integrity kernel [2]. However, TrustZone does not include support for directly detecting the execution of unverified code. Intel Trusted Execution Technology and AMD Secure Virtual Machine have similar characteristics [10, 1].

TrustVisor creates small VMs that isolate individual functions from a larger overall system and persists their state using TPM-based sealed storage [14]. XIVE monitors and controls the configuration of the whole system, which is largely an orthogonal concern.

The Cell Broadband Engine Isolation Loader permits signed and encrypted applications to be loaded into the Synergistic Processing Elements in the Cell processor [15]. Unlike XIVE, this architecture does not perform any ongoing monitoring of the executed code.

6   Conclusion

IAP is a processor technology that is specifically designed to efficiently support a variety of integrity kernels. It provides high performance, hardware-enforced isolation, high compatibility with target systems and flexible invocation options to ensure visibility into the target system. We demonstrated the utility of IAP by developing XIVE, a code integrity enforcement service with a client component that fits entirely within IAP's protected space, containing 859 instructions. XIVE verifies all the code that ever executes on the target system against a network-hosted whitelist, even in the presence of DMA-capable attackers.

Acknowledgments. This work was supported in part by DOE DE-OE0000097, HHS 90TR0003-01, NSF CNS 09-64392, NSF CNS 09-17218, NSF CNS 07-16626, NSF CNS 07-16421, NSF CNS 05-24695, and grants from the MacArthur Foundation, and Lockheed Martin Corporation. The views expressed are those of the authors only. We thank Samuel T. King and the anonymous reviewers for their helpful feedback. We measured lines of code using David A. Wheeler's 'SLOC-Count'.

References

1. Advanced Micro Devices: AMD64 architecture programmers manual. System Programming, vol. 2. Publication Number: 24593 (June 2010)
2. ARM Limited: ARM security technology—Building a secure system using TrustZone technology. PRD29-GENC-009492C (April 2009)
3. Azab, A.M., Ning, P., Sezer, E.C., Zhang, X.: HIMA: A hypervisor-based integrity measurement agent. In: Proceedings of the 25th Annual Computer Security Applications Conference, ACSAC 2009, Honolulu, HI, USA, pp. 461–470 (December 2009)
4. Azab, A.M., Ning, P., Wang, Z., Jiang, X., Zhang, X., Skalsky, N.C.: HyperSentry: enabling stealthy in-context measurement of hypervisor integrity. In: Proceedings of the 17th ACM Conference on Computer and Communications Security, CCS 2010, Chicago, IL, USA, pp. 38–49 (October 2010)

5. Bellare, M., Rogaway, P., Wagner, D.: The EAX mode of operation. In: Roy, B., Meier, W. (eds.) FSE 2004. LNCS, vol. 3017, pp. 389–407. Springer, Heidelberg (2004)
6. Bhatkar, S., DuVarney, D.C., Sekar, R.: Address obfuscation: An efficient approach to combat a board range of memory error exploits. In: Proceedings of the 12th USENIX Security Symposium, Security 2003, Washington, DC, USA (August 2003)
7. Buchanan, E., Roemer, R., Shacham, H., Savage, S.: When good instructions go bad: Generalizing return-oriented programming to RISC. In: Proceedings of the 15th ACM Conference on Computer and Communications Security, CCS 2008, Alexandria, VA, USA, pp. 27–38 (October 2008)
8. Dolev, D., Yao, A.: On the security of public key protocols. IEEE Transactions on Information Theory 29(2), 198–208 (1983)
9. Duflot, L., Levillain, O., Morin, B., Grumelard, O.: Getting into the SMRAM: SMM reloaded. In: CanSecWest 2009, Vancouver, Canada (March 2009)
10. Intel: Intel trusted execution technology software development guide. Document Number: 315168-006 (December 2009)
11. International Business Machines: IBM X-Force 2010 mid-year trend and risk report (August 2010), http://www.ibm.com/services/us/iss/xforce/trendreports/
12. LeMay, M., Gunter, C.A.: Cumulative Attestation Kernels for Embedded Systems. In: Backes, M., Ning, P. (eds.) ESORICS 2009. LNCS, vol. 5789, pp. 655–670. Springer, Heidelberg (2009)
13. Litty, L., Lagar-Cavilla, H.A., Lie, D.: Hypervisor support for identifying covertly executing binaries. In: Proceedings of the 17th USENIX Security Symposium, Security 2008, San Jose, CA, USA, pp. 243–258 (July 2008)
14. McCune, J.M., Li, Y., Qu, N., Zhou, Z., Datta, A., Gligor, V., Perrig, A.: TrustVisor: Efficient TCB reduction and attestation. In: Proceedings of the 31st IEEE Symposium on Security and Privacy, Oakland, CA, USA, pp. 143–158 (May 2010)
15. Murase, M., Shimizu, K., Plouffe, W., Sakamoto, M.: Effective implementation of the cell broadband engine(TM) isolation loader. In: Proceedings of the 16th ACM Conference on Computer and Communications Security, CCS 2009, Chicago, IL, USA, pp. 303–313 (November 2009)
16. Sailer, R., Zhang, X., Jaeger, T., van Doorn, L.: Design and implementation of a TCG-based integrity measurement architecture. In: Proceedings of the 13th USENIX Security Symposium, Security 2004, San Diego, CA, USA (August 2004)
17. Seshadri, A., Luk, M., Perrig, A., van Doorn, L., Khosla, P.: SCUBA: Secure code update by attestation in sensor networks. In: Proceedings of the 5th ACM Workshop on Wireless Security, WiSe 2006, Los Angeles, CA, USA, pp. 85–94 (September 2006)
18. Seshadri, A., Luk, M., Qu, N., Perrig, A.: SecVisor: A tiny hypervisor to provide lifetime kernel code integrity for commodity OSes. In: Proceedings of the 21st ACM SIGOPS Symposium on Operating Systems Principles, SOSP 2007, Stevenson, WA, USA, pp. 335–350 (October 2007)
19. SHA-3 proposal BLAKE, http://131002.net/blake/
20. Wang, J., Stavrou, A., Ghosh, A.: HyperCheck: A hardware-assisted integrity monitor. In: Proceedings of the 13th international symposium on Recent Advances in Intrusion Detection, RAID 2010, Ottawa, ON, CA , pp. 158–177 (September 2010)

Home-Network Threats and Access Controls

Mark Baugher[1] and Victor Lortz[2]

[1] Cisco Systems
mbaugher@cisco.com
[2] Intel Corporation
Victor.Lortz@intel.com

Abstract. This paper describes major risks, threats and attacks on home networks in general, and UPnP™ home networks in particular. Also considered are the strengths and weaknesses of technologies used to protect home-network and personal devices. The authors describe the effort to address these issues with a new security service for UPnP Device Control Protocols, called "UPnP Device Protection," which features a three-tier authorization policy, peer-to-peer design, an industry-standard pairing mechanism based on WiFi Protected Setup, and a gossip protocol. The paper also considers some future issues such as the need for a richer policy infrastructure on home networks.

Keywords: Home networking, security, access controls, UPnP.

1 Introduction

Attacks on individual Internet users result in very real and sizable monetary losses. In the U.S. in 2008, over seventy thousand formal complaints of Internet fraud have had documented losses of over a quarter-billion dollars [1]. Much of these costs are passed on to the detriment of all credit card holders, shareholders or taxpayers, so the loss is not limited to an individual victim of an attack. These estimates do not take into account the enormous costs inflicted by home-borne botnets on businesses, individuals, governments and other organizations [2].

Protection from attacks in commercial enterprises, government and military relies on strong cryptography and trained professional staff. Particularly in large and mid-size organizations, a dedicated organization is chartered to develop processes and ensure that users have the appropriate tools and procedures to follow security policies. Home-networks are typically self-managed or completely unmanaged, however, and the typical user is left to configure and maintain their own software, hardware and applications.

Configuration and management of home-network devices are the primary use cases addressed in this paper. This class of networked, personal devices includes wireless gateways, network-attached storage, and other infrastructure products that people share. Secure configuration, management and operation of network, storage and other shared devices are difficult for any novice to do; people who cannot rely on the help of an expert friend or paid support are at the mercy of the quality of the user interface and security features found in the particular home-network product.

J.M. McCune et al. (Eds.): TRUST 2011, LNCS 6740, pp. 217–230, 2011.
© Springer-Verlag Berlin Heidelberg 2011

From the perspective of home-network device vendors, moreover, any feature that negatively affects usability can be fatal to a mass-market product such as a network gateway product. Security has a significant impact on usability and user experience, and home-network products often sacrifice security in order to improve usability. The problem of securing home-network products becomes even more challenging when the risks and costs of attacks become socialized.

Risk socialization occurs when threats to individual privacy and security affect the public as a whole: An organization or individual who collects information from a large number of individuals might gain power relative to others who lack such information [3]. Many malware programs are now designed to protect the host and minimize the impact on the individual PC user in order to attack a larger, more lucrative target. In this respect, the costs of malware, phishing, fraud and other attacks are socialized whereas the costs of prevention are private. A careless user who tolerates (knowingly or unknowingly) seemingly benevolent malware may not be personally affected, but botnets using such malware are a severe threat to others.

In response to some well-publicized attacks, the UPnP Forum started an effort two years ago to develop a new security framework for UPnP services called Device Protection [4]. One of the goals of Device Protection was to address the usability and architectural issues that have prevented the previous UPnP Device Security service [5] from being widely deployed. This paper gives background, motivation and rationale for the design of UPnP Device Protection.

Device Protection, like any home-network security service, needs to address a set of documented threats: Section 2 considers home-network threats and some of the shortcomings of security technologies for home users. Section 3 describes a set of principles for home network access controls that influenced the design of UPnP Device Protection. Section 4 gives an overview of the rationale and features of the Device Protection service. Previous work in home-network access control is considered in Section 5, followed by the Conclusion.

2   The Security of Unmanaged Networks

On home networks, the most common attack vector is personal computer malware such as computer viruses, email attachments, URI links, and scripts that are downloaded and executed on the PC [2]. Arguably, the gateway is the most critical resource on the home network. Home gateways are vulnerable to attacks from malware, war drivers and the exploitation of unauthenticated gateway services. These attacks fall into several classes.

- Attacks against a gateway using a specific execution platform such as the Adobe Flash Network API [6].
- Attacks against a gateway from a class of application programs, such as cross-site request forgery attacks launched from browsers [7].
- Malware use of gateway services, such UPnP NAT Traversal to distribute botnet command and control and for other purposes [8, 9].
- Attacks against implementations of poorly written specifications that suffer from ambiguities and other issues [10].

A common source of many problems is the lack of effective access controls in home-network products. It is a challenge to add usable access controls to consumer devices: These products are unmanaged, for all practical purposes, and have "the primary goal of making devices and protocols 'just work' reliably and responsively in a wide variety of contexts and for a wide variety of applications, without requiring configuration or technical knowledge on behalf of the user" [11].

One of the biggest vulnerabilities today is that many home gateways allow public access to their configurations through the widespread use of well-known passwords. Vendors intend such passwords to be used just once when the product is installed. However, because many users never properly install the product, their gateways are openly accessible to any interior computer that can provide the well-known system password. Malware can take ownership of a device that operates with a well-known password and then attack DNS, DHCP, firewall, forwarding, file storage and other services.

Rather than a day-zero failure caused by a well-known password, the type of failure that is considered in this paper is caused by the lack of access controls in service suites such as UPnP™ and some Apple™ networking products. For example, certain UPnP services can reconfigure a router's DNS server address through an unauthenticated back door [10]. Malicious DNS configuration can give the attacker control over where the user goes on the Internet and complete knowledge about where the user has been [6].

To prevent such unauthorized reconfiguration of the device, some hands-on configuration is needed at installation time. Simply pointing a configuration program to the gateway's address and port alone, for example, cannot accomplish secure installation because malware can easily exploit these same mechanisms. Instead, the owner of the product needs to perform a "ceremony" [12] (also called an "introduction protocol" [11]). PGP signing parties and the recitation of a "short authentication string" [13] are examples of ceremonies. On home networks, ceremonies typically prove physical locality and control of the device as well as user involvement through knowledge of a secret that is displayed on the product, by pushing a button, use of near-field communications, or similar means [14, 15].

A proliferation of methods to associate a user device with another device is likely to confuse non-technical users. Still, improved methods are needed, and strong access-control methods are required for critical home-network services such as wireless LANs. Beyond WiFi, access controls are needed to protect a variety of other home-network assets from significant risks, which are considered in the next section.

2.1 Assets and Risks

Gateways, network storage, and other home-network devices have critical assets such as DNS proxies, packet forwarding services, file storage, passwords, and firewalls. Among the biggest risks to these assets are the re-configuration of network devices, the theft of personal passwords, and misuse by automated programs as illustrated by the following attacks.

2.2 Threats and Attacks

In recent years, there have been publicized attacks against gateway products that fraudulently re-configure the gateway or use gateway services to further the propagation of malware.

2.2.1 Malware

For example, the UPnP Internet Gateway Device (IGD) protocol has an optional service that re-configures the DNS server address in the home gateway. As shown in Figure 1, the Internet gateway device accepts a new DNS server address from a UPnP control point and updates its configuration, which will overwrite the existing server address. One UPnP service allows any UPnP *control point* to change this field without performing identification, authentication or authorization of the requester [10]. This lack of access control to UPnP configuration services coupled with the predictability of UPnP configuration service addresses and the ability to perform the unauthenticated action with a single UDP packet, led to a serious UPnP attack exploiting a hole in the Adobe Flash platform.

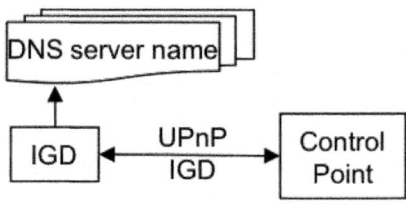

Fig. 1. UPnP Internet Gateway Device (IGD)

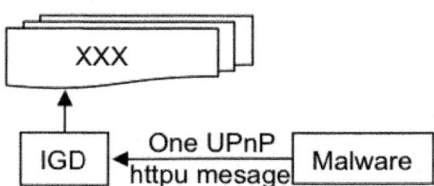

Fig. 2. Attack on UPnP IGD

The so-called "UPnP Flash Attack" uses an off-the-shelf PC to accept an Adobe Flash file from a web site. This file contains a script for the Adobe runtime system; the script formats a UPnP IGD HTTP request over UDP (HTTPU) and requests a change to the DNS server address in the gateway [6]. As shown in Figure 2, malware can use the Flash Attack to direct users' DNS requests to any server it chooses, and then to sites that "phish" usernames and passwords.

Since last year, Adobe has fixed the problem that allowed its API to be used in this way, and no gateway vendor is known to ship the risky IGD service that is vulnerable to this particular attack. However, many of these counter measures address only one chain of weaknesses. Other opportunities exist for malware and other attackers in a variety of home-network services.

There are today hundreds of cross-site request forgery and cross-site scripting attacks that exploit web browsers and spread from there [7]. Gateway user interfaces are not immune from such attacks since most retail gateways use a web interface to configure the product. Therefore, web browsers are vulnerable to cross-site scripting and request forgery attacks on gateway services.

2.2.2 War Drivers and Uninvited Guest

Another attack vector is "war driving", by which an intruder uses an open wireless LAN to gain unauthorized access to a residential network device.

The easiest way to stop a war driver is to ensure that Wi-Fi Protected Access (WPA) or equivalent is enabled on the home wireless LAN. Thus, practically all commercial-gateway products strongly recommend use of WPA, although it is rare for a vendor of a customer-managed gateway to ship their product with WPA enabled by default. In order to re-configure the device to use WPA, a home user needs to use gateway "admin" access or else use Wi-Fi Protected Setup (WPS).

WPS features a few methods to configure WiFi Protected Access such as by PIN, push-button, and near-field communications [14]. These methods involve physical interactions with devices through I/O channels inaccessible to malware. It is not clear how widely used are the WPS methods today; many of the major product vendors direct the customer to a CD installation. Typically, the installation program automatically logs in to the admin account with no human action required and thereby gets full access to the entire system configuration. To automate this process, the gateway uses a well-known password or no password at all, a problem discussed above.

Wireless LAN security can protect against war drivers but is ineffective in stopping threats from home-network malware. Other methods are therefore needed.

2.3 The Risks of Access Controls

When malware runs from a privileged account, it can automatically gain full access to those privileges, such as by using the credentials of a gateway administrator. One approach to this problem is to make access less automatic and require the user to enter a password before a privileged action is performed. For devices that control home-network gateways or other critical resources, multi-factor authentication can restrict privileged access to certain devices based on their public-key and private-key authentication as one factor that is coupled with a user-prompted password. The second factor is the password authentication, which puts the user in the loop. But there is a potential human-factors problem when the user is always in the authorization loop: The user might be conditioned to approve every action or to enter the passphrase whenever prompted to do so. Password-based authentication comes with additional risks.

2.3.1 Problems with Passwords

In general, passwords are a poor authentication method; this has been true for some time [16, 17] and is truer today given advances in hardware speeds and password cracking [18]. There is no proven, usable method to ensure that passwords are strong and unique across unmanaged network devices. Use of identical and similar passwords for a variety of purposes such as for gateway access and online banking, increase the risks of password compromise *via* social-engineering attacks and resident malware.

Today's home network security standards [14, 5, 19] reference various alternatives to poor passwords such as public-key cryptography, password checkers, strong pre-shared symmetric keys, hardware token devices and other means. But these methods are rare in home products today: In practice, most home users do not choose to use cryptographic security techniques in a personally managed or unmanaged home network[1]. Network services such as NAT traversal and firewall control continue to be unauthenticated.

Authentication is hard to do: Means are needed to strictly identify a user, personal device or both; a ceremony is needed to establish an authorization and a credential, and the solution must scale beyond a single device: If a user has a client device that uses N server devices, for example, it is likely that the typical user will refuse to run N secure introductions. Use of an epidemic or gossip protocol [11] is one approach to scale secure introduction to multiple devices whereby one device can introduce another to a group of devices. This is an advanced technique for propagating authentication information, but even the most basic point-to-point authentication is rarely used in most network products that are sold through retail channels.

2.3.2 Well-Known Passwords

As considered at length above, the failure to change a well-known password is probably the most dangerous attack vector to unmanaged network products, but it is only one of several problems with password use on home networks.

2.4 Other Sources of Risk

Protocols that are poorly specified, poorly implemented, and that undergo no security review provide fertile ground for attacks [10]. Often there is a chain of failures in specification, implementation and testing that result in a successful attack such as the UPnP Flash attack, which exploited weaknesses in two unrelated products. The absence of a security review in standards bodies and development organizations allows other failures to be deployed and exploited in real-world attacks. It is clear that any security service needs to be subject to extensive, if not public review to at least partially addresses these other sources of risk. Effective security processes and governance are essential requirements for any organization that attempts to develop security standards. Remarkably few standards development organizations have these.

3 Security Principles for Home Networks

As stated above, two major attack vectors on the home network originate from (1) malware that runs on an interior computer and (2) interlopers that gain access through an open wireless network or by visiting the home. Of the two threats, malware is generally the most serious since it easily circumvents common home-network access controls such as wireless LAN security. Both malware and network interlopers can launch highly effective attacks, moreover, when critical services are available through a well-known password or without any effective access control.

A properly designed access control scheme can prevent or at least impede the ability of malware to operate against home-network devices by limiting the sources and the scope of attacks. Fundamental to this problem is limiting the privilege of users.

---

[1] UPnP Device Security 1.0 is a state of the art security system that has not been deployed. Even successful crypto-systems such as PGP mail and personal voice security systems are rarely used for personal mail and VoIP.

3.1 Least Privilege

In 1975, Saltzer and Schroeder wrote: "Every program and every user of the system should operate using the least set of privileges necessary to complete the job" [20]. In practically all of today's home network products, however, a permission to change anything is a permission to change everything. Thus, the current practice of configuring wireless security and other subsystems from the main configuration screens violates the principle of least privilege. For this reason, the configuration of popular services such as Wi-Fi Protected Access needs to be separated from system configuration and administrative privilege. With proper access control design, a management program such as UPnP can never escalate a privilege.

3.1.1 Escalation

Privilege escalation occurred in the UPnP Flash Attack when a device gained the privilege to change the DNS server address, which is typically protected by a password in gateway vendor's administrative interface. Even a very strong administrative password is useless if the implementation escalates the privilege of a request based solely on the protocol used by the requester.

Privilege escalation can be intrinsic to a poorly designed protocol. In general, a privilege to perform one type of gateway action must not be transitive to all actions. Thus, the privilege to *access* a service must not escalate into the privilege to *grant* access to another to use the service.

As long as there are only two levels of authorization, such as *public* and *admin*, escalation to administrative privilege is needed for any change made to any portion of the device configuration. It may be reasonable for a gateway to allow any device to get Internet access, but a higher level of authorization may be desired for access to in-home devices such as gateways, attached storage and PCs. An even higher level of authorization is of course needed for access to the entire network configuration or to make changes that affect devices other than the one making the request. Thus, at least three levels of privilege are needed when unauthenticated services are supported.

3.1.2 Isolation

To limit the scope of an attack, it may help to separate privileges that affect only one system, like establishing a NAT port mapping to a requesting device, from privileges that affect other systems, such as requesting a port mapping for another device or shutting down the gateway's broadband interface to the entire network.

Thus, a single configuration action that allows a requester to request an action for itself and for others is a candidate for being separated into two different actions. The "lesser privilege" action affects only a single end system, the one making the particular request. A "higher privilege" in this context requires administrator-level authorization to alter the configuration in a way that affects others.

3.2 Strong Identification and Authentication

It is necessary to strongly identify an administrator and also a privileged user, such as one whose device is allowed to access other devices on the home network. There are well-known use cases on the home network where multiple users share a device.

Often, a shared device will have a shared password or no user-level access control. This case can benefit from device-based public/private key cryptography (PKC) for strong identification and authentication so that service requests can at least be authenticated at the device level.

For administrative or other privileged actions that affect the device, both PKC and password-based authentication are needed. In this case, the user's handheld device can both employ PKC and prompt the user to perform password-based authentication.

3.3 Summary: Three Levels of Privilege

In today's home network products, there are typically two levels of access, *public* (or unauthenticated access) and *admin* or complete access to the particular device. In most home-network infrastructure devices, however, at least two privilege levels are needed to separate specific configuration tasks such as establishing WiFi Protected Access from complete access to change the system configuration. Thus, UPnP Device Protection uses three levels of authorization for (1) public access that requires no identification or authentication, (2) user-level access to a home-network service such as WLAN security or NAT Port Mapping service, and (3) administrator-privilege access to a critical resource such as the gateway admin account.

UPnP Device Protection supports three privilege levels through three "roles" as described in the next section.

4 UPnP Device Protection

In response to some well-publicized attacks on the UPnP Internet Gateway Device (IGD) protocol and the lack of deployment of UPnP Device Security 1.0, The UPnP Forum initiated work in 2008 to address these problems. The solution has four major features.

1. The introduction of roles or authorization levels with a default of three levels for *public*, *basic* and *admin* authorization.
2. Use of well-established mechanisms based on the WiFi Protected Setup standard for pairing a device that offers a service with a device that wants access to that service.
3. Use of the well-established security protocol, TLS, and X.509 v3 digital certificates.
4. Peer-to-peer operation that does not require configuration of a third device for authorization and authentication.

4.1 Authorization Levels

UPnP Device Protection is a service for UPnP Device Control Protocols (DCP) such as the Internet Gateway Device DCP. It is thus applicable to other UPnP DCPs such as those that provide Device Management and Audio/Video services. Given the wide variety of potential applications and uses, the Device Protection design provides default values for authorization levels (called "roles") and also allows roles to be defined by a particular DCP or by a particular vendor of the ultimate product.

The recommended default for the number of roles, however, is three levels. The *public* level is what is available in today's UPnP: since UPnP Device Security 1.0 was never deployed, there is no authentication in UPnP systems today. Many services such as packet forwarding by an Internet gateway arguably do not need authorization but can be run "plug and play." The most widely used service in UPnP IGD, moreover, is UPnP NAT traversal, which consists of a requesting device (called a "control point") that directs the gateway to open an external port for its use. In order to open a port for another device on the home network, however, the device by default must first establish that it is authorized[2].

By default, the *basic* level of authorization requires that a control point device be paired with the resource device. UPnP Device Protection supports a pairing protocol that results in the resource device accepting the self-signed certificate of the control point and granting that control point *basic* authorization. The resource device also maintains an access control list (ACL) of the control points that it has so authorized.

In Device Protection, the highest default level of privilege is *admin* privilege, which is obtained by first acquiring *basic* authorization and then proving knowledge of the resource device's, admin password. A control point must first gain *basic* access through pairing before it is allowed to log in (over TLS) with an admin password. This higher-level of authorization is needed because UPnP is generally only one type of service that is found on a home gateway, NAS, Audio/Video device, or other product. Each product has its own methods of controlling access to its configuration. To prevent the kind of privilege escalation exemplified by the UPnP Flash Attack, Device Protection uses two levels of access controls: *Basic* authorization is needed to use a privileged service plus *admin* authorization when a change is protected by an admin password or other means on the hosting device.

4.2 Device Pairing

Device Protection authorizations require that a requesting control-point device be paired with the device that owns the particular resource. UPnP Device Protection uses the WiFi Protected Setup standard protocol [14] for this task. Note that although the WPS registration protocol is used, the transport of that protocol in Device Protection is over UPnP, and there is no requirement that the network be wireless. WPS supports three methods of device pairing.

1. Short string or PIN
2. Near-field communications
3. Push-button control

With the exception of push-button control (PBC), WPS provides strong identification and authentication. The PBC method provides only weak identification, but its vulnerabilities are mitigated somewhat by detecting multiple simultaneous access attempts during an interval called the "walk time" and aborting the WPS operation in this case. Furthermore, if the PBC method is properly implemented, it requires user interaction and use of I/O channels inaccessible to malware.

---

[2] Apple's NAT Port Mapping Protocol does not allow a device to open a port for another device. Although this is "spoofable" at the MAC layer, such a requirement makes abuse of this service somewhat harder.

UPnP Device Protection adapts both the WPS pairing methods and its registration protocol for establishing locality and control of a resource device by a human user, who is also in control of the UPnP control-point device. By using WPS, the proliferation of different pairing methods is minimized in the hope of providing a simpler environment for the user.

There is a well-known problem when device pairing is extended beyond a single resource device, such as a gateway, to other devices such a network-attached storage, home automation and A/V devices: Simple pairing forces the user to pair a general-purpose control point, such as a smart phone, with each of the devices it needs to control. To simplify this task for the user, Device Protection uses a gossip protocol among devices that offer services on the home network. Using this method, a control point that pairs with one resource device is *identified* to the other devices on the home network, but no authorization is established for the control point. It is necessary for an authorized administrator to set the authorization of the control point on other devices so as to avoid automatic authorization on all devices whenever pairing is done on one device.

4.3   TLS and X.509 v3 Digital Certificates

For authorizing resource requests, UPnP Device Protection uses X.509 v3 Digital Certificates and Transport Level Security (TLS) for on-the-wire protection. The resource and control-point devices create and self-sign their certificates, which are exchanged during the pairing process. As mentioned above, passwords may be used in addition to a digital certificate when user-level authentication is also desired.

The presence of standard certificates and Transport-Layer Security is of course transparent to the users, but these standards hopefully make deployment much simpler for the device vendor, who typically ships TLS and X.509 software and firmware in existing products. The fact that these are publicly developed and reviewed standards, moreover, improves the overall security of the Device Protection standard.

4.4   Peer-to-Peer Operation

In natural human relationships, an initial introduction process of some sort always takes place to establish mutual recognition and trust. Therefore, if we follow this natural model in the design of a security framework, the result will be easy to understand. For example, it is easy to understand pair-wise introduction of two devices someone intends to use together. If someone already has a networked media renderer such as a digital TV, and if they subsequently add a media server to their network, then it is intuitively clear that they want these two devices to discover and "talk to" each other. The natural model is for the user to "tell" one or both of the devices about the other at the time the new device is added to the network. Conversely, alternative models based on more complex concepts such as centralized authorities are inherently more difficult for most people to understand and use.

Some home-network security protocols use a third device for storing authorizations and performing authentication of requesters. The need to configure a third device for security was judged to be too much complexity for Device Protection and for the home user, who typically is unwilling to take additional steps to configure security in home and personal devices. There are also serious deployment challenges around security designs that require the presence of administrative devices on home networks because a device vendor cannot know in advance that a home network will include such a device. For these reasons, the use of a "registrar" as found in WiFi Protected Setup or a "security console" as found in UPnP Device Security 1.0 is forsaken in favor of a simpler model in which the device that owns the resource or service manages its own authorization and authentication.

There are cases where a resource device needs to have more capabilities than what is required for the "two-device" model. In the case of extending the pairing methods with a gossip protocol, for example, Device Protection requires that the resource device contain an embedded control-point that shares information about user devices that have been paired with it.

4.5   The Security of Device Protection

Device Protection uses WiFi Protected Setup and TLS standards. How these standards were applied and the specific parameters used have been subject to a considerable review, which is beyond the scope of this paper.

Ultimately, the security of a device rests on the choices made by vendors and users. If a vendor ships with a well-known password, then a user who does not change that password will not have a secure system; the Device Protection service provides some protection of preconfigured passwords by only allowing them to be used over a TLS connection authenticated by a prior pair-wise introduction. However, if a well-known password is also used to authenticate browser-based access to the device configuration, then the device will remain vulnerable to attack. Whether the vendor even offers Device Protection and how it offers it (e.g. without a downgrade vulnerability) are beyond the scope of Device Protection.

Much of the security of Device Protection rests on the standards that it uses: WiFi Protected Setup and TLS. Device Protection integrates these methods to support a three-tier authorization framework for UPnP Internet Gateway Device protocol and other UPnP DCPs. As described in this section, the default Device Protection policy introduces three privilege levels rather than all-or-nothing access.

5   Prior Work

Device Protection both builds on and replaces the earlier UPnP Device Security service [5]. DP replaces Device Security's "three device" security model by requiring only two devices to establish authorizations and perform authentication. Device Protection also uses X.509 v3 certificates whereas Device Security uses SPKI certificates. Moreover, Device Security was developed prior to the standardization of WiFi Protected Setup (WPS), and Device Protection uses WPS methods for pairing devices and establishing authorizations between devices.

The use of pair-wise introduction ceremonies is well established in WiFi Protected Setup (WPS), Apple TV™, and many other home and personal devices. There is a substantial body of innovative work on device pairing using short authentication strings, buttons, cameras, near-field communications and other methods [21, 14, 22, 23, 15].

In principle, Device Protection is extensible to encompass new pair-wise introduction methods, but only the WPS methods are available in the first release.

Device Protection reduces the number of pair-wise introduction ceremonies by means of a gossip protocol, which communicates namespace changes when an introduction ceremony succeeds and a device is added to a network of personal devices [11]. After the WPS exchange, Device Protection "gossips" [24] the identity of the new member to known UPnP devices; the Device Protection device communicates the change to its namespace (i.e. Control Point identities in its access control list) to previously introduced devices. There are issues with the correctness of "gossiped" information and with the revocation of information established through such means. Device Protection restricts the use of gossip to allow only the identification of a newly paired device and requires an additional administrative step to assign an authorization (i.e. a Device Protection role) to the gossiped identity. This is the default policy.

Device Protection policies are static; there is a pre-defined set of roles, default or otherwise; devices map roles onto allowable UPnP actions, and these assignments don't change once the UPnP device is provisioned and operational. More recent work considers pre-set policy "suites" that allow the user to select a category of policy for a particular authorization [25].

6 Conclusion

Defining an access control framework suitable for home use is extremely challenging for a variety of reasons. Home environments are more diverse than corporate IT environments both in terms of types of devices and in terms of technical expertise and motivation of the people who manage and use the devices. The mix of devices grows organically over time with no central planning of replacement cycles for upgrading equipment in a coordinated fashion. This means traditional notions of securing a "network" by upgrading all of the devices to support a new protocol are entirely inappropriate in a home environment. Furthermore, although home users often do care about security, they should not be expected to develop a deep understanding of security issues. The security properties of the network should emerge automatically from simple and intuitive actions and choices that relate directly to concepts that even technically non-technical users understand.

To address the usability, deployment, and security challenges of home networks, Device Protection has abandoned the centralized model and has instead embraced a fully-distributed model in which devices establish security relationships pair-wise as a result of a local introduction process using self-signed certificates and well-known protocols such as TLS and WPS. Device Protection also introduces a simple role-based policy framework with three default roles. This new UPnP service does not address all of the security risks in home networks, such as well-known passwords and PC malware, but it represents an important advance in addressing the risks associated with previously unprotected UPnP protocols.

The UPnP Forum has recently published the Device Protection specifications [4]. These specifications are part of the UPnP IGD version 2 release, which also includes IPv6 enablement of the gateway protocol.

Acknowledgements

Mika Saaranen of Nokia co-authored the Device Protection specification and chaired the UPnP Gateway Working Committee whose members also contributed much to this work.

References

1. U.S. Federal Bureau of Investigation, Internet Crime: Complaints and Losses on the Rise, Federal Bureau of Investigation (2009),
   http://www.fbi.gov/page2/march09/internet_033009.html
2. OECD, Malicious Software (Malware): A security threat to the Internet Economy, OECD Ministerial Meeting on the Future of the Internet Economy, DSTI/ICCP/REG(2007)5/FINAL, OECD / OCDE (2008),
   http://www.oecd.org/dataoecd/53/34/40724457.pdf
3. Lessig, L.: The Architecture of Privacy. In: Proceedings of Taiwan NET 1998, Taipei, Taiwan (1998),
   http://www.lessig.org/content/articles/works/architecture_priv.pdf
4. UPnP Forum, UPnP Device Protection (March 2, 2011),
   http://upnp.org/specs/gw/deviceprotection1
5. Ellison, C.: DeviceSecurity:1, UPnP Forum (2003),
   http://www.upnp.org/standardizeddcps/documents/DeviceSecurity_1.0cc_001.pdf
6. Gnu Citizen, http://www.gnucitizen.org/blog/flash-upnp-attack-faq
7. US-CERT Current Activity for (October 10, 2008), http://www.us-cert.gov/current/archive/2008/10/10/archive.html
8. Porras, P., Saidi, H., Yegneswaran, V.: An Anaysis of Conficker's logic and Rendezvous Points, SRI International (March 19, 2009), http://mtc.sri.com/Conficker/
9. Indian Computer Emergency Response Team, WIN32/Conficker (May 13, 2009),
   http://www.cert-in.org.in/virus/win32_conficker.htm
10. Hemel, A.: Universal Plug and Play: Dead simple or simply deadly. In: 5th System Administrator and Network Engineering Conference, SANE 2006 (May 15-19, 2006),
    http://www.sane.nl/sane2006/program/final-papers/R6.pdf
11. Ford, B.: UIA: A Global Connectivity Architecture for Mobile Personal Devices, PhD Thesis, MIT (2008), http://www.brynosaurus.com/pub/net/phd.pdf
12. Walker, J., Ellison, C.: UPnP Security Ceremonies Design Document (2003),
    http://www.upnp.org/download/standardizeddcps/UPnPSecurityCeremonies_1_0secure.pdf
13. Zimmermann, P., Johnston, A., Callas, J.: ZRTP: Media Path Key Agreement for Secure RTP, IETF RFC 6189 (2011)
14. Wi-Fi Protected Setup, Wikipedia (February 2009),
    http://en.wikipedia.org/wiki/Wi-Fi_Protected_Setup
15. Kobsa, A., Sonawalla, R., Tsudik, G., Uzun, E., Wang, Y.: Serial Hook-Ups: A Comparative Usability Study of Secure Device Pairing Methods. In: The Fifth Symposium on Usable Privacy and Security (2009)
16. Neumann, P.: Risks of Passwords (1994),
    http://portal.acm.org/citation.cfm?id=175289

17. Morris, R., Thompson, K.: Password security: A case history. Communications of the ACM 22(11), 594–597 (1979)
18. Elcomsoft Corporation News, ElcomSoft Breaks Wi-Fi Encryption Faster with GPU Acceleration (October 2008), http://www.elcomsoft.com/news/268.html
19. Stark, B. (ed.): LAN-Side DSL CPE Configuration, DSL Forum (2004), http://www.broadband-forum.org/technical/download/TR-064.pdf
20. Saltzer, J.H., Schroeder, M.D.: The Protection of Information in Computer Systems. Proceedings of the IEEE 63, 1278–1308 (1975)
21. Stajano, F., Anderson, R.: The Resurrecting Duckling: Security Issues for Ad-hoc Wireless Networks. In: 7th International Workshop on Security Protocols, vol. (1796). Springer, Heidelberg (1999)
22. McCune, J.M., Perrig, A., Reiter, M.K.: Seeing is Believing: Using Camera Phones for Human-Verifiable Authentication. In: IEEE Symposium on Security and Privacy (2005)
23. Vaudenay, S.: Secure communications over insecure channels based on short authenticated strings. In: Shoup, V. (ed.) CRYPTO 2005. LNCS, vol. 3621, pp. 309–326. Springer, Heidelberg (2005)
24. Demers, A., et al.: Epidemic algorithms for replicated database maintenance. In: 6th ACM Symposium on Principles of Distributed Computing, pp. 1–12 (1987)
25. Kim, T.H., Bauer, L., Newsome, J., Perrig, A., Walker, J.: Challenges in Access Right Assignment for Secure Home Networks. In: Proceedings of the 5th USENIX Workshop on Hot Topics in Security, HotSec (August 10, 2010)

Contego: Capability-Based Access Control for Web Browsers

(Short Paper)

Tongbo Luo and Wenliang Du*

Department of Electrical Engineering & Computer Science,
Syracuse University, Syracuse, New York, USA
{toluo,wedu}@syr.edu

Abstract. Over the last two decades, the Web has significantly transformed our lives. Along with the increased activities on the Web come the attacks. A recent report shows that 83% of web sites have had at least one serious vulnerability. As the Web becomes more and more sophisticated, the number of vulnerable sites is unlikely to decrease. A fundamental cause of these vulnerabilities is the inadequacy of the browser's access control model in dealing with the features in today's Web. We need better access control models for browsers.

Today's web pages behave more and more like a system, with dynamic elements interacting with one another within each web page. A well-designed access control model is needed to mediate these interactions to ensure security. The capability-based access control model has many properties that are desirable for the Web. This paper designs a capability-based access control model for web browsers. We demonstrate how such a model can be beneficial to the Web, and how common vulnerabilities can be easily prevented using this model. We have implemented this model in the Google Chrome browser.

1 Introduction

Over the last two decades since the Web was invented, the progress of its development has been tremendous. From the early day's static web pages to today's highly dynamic and interactive ones, the Web has evolved a lot. During the technology evolution, security has often been overlooked. A recent report produced by WhiteHat Security indicates that 83% of websites *have had* at least one serious vulnerability, 64% *currently have* at least one serious vulnerability, and the average number of serious vulnerabilities per website is 16.7 [13]. These numbers are quite alarming.

A fundamental cause for many of these problems is the browser's failure to mediate the interactions within each web page. In terms of access control, the Web has adopted a policy called Same-Origin Policy (SOP), which gives all the contents from the same origin the same privileges. Such a policy, sufficient for early day's Web, is not appropriate anymore. The inadequacy of these access control models has been pointed out by various studies [1, 2, 4, 7, 8, 10, 12]. A fundamental problem of SOP is in its coarse

* This work was supported by Award No. 1017771 from the US National Science Foundation.

J.M. McCune et al. (Eds.): TRUST 2011, LNCS 6740, pp. 231–238, 2011.

granularity. Today's web page can simultaneously contain contents with varying levels of trustworthiness. For example, advertisements from a third party and inputs from users are less trustworthy than the first-party contents produced by the websites themselves. These untrusted contents should not be given the same privileges as those trusted first-party contents.

To solve the access control problems faced by SOP, our earlier work, Escudo [5], proposes a ring access control model for web browsers. This model allows web application servers to put contents in different rings, based on their trustworthiness: contents that are more trustworthy are put in the higher privileged rings. Escudo ensures that contents in the lower-privileged rings cannot access contents in the higher-privileged rings. While Escudo has helpped solve a number of security problems on the Web, its granularity on privileges is not fine enough.

There are two typical types of privileges within a web page. One is the privileges to access certain objects, we call these privileges the *object-based privileges*. The other type is the privileges to access certain actions, such as invoking AJAX APIs, issuing HTTP POST requests, accessing cookies, etc. Whether a principal can access these actions or not has security consequences. We call this type of privileges the *action-based privileges*. Escudo can deal with the object-based privileges quite well, but it is inappropriate for controlling the action-based privileges, because no specific objects are associated to the action-based privileges. As a result, a principal in Escudo basically has all the action-based privileges entitled to its origin, regardless of which ring it is in. This is undesirable according to the least-privilege principle: if a Javascript code from a semi-trusted third party only needs to send HTTP GET requests, we should not give this code the privilege to invoke AJAX APIs or send HTTP POST requests.

To secure the Web, controlling the uses of action-based privileges must be built into the browser's access control model. This objective can be achieved using capability-based access control. The main idea of capability is to define a "token" (called capability) for each privilege; a principal needs to possess the corresponding tokens if it wants to use certain privileges. Because of these fine-grained capabilities, we can assign the least amount of privileges to principals.

The Web has evolved to a stage where it becomes too risky to assign all the action-based privileges to the principals within a web page. These privileges should be separated, and assigned to principals based on their needs and trustworthiness. The same-origin policy model does not separate these privileges, neither does Escudo. To handle the web applications with ever-increasing complexity and to reduce the risks of web applications, we believe that web browsers should adopt the capability model in its access control. As a first step towards this direction, we have designed Contego, a capability-based access control system for web browsers; we have implemented our design in the Google Chrome browser, and have conducted case studies using our implementation. Due to the page limitation, details of the case studies are not included in this paper; they can be found in the extended version of the paper [9].

2   Capability for Browsers

Access control is the ability to decide who can do what to whom in a system. An access-control system consists of three components: principals, objects, and an access-control model. Principals (the who) are the entities in the system that can manipulate resources. Objects (the whom) are the resources in the system that require controlled access. An access-control model describes how access decisions are made in the system; the expression of a set of rules within the model is an access-control policy (the what). A systematic design of an access-control model should first identify the principals and objects in the system.

Principals in a web page are elements that can initiate actions. There are several types of principals inside a web page: (1) Dynamic contents, such as Javascript code, are obvious principals. (2) Many HTML tags in a web page can initiate actions, such as a, img, form, iframes, button, meta[1], etc. These tags are considered as principals. (3) Plugins can also initiate actions, so are also considered as principals. Objects include everything in a web page or those associated with a web page. DOM objects are obviously considered as objects in our access control system. Cookies are another type of objects.

There are three major components in a capability-based access control: the list of capabilities supported by the system, how capabilities are binded to principals, and how access control is enforced. We will discuss each of these components in this section.

2.1 Capabilities

Learning from the history of capability design in Linux, we know that the development of capabilities is an evolving process: in this process, rarely used capabilities may be eliminated, more desirable capabilities may be added, new privileges may be introduced, and so on. Therefore, we do not intend to come up with a list of capabilities that are complete. We consider our efforts of introducing capabilities in web browsers only as the first step in such an evolution. In this initial step, we have identified a list of capabilities. They are classified into five categories:

- *Access sensitive resources*: bookmarks, cookies, certificates, HTML5 local storage, and custom protocol handlers.
- *Access history resources*: web cache, history, downloaded item, etc.
- *Access DOM elements*, such as whether a principal is allowed to access DOM objects, register an event handler, or to access the attribute settings of DOM objects.
- *Send HTTP Requests*, Ajax GET/POST and HTTP GET/POST requests.
- *Execute Javascript or plug-in programs*, including Flash, PDF, video, audio, etc.

As a proof of concept, we have only implemented a subset of the above capabilities in our prototype, including capabilities to set cookies, read cookies, use cookies (i.e. attaching cookies to HTTP requests), capabilities to send AJAX GET/POST requests, capabilities to send HTTP GET/POST requests, and capabilities to click hyperlinks and buttons. We use a bitmap string to represent capability lists, with each bit of the bitmap string representing one specific capability.

---

[1] The meta tag is supposed to be put in the header of a web page only, but most web browsers accept it if it is embedded in the body of the page.

2.2   Binding of Capabilities

To use capabilities in access control within a web page, web developers, when constructing a web page, need to assign capabilities to the principals in the page, based on the actual needs of principals. As we have discussed before, principals are DOM elements of a web page. In Escudo, the HTML div tag is used for assigning the ring label to each DOM element. HTML div tags were originally introduced to specify style information for a group of HTML tags; Escudo introduces a new attribute called the ring attribute for the div tag. To be consistent with Escudo, we take the same approach. We add another attribute called cap for the div tag. This attribute assigns a capability list to all the DOM elements within the region enclosed by its corresponding div and /div tags. An example is given in the following:

```
<div cap="11000110"> ... contents ...  </div>
```

In the above example, the privileges of the contents within the specified div region are bounded by capabilities 1, 2, 6, and 7; namely no DOM elements within this region can have any capability beyond these four.

2.3   Capability Enforcement

Enforcement in capability-based access control is well defined in the capability model: an access action is allowed only if the initiating principal has the corresponding capability. The main challenge in a capability system is to identify the initiating principals and their associated capabilities. In general, identifying principals is not so difficult: whenever an action is initiated (either by Javascript code or by HTML tags), the browser can easily identify the div region of the code or tags, and can thus retrieve the capabilities binded to this region. Unfortunately, as a proverb says, the devil is in the details; identifying principals is quite non-trivial. We describe details of capability enforcement in the Implementation section.

2.4   Ensuring Security

The key to capability enforcement is the integrity of the configuration (i.e., capability assignment) provided by the application. We describe additional measures to prevent the configuration from being tampered with.

Configuration Rule: Protecting against Node Splitting. Any security configuration that relies on HTML tags are vulnerable to node-splitting attacks [6]. In a node-splitting attack, an attacker may prematurely terminate a div region using </div>, and then start a new div region with a different set of capability assignments (potentially with higher privileges). This attack escapes the privilege restriction set on a div region by web developers. Node-splitting attacks can be prevented by using the markup randomization techniques, such as incorporating random nonces in the div tags [3, 11]. Contego-enhanced browsers will ignore any </div> tag whose random nonce does not match the number in its matching div tag. The random nonces are dynamically generated when a web page is constructed, so adversaries cannot predict them before inserting malicious contents into a web page.

Scoping Rule. When contents are from users, they are usually put into div regions with limited privileges. However, user contents may also include div tags with the capability attribute. If web applications cannot filter out these tags, attackers will be able to create a child div region with an arbitrary list of capabilities. To prevent such a privilege-escalation attack, Contego defines the following *scoping rule*: The actual capabilities of a DOM element is always bounded by the capabilities of its parent. Formally speaking, if a div region has a capability list L, the privileges of the principals within the scope of this div tag, including all sub scopes, are bounded by L.

Access Rule for Node Creation/Modification. Using DOM APIs, Javascript programs can create new or modify existing DOM elements in any div region. To prevent a principal from escalating its privileges by creating new or modify existing DOM elements in a higher privileged region, Contego enforces the following access rule: A principal with capabilities L can create a new or modify an existing DOM element in another div region with capabilities L' if L' is a subset of L, i.e., the target region has less privilege than the principal.

Cross-Region Execution Rule. In most web applications, Javascript functions are often put in several different places in the same HTML page. When a Javascript program from one div region (with privilege $\mathcal{A}$) invokes a function in another div region (with privilege $\mathcal{B}$), Contego enforces the following rule: when the function is invoked, the privilege of the running program becomes the conjunction of $\mathcal{A}$ and $\mathcal{B}$, i.e., $\mathcal{A} \wedge \mathcal{B}$. Namely, the privilege will be downgraded if $\mathcal{B}$ has less privilege than $\mathcal{A}$. After the function returns back to the caller, the privilege of the running program will be restored to $\mathcal{A}$ again.

3   Implementation

3.1   System Overview

We have implemented Contego in the Google Chrome browser[2]. In Chrome, there are four major components related to our implementation: Browser Process (Kernel), Render Engine, Javascript Interpreter (V8), and sensitive resources. We added two sub-systems: *Binding System*, and *Capability Enforcement System*. Figure 1 depicts the positions of our additions within Chrome. We also evaluated our model on multiple web applications; see our full paper [9] for details.

Binding System. The purpose of the binding system is to find the capabilities of a principal, and store them in data structures where the enforcement module can access. The capability information of each principal is stored inside the browser core. Only the browser's code can access the capability information; the information is not exposed to any code external to the browser's code base (e.g. Javascript code).

Effective Capabilities. When an access action is initiated within a web page, to conduct access control, the browser needs to know the corresponding capabilities of this

---

[2] We use Version 3.0.182.1. We plan to port our implementation to the most recent version.

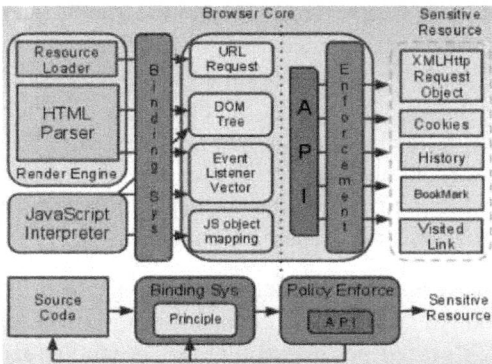

Fig. 1. System Overview

access. We call these capabilities the *effective capabilities*. Identifying effective capabilities is nontrivial: in the simplest case, the effective capabilities are those attached to the principal that initiates the action. Javascript code makes the situation much more complicated. A key functionality of our binding system is to keep track of the effective capabilities within a web page. We will present the details later in this section.

Capability Enforcement. Our implementation takes advantage of the fact that every user-level access to sensitive resources goes through the browser kernel, precisely, through the local APIs. When they are invoked, the enforcement system checks whether the effective capabilities have the required capabilities for the invoked APIs.

Actions. Within a web page, there are several types of actions. For each type, when it takes place, we need to identify the *effective capabilities* that should be applied to the actions. We discuss these different types of actions in the following subsections.

3.2 HTML-Induced Actions

Some actions are triggered by HTML tags. The effective capabilities of these HTML-induced actions are the capabilities assigned to the tag's `div` region. These capabilities will be extracted by the HTML parser, delivered to the binding system, and stored in a *shadow DOM* tree. This shadow DOM tree stores capabilities of each DOM node, and it can only be accessed by the binding system. Although Javascript programs can modify the attributes of DOM objects through various APIs, these APIs cannot be used to modify the capability attributes, because the values of the capability attributes are stored in the shadow tree, not the original tree; no shadow-tree API is exposed to Javascript. When an action is initiated from an HTML tag, the enforcement system identifies its DOM object, retrieves the capabilities from its shadow object, and finally checks whether the capabilities are sufficient. If not, the action will not be carried out.

3.3 Javascript-Induced Actions

Some actions are triggered by Javascript code. Identifying the effective capabilities of these Javascript-induced actions is quite complicated. This is because a running sequence of Javascript can span *multiple* principals with different sets of capabilities. The system will trace the executing principal and record the effective capabilities. We use a stack data structure in our binding system to store the effective capabilities in the runtime (we call it the capability stack). When a Javascript program gets executed, the capabilities of the corresponding principal will be pushed into the stack as the first element of the stack. The top element of the stack is treated as the *effective capabilities*, denoted as E. When code in another principal (say principal B) is invoked, the updated effective capabilities $E \wedge Cap(B)$ will be pushed into the stack, where $Cap(B)$ represents the capabilities assigned to B. When the code in B returns, the system will pop up and discard the top element of the stack.

3.4 Event-Driven Actions

Some actions are triggered by events, not directly by principals. When these actions are triggered, we need to find the capabilities of the responsible principals. Some events are statically registered via HTML code; for them, it is quite easy to find their principals by identifying the DOM nodes they belong to. Many other events are however registered dynamically, during the runtime, such as timer events, AJAX callback events, and those dynamically registered to DOM objects by Javascript code. Since the principals can be easily identified during registration, Contego binds the capabilities of the principals to the event handlers when the handlers are registered to events. Therefore, when these events are triggered, Contego can retrieve the capabilities from the event handlers.

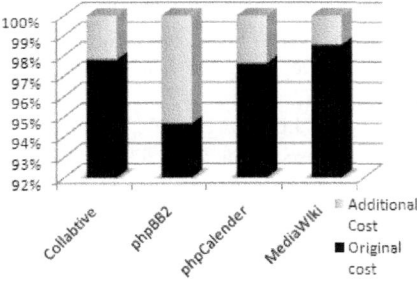

Fig. 2. Performance

3.5 Performance Overhead

To evaluate the performance of our implementation, we have conducted experiments to measure the extra cost our model brings to the Chrome. We measured how long it takes a page to be rendered in our modified browser versus in the original browser. We used some of the built-in tools in Chrome to conduct the measurement. In our evaluation, we tested four web applications: Collabtive, phpBB2, phpCalendar and MediaWiki; we measured the total time spent on rendering pages and executing Javascript code. The configuration of the computer is the following: Inter(R) Core(TM)2 Quad CPU Q6600 @ 2.40GHz, 3.24 GB of RAM. The results are plotted in Figure 2.

The results show that the extra cost caused by the model is quite small. In most cases, it is around three percent. For phpBB2, it is a little bit higher, because phpBB2 uses more Javascript programs than the others.

4 Conclusion and Future Work

To enhance the security infrastructure of the Web, we have designed a capability-based access control for web browsers. This access control model, widely adopted in operating systems, provides a finer granularity than the existing models in browsers. We have implemented this model in Google Chrome. Using case studies, we have demonstrated that many of the hard-to-defend attacks faced by the Web can be easily defended using the capability-based access control model within the browser. The full details of this work can be found in the extended version of the paper [9].

References

1. Crockford, D.: ADSafe, http://www.adsafe.org
2. Dalton, M., Kozyrakis, C., Zeldovich, N.: Nemesis: Preventing authentication & access control vulnerabilities inweb applications. In: Proceedings of the Eighteenth Usenix Security Symposium (Usenix Security), Montreal, Canada (2009)
3. Gundy, M.V., Chen, H.: Noncespaces: Using randomization to enforce information flow tracking and thwart cross-site scripting attacks. In: Proceedings of the 16th Annual Network and Distributed System Security Symposium (NDSS), San Diego, CA (February 2009)
4. Jackson, C., Bortz, A., Boneh, D., Mitchell, J.C.: Protecting browser state from web privacy attacks. In: WWW 2006 (2006)
5. Jayaraman, K., Du, W., Rajagopalan, B., Chapin, S.J.: Escudo: A fine-grained protection model for web browsers. In: Proceedings of the 30th International Conference on Distributed Computing Systems (ICDCS), Genoa, Italy (June 21-25, 2010)
6. Jim, T., Swamy, N., Hicks, M.: Defeating script injection attacks with browser-enforced embedded policies. In: WWW 2007,
7. Karlof, C., Shankar, U., Tygar, J.D., Wagner, D.: Dynamic pharming attacks and locked same-origin policies for web browsers. In: CCS 2007 (2007)
8. Livshits, B., Erlingsson, U.: Using web application construction frameworks to protect against code injection attacks. In: PLAS 2007 (2007)
9. Luo, T., Du., W.: Contego: Capability-based access control for web browsers (full version), http://www.cis.syr.edu/~wedu/Research/paper/contego_full.pdf
10. Meyerovich, L.A., Livshits, V.B.: Conscript: Specifying and enforcing fine-grained security policies for javascript in the browser. In: IEEE Symposium on Security and Privacy, pp. 481–496 (2010)
11. Nadji, Y., Saxena, P., Song, D.: Document structure integrity: A robust basis for cross-site scripting defense. In: Proceedings of the 16th Annual Network and Distributed System Security Symposium (NDSS), San Diego, CA (February 2009)
12. Parno, B., McCune, J.M., Wendlandt, D., Andersen, D.G., Perrig, A.: CLAMP: Practical prevention of large-scale data leaks. In: Proc. IEEE Symposium on Security and Privacy, Oakland, CA (May 2009)
13. WhiteHat Security. Whitehat website security statistic report, 10th edn. (2010)

Efficient Techniques for Privacy-Preserving Sharing of Sensitive Information

Emiliano De Cristofaro, Yanbin Lu, and Gene Tsudik

University of California, Irvine
{edecrist,yanbinl,gts}@uci.edu

Abstract. The need for privacy-preserving sharing of sensitive information occurs in many different and realistic everyday scenarios, ranging from national security to social networking. A typical setting involves two parties: one seeks information from the other without revealing the interest while the latter is either willing, or compelled, to share only the requested information. This poses two challenges: (1) how to enable sharing such that parties learn no information beyond what they are entitled to, and (2) how to do so efficiently, in real-world practical terms. This paper explores the notion of Privacy-Preserving Sharing of Sensitive Information (PPSSI), and provides a concrete and efficient instantiation, modeled in the context of simple database querying. Proposed approach functions as a *privacy shield* to protect parties from disclosing more than the required minimum of their respective sensitive information. PPSSI deployment prompts several challenges, which are addressed in this paper. Extensive experimental results attest to the practicality of attained privacy features and show that our approach incurs quite low overhead (e.g., 10% slower than standard MySQL).

1   Introduction

In today's increasingly digital world, there is often a tension between safeguarding privacy and sharing information. Although, in general, sensitive data clearly needs to be kept confidential, data owners are often motivated, or forced, to share sensitive information. Consider several examples:

- *Aviation Safety:* The US Department of Homeland Security (DHS) checks whether any passengers on each flight from/to the United States must be denied boarding or disembarkation, based on several secret lists, including the *Terror Watch List* (TWL). Today, airlines surrender their passenger manifests to the DHS, along with a large amount of sensitive information, including credit card numbers [6]. Besides its obvious privacy implications, this modus operandi poses liability issues with regard to (mostly) innocent passengers' data and concerns about possible data loss.[1] Ideally, the DHS would obtain information pertaining *only* to passengers on one of its watch-lists, without disclosing any information to the airlines.

---

[1] See [3] for a litany of recent incidents where large amounts sensitive data were lost or mishandled by government agencies.

J.M. McCune et al. (Eds.): TRUST 2011, LNCS 6740, pp. 239–253, 2011.
© Springer-Verlag Berlin Heidelberg 2011

- *Law Enforcement:* An investigative agency (e.g., the FBI) needs to obtain electronic information about a suspect from other agencies, e.g., the local police, the military, the DMV, the IRS, or the suspect's employer. In many cases, it is dangerous (or simply forbidden) for the FBI to disclose the subjects of its investigation. Whereas, the other party cannot disclose its entire data-set and trust the FBI to only obtain desired information. Furthermore, FBI requests might need to be pre-*authorized* by some appropriate authority, e.g., a federal judge. This way, the FBI can only obtain information related to legitimate authorized requests.
- *Healthcare:* A health insurance company needs to retrieve information about its client from other insurance carriers and/or hospitals. The latter cannot provide any information on other patients and the former cannot disclose the identity of the target client.

Other examples of sensitive information sharing include collaborative botnet detection [22], where parties share their logs for the sole purpose of identifying common anomalies.

Motivated by these examples, this paper develops the architecture for **Privacy-Preserving Sharing of Sensitive Information (PPSSI)**, and proposes one efficient and secure instantiation that functions as a *privacy shield* to protect parties from disclosing more than the required minimum of sensitive information. We model PPSSI in the context of simple database-querying applications with two parties: a *server* that has a database, and a *client*, performing simple disjunctive equality queries. In terms of the airline safety example above, the airline (server) has a database with passenger information, while DHS (client) poses queries corresponding to its TWL.

Intended Contributions. We explore the notion of Privacy-Preserving Sharing of Sensitive Information (PPSSI). Our main building blocks are Private Set Intersection (PSI) techniques. As part of PPSSI design, we address several challenges stemming from adapting PSI to realistic database settings. In particular, we propose a novel encryption method to handle "multi-sets" and "data pointers" challenges and propose a new architecture with an *Isolated Box* to deal with "bandwidth" and "liability" challenges. Our experimental evaluation demonstrates that our approach incurs very low overhead: about 10% slower than standard (not privacy-preserving) MySQL. All source code is publicly available.[2]

Organization. The next section introduces the PPSSI syntax and privacy requirements as well as PSI terminology. After reviewing related work in Section 3, Section 4 discusses the inadequacy of a strawman approach obtained via naïve adaptation of PSI techniques to PPSSI. Then, Section 5 develops a secure PPSSI architecture and addresses all challenges shown in the strawman approach. Section 6 presents experimental results, and Section 7 concludes this paper.

---

[2] Source code is available at http://sprout.ics.uci.edu/projects/iarpa-app/index.php?page=code.php

2   Preliminaries

This section introduces PPSSI and overviews PSI techniques.

2.1   PPSSI Syntax and Notation

PPSSI can be viewed in the context of simple database querying. A server maintains a database, DB, containing w records with m attributes $(attr_1, \cdots, attr_m)$. We denote $DB = \{(R_j)\}_{j=1}^{w}$. Each record $R_j = \{val_{j,l}\}_{l=1}^{m}$, where $val_{j,l}$ is R_j's value for attribute $attr_l$. A client poses simple disjunctive SQL queries, such as:

$$\text{SELECT * FROM DB WHERE } (attr_1^* = val_1^* \text{ OR } \cdots \text{ OR } attr_v^* = val_v^*) \quad (1)$$

As a result of its query, the client gets all records in DB satisfying *where* clause, and nothing else. Whereas, the server learns nothing about any $\{attr_i^*, val_i^*\}_{1 \leq i \leq v}$. We assume that the database schema (format) is known to the client. Furthermore, without loss of generality, we assume that the client only queries searchable attributes.

In an alternative version supporting *authorized queries*, we require the client to obtain query authorizations from a mutually trusted offline *Certification Authority* (CA) prior to interacting with the server. That is, the client learns matching records only if it has pertinent authorizations for $(attr_i^*, val_i^*)$.

Our notation is reflected in Table 1. In addition, we use $Enc_k(\cdot)$ and $Dec_k(\cdot)$ to denote, respectively, symmetric key encryption and decryption, under key k. Public key encryption and decryption, under keys pk and sk, are denoted as $E_{pk}(\cdot)$ and $E_{sk}(\cdot)^{-1}$, respectively. $\sigma = \mathsf{Sign}_{sk}(M)$ is a digital signature computed over message M using secret key sk. Operation $\mathsf{Vrfy}_{pk}(\sigma, M)$ returns 1 or 0 indicating whether σ is a valid signature on M. $\mathbb{Z}_N^*$ refers to a composite-order RSA group, where N is the RSA modulus. We use d to denote RSA private key and e to denote corresponding public key. We use $\mathbb{Z}_p^*$ to denote a cyclic group with a subgroup of order q, where p and q are large primes, and $q|p - 1$. Let G_0, G_1 be two multiplicative cyclic groups of prime order p. We use $\hat{e} : G_0 \times G_0 \rightarrow G_1$ to denote a bilinear map. $ZKPK$ denotes zero-knowledge proof of knowledge. We use $H(\cdot), H_1(\cdot), H_2(\cdot), H_3(\cdot)$ to denote different hash functions. In practice, we implement $H(m), H_1(m), H_2(m), H_3(m)$ as $\text{SHA-1}(0||m), \text{SHA-1}(1||m), \text{SHA-1}(2||m), \text{SHA-1}(3||m)$.

2.2   Adversary Model

We consider both Honest-but-Curious (HbC) adversaries and malicious adversaries. An HbC adversary is assumed to faithfully follow all protocol's specifications. However, it attempts to infer additional information during or after protocol execution. Whereas, a malicious adversary might arbitrarily deviate from the protocol.

Table 1. Notation

$attr_l$	lth attribute in the database schema	$ctr_{j,l}$	number of times where $val_{j',l} = val_{j,l}, \forall j' <= j$
R_j	jth record in the database	$tag_{j,l}$	tag for $attr_l, val_{j,l}$
$val_{j,l}$	value in R_j corresponding to $attr_l$	$k'_{j,l}$	key used to encrypt k_j
k_j	key used to encrypt R_j	$k''_{j,l}$	key used to encrypt index j
er_j	encryption of R_j	$ek_{j,l}$	encryption of key k_j
$tk_{j,l}$	token evaluated over $attr_l, val_{j,l}$	$eind_{j,l}$	encryption of index j

2.3 Privacy Requirements

– *Server Privacy.* The client learns no information about any record in server's database that does not satisfy the *where* $(attr_i^* = val_i^*)$ clause(s).
– *Server Privacy (Authorized Queries).* Same as "Server Privacy" above, but, in addition, the client learns no information about any record satisfying the *where* $(attr_i^* = val_i^*)$ clause, unless the $(attr_i^*, val_i^*)$ query is authorized by the CA.
– *Client Privacy.* The server learns nothing about any client query parameters, i.e., all $attr_i^*$ and val_i^*, nor about its authorizations, (for authorized queries).
– *Client Unlinkability.* The server cannot determine (with probability non-negligibly exceeding $1/2$) whether any two client queries are related.
– *Server Unlinkability.* For any two queries, the client cannot determine whether any record in the server's database has changed, except for the records that are learned (by the client) as a result of both queries.
– *Forward Security (Authorized Queries).* The client cannot violate Server Privacy with regard to prior interactions, using authorizations obtained later.

Note that Forward Security and Unlinkability requirements are crucial in many practical scenarios. Referring to the second example in Section 1, suppose that FBI agent frivolously queries a company's employee database without having authorization for an individual, e.g., Alice. Server Privacy (Authorized Queries) ensures that FBI does not obtain any information about Alice. However, unless Forward Security is guaranteed, if FBI later obtains authorization for Alice, it could inappropriately recover her file from the (recorded) protocol transcript. Whereas, Unlinkability keeps one party from noticing changes in other party's input. In particular, unless Server Unlinkability is guaranteed, the client can always detect whether the server updates its database between two interactions. Unlinkability also minimizes the risk of privacy leaks. Without Client Unlinkability, if the server learns that the client's queries are the same in two interactions and one of these query's contents are leaked, the other query would be immediately exposed.

2.4 Private Set Intersection (PSI)

PSI [12] constitutes our main building block. It allows two parties – server and client – to interact on their respective input sets, such that the client only learns the intersection of the two sets, while the server learns nothing beyond client's set size. Below, we review two recent PSI variants [17,7]. They involve linear communication and computational complexities, in terms of client and server set sizes.

PSI with Data Transfer (PSI-DT): involves a server, on input a set of w items, each with associated data record, $S = \{(s_1, data_1), \cdots, (s_w, data_w)\}$, and a client, on input of a set of v items, $C = \{c_1, \cdots, c_v\}$. It results in the client outputting $\{(s_j, data_j) \in S \mid \exists c_i \in C \text{ s.t. } c_i = s_j\}$ and the server – nothing except v. PSI-DT is useful whenever the server holds a set of records, rather than a simple set of elements.

Authorized PSI-DT (APSI-DT): ensures that client input is *authorized* by a mutually trusted offline CA. Unless it holds pertinent authorizations, the client does not learn whether its input is in the intersection. At the same time, the server does not learn whether client's input is authorized, i.e., verification of client's authorizations is performed obliviously. More specifically, APSI-DT involves a server, on input of a set of w items: $S = \{(s_1, data_1), \cdots, (s_w, data_w)\}$, and a client, on input of a set of v items with associated authorizations (typically, in the form of digital signatures), $C = \{(c_1, \sigma_1) \cdots, (c_v, \sigma_v)\}$. It results in client outputting $\{(s_j, data_j) \in S \mid \exists (c_i, \sigma_i) \in C \text{ s.t. } c_i = s_j \wedge \mathsf{Vrfy}_{pk}(\sigma_i, c_i) = 1\}$ (where pk is CA's public key).

We also distinguish between (A)PSI-DT protocols based on whether or not they support *pre-distribution*:

(A)PSI-DT with pre-distribution: The server can "pre-process" its input independently from client input. This way, the server can *pre-distribute* its (processed) input before protocol execution. Both pre-processing and pre-distribution can be done offline, once for all possible clients.

(A)PSI-DT without pre-distribution: The server cannot pre-process and pre-distribute its input.

Note that pre-distribution precludes Server Unlinkability, since server input is assumed to be fixed. Similarly, in the context of authorized protocols with pre-distribution, Forward Security cannot be guaranteed.

3   Related Work

A number of cryptographic primitives provide privacy properties resembling those listed in Section 2.3. We overview them below.

Secure Two-Party Computation (2PC). 2PC allows two parties, on input x and y, respectively, to privately compute the output of a public function f over (x, y). Both parties learn nothing beyond what can be inferred from the output of the computation. Although one could implement PPSSI with generic 2PC, it is usually far more efficient to have dedicated protocols, as 2PC incurs high computational overhead and involves several communication rounds.

Oblivious Transfer (OT). OT [24] involves a sender holding n secret messages and a receiver willing to retrieve the i-th sender's message. OT ensures that the sender does not learn which message is retrieved, and the receiver learns no other messages. While the OT functionality resembles PPSSI requirements, note that, in PPSSI, receiver's inputs are queries, whereas, in OT, they are indexes.

Private Information Retrieval (PIR). PIR [5] allows a client to retrieve an item from a server database while not revealing which item it is retrieving, with communication overhead strictly lower than $O(n)$, where n is database size. In PIR, server database is not private – the client may receive additional information, besides specific records requested. Symmetric PIR (SPIR) [13] also offers server privacy, thus achieving OT with communication overhead lower than $O(n)$. However, similar to OT, the client in symmetric PIR needs to input the index of the desired item in server's database – an unrealistic assumption for PPSSI. An extension supporting keyword-based retrieval is known as Keyword-PIR (KPIR) [4]. However, it does not consider server privacy and involves multiple rounds of PIR.

Searchable Encryption (SE). Symmetric Searchable Encryption (SSE) [25] allows the client to store, on an untrusted server, messages encrypted using a symmetric-key cipher under its own secret key. Later, the client can search for specific keywords by giving the server a trapdoor that does not reveal keywords or plaintexts. Boneh et al. [2] extended SSE to the public-key setting, i.e., anyone can use client's public key to encrypt and route messages through an untrusted server (e.g., a mail server). The client can then generate search tokens, based on its private key, to let the server identify messages including specific keywords. We conclude that Searchable Encryption is targeted at related yet different scenarios from PPSSI.

Privacy-Preserving Database Querying (PPDQ). PPDQ techniques can be partitioned into two types. One is similar to SSE: the client encrypts its data and outsources it to the untrusted server for subsequent querying. In addition to simple equality predicates supported by SSE, techniques such as [14,16] support more general SQL operations. The setting is different from PPSSI, since data, although stored at the server, belongs to the client. Thus, there is no privacy restriction against the client. Moreover, these techniques do not offer provable security guarantees, as they are based on statistical methods.

The second types of PPDQ is closely related to private predicate matching. Olumofin and Goldberg [23] propose a transition from block-based PIR to SQL-enabled PIR. In contrast with PPSSI, server database is assumed to be public. Kantarcioğlu and Clifton [18] consider a scenario where client matches classification rules against server's database. However, they assume the client's rule set is fixed *a priori* and known to the server. Murugesan et al. [21] also allow "fuzzy" matching. However, it requires a number of (expensive) cryptographic operations (i.e., public-key homomorphic operations) quadratic in the size of parties' inputs. Whereas, our goal is to construct scalable techniques with linear complexity.

4   A Strawman Approach

Based on the definitions in Section 2.4, it seems that PPSSI can be trivially realized by applying efficient PSI-DT protocols, or APSI-DT for authorized queries. We outline this *strawman* approach below and show that it is insecure.

For each record, consider the hash of every attribute-value pair $(attr_l, val_{j,l})$ as a set element, and R_j as its associated data. Server "set" then becomes:

$$\mathcal{S} = \{(H(attr_l, val_{j,l}), R_j)\}_{1 \leq l \leq m, 1 \leq j \leq w}$$

Client "set" is: $\mathcal{C} = \{H(attr_i^*, val_i^*)\}_{1 \leq i \leq v}$, i.e., elements corresponding to the *where* clause in Equation 1. Optionally, if authorized queries are enforced, $\mathcal{C}$ is accompanied by signatures σ_i over $H(attr_i^*, val_i^*)$, following the APSI-DT syntax. Parties engage in an (A)PSI-DT protocol, at the end of which, the client obtains all records matching its query.

The strawman approach has four security issues:

Challenge 1: Multi-Sets. While most databases include duplicate values (e.g., "gender=male" or "age=33"), PSI-DT and APSI-DT definitions assume distinct set elements.[3] If server set contains duplicated values, corresponding messages (e.g. PRF outputs computed over duplicate values) to the client would be identical and the client would learn all patterns and distribution frequencies. This is a serious concern, since actual values can be often inferred from their frequencies. For example, if the database has an attribute "patient blood type", since blood type frequencies are well-known for general population, frequency distribution of this attribute would essentially reveal the plaintext.

Challenge 2: Data Pointers. To enable querying by any attribute, each record R_j must be separately encrypted m times, once for each query-able attribute. Since this would result in high storage/bandwidth overhead, we could encrypt each R_j with a unique symmetric key k_j and then use k_j (instead of R_j) as data associated with $H(attr_l, val_{j,l})$. Although this would reduce overhead, it would trigger another issue: in order to use the key – rather than the actual record – as the associated "data" in the (A)PSI-DT protocol, we would need to store a pointer to the encrypted record alongside each $H(attr_l, val_{j,l})$. This would allow the client to determine all $H(attr_l, val_{j,l})$ corresponding to a given encrypted record by simply identifying all $H(attr_l, val_{j,l})$ with associated data pointers equal to the given record. Such a (potential) privacy leak would be aggravated if combined with the previous "attack" on multi-sets: given two encrypted records, the client could establish their similarity based on the number of identical attributes.

Challenge 3: Bandwidth. If server database is very large and/or communication takes place over a slow channel, bandwidth overhead incurred by encrypted database transfer may become prohibitive.

---

[3] Note that some PSI constructs (e.g., [20]) support multi-sets, however, their performance is relatively poor, as they incur quadratic computational overhead, as opposed to more recent (A)PSI-DT protocols with linear complexity (e.g., [17,9,7]). Also, they support neither *data transfer* nor *authorization*.

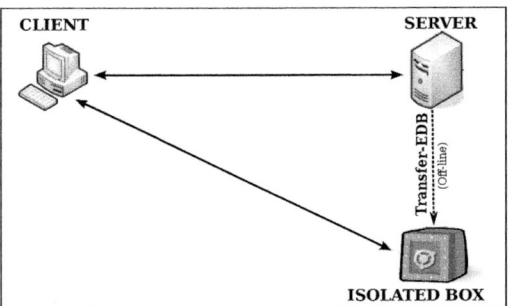

Fig. 1. Architecture with Isolated Box

Challenge 4: Liability. Transfer of the entire encrypted database also prompts the problem of long-term data safety and associated liability. An encryption scheme considered strong today might gradually weaken in the long term. While we can ensure that the client cannot decrypt records outside its query, it is not too far-fetched to imagine that the client might decrypt the entire database in reasonably near future, e.g., 10 or 20 years later. However, data sensitivity might not dissipate over time. For example, suppose that a low-level DoD employee is only allowed to access unclassified data. By gaining access to the encrypted database containing top secret data and patiently waiting for the encryption scheme to "age", the employee might obtain still-classified sensitive information. Furthermore, in several settings, parties (e.g., banks) may be prevented, by regulation, from releasing copies of their databases (even if encrypted).

5   PPSSI Design

We now discuss the design of PPSSI. First, we describe our system architecture with additional trust assumption and show a general framework for adapting (A)PSI-DT protocols to PPSSI. Next we propose a new database encryption and query lookup method for that framework. Finally, we discuss challenges and limitations.

5.1   Architecture

We propose a new system architecture shown in Figure 1. It includes a new component: *"Isolated Box"* (IB), a non-colluding, untrusted party connected with both the server and the client.

The new interaction involving the IB is shown in Figure 2. During the offline setup phase, the server encrypts its database, using EncryptDatabase (Algorithm 1, explained in Section 5.2), and transfers the encrypted database to the IB. During the online phase, in step 1, the client and the server engage in *oblivious* computation of the Token function: as a result, the client obtains $tk_i = \text{Token}(c_i)$, where $c_i = H(attr_i^*, val_i^*)$. Note that the server learns nothing

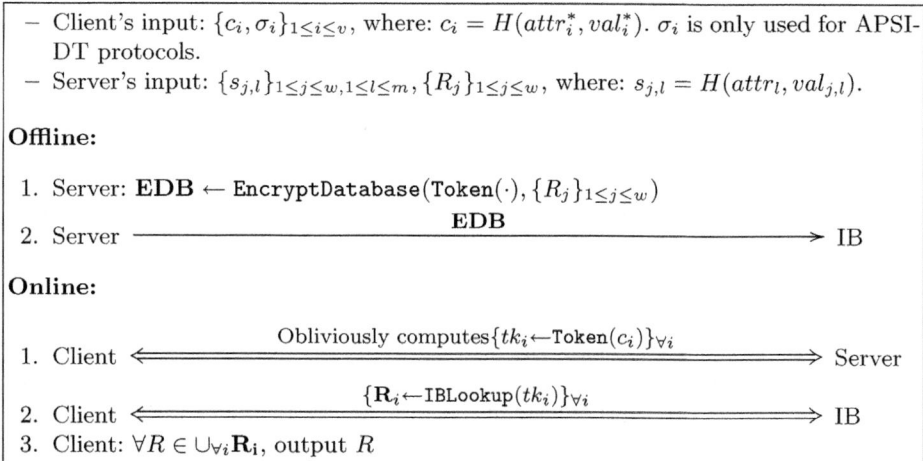

- Client's input: $\{c_i, \sigma_i\}_{1 \leq i \leq v}$, where: $c_i = H(attr_i^*, val_i^*)$. σ_i is only used for APSI-DT protocols.
- Server's input: $\{s_{j,l}\}_{1 \leq j \leq w, 1 \leq l \leq m}, \{R_j\}_{1 \leq j \leq w}$, where: $s_{j,l} = H(attr_l, val_{j,l})$.

Offline:

1. Server: $\mathbf{EDB} \leftarrow \texttt{EncryptDatabase}(\texttt{Token}(\cdot), \{R_j\}_{1 \leq j \leq w})$
2. Server $\xrightarrow{\hspace{2.5cm} \mathbf{EDB} \hspace{2.5cm}}$ IB

Online:

1. Client $\xleftarrow{\quad \text{Obliviously computes} \{tk_i \leftarrow \texttt{Token}(c_i)\}_{\forall i} \quad}$ Server
2. Client $\xleftarrow{\quad \{\mathbf{R_i} \leftarrow \texttt{IBLookup}(tk_i)\}_{\forall i} \quad}$ IB
3. Client: $\forall R \in \cup_{\forall i} \mathbf{R_i}$, output R

Fig. 2. Outline of our PPSSI approach based on IB

about c_i or tk_i due to the oblivious computation protocol whose instantiation relies on specific (A)PSI-DT protocols. The server can also evaluate Token over its own inputs without involving the client. Next, for each computed token, the client runs the IBLookup procedure (Algorithm 2, explained in Section 5.3) with the IB to retrieve matching records.

The Token($\cdot$) functionality is instantiated using (A)PSI-DT *with* pre-distribution protocols. Specifically, we select the construction from [9] (denoted as **DT10-2**), [17] (denoted as **JL10**) and [7] (denoted as **IBE-APSI**). Our choices are based on these protocols' efficiency and security models. Our experiments – in the full version of this paper [8] – show that DT10-2, secure in the presence of HbC adversaries, is the most efficient construction, while JL10 combines reasonable efficiency with security against malicious adversary. IBE-APSI is the only APSI-DT with pre-distribution, and it is secure against HbC adversaries. Note that (A)PSI-DT with pre-distribution protocols, by themselves, preclude Server Unlinkability and Forward Security. However, in Section 5.5, we show these security issues can be avoided in the new architecture with IB.

For the sake of completeness, we define Token function for the selected (A)PSI-DT constructions in Table 2. Note that Token definitions only rely on server's secret parameters (d, k, z) and that is why the server can evaluate it directly while the client has to interact with the server to evaluate it. Complete details, for each oblivious instantiation, are presented in [8].

Trust Assumptions. The Isolated Box is assumed not to collude with either the server or the client. (Although, we discuss the consequences of collusion in Section 5.5.) We remark that the use of non-colluding parties in the context of Secure Computation was first suggested by [10], and then applied in [19,18,1].

While our requirement for the presence of IB might seem like a "strong" assumption, we stress that the IB is only trusted not to collude with other parties. It simply stores server's encrypted database and returns ciphertexts matching

Table 2. Token for (A)PSI-DT with pre-distribution (d, k, z are server's private parameters)

Scheme name	Token definition
DT10-2 (Figure 4 of [9])	$\text{Token}(c) = (c)^d \bmod N$
JL10 (Figure 2 of [17])	$\text{Token}(c) = ((c)^{(p-1)/q})^k \bmod p$
IBE-APSI (Figure 5 of [7])	$\text{Token}(c) = \hat{e}(Q, c)^z$ where Q is CA's public parameter

---

Algorithm 1. EncryptDatabase Procedure

---

input : Function Token($\cdot$) and record set $\{R_j\}_{1 \le j \le w}$
output: Encrypted Database **EDB**

1: Shuffle $\{R_j\}_{1 \le j \le w}$
2: $maxlen \leftarrow$ max length among all R_j
3: **for** $1 \le j \le w$ **do**
4:     Pad R_j to $maxlen$;
5:     $k_j \xleftarrow{r} \{0,1\}^{128}$;
6:     $er_j \leftarrow Enc_{k_j}(R_j)$;
7:     **for** $1 \le l \le m$ **do**
8:         $s_{j,l} \leftarrow H(attr_l, val_{j,l})$;
9:         $tk_{j,l} \leftarrow \text{Token}(s_{j,l})$;
10:        $tag_{j,l} \leftarrow H_1(tk_{j,l}||ctr_{j,l})$;
11:        $k'_{j,l} \leftarrow H_2(tk_{j,l}||ctr_{j,l})$;
12:        $k''_{j,l} \leftarrow H_3(tk_{j,l}||ctr_{j,l})$;
13:        $ek_{j,l} \leftarrow Enc_{k'_{j,l}}(k_j)$;
14:        $eind_{j,l} \leftarrow Enc_{k''_{j,l}}(j)$;
15:        **LTable**$_{j,l} \leftarrow$
               $(tag_{j,l}, ek_{j,l}, eind_{j,l})$
16:     **end for**
17: **end for**
18: Shuffle **LTable** w.r.t. j and l;
19: **EDB** $\leftarrow \{$**LTable**, $\{er_j\}_{1 \le j \le w}\}$;

---

client's encrypted queries (i.e., *tags*), without learning any information about records and queries. Also note that, in practice, the IB can be either instantiated as a (non-colluding) cloud server or as a piece of secure hardware installed on server's premises: it is only important to ensure that the server does not learn *what* the IB reads from its storage and transfers to the client.

5.2 Database Encryption with Counters

We illustrate EncryptDatabase procedure in Algorithm 1. It takes as input the definition of the Token function, and server's record set. It consists of two "phases": (1) *Record-level* and (2) *Lookup-Table* encryptions.

Record-level encryption is relatively trivial (lines 1–6): first, the server shuffles record locations; then, it pads each R_j up to a fixed maximum record size, picks a random symmetric key k_j, and encrypts R_j as $er_j = Enc_{k_j}(R_j)$.

Lookup-Table (LTable) encryption (lines 8–15) pertains to attribute name and value pairs. It enables efficient lookup and record decryption. In step 8, the server hashes an attribute-value pair and uses the result as input to Token function in step 9. In step 10, we use the concatenation of Token output and a counter, $ctr_{j,l}$, in order to compute the tag $tag_{j,l}$, later used as a lookup tag during client query. We use $ctr_{j,l}$ to denote the index of duplicate value for the l-th attribute. In other words, $ctr_{j,l}$ is the counter of occurrences of $val_{j',l} = val_{j,l}, \forall j' <= j$. For example, the third occurrence of value "Smith" for attribute "Last Name" will

---

Algorithm 2. IBLookup Procedure

Client's input : tk_i

IB's input   : $\mathbf{EDB} = \{\mathbf{LTable}, \{er_j\}_{1 \le j \le w}\}$

Client's output: Matching record set $\mathbf{R}$

1. Client: $ctr \leftarrow 1$
2. Client: $tag_i \leftarrow H_1(tk_i \| ctr)$
   $k_i'' \leftarrow H_3(tk_i \| \| ctr)\}$
3. Client $\xrightarrow{tag_i, k_i''}$ IB
4. IB: If ($\exists tag_{j,l} \in \mathbf{LTable}_{j,l}$
   s.t. $tag_{j,l} = tag_i$)
   $j' \leftarrow Dec_{k_i''}(eind_{j,l})$
   $ret \leftarrow \{ek_{j,l}, er_{j'}\}$
   else
   $ret \leftarrow \perp$

5. IB $\xrightarrow{ret}$ Client
6. Client: If ($ret = \perp$)
   abort
   else
   $k_i' = H_2(tk_i \| ctr)$
   $k_i = Dec_{k_i'}(ek_{j,l})$
   $R_i = Dec_{k_i}(er_{j'})$
   $\mathbf{R} \leftarrow \mathbf{R} \cup R_i$
   $ctr \leftarrow ctr + 1$
   Goto step 2

---

have the counter equal to 3. The counter guarantees that duplicate $(attr, val)$ pairs correspond to different tags, thus addressing Challenge 1. Next, the server computes $k_{j,l}' = H_2(tk_{j,l} \| ctr_{j,l})$ and $k_{j,l}'' = H_3(tk_{j,l} \| ctr_{j,l})$. Note that $k_{j,l}'$ is used for encrypting symmetric key k_j. Whereas, $k_{j,l}''$ is used for encrypting the index of R_j. In step 13, the server encrypts k_j as $ek_{j,l} = Enc_{k_{j,l}'}(k_j)$. Then, the server encrypts $eind_{j,l} = Enc_{k_{j,l}''}(j)$. The encryption of index (data pointer) guarantees that the client cannot link two tags belonging to the same record, thus addressing Challenge 2. In step 15, the server inserts each $tag_{j,l}$, $ek_{j,l}$ and $eind_{j,l}$ into LTable, which is $\{tag_{j,l}, ek_{j,l}, eind_{j,l}\}_{1 \le j \le w, 1 \le l \le m}$. Next, the server shuffles LTable (step 18). The resulting encrypted database, $\mathbf{EDB}$, is composed of LTable and $\{er_j\}_{j=1}^w$ (step 19).

5.3 Query Lookup

IBLookup procedure is used by the client to obtain records matching client's query. It is shown in Algorithm 2. The client runs the lookup procedure after obtaining search tokens (via oblivious computation of Token – online step 1 in Figure 2). For each derived token, tk_i, it invokes IBLookup to retrieve from the IB all records matching tk_i.

We use the term *transaction* to denote a complete query procedure, for each tk_i (from the time the first query for tk_i is issued, until the last response from the IB is received). *Retrieval* denotes the receipt of a single response record during a transaction. A transaction is composed of several retrievals between the client and the IB. The client retrieves records one by one from the IB, by gradually incrementing the counter ctr. In step 1, the client sets ctr to 1. In step 2, the client derives tag_i and an index decryption key k_i'' from token tk_i. After receiving tag_i and k_i'' in step 3, the IB searches for matching tags in the lookup table in step 4. If there is a match, the IB recovers the index j' by decrypting $eind_{j,l}$ with k_i'', assembles the corresponding record $er_{j'}$ and the ciphertext of its decryption key $ek_{j,l}$ into ret and transmits ret to the client in step 5. Otherwise, $\perp$ is transmitted. If the client receives $\perp$, it aborts. Otherwise, it decrypts $ek_{j,l}$ into k_i with k_i' and recovers record R_i from $er_{j'}$ using k_i. Then, it increments ctr and starts another retrieval by returning to step 2.

5.4   Challenges Revisited

We claim that our approach addresses all challenges discussed in Section 4. The reasons are as follows:

Multi-sets: The use of counters during database encryption makes each $tag_{j,l}$ (resp. $ek_{j,l}$, $eind_{j,l}$) distinct in **LTable**, thus hiding plaintext patterns.

Data Pointers: Storing $eind_{j,l}$ (rather than j) in **LTable**, prevents the server from exposing the relationship between an entry **LTable**$_{j,l}$ and its associated record R_j.

Bandwidth: Once the server transfers its database (offline) to the IB, the latter returns to the client only records matching its query. Therefore, bandwidth consumption is minimized.

Liability: Since the IB holds the encrypted database, the client only obtains the result of its queries, thus, ruling out any potential liability issues.

5.5   Discussion

Privacy Revisited. The introduction of the IB does not violate Client or Server Privacy. Client Privacy is preserved because the client (obliviously) computes a token, which is not learned by the server. The IB does not learn client's interests, since client's input to the IB (tag) is statistically indistinguishable from a random value. Server Privacy is preserved because the client does not gain any extra information by interacting with the IB. Finally, the IB only holds the encrypted database and learns no plaintext.

The introduction of the IB also enables Server Unlinkability and Forward Security, despite the fact that we use (A)PSI-DT *with* pre-distribution techniques. Indeed, records not matching a query are never available to the client, thus, it does not learn whether they have changed. Similarly, the client cannot use future authorizations to maliciously obtain information from previous (recorded) interactions. We defer formal security proofs of our IB-based PPSSI approach to the full version of the paper [8].

Removing Online Server. Although it only needs to perform oblivious computation of tokens, we still require the server to be online. Inspired by [15] and [11], we can replace the online server with a tamper-proof smartcard, dedicated to computing Token function. The server only needs to program its secret key into the smartcard, which protects the key from being accessed by the client. This way, after handing the smartcard to the client, the server can go offline. The smartcard is assumed to enforce a limit on the number of Token invocations.

Limitations. We acknowledge that our second PPSSI approach has some limitations. Over time, as it serves many queries, the IB gradually learns the relationship between tags and encrypted records through pointers associated with each tag. This issue can be mitigated by letting the server periodically re-encrypt the database. IB also learns database access patterns generated by query executions. Nonetheless, without knowing the distribution of query predicates, the access pattern of encrypted data leaks very little information to the IB. Next, if the server and the IB collude, Client Privacy is lost, since the IB learns the *tag* that the client seeks, and the server knows the $(attr, val)$ pair each *tag* is related to. On the other hand, if the client and the IB collude, the client can access the entire encrypted database, thus, liability becomes a problem. Last, Server Unlinkability is protected only with respect to the client. Server Unlinkability with respect to the IB is not guaranteed, since the IB learns about all changes in server's database. Finally, note that PPSSI currently supports only equality and disjunctive queries. Enabling conjunctive queries would require treating all combinations of $(attr, val)$ pairs as server's set elements. Thus, client's input would become exponential in terms of the number of attributes. This remains an interesting challenge left as part of future work.

6   Performance Evaluation

In this section, we evaluate the performance our IB-based PPSSI approach by measuring it against standard (non privacy-preserving) MySQL.

We build our PPSSI approach based on GMP library (ver.5.0.1) and PBC library (ver.0.5.11). We deploy the server and the IB on an Intel Harpertown server with Xeon E5420 CPU (2.5 GHz, 12MB L2 Cache) and 8GB RAM inside. Client runs on a laptop with Intel Core 2 Duo CPU (2.2 GHz) and 4GB RAM inside.

On a conservative stance, we use MySQL with indexing enabled on each searchable attribute. We run the IB and the server on the same machine. Client is connected to the server and the IB through a $100Mbps$ link. The testing database has 45 searchable attributes and 1 unsearchable attribute (type "LARGEBLOB") used to pad each record to a uniform size. There are, in total, $100,000$ records. All records have the same size, which we vary during experiments.

First, we compare the *index lookup time*, defined as the time between SQL query issuance and the receipt of the first response from the IB. We select a set of SQL queries that return 0, 1, 10, 100, 1000, 10000 ($\pm10\%$) responses, respectively, and fix each record size at 500KB. Figure 3(a) shows index lookup time for our PPSSI approach (all underlying (A)PSI-DT instantiations), as well as MySQL, with respect to the response set size. All proposed schemes' cost are slightly more expensive than MySQL and are independent of the response size.

Next, we test the impact of the response set size on the *total query time*, which we define as the time between SQL query issuance and the arrival of the last response from the IB. Figure 3(b) shows the time for the client to complete a query for a specific response set size divided by the time taken by MySQL (again, for all underlying (A)PSI-DT instantiations). Results gradually converge

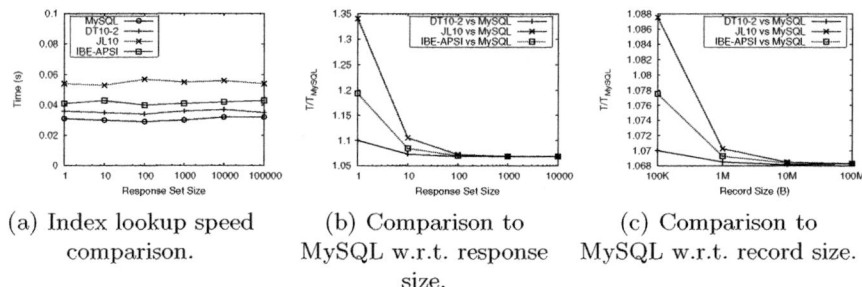

(a) Index lookup speed comparison.   (b) Comparison to MySQL w.r.t. response size.   (c) Comparison to MySQL w.r.t. record size.

[DT10-2, JL10, IBE-APSI labels indicate variants of the Token function in PPSSI]

Fig. 3. Performance comparison between our PPSSI approach and MySQL

to 1.1 for increasing response set sizes, i.e., our approach is only 10% slower than standard MySQL. This is because the extra delay incurred by cryptographic operations (in the oblivious evaluation of Token) is amortized by subsequent data lookups and decryptions. Note that we can also infer the impact of various client query set size by multiplying the client query set size with each single query delay.

Last, we test the impact of record size on the total query time. We fix response set size at 100 and vary each record size between $100KB$ and $100MB$. Figure 3(c) shows the ratio between our PPSSI approach and MySQL, once more for all underlying (A)PSI-DT instantiations. Again, results gradually converge well below 1.1 with increasing record size. This occurs because, with bigger records, the overhead of record decryption becomes the "bottleneck".

7   Conclusion

In this paper, we proposed a novel architecture for Privacy-Preserving Sharing of Sensitive Information (PPSSI), based on efficient PSI techniques. It enables a client and a server to exchange information without leaking more than the required minimum. Privacy guarantees are formally defined and achieved with provable security. Experimental results show that our approach is sufficiently efficient for real-world applications.

Acknowledgements. This research was supported by the US Intelligence Advanced Research Projects Activity (IARPA) under grant number FA8750-09-2-0071. We also would like to thank Xiaomin Liu and Stanislaw Jarecki for their helpful comments.

References

1. Asonov, D., Freytag, J.-C.: Almost optimal private information retrieval. In: PETS (2003)
2. Boneh, D., Di Crescenzo, G., Ostrovsky, R., Persiano, G.: Public key encryption with keyword search. In: Cachin, C., Camenisch, J.L. (eds.) EUROCRYPT 2004. LNCS, vol. 3027, pp. 506–522. Springer, Heidelberg (2004)

3. Caslon   Analytics.   Consumer   Data   Losses,   `http://www.caslon.com.au/datalossnote.htm`
4. Chor, B., Gilboa, N., Naor, M.: Private information retrieval by keywords. Manuscript (1998)
5. Chor, B., Kushilevitz, E., Goldreich, O., Sudan, M.: Private information retrieval. Journal of the ACM 45(6), 965–981 (1998)
6. Davidoff, S.: What Does DHS Know About You?, `http://tinyurl.com/what-dhs-knows`
7. De Cristofaro, E., Jarecki, S., Kim, J., Tsudik, G.: Privacy-preserving policy-based information transfer. In: Goldberg, I., Atallah, M.J. (eds.) PETS 2009. LNCS, vol. 5672, pp. 164–184. Springer, Heidelberg (2009)
8. De Cristofaro, E., Lu, Y., Tsudik, G.: Efficient techniques for privacy-preserving sharing of sensitive information. Cryptology ePrint Archive, `http://eprint.iacr.org/2011/113`
9. De Cristofaro, E., Tsudik, G.: Practical private set intersection protocols with linear complexity. In: Sion, R. (ed.) FC 2010. LNCS, vol. 6052, pp. 143–159. Springer, Heidelberg (2010)
10. Feige, U., Killian, J., Naor, M.: A minimal model for secure computation (extended abstract). In: STOC (1994)
11. Fischlin, M., Pinkas, B., Sadeghi, A.-R., Schneider, T., Visconti, I.: Secure set intersection with untrusted hardware tokens. In: CT-RSA (2011)
12. Freedman, M.J., Nissim, K., Pinkas, B.: Efficient private matching and set intersection. In: Cachin, C., Camenisch, J.L. (eds.) EUROCRYPT 2004. LNCS, vol. 3027, pp. 1–19. Springer, Heidelberg (2004)
13. Gertner, Y., Ishai, Y., Kushilevitz, E., Malkin, T.: Protecting data privacy in private information retrieval schemes. In: STOC (1998)
14. Hacigümüş, H., Iyer, B., Li, C., Mehrotra, S.: Executing SQL over encrypted data in the database-service-provider model. In: SIGMOD (2002)
15. Hazay, C., Lindell, Y.: Constructions of truly practical secure protocols using standard smartcards. In: CCS (2008)
16. Hore, B., Mehrotra, S., Tsudik, G.: A privacy-preserving index for range queries. In: VLDB (2004)
17. Jarecki, S., Liu, X.: Fast secure computation of set intersection. In: Garay, J.A., De Prisco, R. (eds.) SCN 2010. LNCS, vol. 6280, pp. 418–435. Springer, Heidelberg (2010)
18. Kantarcioğlu, M., Clifton, C.: Assuring privacy when big brother is watching. In: DMKD (2003)
19. Kantarcioglu, M., Vaidya, J.: An architecture for privacy-preserving mining of client information. In: CRPIT (2002)
20. Kissner, L., Song, D.: Privacy-preserving set operations. In: Shoup, V. (ed.) CRYPTO 2005. LNCS, vol. 3621, pp. 241–257. Springer, Heidelberg (2005)
21. Murugesan, M., Jiang, W., Clifton, C., Si, L., Vaidya, J.: Efficient privacy-preserving similar document detection. In: VLDB (2010)
22. Nagaraja, S., Mittal, P., Hong, C., Caesar, M., Borisov, N.: BotGrep: Finding Bots with Structured Graph Analysis. In: Usenix Security (2000)
23. Olumofin, F., Goldberg, I.: Privacy-preserving queries over relational databases. In: Atallah, M.J., Hopper, N.J. (eds.) PETS 2010. LNCS, vol. 6205, pp. 75–92. Springer, Heidelberg (2010)
24. Rabin, M.: How to exchange secrets by oblivious transfer. TR-81. Harvard Aiken Computation Lab (1981)
25. Song, D., Wagner, D., Perrig, A.: Practical techniques for searches on encrypted data. In: S&P (2000)

CertainLogic: A Logic for Modeling Trust and Uncertainty
(Short Paper)

Sebastian Ries[1], Sheikh Mahbub Habib[1], Max Mühlhäuser[1],
and Vijay Varadharajan[2]

[1] Technische Universität Darmstadt, CASED
Darmstadt, Germany
[2] Macquarie University
Sydney, Australia

Abstract. The evaluation of the trustworthiness of complex systems is a challenge in current IT research. We contribute to this field by providing a novel model for the evaluation of propositional logic terms under uncertainty that is compliant with the standard probabilistic approach and subjective logic. Furthermore, we present a use case to demonstrate how this approach can be applied to the evaluation of the trustworthiness of a system based on the knowledge about its components and subsystems.

1 Introduction

The evaluation of the trustworthiness of complex systems is one of the major challenges in current IT research, as – following the visions of the Internet of Services, the Future Internet and Cloud Computing – IT systems become highly distributed, dynamically composed, and hosted and managed by multiple parties. For example, in the field of Cloud Computing, people and enterprises are still hesitating to *move to the Cloud* due to missing transparency and security concerns. However, it is not only the users who are interested in evaluating the trustworthiness of a service, infrastructure, or platform, but also the providers and accreditation authorities.

Currently, there are several approaches supporting those stakeholders in assessing the trustworthiness of such kind of systems, e.g., from the field of trusted computing, experience-based trust and reputation models, and security [1]. However, for complex systems there is a lack of models that provide means for deriving the trustworthiness of the overall system considering (1) the trustworthiness of the subsystems and atomic components (independently from how these trust values are assessed), (2) the uncertainty associated to this information. For example, reputation values might be based on insufficient information and current solutions from the field of trusted computing cannot effectively capture dynamic changes in trust [2]. Also when considering the recent advances in the field of property-based attestation (e.g., [3]), there is a need for modeling trust and uncertainty in order to deal with the fact that (1) the state of the system that was measured at the time of booting does not necessarily reflect the state of the

J.M. McCune et al. (Eds.): TRUST 2011, LNCS 6740, pp. 254–261, 2011.
© Springer-Verlag Berlin Heidelberg 2011

system at the time of attestation and (2) that the authority that provides the property certificates might only be trusted to a certain degree [4].

As the core contribution of this paper, we define operators for AND, OR, and NOT for the evaluation of propositional logic terms under uncertainty and we give the properties of these operators. The operators have been designed to be compliant to the standard probabilistic approach and subjective logic [5, 6], which also provides the justification for the mathematical validity of the model. Furthermore, we introduce a use case to show how this approach could be used for evaluating the trustworthiness of a system in a Cloud Computing scenario and to show how the evaluation of the trustworthiness of a complex system relates to the evaluation of propositional logic terms. The paper is structured as follows: Sec. 2 presents the related work, Sec. 3 introduces a use case and Sec. 4 presents the model. Finally, we draw our conclusions in Sec. 6.

2   Related Work

In the field of trust modeling – for a definition of trust see [7] – there is a number of approaches modeling the (un-)certainty of a trust value, well-known approaches are given in [8, 9, 10, 11]. However, those approaches do not tackle the issue of deriving the trustworthiness of a system based on the knowledge about its subsystems and components, instead the challenge of these approaches is to find good models for deriving trust from direct experience of a user, recommendations from third parties, and sometimes additional information, e.g. social relationships. Especially, those models aim on providing robustness to attacks, e.g., misleading recommendations, re-entry, Sybil attacks. For those tasks they usually provide operators for combining evidence from different sources about the same target (also called consensus) and for weighting recommendations based on the trustworthiness of the source (also called discounting).

Although, there are researchers in the field of trust focusing on modeling (un-)certainty [5, 9, 12, 13], they do not provide operators for the evaluation of propositional logic terms, except for "subjective logic" [5, 6].

Furthermore, there are well-known approaches for modeling uncertainty outside the trust field. At first, there is the standard probabilistic approach. However, this approach only allows to deal with the uncertainty of the outcome of the next event, but probabilities are assumed to be known.

Fuzzy logic [14] seems to be related, however, it models another type of uncertainty, which could be typed as linguistical uncertainty or fuzzyness.

There is the field of (Dempster-Shafer) belief theory, which again leads to "subjective logic" [5]. The main drawback of this model is that the parameters for *belief*, *disbelief*, and *uncertainty* are dependent on each other, which introduces an unnecessary redundancy from the perspective of modeling and prevents one from re-assign just a single parameter.

Beyond subjective logic there are numerous other approaches for probabilistic reasoning, see e.g. [15]. However, as we argue for the mathematical validity of our model based on its compliance to subjective logic and the standard probabilistic approach, we do not provide a discussion of probabilistic reasoning in general.

Finally, it is possible to model uncertainty using Bayesian probabilities [16], this usually leads to probability density functions, e.g., the Beta probability density function. For the approaches in [13,5], it has been shown that there are bi-directional mappings between the representations proposed in those papers and the Beta probability density function. It is possible to apply the propositional standard operators to probability density functions, however, this leads to complex mathematical operations and multi-dimensional distributions, which are also hard to interpret and to visualize. In our proposed approach, we will not increase the dimensions when calculating AND and OR.

3   Use Case

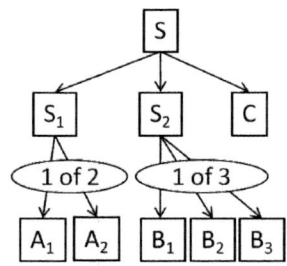

We introduce a scenario from the field of Cloud Computing, and show how the evaluation of the trustworthiness of the overall system can be carried out, if there is an appropriate approach for the evaluation of propositional logic terms (see also [17]). We evaluate the trustworthiness of a simple Customer Relationship Management (CRM) system focusing on the availability of the system.

Fig. 1. System architecture (incl. information about redundant components)

In the example (see Fig. 1), the CRM system S directly relies on two subsystems, S_1 providing authentication capabilities, S_2 offering storage capacity for sales data and data mining capabilities, and an atomic component C for the billing. Subsystem $S1$ consist of two authentication servers (A_1 and A_2), where at least one of the servers has to be available. Similarly, subsystem $S2$ is composed of three redundant databases servers (only one needs to be available).

Based on the description above and assuming that the information about the trust values of the atomic components is known, the evaluation of the trustworthiness of the complete system in the context of availability, can be carried out by evaluating the following propositional logic term:

$$(A_1 \vee A_2) \wedge (B_1 \vee B_2 \vee B_3) \wedge C$$

where A_1 is a proposition that is true if the component A_1 behaves as expected (e.g., the component replies to requests within a certain time limit); the interpretations of the other propositions are assigned in the same way. Although, we restricted the scope of our example to availability, please note that it is possible to model statements about the fulfillment of other relevant properties (e.g., attested / self-evaluated security properties or reputation of a component or subsystem) as propositions and to consider them in the evaluation of the overall trustworthiness of the system using propositional logic terms. However, as the knowledge about the fulfilment of the propositions is subject to uncertainty, the evaluation method has to take this uncertainty into account when calculating the trustworthiness of the overall system.

4   CertainLogic

In the following, we introduce a novel model, which we call *CertainLogic*, for evaluating propositional logic terms that are subject to uncertainty. Especially, we define the standard operators of propositional logic: *AND*, *OR*, and *NOT*. However, before introducing these operators, we have to introduce a way for modeling probabilities and uncertainty.

4.1   CertainTrust - Representation

The model for expressing opinions, this is how we call the construction for modeling probabilities that are subject to uncertainty (in accordance with [5]), is called *CertainTrust* [13]. CertainTrust (CT) bas been designed as a representation for evidence-based trust, but may also serve as a representation for uncertain probabilities. Additionally, it supports users with a graphical, intuitively interpretable interface (see [13, 18]).

Definition 4.1 (Representation CertainTrust). *In CertainTrust, an opinion o_A about the truth of a proposition A is given as $o_A = (t, c, f)$ where the parameters are called* average rating $t \in [0, 1]$, certainty $c \in [0, 1]$, *and* initial expectation value $f \in]0, 1[$. *If it holds $c = 0$ (complete uncertainty), the expectation value (see Def. 4.2) depends only on f, however, for soundness we define $t = 0.5$ in this case.*

The following introduces the basic semantics of the parameters[1]. The *average rating* t indicates the degree to which past observations (if there are any) support the truth of the proposition. It can be associated to the relative frequency of observations supporting the truth of the proposition. The extreme values can be interpreted as follows:

- average rating = 0: There is only evidence contradicting the proposition.
- average rating = 1: There is only evidence supporting the proposition.

The *certainty* c indicates the degree to which the average rating is assumed to be representative for the future. It can be associated to the number of past observations (or collected evidence units). The higher the certainty of an opinion is, the higher is the influence of the average rating on the expectation value in relation to the initial expectation. When the maximum level of certainty ($c = 1$) is reached, the average rating is assumed to be representative for the future outcomes. The extreme values can be interpreted as follows:

- certainty = 0: There is no evidence available.
- certainty = 1: The collected evidence is considered to be representative.

The *initial expectation* f expresses the assumption about the truth of a proposition in absence of evidence.

---

[1] There are additional parameters defined in [13], i.e., the *weight* w of the initial belief, the *number of expected evidence units* N, and a parameter for considering the *age* of evidence. When deriving the parameters (t, c, f) from past evidence, one could assume $w = 1$ and $\lim N \to \infty$. The param. *age* is not directly relevant for this paper.

Table 1. Definition of the operators

OR	$c_{A \vee B} = c_A + c_B - c_A c_B - \dfrac{c_A(1-c_B)f_B(1-t_A) + (1-c_A)c_B f_A(1-t_B)}{f_A + f_B - f_A f_B}$ $t_{A \vee B} = \begin{cases} \frac{1}{c_{A \vee B}}(c_A t_A + c_B t_B - c_A c_B t_A t_B) & \text{if } c_{A \vee B} \neq 0 \text{ ,} \\ 0.5 & \text{else .} \end{cases}$ $f_{A \vee B} = f_A + f_B - f_A f_B$
AND	$c_{A \wedge B} = c_A + c_B - c_A c_B - \dfrac{(1-c_A)c_B(1-f_A)t_B + c_A(1-c_B)(1-f_B)t_A}{1 - f_A f_B}$ $t_{A \wedge B} = \begin{cases} \frac{1}{c_{A \wedge B}}\left(c_A c_B t_A t_B + \frac{c_A(1-c_B)(1-f_A)f_B t_A + (1-c_A)c_B f_A(1-f_B)t_B}{1-f_A f_B}\right) & \text{if } c_{A \wedge B} \neq 0, \\ 0.5 & \text{else .} \end{cases}$ $f_{A \wedge B} = f_A f_B$
NOT	$t_{\neg A} = 1 - t_A,\ c_{\neg A} = c_A,\ \text{and } f_{\neg A} = 1 - f_A$

The assessment of those parameters can be achieved in multiple ways, e.g., direct assessment by an expert, or derived from a Bayesian reputation system, subjective logic, or a Beta probability distribution.

Definition 4.2 (Expectation value of CT). *The* expectation value *of an opinion* $E(t, c, f) \in [0, 1]$ *is defined as* $E(t, c, f) = t * c + (1 - c) * f$.

It expresses the expectation about the truth of the proposition taking into account the initial expectation, the average rating and the certainty.

4.2 Logical Operators

Having introduced the representational model, we define the operators of propositional logic (*OR*, *AND*, and *NOT*). These operators are defined in a way that they are compliant with the evaluation of propositional logic terms in the standard probabilistic approach. However, when combining opinions, those operators will especially take care of the (un-)certainty that is assigned to its input parameters, and reflect this (un-)certainty in the result.

Operator *OR*. The operator *OR* is applicable when opinions for two independent propositions need to form a new opinion reflecting the degree of truth for at least one out of both propositions.

Definition 4.3 (Operator *OR*). *Let A and B be two independent propositions and the opinions about the truth of these propositions be given as* $o_A = (t_A, c_A, f_A)$ *and* $o_B = (t_B, c_B, f_B)$, *respectively. Then, the resulting opinion is denoted as* $o_{A \vee B} = (t_{A \vee B}, c_{A \vee B}, f_{A \vee B})$ *where* $t_{A \vee B}$, $c_{A \vee B}$, *and* $f_{A \vee B}$ *are defined in Table 1 (OR). We use the symbol* $'\vee'$ *to designate the operator OR and we define* $o_{A \vee B} \equiv o_A \vee o_B$.

Operator *AND*. The operator *AND* is applicable when opinions for two independent propositions need to be aggregated to produce a new opinion reflecting the degree of truth of both propositions simultaneously.

Definition 4.4 (Operator AND**).** *Let* A *and* B *be two independent proposi-tions and the opinions about the truth of these propositions be given as* $o_A = (t_A, c_A, f_A)$ *and* $o_B = (t_B, c_B, f_B)$*, respectively. Then, the resulting opinion is denoted as* $o_{A \wedge B} = (t_{A \wedge B}, c_{A \wedge B}, f_{A \wedge B})$ *where* $t_{A \wedge B}$*,* $c_{A \wedge B}$*, and* $f_{A \wedge B}$ *are defined in Table 1 (AND). We use the symbol* $'\wedge'$ *to designate the operator* $'AND'$ *and we define* $o_{A \wedge B} \equiv o_A \wedge o_B$*.*

Operator NOT**.** The operator NOT is applicable when an opinion about an proposition needs to be negated.

Definition 4.5 (Operator NOT**).** *Let* A *be a proposition and the opinion about the truth of this proposition be given as* $o_A = (t_A, c_A, f_A)$*. Then, the re-sulting opinion is denoted as* $\neg o_A = (t_{\neg A}, c_{\neg A}, f_{\neg A})$ *where* $t_{\neg A}$*,* $c_{\neg A}$*, and* $f_{\neg A}$ *are given in Table 1 (NOT). We use the symbol* $'\neg'$ *to designate the operator NOT and we define,* $o_{\neg A} \equiv \neg o_A$

The operators for AND and OR are commutative and associative. The proofs for Theorem 4.1 and Theorems 4.2 are given in [19].

Theorem 4.1 (Commutativity). *It holds* $o_{A \wedge B} = o_{B \wedge A}$ *and* $o_{A \vee B} = o_{B \vee A}$*.*

Theorem 4.2 (Associativity). *It holds* $o_{A \wedge (B \wedge C)} = o_{(A \wedge B) \wedge C}$ *and* $o_{A \vee (B \vee C)} = o_{(A \vee B) \vee C}$*.*

The operators are *not distributive*, i.e., it does not hold that $o_{A \wedge (B \vee C)} = o_{(A \wedge B) \vee (B \wedge C)}$, as $A \wedge B$ and $A \wedge C$ are not independent propositions. Finally, it can be shown that the evaluation of the operators is compliant to the standard probabilistic approach as well as to subjective logic (see [19]).

5   Evaluation of the Use Case

In this section, we show how the operators of CertainLogic can be applied to the use case presented in Section 3. The propositional logic term for evaluating the trustworthiness of the system in the use case has been given as $(A_1 \vee A_2) \wedge (B_1 \vee B_2 \vee B_3) \wedge C$.

For the evaluation, we assume that we have good knowledge about the compo-nents of subsystem S_1 (consisting of A_1 and A_2) and subsystem S_2 (consisting of B_1, B_2, and B_3) and that the components are highly available. The opin-ions for the components as well as for the resulting subsystems are given in table 2. In both cases, the subsystems are highly trustworthy ($E(o_{S_1}) = 0.9963$ and $E(o_{S_2}) = 0.9964$) and the certainty for both systems is high.

We show the advantage of the new operators presenting different scenarios regarding the trustworthiness of the atomic component C. Depending on whether the component is hosted by the owner of the overall system or by a third party, the certainty about the behavior of this component might be higher or lower. Here we consider two cases:

Case 1: We assume that the trustworthiness of C is given as $o_C = (0.9, 0.9, 0.5)$ [*high certainty*] or as $o_C = (0.9, 0.1, 0.5)$ [*low certainty*]. For this case, the trust-worthiness of the overall system S (consisting of S_1, S_2, and C) are given in Table

Table 2. Resulting opinions for S_1 (left) and S_2 (right)

o_{A_1}	$(0.90, 0.98, 0.5)$
o_{A_2}	$(0.99, 0.95, 0.5)$
$o_{A_1 \vee A_2} = o_{S_1}$	$(0.9974, 0.9956, 0.75)$

o_{B_1}	$(0.9, 0.8, 0.5)$
o_{B_2}	$(0.95, 0.8, 0.5)$
o_{B_3}	$(0.9, 0.9, 0.5)$
$o_{B_1 \vee B_2 \vee B_3} = o_{S_2}$	$(0.9978, 0.9894, 0.875)$

3 (left). In the first row, we see that the *high certainty in o_C* is also reflected in the resulting opinion ($c_S = 0.9229$), whereas the *low certainty in o_C* is reflected in the resulting opinion ($c_S = 0.3315$) in the second row. In this example, we have different expectation values for o_C (depending on the certainty), and thus also different expectation values for o_S.

Case 2: We assume that the trustworthiness of C is given as $o_C = (0.9, 0.9, 0.9)$ [*high certainty*] or as $o_C = (0.9, 0.1, 0.9)$ [*low certainty*]. Here, both opinions lead to the same expectation value. The expectation value for the trustworthiness of the overall system is also the same (due to the compliance with the standard probabilistic approach). However, in our approach the different values for the certainty in the input parameters are still visible in the final result, for the certainty it holds $c_S = 0.9704$ [*high certainty*] and $c_S = 0.7759$ [*low certainty*] (see Table 3 (right)).

Table 3. Resulting opinions for S – Case 1 (left) & Case 2 (right)

	o_C	$o_{S_1 \wedge S_2 \wedge C} = o_S$		o_C	$o_{S_1 \wedge S_2 \wedge C} = o_S$
high certainty	$(0.9, 0.9, 0.5)$	$(0.8978, 0.9229, 0.3281)$ $E(o_S) = 0.8538$	high certainty	$(0.9, 0.9, 0.9)$	$(0.9028, 0.9704, 0, 5906)$ $E(o_S) = 0.8935$
low certainty	$(0.9, 0.1, 0.5)$	$(0.9556, 0.3315, 0.3281)$ $E(o_S) = 0.5361$	low certainty	$(0.9, 0.1, 0.9)$	$(0.981, 0.7759, 0.5906)$ $E(o_S) = 0.8935$

6   Conclusion

In this paper, we proposed a novel model for the evaluation of propositional logic terms under uncertainty. The operators for AND and OR can be shown to be associative and commutative, which is essential for the evaluation of propositional logic terms. Additionally, the operators can be shown to be compliant with the standard probabilistic evaluation of propositional logic terms and with subjective logic, which finally provides the justification for the mathematical validity of our model. However, the proposed approach is more expressive than the standard probabilistic approach, and although it is as expressive as subjective logic, it provides a simpler representation since it is based on independent parameters and it provides a more intuitive and more expressive graphical representation.

Finally, we have briefly indicated how the model can be applied when evaluating the trustworthiness of a system in a Cloud Computing scenario. The model provides a means (1) to derive the trustworthiness of the overall system based on the knowledge about its components, (2) to take into account multiple criteria (modeled by propositions), and (3) to explicitly model the uncertainty associated to the truth of a proposition. Thus, we consider this approach an appropriate, expressive, and well-founded tool for the evaluation of the trustworthiness of complex systems.

While we have used the Cloud Computing scenario as a descriptive example, the model could also be used for reasoning under uncertainty in other fields such as those involving contextual information. Such information is also subject to uncertainty; for instance, information collected by sensors.

References

1. Schneier, B.: Attack trees: Modeling security threats. Dr. Dobb's Journal 24 (1999)
2. Varadharajan, V.: A note on trust-enhanced security. IEEE Security and Privacy 7, 57–59 (2009)
3. Sadeghi, A., Stüble, C.: Property-based attestation for computing platforms: caring about properties, not mechanisms. In: Workshop on New Security Paradigms (2004)
4. Nagarajan, A., Varadharajan, V.: Dynamic trust enhanced security model for trusted computing platform based services. Future Generation Comp. Sys. (2010)
5. Jøsang, A.: A logic for uncertain probabilities. International Journal of Uncertainty, Fuzziness and Knowledge-Based Systems 9(3), 212–279 (2001)
6. Jøsang, A., McAnally, D.: Multiplication and comultiplication of beliefs. International Journal of Approximate Reasoning 38(1), 19–51 (2005)
7. Gambetta, D.: Can we trust trust? In: Gambetta, D. (ed.) Trust: Making and Breaking Cooperative Relations, pp. 213–237. Basil Blackwell, New York (1990)
8. Buchegger, S., Le Boudec, J.Y.: A Robust Reputation System for Peer-to-Peer and Mobile Ad-hoc Networks. In: P2PEcon 2004 (2004)
9. Teacy, W., et al.: Travos: Trust and reputation in the context of inaccurate information sources. Aut. Agents and Multi-Agent Systems 12(2), 183–198 (2006)
10. Jøsang, A., Ismail, R.: The beta reputation system. In: Proceedings of the 15th Bled Conference on Electronic Commerce (2002)
11. Ries, S., Heinemann, A.: Analyzing the robustness of CertainTrust. In: 2nd Joint iTrust and PST Conf. on Privacy, Trust Management and Security, pp. 51–67 (2008)
12. Wang, Y., Singh, M.P.: Formal trust model for multiagent systems. In: Proceedings of the 20th International Joint Conference on Artificial Intelligence, IJCAI (2007)
13. Ries, S.: Extending bayesian trust models regarding context-dependence and user friendly representation. In: ACM Symp. on Applied Computing, pp. 1294–1301 (2009)
14. Zadeh, L.A.: Fuzzy logic and approximate reasoning. Synthese 30, 407–428 (1975)
15. Haenni, R.: Towards a unifying theory of logical and probabilistic reasoning. In: 4th Int. Symp. on Imprecise Probabilities and Their Applications, pp. 193–202 (2005)
16. Bolstad, W.M.: Introduction to Bayesian Statistics. John Wiley & Sons, Inc., Chichester (2004)
17. Schryen, G., Volkamer, M., Ries, S., Habib, S.M.: A formal approach towards measuring trust in distributed systems. In: ACM Symp. on Applied Comp. (2011)
18. Ries, S.: Trust in Ubiquitous Computing. PhD thesis, Technische Universität Darmstadt (2009)
19. Ries, S., Habib, S.M., Mühlhäuser, M., Varadharajan, V.: CertainLogic: A Logic for Modeling Trust and Uncertainty. Technical report, Technische Universität Darmstadt (2011)

AS-TRUST: A Trust Quantification Scheme for Autonomous Systems in BGP⋆

Jian Chang, Krishna K. Venkatasubramanian, Andrew G. West,
Sampath Kannan, Boon Thau Loo, Oleg Sokolsky, and Insup Lee

Department of Computer and Information Science,
University of Pennsylvania, Philadelphia, PA, 19104
{jianchan,vkris,westand,kannan,boonloo,sokolsky,lee}@cis.upenn.edu

Abstract. The Border Gateway Protocol (BGP) works by frequently exchanging updates that disseminate *reachability information* about IP prefixes (*i.e.*, IP address blocks) between Autonomous Systems (ASes) on the Internet. The ideal operation of BGP relies on three major *behavioral assumptions* (BAs): (1) information contained in the update is legal and correct, (2) a route to a prefix is stable, and (3) the route adheres to the valley free routing policy. The current operation of BGP implicitly trusts all ASes to adhere to these assumptions. However, several documented violation of these assumptions attest to the fact that such an assumption of trust is perilous. This paper presents *AS-TRUST*, a scheme that comprehensively characterizes the trustworthiness of ASes with respect to their adherence of the behavioral assumptions. AS-TRUST quantifies trust using the notion of *AS reputation*. To compute reputation, AS-TRUST analyzes updates received in the past. It then classifies the resulting observations into multiple types of *feedback*. The feedback is used by a *reputation function* that uses Bayesian statistics to compute a probabilistic view of AS trustworthiness. This information can then be used for improving quotidian BGP operation by enabling improved route preference and dampening decision making at the ASes. Our implementation of AS-TRUST scheme using publicly available BGP traces demonstrates: (1) the number of ASes involved in violating the BGP behavioral assumptions is significant, and (2) the proposed reputation mechanism provides multi-fold improvement in the ability of ASes to operate in the presence of BA violations.

1 Introduction

Large IP domains, called *Autonomous Systems* (ASes) use the Border Gateway Protocol (BGP) as the standard communication protocol. BGP enables ASes to exchange IP prefix (*i.e.*, IP address blocks) reachability information with each other through periodic propagation of BGP *update* messages. The *reachability information* within a BGP update consists of IP prefixes, and an ordered list of

---

⋆ This research was supported in part by ONR MURI N00014-07-1-0907. POC: Insup Lee, lee@cis.upenn.edu

ASes, called *AS_PATH*, through which the prefix is reachable. Additionally, BGP relies on three major *behavioral assumptions* (BAs) to operate: (1) information contained in the update is legal and correct, (2) a route to a prefix is stable, and (3) the route adheres to the valley free routing policy. Violation to any of these behavioral assumptions can have severe consequences for the inter-domain routing. The past decade has seen numerous incidences of BA violations. For instance *prefix hijacking*, when an AS claims to directly reach (*i.e.*, own) a prefix contrary to its actual capability [5] and [8]; *valley route*, which might prevent BGP convergence [2]; and *unstable or potentially spoofed link insertion* in the *AS_PATH* to make the route more attractive [20].

In this paper, we present *AS-TRUST*, a novel scheme for quantifying the level of trust[1] one can have on the ASes based on their adherence to the BAs. This trust quantification has many benefits: (1) obtain a succinct but global view of the current state of inter-domain routing and the extent to which it is plagued by the aforementioned hijacking, stability and policy violation issues, (2) potentially minimize the ASes that violate BAs by making the AS trustworthiness information available to the entire BGP community, and (3) use the information to make informed policy decisions about any new updates received from the ASes.

In AS-TRUST, trust is quantified using the notion of *AS reputation*. This is based on the observation that AS behavior is repetitive. To compute the reputation of an AS, AS-TRUST evaluates past BGP updates received for exhibition of specific behaviors, based on well-defined properties. The behavior evaluation provides feedback to a Bayesian reputation function to generate a probabilistic view of the trustworthiness of all the observable ASes in the Internet. Note that, a low reputation for an AS does not mean it is necessarily malicious. It simply means it has violated one or more of the behavioral assumptions. It could have done it for a variety of reasons including misconfiguration, traffic engineering purposes, as well as malice. We argue that, as it has been shown that violating these individual assumption has consequences for the inter-domain routing space [2] [5] and [20], one needs to be aware of their occurrence. The AS-TRUST reputation values allow us to achieve this sense of awareness. Our implementation of AS-TRUST demonstrates the following: (1) incidents of BA violation are consistently present, (2) a considerable percentage of ASes (5-6%) are involved in some form of BA violation with a handful exhibiting poor behavior exclusively, and (3) the proposed reputation mechanism significantly improves the ability of ASes to operate in the presence of BA violations. To the best of our knowledge, this is the first attempt to quantify the behavioral assumptions of BGP in a systematic manner.

The paper is organized as follows. Section 2 presents background on BGP and the problem statement. Section 3 presents details of AS-TRUST including the notion of BGP service, feedback mechanism, and the reputation function employed. Section 4 presents the properties for evaluating the BGP services. Section 5 presents the AS reputation computation and analysis. Section 6 presents the related work, followed by Section 7, which concludes the paper.

---

[1] Trust is defined as the competence of an entity to exhibit a specific behavior(s) [14].

2   Preliminaries

2.1   The Border Gateway Protocol

The Border Gateway Protocol is a path-vector routing protocol for exchanging information about reaching IP prefixes. Using BGP, each AS informs its neighbors about the best available route to prefixes it can reach. In this regard, AS sends out a BGP update message *announcing* the prefix. Similarly, an AS can *withdraw* a prefix that it has previously announced. Each AS through which the update passes adds its AS number to the message. This ordered list of ASes called the *AS_PATH* informs an AS receiving the update, the path through which the prefix can be reached. When an update is received by an AS containing a prefix announcement, it has to determine whether it should be accepted or not. Acceptance means that the AS is willing to add the route to its routing information base. Each AS has its own policies that determine whether it accepts a BGP update and whether it forwards it (the update) to its neighbors. Routing policies serve an important purpose in BGP and provide an AS with not only the capability to prefer routes over others to reach a prefix, but also to filter and/or tag an update to change the route's relative preference downstream.

2.2   Problem Statement and Approach

The current version of BGP [1] was designed with only effectiveness in mind. It implicitly assumes ASes can be trusted to adhere to certain *behavioral assumptions* (BAs). We say that an AS is violating (*i.e.*, not adhering to) the BAs, if it displays any of the following five behaviors:

- *Illegality:* The values of the AS number and the prefixes in the update are from a restricted range, that is the AS numbers are private or the prefixes are bogons.
- *Hijack:* An AS falsely claims to own a prefix in the update. Such false claims on someone else's prefixes can have adverse consequences including loss of service [8], or can be used for spamming purposes [23].
- *Vacillation:* An update is deemed vacillating if it is part of a quick succession of announcements and withdrawals involving a specific prefix perpetuated by an AS that owns it. Vacillation can cause frequent route-flapping at the upstream ASes, which is detrimental to BGP stability and router performance [10].
- *Valley Route:* The *AS_PATH* of an update has one or more ASes that form a valley. An AS in the *AS_PATH* is said to form a valley if: (1) it forwards a route received from its provider[2] to another provider, or (2) it forwards a route with an existing peer-to-peer link to one of its own peers. Most ASes try to follow a *valley-free routing* (VFR) guideline in their export policy settings [21] as VFR have been shown to be a sufficient condition to ensure that convergence of BGP [13].

---

[2] ASes and their neighbors usually have one of the four relationships: provider-to-customer (Pv2C), customer-to-provider (C2Pv), sibling-to-sibling (S2S), and (P2P) peer-to-peer[13].

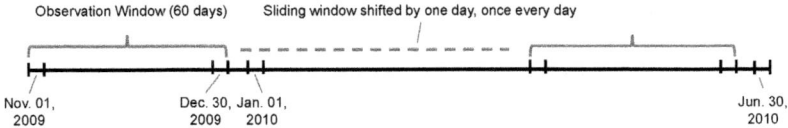

Fig. 1. Data Source Time Windows

- *Unstable AS-Links:* An AS propagates updates through a short-lived AS-link (*i.e.,* a hop between individual ASes in the *AS_PATH*). Detecting such unstable AS-link bindings is important, since ASes which chose a path with one or more unstable AS-links may increase the latency of data delivery, increase the number of BGP updates exchanged within the inter-domain routing space, and may be indicative of link spoofing [18].

The principal question this paper tries to address is *"what is the probability with which an AS adheres and violates the behavioral assumptions of BGP?"* In this regard, we use the notion of reputation. *Reputation* is a quantitative measure of an entity's likelihood to perform a specific task based on its past behavior [16]. The idea is to compute the reputation for all the ASes in the Internet based on the updates received in the past and analyze them for adherence to the BAs. This is done in four steps: (1) collecting BGP updates in a database; (2) evaluating the data in the database, over a well-defined duration called the *observation window*, for the exhibition of the aforementioned five behaviors; (3) recording the results of the analysis as feedback; and (4) using feedback to compute reputation for the ASes. Reputation is a dynamic value which changes as the AS behavior changes, over time. This is accomplished by repeating the evaluation process over a sliding observation window and generating updated feedback.

2.3   Experiment Setup

We implemented the proposed scheme and conducted a six month long experiment measuring the evolving trustworthiness of ASes, on an Internet-scale. To receive the latest BGP updates, we use the RouteViews BGP trace collector, maintained by University of Oregon [9]. The RouteViews trace collector is a group of BGP routers which peer with a large number of ISPs via BGP sessions. At the time of writing, the RouteViews received BGP updates from 46 ASes. It has been shown in [24] that RouteViews receives updates from almost all the ASes currently active within the Internet and is therefore a good source for computing reputation of ASes. Just as many of the past works in BGP security [22], we assume the RouteViews repository to be trustworthy and provides us with accurate information.

In this work, we use BGP update data from Nov. 1, 2009 - Jun. 28, 2010 (see Figure 1). We take BGP updates received over a 60 day period called the *observation window*, evaluate the AS behavior, and compute reputation for the ASes on the 61st day. For example, data from Nov. 1, 2009 to Dec. 30, 2009 is analyzed to compute AS reputation on Jan. 1, 2010. The observation window is then slid forward by one day and the process is repeated. In order to be fair to the ASes, we did not consider updates announced within 24 hours of the end of the observation window in computing the reputation of the ASes as they have not had enough time to prove themselves. There are over 180 observation windows between Nov 1, 2009 and Jun. 28, 2010. The 60 day observation window was chosen as it was long enough to prevent the behavior evaluation from being biased by transient AS behavior.

3   AS-TRUST Reputation Computation

This section provides an overview of the principal aspects of computing trustworthiness of ASes by AS-TRUST. We begin by formalizing the notion of *BGP service* which forms the basis of the whole process. We then present the mechanism for obtaining feedbacks. In the subsequent sections we describe the evaluation process and reputation computation, respectively.

3.1   BGP Service

The principal task of BGP is to facilitate the dissemination of reachability information through updates. We model this dissemination using a novel notion of *BGP service*. A BGP service is a formal way of viewing reachability information provided collectively by the ASes in the AS_PATH, called *providers*[3], to an *observer* AS receiving a BGP update. It is defined as: $S_i = \{p_i, AS\_PATH = [AS_0, \ldots, AS_N]\}$. Here S_i is the service identifier indexed by i, p_i is the prefix being announced by AS_0 as a part of the service S_i, and $AS_0, \ldots, AS_N \in AS\_PATH$ are the provider ASes which forward the reachability information as a part of the service S_i. Figure 2 (a) illustrates the principal concepts and entities of a BGP service. A service said to have *started* when a provider AS announces a particular prefix and *ended* when the prefix is withdrawn. A service can therefore be in two modes: *active* and *inactive*. A service is said to be active if it has started but not ended; and inactive otherwise. An inactive service has to have been active, at least once, in the past. Each time a service is active, it is called an *instance* of that service. The bottom half of the Figure 2 (a) illustrates some of these concepts over a *time-line* of a service.

A BGP service can be decomposed into three orthogonal *service elements*, each of which are provided by a subset of providers: (1) *AS-prefix binding:* a tuple of the form (AS_0, p), which is established when an AS_0 announces a prefix p and is broken when the prefix is withdrawn. Each BGP service has one AS-prefix binding in it. This service element is provided by AS_0. (2) *AS-path vector:* is synonymous with the AS_PATH in the service. It is said to be provided *collectively* by all the providers; and (3) *AS-link binding:* a tuple of the form (AS_i, AS_j), which is established when AS_i forwards an update to AS_j.

---

[3] These are different from notion used in the context of VFR. Here, the term provider ASes mean the provider of a service. In the rest of the paper, unless otherwise specified, the term provider refers to provider ASes.

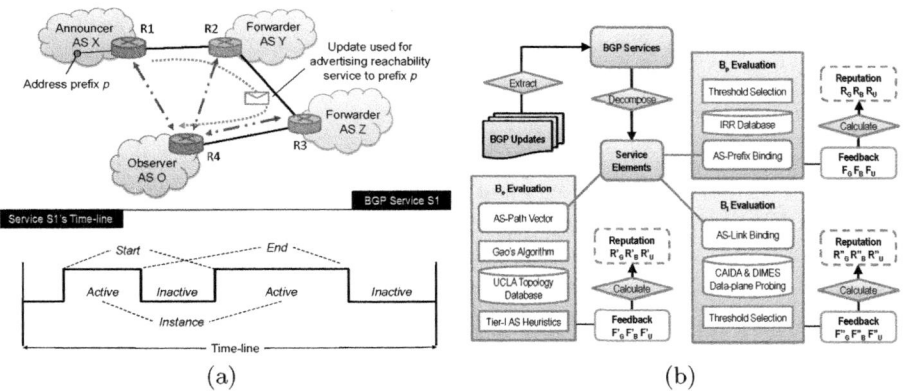

Fig. 2. (a) BGP Service and Timeline, (b) AS-TRUST Service Analysis

The AS-link binding is broken when no service uses it. A service has $N - 1$ AS-link bindings; one between each of the N ASes in the AS_PATH. This service element is said to be provided *individually* by all the providers in the AS_PATH to the observer. In the rest of the paper, we use the term AS-link bindings and AS-links, interchangeably.

Upon observing a BGP service, the observer decomposes it into its constituent service elements, each of which is then evaluated on its validity. The results of the evaluation act as a feedback on the providers of the service element. The next sub-section details how the behaviors described in Section 2.2 can be evaluated for the service elements, followed by the feedback mechanism used. *Note that, as the feedback is generated locally, we do not have to consider the case of potentially dishonest external feedback affecting our reputation computation outcome.*

3.2   Behavior Evaluation

We propose three behavior sets, one corresponding to each service element, for behavior evaluation. The three *behavior sets* comprehensively cover the behavioral assumptions on which BGP operates. They are: (1) *Prefix Behavior Set (Bp)*: Requires that AS in the AS-prefix binding service element *does not* exhibit prefix value illegality, hijacking or vacillating behavior; (2)*Path Behavior Set (Bo)*: Requires that *none* of the ASes in the AS-path vector service element form a valley or exhibit AS number illegality[4]; (3) *Link Behavior Set (Bl)*: Requires that *none* of the ASes create an AS-link binding service element that is short-lived.

It can be seen that there is a one-to-one mapping between the service elements and the behavior sets. Therefore, evaluating a service involves evaluating whether AS-prefix binding, AS-path vector, and AS-link binding service elements satisfy B_p, B_o, and B_l, respectively. However, before we delve into the details

---

[4] A 16-bit AS number is *illegal* if its value is in the range of 64496-64511, which is reserved for use in documentation and sample code, 64512-65534, which is designated for private use, or 65535, which is reserved [6].

of evaluation, we provide an overview of our feedback mechanism, which is essential for reputation computation, and forms an integral part of the evaluation process.

3.3   Feedback Mechanism

Evaluation of a BGP service element provides one of three mutually exclusive feedbacks. The feedback can have one of three values: (1) *Feedback G:* this feedback is given on the providers that satisfies the requirements of the appropriate behavior set; (2) *Feedback B:* this feedback is given on the providers that do *not* satisfy the requirements of the behavior sets, however, they do not disrupt BGP operation; and (3) *Feedback U:* this feedback is given on the providers that not only violate the requirements of the behavior sets, but also disrupt BGP operation.

   In the rest of the paper, we use the term *GBU feedbacks* to refer to our feedback types. When the service element implemented by the provider(s) receives *Feedback G*, it is referred to as *good behavior*. Conversely, a *Feedback B* or a *Feedback U* for an AS is referred to as the demonstration of *poor behavior*. Essentially, a good behavior adheres to the behavioral assumptions, while poor behaviors violates them. In general, there exists a 3×3 feedback matrix for every provider AS_a, at the observer, of the form:

$$F_a = \begin{pmatrix} F_G & F_B & F_U \\ F_G' & F_B' & F_U' \\ F_G'' & F_B'' & F_U'' \end{pmatrix}$$

where the element $F_a(1,j)$, $F_a(2,j)$, and $F_a(3,j)$ stores the details of the BGP service, which AS a provided when evaluated with respect to B_p, B_o, and B_l, respectively. Finally, as the feedback are generated locally at the observer AS, we do not have to consider the case of potentially dishonest feedback affecting our reputation computation outcome.

4   BGP Service Evaluation and Feedback

In this section, we describe the metrics used in the behavior evaluation of service elements. These metrics allow the feedback matrix to be populated, which will subsequently be used to compute reputation. As mentioned earlier, the behavior evaluation considers BGP services received during a 60 day observation window and produces feedback on the providers. Figure 2 (b) illustrates the work-flow of the evaluation process discussed in this section. The boxes with dashed outlines illustrate the output produced at the end of analyzing a service based on each of three behavior sets.

4.1   Evaluation of Service Using B_p

Determining whether an AS-prefix binding (AS_0, p) exhibits B_p builds on [11]. Therefore, in the rest of the section we briefly summarize the metrics used and evaluation described therein. The evaluation is a three step process:

Table 1. Feedback for Behavior Evaluation based on B_p

Prevalence	Persistence	Classification	Feedback
high	high	Good	F_G
high	low	Vacillation	F_B
low	high	Good	F_G
low	low	Hijack	F_U

- *Stability Analysis:* For each (AS_0, p) observed during the observation window, we compute two temporal metrics: persistence and prevalence[5]. *Prevalence* (Ps), is the total percentage of time an AS-prefix binding is active within the observation window. *Persistence (Pr)*, on the other hand, is the average duration of time an AS-prefix binding is active, within the observation window.
- *Providing Feedback:* The value of the Ps and Pr are compared against a set of thresholds T_{pr} (1% of the observation window) and T_{Ps} (10 hours)[6] and feedback provided. Table 1 shows the feedback matrix element updated for different Pr and Ps values.
- *Detecting Bogons:* (AS_0, p) is also statically checked for the presence of bogons, and their discovery results in F_U element being updated in the feedback matrix F_a associated with AS_0.

The case of Pr being high and Ps being low demonstrates a *vacillating* nature of an AS-prefix binding. Detailed analysis of such bindings demonstrate that they are usually legitimate [11]. However, the AS-prefix binding service element itself vacillates between being active and inactive at a rate which is not conducive for data communication. Further, it causes significant increase in the number of updates exchanged to manage the changes causing frequent route flapping [11]. Consequently, we give such vacillating behavior *Feedback B* because the ASes execute BGP's functionality correctly but fail to meet the requirement of the behavior set. As for bogons, we believe their announcement subverts the operation of BGP and we therefore give them *Feedback U*.

The results of the evaluation, based on B_p, are summarized in Figure 3. An average of 421704.1 AS-prefix bindings were observed every observation window, out of which an average of 4.0% were found to be hijacked[7] involving 1.7% of all the ASes. Similarly, about 6.9% of AS-prefix bindings were classified as vacillating, involving 3.1% of all the ASes. The number of ASes displaying exclusively poor behaviors is lower still. Finally, we observed zero occurrence of AS-prefix bindings with bogon prefixes during any of the observation windows. We believe this is because bogons are invariably filtered out by ASes that detect them.

---

[5] The principle idea of evaluating temporal characteristics comes from the observation that legitimate AS-prefix pairs last long periods of time [17].

[6] Both the thresholds have been established empirically, based on lowest false positive and false negative rates when compared with Internet Route Registries (IRR) [11].

[7] This number is unusually high due to the Internet-scale prefix hijacking attempt on April 8th, 2010 by AS_{23724}.

Behavior Evaluation Results from Jan. 1, 2010 and Jun. 30, 2010

(For each day, the analysis considers: I. BGP updates from the past *60* days for B_p and B_l, and II. AS relationship annotated topologies of the past 24 hours for B_o)

Analysis of B_p *			Property	Value	Analysis of B_o		
			Avg. # unique AS Observed	35448.2	Property		Value
Property		**Value**	Avg. # of AS with Feedback B	1132.8	Avg. # of Paths		661395.7
Avg. # of ASPB** Observed		421704.1	Avg. # of AS with Feedback U	605.5	Avg. # of Valley Routes		3447.8
Avg. # of ASPB Provide Feedback U		6955.61***	Avg. # of AS with Only Feedback B	17.8	Avg. # of AS Creating Valley Routes		89.2
Avg. # of ASPB Provide Feedback B		29256.6	Avg. # of AS with Only Feedback U	54.3	Avg. # of BGP Services Containing Illegal AS Number		44.1

	Analysis of B_l			
Property	Value	Property	Value	
Avg. # of AS-links Observed	94754.2	Avg. # of Unique AS Observed	35667.2	
Avg. # of Stable AS-links	91143.6	Avg. # of AS Using Unstable AS-links	1945.7	
Avg. # of Unstable AS-links	3610.6	Avg. # of AS Only Using Unstable AS-links	67.4	

* No bogons were observed during the experiment periods
** ASPB: AS-prefix bindings
*** The actual value was higher, due to the Internet scale prefix hijacking mounted by AS23724 on Apr. 8, 2010.

Fig. 3. AS Behavior Evaluation Statistics

The results demonstrate that a relatively large number of ASes (3-5%) are involved in announcing vacillating and hijacked prefixes.

4.2   Evaluation of Service Using B_o

To evaluate an AS-path vector based on B_o is a four step process: (1) *Generating AS Relationship Map:* We download that day's annotated topology from the UCLA's Internet topology site [24] and merge it with a topology inferred by applying Gao's algorithm [13] to the previous day's RouteViews data; (2) *Introduce Peers:* We obtain the list of all tier-1 ASes from [2]. All links between tier-1 ASes are re-labeled peer-to-peer (P2P), and links between tier-1 AS and lower-tier AS are re-labeled Pv2C where the tier-1 AS is the provider (Pv); (3) *Providing Feedback:* Once the merged annotated topology has been created, the AS-path service element of all the services announced that day is evaluated for the existence of ASes which might violate VFR. If such an AS is found, then its F'_B entry in its feedback matrix is updated; and (4) *Identifying Illegal ASes:* The *AS_PATH* is finally examined for illegal AS numbers. This is done based on a static check. The first legal AS, after the set of illegal ones is blamed and its F'_B updated.

The use of two well-known AS topology relationship inference techniques increases the confidence of our own relationship labeling. The violation of VFR is given *Feedback B* because, though not good in the long run, it does not necessarily affect the operation of BGP in providing knowledge about routes to prefixes. In the case of illegal ASes, the first legal AS after a set of private ASes is blamed because such leaking of private numbers usually happens when an AS forgets to filter out local AS numbers before forwarding the update [18].

The results of the evaluation, based on B_o, are summarized in Figure 3. We found that, an average of 661395.7 paths were observed per day. Out of these, 0.5% paths were found to violate VFR per day. Finally, an average of 89.2 providers out of over 35K were seen violating VFR per day. On average, we found only about 44.1 ASes involved in allowing illegal AS numbers in the *AS_PATH*, per day, during the six months of behavior analysis with respect to B_o. *In summary, the violation to B_o, especially valley routes are prevalent and a recurring event in the day to day operation of BGP.*

Table 2. Feedback for Behavior Evaluation based on B_l

Prevalence	Persistence	Classification	Feedback
high	high	Good	F_G''
high	low	Good	F_G''
low	high	Good	F_G''
low	low	Unstable	F_U''

4.3   Evaluation of Service Using B_l

Computing the stability of an AS-link binding (AS_i, AS_j) in the *AS_PATH* follows a similar approach to AS-prefix binding stability evaluation and uses the *prevalence* and *persistence* metrics. The evaluation and feedback with respect to B_l is done in three steps: (1) *Identifying AS-link Bindings:* This generates a set L of all the AS-link bindings, decomposed from the services observed during the observation window; (2) *Computing Stability Metrics:* This step computes the prevalence (Pr) and persistence (Ps) for each of the AS-link in set L; (3) *Providing Feedback:* The computed Pr and Ps values are then compared with a threshold Tl_{Pr} and Tl_{Ps} and a feedback is provided. Table 2 shows the feedback matrix element updated for different Pr and Ps values.

The reason we give unstable AS-links the *Feedback U* because it is possible that poor AS-link stability is due to an attempted link spoofing which could subvert the intended BGP operation. It should be noted that it is difficult to get conclusive proof for the spoofing given a lack of ground truth, though we find an interesting result which strengthens the case for their occurrence (see Section 5.2). We therefore argue that the potential of spoofing merits a punitive feedback for ASes involved in unstable AS-links. The value of thresholds Tl_{Pr} and Tl_{Ps} are set to 1% of the observation window and one hour, respectively. These values are established empirically based on comparison with a set of AS-links D. The set D is obtained from data-plane probing database provided by the CAIDA [3] and DIMES [4] projects. The thresholds are the values below which, all the AS-links in the set L, with the particular Pr and Ps, have the smallest intersection with the set D. Data-plane probing is used because if a AS-link is ephemeral, it has a low probability of being found in data-plane probing. Further, it is the only form of ground-truth available that can reliably identify AS-links stable enough to allow data traffic to pass through them [19].

Figure 3 shows the results of analysis, based on B_l. An average of 95640.4 AS-links were observed during the each of the observation windows. Out of these over 96.1% AS-links received *Feedback G*. From the perspective of the ASes, on average of 35667 ASes were seen every observation window, out of which 5.4% ASes announced unstable AS-links at least once. Only about an average of 0.18% of ASes announced purely unstable AS-links. Figure 4(a) visualizes 4625 unstable AS-links seen each month over the course of the experiment involving 2305 ASes. The dots are the ASes and the lines between them are unstable AS-links. The red dots represent the 149 ASes which have established unstable AS-links at least once every month, during the course of our experiment. *In summary, these*

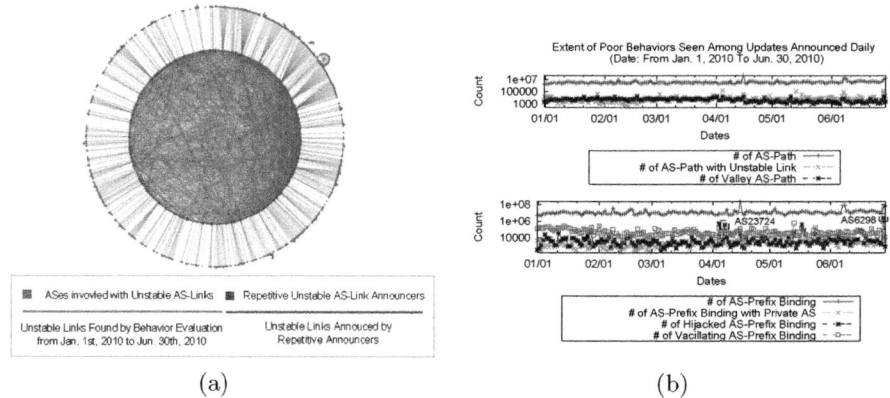

(a)   (b)

Fig. 4. (a) Visualization of Unstable AS-Links and the Provider ASes Involved, (b) Extent of Poor Behaviors in the Internet

results demonstrate that unstable AS-links are a repetitive phenomena, affecting a substantial number (5-6%) of ASes.

Figure 4(b) presents the extent of poor behavior seen every day between Jan. 1, 2010 and Jun. 30, 2010. The trend graphs provide an overview of the extent the poor behaviors of ASes afflicting inter-domain routing and how they have evolved over time. The numbers are raw-values and include all AS-prefix bindings, *AS_PATHS* and AS-links, decomposed from the observed BGP services. Overall, the problem of poor behavior is consistently present over the course of the six months and is largely stable in its intensity, with occasional spikes. These results do indicate the importance of monitoring AS-prefix binding vacillation, AS-link stability and presence of valley route with the same diligence as prefix hijacking.

5   Reputation Computation

At the end of behavior evaluation, we have a feedback matrix for each AS. This will now be used to compute reputation. The reputation will allow the observer AS to know *the probability of a service element in a BGP service provided by an AS, being given Feedback G (or Feedback B or Feedback U)*. Given the service elements are orthogonal to each other, the reputation for an AS a is computed as a 3×3 matrix (just like F_a).

$$R_a = \begin{pmatrix} R_G & R_B & R_U \\ R_G' & R_B' & R_U' \\ R_G'' & R_B'' & R_U'' \end{pmatrix}$$

Here, the rows correspond to the reputation of the AS with respect to an AS-prefix binding, AS-path, and AS-link binding service elements, respectively. We do not arrive at a single number for reputation here, as it would not be able to describe the behavior of an AS with the same level of detail.

5.1   Reputation Computation

To calculate the reputation we use Bayesian statistics. Intuitively, if we have random events with k possible outcomes, we can compute the posteriori probabilities, *i.e.,* the probabilities of observing these behaviors, using the Dirichlet distribution if we assume the prior to be a Dirichlet distribution as well [7]. Then, the reputation is the expected value of a posteriori probability distribution. The reputation model presented here is a generalization of [16].

An important property of the Internet is that poor behaviors usually have very short duration [11] [20]. Reputation value is designed to determine *the expected probability of a service element in active service provided by an AS being given Feedback G.* Consequently, the reputation is calculated by weighing the entries in the feedback set to a value proportional to the time the service remained active within an observation window. In other words, after M trials, let $|F_X|$ be the count of BGP services contained in F_X, where $X \in \{G, B, U\}$, and $|F_G| + |F_B| + |F_U| = M$. Then, we define $|F_X| = \sum_{i=1}^{k} t(s_i)$, where k is the total number of BGP services in F_X and $t(s_i)$ is the percentage of time a BGP service s_i in F_X is active within the observation window. As good behaviors last a long duration compared to poor ones, at any given time within our observation window, the probability of an active service having good service elements will be much higher than probability of an active service with poor service elements. *Example:* Let an $AS0$ provide four services $S1$, $S2$, $S3$, $S4$ where $t(S1) = 0.95$, $t(S2) = 0.70$, $t(S3) = 0.05$ and $t(S4) = 0.40$, respectively. After evaluating the services based on B_p, let $S1$ and $S2$ be give the *Feedback G*, $S3$ is given *Feedback B* and $S4$ is given *Feedback U*. As each service element in a service is independent of the others, $t(S1) + t(S2)$ may be greater than 1. The reputation of ASes is given by: $|F_G| = 0.95 + 0.70 = 1.65$, $|F_B| = 0.05$, $|F_U| = 0.4$, resulting in $R_G = (1.65 + 1)/(1.65 + 0.05 + 0.4 + 3) = 0.51$, $R_B = (0.05 + 1)/(1.65 + 0.05 + 0.4 + 3) = 0.21$, and $R_U = (0.4 + 1)/(1.65 + 0.05 + 0.4 + 3) = 0.28$. The value one added encodes the prior observation. We can compute reputation values corresponding to other two behavior sets in a similar manner. It can be seen that the reputation function redistributes the probability of poor behavior in a manner proportional to the duration for which the service was active.

5.2   Reputation Analysis

In this section, we analyze the reputation of ASes, generated over a period of six months from Jan. 1, 2010 - Jun. 30, 2010. We focus on presenting only the results of the reputation due to poor behaviors. The reputation due to good behavior is a complement of the results and can be easily extracted from these. Figure 5 (a) shows the CDF of reputations of ASes which have at least one *Feedback B* or *Feedback U* for B_p, B_o and B_l. As reputation of ASes is computed every day, we illustrate the CDFs for a sampling of six days during the six month period. These graphs demonstrate three important points: (1) among the ASes that do demonstrate poor behaviors, over 85% of them do so infrequently (in the case of B_o this number is over 99%); (2) about 2-8% of the ASes which

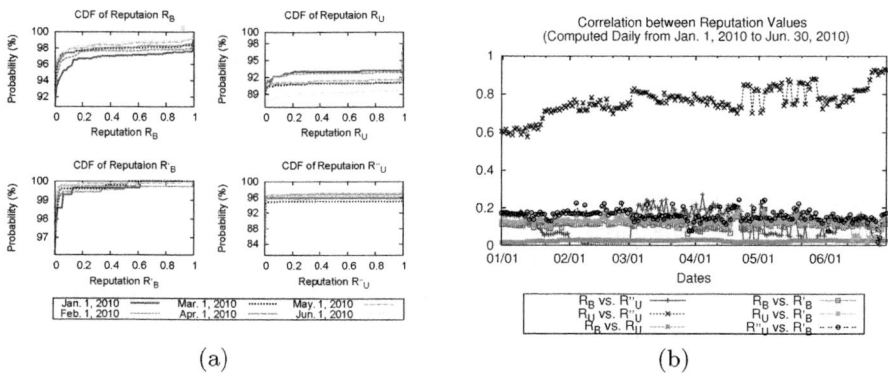

Fig. 5. (a) CDF of ASes with Poor Reputation Values, (b) Correlation between Various Reputation Values

demonstrate poor behavior do so exclusively (*i.e.*, the spike near the very end of the distribution) for B_p and B_l; and (3) over 99% of the ASes have a reputation close to zero for B_o, which means they are rarely involved in valley routes. This result demonstrates the *sensitivity of the reputation metric* as it is able to capture even those ASes which seldom violate BAs.

The availability of a quantitative value for different aspects of AS trustworthiness in the form of reputation allows us to mine emergent AS behavior trends that were heretofore difficult to identify. Figure 5 (b) illustrates the results of the correlation between different elements of the reputation matrix. Interestingly, we find R_U (*i.e.*, prefix hijacking) and R_U'' (*i.e.*, unstable AS-links) have a very high correlation, over the six months of our experiments. This is very intriguing as it increases the potential for low stability AS-links to be malicious (spoofed links). None of the other reputation values are strongly correlated.

One of the ways of using the AS reputation information is to improve the routing policies at ASes in order to minimize the effects of BA violations. In this regard, we built a BGP simulator that uses AS reputation information to make policy decisions about route-preference and route-dampening (*i.e.*, a process that prevents routers from thrashing while trying to incorporate a large number of route updates, thus producing a more stable routing table). The idea is to demonstrate that reputation information improves the number of quality routes added to the routing tables of an AS compared to reputation-less scheme. We find that, the reputation-based policy is particularly effective for reducing hijacked entries in the routing table, with an average 13 fold reduction compared to non-reputation case. Additionally, the reputation-based policy achieves two and four fold reduction in adding valley routes and routes with unstable-links, respectively. For more details on the simulation please refer to Section 6 in the technical report [12].

6   Related Work

Little work has been done with respect to characterizing AS behaviors. Most of the work has focused on detecting prefix hijacking using control-plane [17] [20] or data-plane probing [15] [25]. In [11], we present a preliminary version of this system called AS-CRED. AS-CRED, computes reputations for ASes based on their tendencies to hijack or announce short-lived prefixes as in this work. AS-TRUST, on the other hand, considers many more aspects in reputation computation including valley free routing and AS-link stability. However, the principal difference between the two is in the semantics of the reputation value. For example, in AS-TRUST R_U indicates how many prefix hijacking an AS performed. This value is indifferent to the number of stable AS-prefix bindings the AS had. For AS-CRED, reputation is simply a statement of how many prefix hijacking an AS has mounted. AS-CRED reputations can therefore be compared with the reputations of other ASes to see how they fare in comparison. With AS-TRUST, each row in the reputation matrix is a normalized value and has a probabilistic meaning. Therefore, poor behaviors of an AS cannot be seen independently of its good behaviors. We believe, reputation values of AS-TRUST thus provide a complimentary view of the AS behavior compared to the one provided by AS-CRED.

7   Conclusions

In this paper we presented AS-TRUST, a reputation-based trust quantification scheme with respect to the adherence of an AS to the three behavioral assumptions of BGP. Reputation is computed by evaluating past updates announced by each observable AS in the Internet for the exhibition of specific behaviors. The evaluation utilizes well-defined properties for this purpose including the presence of stable AS-prefix binding, stable AS-links, and valley free routes. It then classifies the resulting observations into multiple types of feedback. The feedback values are input into a reputation function that provides a probabilistic view of trust. Analysis of AS-TRUST shows that the incidents of assumption violation is consistently present, and that the proposed reputation mechanism can significantly improves the ability of ASes to function in the presence of violations of behavioral assumptions. In the future, we plan to study the effectiveness of other possible ways of using AS reputation to improve AS' policies.

References

1. A Border Gateway Protocol 4 (BGP-4) RFC, http://www.rfc-editor.org/rfc/rfc4271.txt
2. BGP Routing Leak Detection System Routing Leak Detection System, http://puck.nether.net/bgp/leakinfo.cgi
3. Macroscopic Topology Measurements, http://www.caida.org/projects/macroscopic/
4. The DIMES project, http://www.netdimes.org/new/
5. 7007 Explanation and Apology, http://www.merit.edu/mail.archives/nanog/1997-04/msg00444.html/
6. Autonomous System (AS) Numbers, http://www.iana.org/assignments/as-numbers/
7. Dirichlet distribution, http://www.cis.hut.fi/ahonkela/dippa/node95.html

8. Pakistan hijacks YouTube, `http://www.renesys.com/blog/2008/02/pakistan_hijacks_youtube_1.shtml/`
9. RouteViews, `http://www.routeviews.org/`
10. Caesar, M., Rexford, J.: BGP routing policies in ISP networks. IEEE Network 19(6), 5–11 (2005)
11. Chang, J., Venkatasubramanian, K., West, A.G., Kannan, S., Lee, I., Loo, B., Sokolsky, O.: AS-CRED: Reputation service for trustworthy inter-domain routing. In: University of Pennsylvania Technical Report, MS-CIS-10-17 (April 2010)
12. Chang, J., Venkatasubramanian, K., West, A.G., Kannan, S., Loo, B., Sokolsky, O., Lee, I.: AS-TRUST: A trust characterization scheme for autonomous system in BGP. In: University of Pennsylvania Technical Report, MS-CIS-10-25 (August 2010)
13. Gao, L.: On inferring autonomous system relationships in the Internet. IEEE/ACM Trans. Netw. 9(6), 733–745 (2001)
14. Grandison, T., Sloman, M.: A survey of trust in Internet applications. IEEE Communications Surveys and Tutorials 3(4) (August 2000)
15. Hu, X., Mao, Z.M.: Accurate real-time identification of IP prefix hijacking. In: SP 2007: Proceedings of the 2007 IEEE Symposium on Security and Privacy, pp. 3–17. IEEE Computer Society, Washington, DC (2007)
16. Josang, A., Ismail, R.: The beta reputation system. In: Proceedings of the 15th Bled Electronic Commerce Conference (2002)
17. Karlin, J., Forrest, S., Rexford, J.: Autonomous security for autonomous systems. Comput. Netw. 52(15), 2908–2923 (2008)
18. Mahajan, R., Wetherall, D., Anderson, T.: Understanding BGP misconfiguration. In: Proc. of the 2002 Conference on Applications, Technologies, Architectures, and Protocols for Computer Communications, pp. 3–16 (2002)
19. Nicholes, M., Mukherjee, B.: A survey of security techniques for the Border Gateway Protocol (BGP). IEEE Communications Surveys and Tutorials 11(1) (First Quarter 2009)
20. Qiu, J., Gao, L., Ranjan, S., Nucci, A.: Detecting bogus BGP route information: Going beyond prefix hijacking. In: Third International Conference on Security and Privacy in Communications Networks and the Workshops, SecureComm 2007, pp. 381–390 (September 2007)
21. Qiu, S.Y., McDaniel, P.D., Monrose, F.: Toward valley-free inter-domain routing. In: IEEE International Conference on Communications, ICC 2007, pp. 2009–2016 (2007)
22. Qiu, T., Ji, L., Pei, D., Wang, J., Xu, J., Ballani, H.: Locating prefix hijackers using LOCK. In: 18th USENIX Security Symposium (August 2009)
23. Ramachandran, A., Feamster, N.: Understanding the network-level behavior of spammers. SIGCOMM Computation and Communication Review 36(4), 291–302 (2006)
24. Zhang, B., Liu, R., Massey, D., Zhang, L.: Collecting the Internet AS-level topology. SIGCOMM Comput. Commun. Rev. 35(1), 53–61 (2005)
25. Zhang, Z., Zhang, Y., Hu, Y.C., Mao, Z.M., Bush, R.: iSPY: detecting IP prefix hijacking on my own. SIGCOMM Comput. Commun. Rev. 38(4), 327–338 (2008)

Incentivizing Responsible Networking via Introduction-Based Routing*

Gregory Frazier[1], Quang Duong[2], Michael P. Wellman[2], and Edward Petersen[1]

[1] BAE Systems
[2] University of Michigan

Abstract. The Introduction-Based Routing Protocol (IBRP) leverages implicit trust relationships and per-node discretion to create incentives to avoid associating with misbehaving network participants. Nodes exercise discretion through their policies for offering or accepting introductions. We empirically demonstrate the robustness of IBRP against different attack scenarios. We also use empirical game-theoretic techniques to assess the strategic stability of compliant policies, and find preliminary evidence that IBRP encourages the adoption of policies that limit damage from misbehaving nodes. We argue that IBRP scales to Internet-sized networks, and can be deployed as an overlay on the current Internet, requiring no modifications to applications, operating systems or core network services, thus minimizing cost of adoption.

1 Introduction

Militaries, governments, commercial firms, and individuals on the Internet are continually subject to a variety of attacks from a plethora of individual, organized-crime, and nation-state actors. One can identify a proximate cause for each security failure, and there exist research efforts to find mitigations to individual threat vectors as well as engineering efforts by vendors to harden products against attack. These efforts have as yet failed to significantly reduce the degree to which computer systems are being subverted.

A central cause of the widespread corruption on the Internet is the ephemeral nature of the relationship between communicating parties. Whereas there is a concrete (fiduciary, organizational) relationship between an endpoint and its Internet service provider (ISP), and between the adjacent autonomous systems that the packets traverse, the Internet protocol (IP) hides these relationships so that all two communicating endpoints know is each other's IP address. In the physical/kinetic economy, the supply chain is visible, and the resulting economic incentives reinforce good behavior. For example, when it was discovered that toothpaste exported from China contained diethylene glycol, public outrage pressured the U.S. government, which in turn pressured the Chinese government, which (then) enforced product safety laws with the exporters. Without

---

* This research was supported by the Air Force Research Laboratory (AFRL).

J.M. McCune et al. (Eds.): TRUST 2011, LNCS 6740, pp. 277–293, 2011.

the exposed supply chain, consumers would have had no leverage with the exporters. Similarly, there is a supply chain behind every packet that traverses the Internet—but IP (in its current incarnation) hides it.

Introduction-based routing (IBR) seeks to limit misbehavior in a network by: i) exposing the network supply chain, ii) giving network elements authority over with whom they interact, and iii) incorporating feedback, giving participants a basis for making their relationship choices. The ability to choose with whom one interacts creates economic incentives that (in the long run) discourage network elements from interacting with nodes that repeatedly misbehave. An IBR node's decisions with regards to introductions are made by the node's *policy*, a software implementation of a strategy that maximizes the node's utility in a network that may contain corrupt participants.

The IBR protocol is completely decentralized, designed to scale to Internet-sized networks. It presumes no universal authentication mechanism, requires minimal information sharing among participants, and accommodates heterogeneous misbehavior definitions and policy implementations. Through proxy-based implementation, it can be deployed without any modifications to applications, operating systems, or the network backbone.

In the next section we describe the IBR protocol. §3 presents a simulation-based evaluation of the ability of networks of IBR-compliant nodes to create a trusted network capable of resisting various attacks. The analysis of §4 employs (empirical) game-theoretic techniques to evaluate the incentives for compliance with the protocol. In §5 we relate IBR to previous work in network security, and the final section summarizes contributions and suggests future research.

2   Introduction-Based Routing

Fundamental to the introduction-based approach is a node's discretion about whether to participate in an exchange of packets. Under the IBR protocol (IBRP), a packet can enter the network if and only if it is traveling on a *connection* (comparable to a VPN between two nodes). Having entered the network, it can reach only the node at the other end of the connection. Both parties to a connection must consent to participate, and either party can close the connection.

2.1   IBR Protocol

To establish a new connection, a node must be *introduced* by a third party with connections to both the node and the neighbor-to-be. Since no node will be connected to every other (i.e., there is no universal introducer), forming a new connection may require multiple consecutive introductions. To bootstrap participation in the network, a node must have at least one *a priori* connection (a connection that does not require an introduction). The graph of nodes linked by a priori connections defines the network.

There are three parties to an introduction: the *requester* (the node requesting the introduction); the *introducer* (the node asked to make the introduction); and the *target* (the node to which the requester wishes to be introduced). If the introduction offer is accepted, a connection is established between the requester and target and the two nodes can exchange packets and/or request introductions to others. (These labels reflect roles in IBR, not inherent qualities of the nodes. A node may perform different roles at various points.)

A connection exists indefinitely until either party elects to close it. When a connection is closed, the requester and target provide feedback to the introducer regarding the state of the connection at the time of closing. If these nodes were introduced to the introducer, then the feedback is forwarded to those introducers after being processed. The feedback is binary—it is either positive (the other party was well-behaved) or negative. A connection closure is accompanied by messages between the two parties that signify the closure and notify the other party regarding the value of the feedback.

A key difference between IBRP and conventional routing protocols is that nodes have discretion regarding with which nodes they interact. There are two ways that a connection request can be refused. First, the introducer may respond to the introduction request with an *introduction denied* message. Second, the target may respond to the introduction offer with an *introduction declined* message. If the requester cannot find an introducer willing and able to make the introduction, then he will be unable to send packets to the target.

2.2   An Introduction Sequence

We illustrate the basic process of establishing a connection with a simple four-node network (Fig. 1). A priori connections exist between computers Q and M, M and G, and G and N. Suppose a process on Q wishes to communicate with a process on N. Q might start by sending a request to M for an introduction to G. [The policy on] M agrees to this request, and makes the introduction. G decides to accept the introduction, thus establishing a connection between Q and G ($\overline{QG}$). Q can now ask G for an introduction to N, which G agrees to make. N accepts the introduction, establishing $\overline{QN}$ and allowing the process on Q to interact with the process on N.

If either Q or N at a later time closes the connection, both nodes provide feedback about the connection state (positive or negative) to G. The feedback from N is processed by G and is also forwarded to M, since M introduced the subject of the feedback (Q) to G. Nodes may play different roles on different introductions (e.g., G is the target in the first introduction and the introducer

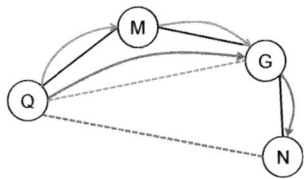

Fig. 1. Simple introduction sequence. Solid lines are a priori connections, curved arrows introductions and requests, and dashed lines the connections established.

in the second). Note also that both the a priori and the introduced connections are logical constructs over the network—they do not entail physical proximity between the nodes and are independent of underlying network architecture. Although the protocol does not levy any particular requirements on a node that will act as an introducer, we anticipate that in a large-scale network, introducers will typically be long-lived, well-established nodes whose capabilities as introducers are well known (possibly advertised via DNS or other lookup services).

2.3   Reputation

The IBR protocol does not specify the basis for nodes deciding whether to offer or accept introductions or when to close a connection. This is intentional, as we anticipate that organizations will craft policies for their nodes that correspond to their economic interests. That being said, we propose a simple model for making these decisions and argue that it i) protects the nodes' interests and globally discourages misbehavior in the network and ii) is stable, remaining an effective policy even when neighboring nodes base their decisions on a different model.

In the simple model, a node maintains a score for every neighbor to which it has a connection. We call that score a *reputation*. Much prior work in reputation-based systems (see §5) has used an explicit sharing of reputation scores as the means to curtail the attacks of a malicious participant. IBR takes a different tack. There is no sharing of reputations, and a node maintains reputation scores only for its current connections. When a target is offered an introduction, it decides whether or not to establish the connection based on the reputation of the *introducer*—not the requester, for whom the target does not have a reputation model. Therein lies the economic incentive exposed by IBR. Introducing a misbehaving node will damage the introducer's subsequent ability to provide introductions. The value of future introduction thereby drives nodes to exercise vigilance and discretion over those they are willing to introduce.

There are several reasons in practice that nodes could obtain positive value from introducing successful connections.

1. Direct benefit from activity on the connection. For instance, in a collaborative project, all participants gain from the ability of others to communicate.
2. Direct or indirect compensation from the requester for facilitating the connection. For instance, the introducer may be an ISP, who charges a fee to the requester for the introduction or more broadly for network services.
3. Implicit compensation through reciprocal action, for example the requester may be more inclined to offer introduction in kind to its existing connections.
4. Since the network itself generates value, all parties indirectly benefit from its growth to new trustworthy nodes.

We expect that factors like these provide sufficient motivation for nodes to preserve their ability to introduce, and thus cultivate and maintain a positive reputation through careful use of their introduction capability.

2.4   Deployment

We are pursuing the implementation of an IBR protocol proxy that is based on a bulk virtual private network (VPN) implementation. This will allow IBR to be deployed without modifications to applications, operating systems, router/switch implementations or the Internet backbone. Hosts need only to identify the IBR proxy as their gateway to participate in the protocol. Misbehavior sensors (e.g., spam detectors, network intrusion detection systems, personal security products, etc.) will be integrated with the proxy, notifying it when to preemptively close a connection and provide negative feedback.

An important element of the IBR implementation is a reliable service for discovering the introduction sequence to a given destination. We are implementing a hill-climbing algorithm, where hosts advertise nodes they accept introductions from that are higher up the hill. To obtain a connection to a given host, a node will request introductions "up the hill" until it has a connection to a node that is above the destination or has a peer that is above the destination, at which point the node requests introductions "down the hill" until it reaches the destination. This algorithm is implemented in the simulation described in the next section. In the simulation, after a warmup period where hosts establish connections to their communication partners, introductions are rarely requested. We anticipate that the same phenomena will occur in a real IBR network.

3   Network Performance Evaluation

Having introduced the IBR protocol, we next assess its impact on raw network performance (throughput) and its ability to discourage and/or prevent misbehavior when there are attackers present on the network.

3.1   Experiment Settings

We evaluate performance using an event-driven simulator. The physical details of the network were not simulated; we assumed that messages travel from source to destination in a single time unit, and we did not restrict the number of messages a node could receive per unit time. We initialized the experimental network with a set of a priori connections. Per the IBR protocol, to send a message to a given destination, a node must first establish a connection via introductions. If the connection cannot be established (due to refusal of an introducer or target server), then the message is not delivered.

Every node in an IBR network is capable of playing any of the three roles in an introduction (requester, introducer, or target). That said, for our simulation communicating nodes are explicitly designated as *clients* or *servers*. Clients generate application messages every ten to fifty time units. Each message generated is addressed to one of the server nodes in the network, selected uniformly. Upon receiving a message, servers send a response message back to the client. Nodes not designated as a client or a server provided introductions but do not participate in the application-level messaging.

Nodes in our IBR simulation monitor reputations and make introduction and connection decisions using a policy we label Compliant. A Compliant node i initializes reputation scores for all a priori connections to 1.95. When i accepts a connection with node j through k's introduction, i sets its reputation score τ_{ij} for j to $0.95\tau_{ik}$ where τ_{ik} is the present reputation score for the introducer k. When its sensors detect attacks carried out by j, i drops τ_{ij} by 1.6 and its trust τ_{ik} for the introducer k by 0.15, while the lack of sensor alerts when communicating with j leads to an increase of 0.17 to τ_{ij} and of 0.1275 to τ_{ik}. Upon receiving negative (positive) feedback from other nodes regarding j's activities, i decreases (increases) its reputation score τ_{ij} for node j by 0.35 (0.01), and decrements the score of the node that introduced j to i by 0.05 (0.0005). During periods of no communication between i and j, τ_{ij} regresses back toward zero with a rate of $5 \times 10^{-6} \times (t - t_{ij}^{\text{last}})^2$, where t_{ij}^{last} records the last time the two nodes exchanged messages. If j is an a priori connection, i will disconnect from j when τ_{ij} drops below 0.8. Otherwise, when τ_{ij} falls below threshold $\theta_{\text{Compliant}} = -0.4$, node i disconnects from j if connected, and stops introducing j to others. We chose the various parameters (e.g., reputation adjustments, thresholds) through an ad hoc tuning exercise using a preliminary set of simulation runs. The strategy implemented by these constants is one of gradually increasing trust for nodes that are consistently well-behaved. When a host misbehaves, it and its introducers' reputations are significantly impacted, but it requires multiple misbehavior events in proximity before a host finds its network access restricted.

In a given experiment, one or more of the clients and/or servers are designated as *attackers*. Each message generated by an attacker node is classified as an *attack message* with some *attack probability* q. For the main experiments reported in §3.2, clients address attacks to servers in a uniform distribution, and attacking servers simply responded to client messages with attacks (with the specified probability). Every client and server in the network is equipped with an attack sensor that has a specified rate of detecting attack messages, as well as a false alarm (false positive) rate. Unless otherwise noted, the detection rate is 0.9 and the false positive rate 0.001 for these experiments. (These rates approximate the accuracy of spam detectors. Other forms of misbehavior and associated sensors will yield different sensitivities and specificities.)

We simulated a 4956-node network comprising 4900 client and server nodes and 56 introduction providers. The initial connection topology (Fig. 2) is a redundant tree, with seven fully connected introducers at the root and the clients and servers at the leaves. Each client and server has a single a priori connection to an introducer, notionally playing the role of ISP. There are 49 ISPs in the network, each with 99 clients and one server attached. Each ISP, in turn, is connected to two of the root introducers. Thus, each client-server connection requires between one and four introductions to establish. There is no limit to the duration of a connection or the number of connections that a node can have—once established, a connection can be used for multiple client-server transactions and is only closed when misbehavior is detected (on sensor true and false positives). We simulated conventional IP by specifying additional a priori connections from

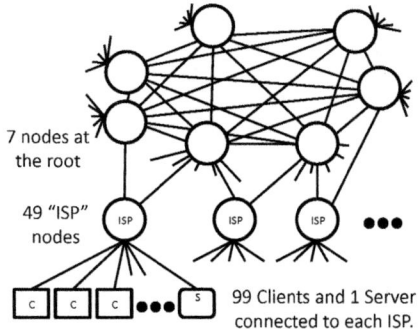

Fig. 2. The topology of a priori connections in the simulated network

every client to every server, and employing the policy Oblivious. The threshold parameter $\theta_{\text{Oblivious}} = -\infty$ means that IP nodes effectively trust all other nodes regardless of evidence about their behavior and thus never close connections. Each simulation instance generates a run that lasts for 10^4 time units, during which every client sends and receives approximately 330 messages (3.2 million application messages per simulation). To account for the stochastic nature of the environment, for each experiment we perform 5 runs to generate one data point.

3.2   Results

The first experiment compared the performance of IBRP to conventional IP with a single attacking node in the network. The probability of attack q was varied from 0.0 to 0.5. The results are shown in Fig. 3. Since the IP network provides no mechanism to prevent attack packets from reaching their destination, the number is directly proportional to q. In the IBR network, the attacker successfully sends approximately 20 attack messages. After approximately three attacks against a given server employing the Compliant policy, that server will cease to accept introductions to the attacker. After approximately five attacks, the Compliant introducer that hosts the the attacker refuses to offer any more introductions. The remaining attacks are sent on connections that the attacker already had open at the time of the fifth attack (hence the marginal drop in the number of attack messages reaching their destination for q exceeding 0.2).

We note that introductions do impose some performance overhead. Under actual networking conditions, the impact is on the latency of the first packet between two hosts. Given the way we account for time in our simulation model, the introduction overhead is reflected by a loss in throughput. Each client can send only one message at a time, and the simulation is terminated after a given number of time units have elapsed. Hence the added latency of waiting to be connected reduces the total number of messages delivered. The introduction delay is experienced in the IBR network both at the beginning of the simulation (when there are no connections between clients and servers) and when a sensor false alarm causes connections to be dropped. In the IP network, a total of 3.3

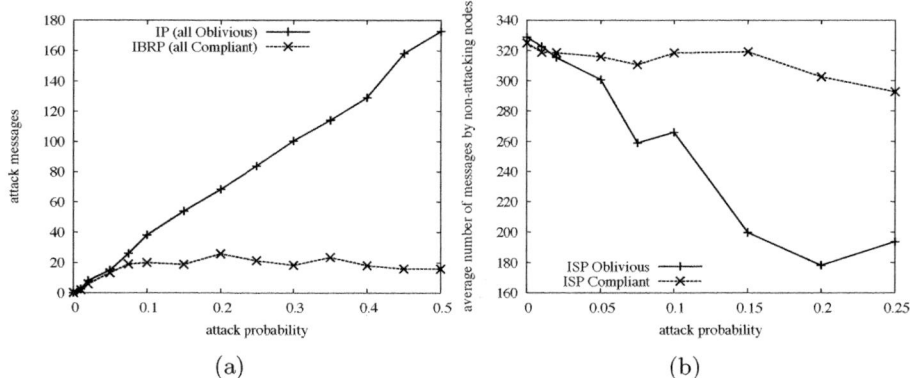

Fig. 3. (a) The number of attack messages that reached their destination per probability of attack, in IP and IBR networks of the same topology and configuration. servers. (b) Throughput experienced by the well-behaved nodes that share an ISP with the attacker, when the attacker's ISP throttles the attack (Compliant) and does not throttle the attacker (Oblivious).

million messages were delivered; in the IBR network, 3.1 million messages were delivered. (The attacker's messages were not counted.)

A tenet of IBR is that it is creating socio-economic incentives for network participants to behave responsibly. This applies not only to the network endpoints, but also to ISPs and other service providers. In the previous experiment, we showed that an ISP that applied the Compliant policy (consistent with the IBR protocol) would block the activity of an attacking node, protecting the rest of the network. However, a selfish ISP might conceivably elect not to block the attacker's activity, rather accruing subscription fees from the attacking node in return for continued service. In §4, we provide some game-theoretic evidence that rational nodes would actually adopt a compliant strategy. Here we show the performance impact on an ISP that chooses not to comply with IBR. Fig. 3 compares the performance of two networks, both of which have five attackers, all connected to the same ISP. The first network is an IBR network in which every node, including the ISP for the attackers, adopts Compliant. The second network is identical except that the attackers' ISP follows the non-compliant Oblivious policy—it continues to provide introductions for the attackers. The graph compares the throughput experienced by the *non-attacking* nodes that share the same ISP as the attackers.

When the ISP does not restrict the attackers' access to the network, all of its customers experience reduced access. This is because the second-tier introducers (the nodes to which the ISP has a priori connections) reduce the non-compliant Oblivious ISP's reputation to the point it impacts the ISP's ability to introduce its well-behaved customers. Specifically, when negative feedback from its neighbors reduces the ISP's reputation below a threshold, the ability of the ISP's customers to reach their destinations drops precipitously. This experiment reveals a phenomenon more comprehensively analyzed in §4: that the possible benefits of providing service to a misbehaving customer will be countered by the damage caused to one's own ability to interact with the network.

3.3 Reputation Attacks

Of particular concern for systems that rely on reputation are attacks that undermine the reliability of information used in reputation assessment. IBR inherently mitigates the risk from such attacks by refraining from sharing reputations among nodes. Nevertheless, there remains the threat of corruption in feedback that nodes offer when closing connections. Specifically, a node might connect to its target only to close the connection and issue spurious negative feedback, hoping to convince the target's ISP to cease to introduce the target.

To assess the impact of corrupt feedback on IBR, we performed an experiment where one client node deploys such a reputation attack. Specifically, the client attacks a particular server. In our experiments, the attack rate was 0.2, which means that for every application message the client attacker generated, it had a probability of 0.2 to be addressed to the victim server. Whenever this server responds to a message from the client, the client closes the connection and sends negative feedback as though it had received an attack message from the server. For messages from all other servers, the attacker behaves like every other node, generating a false positive with probability 0.001.

IBR effectively deals with the attack in this instance. When the server discovers that the client sent negative feedback (the protocol guarantees that it will), it registers the client's misbehavior and drops its reputation. Thus, before the client can cause the server to be disconnected, the server has ceased to accept connections from the client, and the server's continued good behavior quickly restores its reputation with its ISP. In our simulations, the throughput experienced by the victim server was not adversely affected at all by the attack: the average number of messages received actually increased from 32900 to 33000.

Besides this rather mechanistic defense, the server is also shielded by a strongly positive reputation with its ISP; the attacker will have difficulty overcoming this. However, these defenses have limits. A group of coordinated attackers could achieve measurable damage to a server's reputation. This is not really surprising, as *every* protocol is susceptible to defeat by a sufficient number of Byzantine attackers [19].

3.4 Discussion

Our performance experiments have illustrated three key properties that IBR is designed to provide for responsible networking.

1. An ability to prevent hosts from repeatedly attacking.
2. Economic incentives for responsible network management, in the form of a reduced ability for introducers to provide introductions if they continue to introduce hosts that are known to be misbehaving.
3. Resistance to attack on based on reputation feedback.

Although the limited scope of experiments conducted reported to date prevents us from reaching sweeping conclusions, we regard the results thus far as confirming the promise of this approach.

4   Empirical Game Evaluation

We further evaluate whether IBRP indeed leads to a network of trustworthy connections, where malicious activity is effectively deterred and well-behaving nodes can efficiently communicate. This entails assessing to what extent IBR mechanisms induce compliant policies, in the sense that adoption of behaviors following the intended design represents a strategically stable configuration. In particular, is the use of reputation feedback enabled by IBRP for connection and introduction decisions sufficient to keep the network in a predominantly trusted state? In other words, are there plausible policies that nodes can adopt to operate both safely and efficiently? As a start toward answering these questions, we investigate the robustness and game-theoretic stability of specific compliant policies in the face of specified attacks.

4.1   Game Formulation

Consider an IBRP network with n nodes. We construct a game model representing the interaction of these nodes over a set time horizon, as follows.

- Each node $i \in \{1, \ldots, n\}$ is a *player* (agent), who selects a *policy* (strategy) p_i from a space P_i of candidate policies. The policy dictates how the agent makes decisions about introductions, connections, and feedback propagation, as a function of network history.
- Nodes independently choose their policy at the beginning of a scenario run. The configuration $p = (p_1, \ldots, p_n)$ of choices is called a *policy profile*.
- The outcome of a run of the network is summarized by a *payoff* each player receives, based on how well it satisfied its communication objectives through the network over the scenario's time horizon. The payoff for node i is represented by a *utility function*, $u_i : \prod_k P_k \to \Re$.

To define the game for an IBRP scenario, we specify a network topology and assign objectives for communication in the form of a distribution of messaging tasks. Receiving a benign message accrues a unit payoff, whereas a malicious message subtracts 1000 from utility. An introducer's utility is proportional to the number of successful connections it establishes. Given these scenario settings, we estimate the utility function over policy profiles, through simulations configured as described in §3.1.

We consider a policy profile strategically stable if it constitutes an (approximate) *pure-strategy Nash equilibrium* (PSNE) of the IBRP-induced game. At a Nash equilibrium, no player can increase its utility by unilaterally deviating from its policy in the profile. Given sampling noise and our rough modeling of node utility, we consider approximate degrees of strategic stability. For profile p, let us define player i's *regret* $\epsilon_i(p)$ as the maximum gain i can obtain from unilaterally changing its own policy p_i: $\epsilon_i(p_i, p_{-i}) = \max_{p'_i \in P_i \setminus \{p_i\}} u_i(p'_i, p_{-i}) - u_i(p_i, p_{-i})$. The overall regret of a profile $\epsilon(p) = \max_i \epsilon_i(p)$.

4.2 Experiment Settings

Our exploratory empirical study examines simulated small-scale IBRP networks, such as the two networks illustrated in Fig. 4. In Scenario 1 a lone introducer mediates connections between all clients and servers. Scenario 2 consists of a more elaborate network of introducers between the clients and servers.

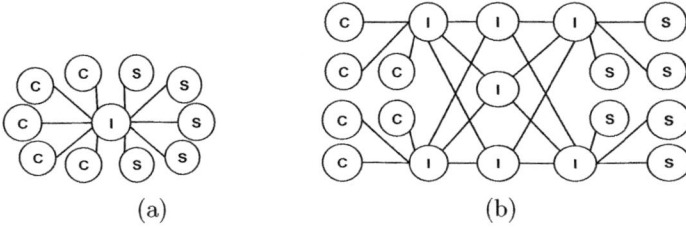

(a)   (b)

Fig. 4. (a) Scenario 1 comprises five clients and four servers, with a single introducer. (b) Scenario 2 includes a network of intermediate introducers.

We consider three candidate policies, and assume that each node chooses one and adheres to that throughout a run. The candidates include the aforementioned policy Oblivious, a parametric variant of Compliant we denote Compliant2, and a less strict version of Compliant2 named RCompliant2. We tuned Compliant2's parameters for the specific small network configurations in this section, where the presence of one attacker has a relatively more profound effect on other nodes than in larger networks. A Compliant2 node i initializes all reputation values to 1.0. Each detected attack by j on i causes i to decrease τ_{ij} by 1.0, and τ_{ik} by 0.5, where k is the node that introduced j to i. Each good transaction increases τ_{ij} by 10^{-4} and τ_{ik} by 5×10^{-5}. Upon receiving negative feedback regarding j's activities, i decreases its reputation score τ_{ij} by 0.5, and decrements the score τ_{ik} by 0.25. Node i increases τ_{ij} by 5×10^{-5} and τ_{ik} by 2.5×10^{-5} on positive feedback about j. During periods of no communication between i and j, τ_{ij} regresses back toward zero with a rate of $10^{-6}(t - t_{ij}^{last})^2$. It further specifies the threshold $\theta_{\text{Compliant2}} = -0.01$ for its neighbors' reputation. RCompliant2 retains all Compliant2's parameters except that $\theta_{\text{RCompliant2}} = -0.1$. These candidate policies, though containing arbitrary elements, are chosen to represent a spectrum of prospective node behaviors. We are interested in comparing and contrasting the intended IBRP behaviors Compliant2 and RCompliant2 and the naive behavior Oblivious employed under IP.

For each scenario, we examine two environment settings and various levels of attack probability q. In the Moderate environment, nodes can perfectly detect malicious messages from their connected nodes, and only one of the client nodes is malicious. Note that since there are no attackers on the server side in Moderate, client policy is irrelevant. In environment Severe, there are attackers on both server and client sides. Moreover, nodes in Severe may mistake benign messages for harmful attacks or vice versa, each with probability 0.005.

4.3   Single Introducer

Under the Moderate setting of Scenario 1, for all tested values of q, profiles in which servers adopt either Compliant2 or RCompliant2 and the sole introducer plays Oblivious are approximate PSNEs. For the case where the attack probability is high, $q = 0.9$, the profile p_{guard} in which the introducer chooses Compliant2 and the servers all play Oblivious is also a PSNE. All other profiles were found to be strategically unstable. Thus, when the sole introducer does not implement any measures to shield the servers from the attackers, the servers have to adopt compliant policies to protect themselves. In the one extreme case of reliable attack the compliant introducer with trusting servers (p_{guard}) achieves the same result. In all cases, the approximate equilibria dictate that either introducer or servers are compliant, with agent(s) of the other role relying on that.

Let p_{sC} (resp. p_{sRC}) denote the approximate PSNE profile where all servers adopt Compliant2 (RCompliant2). Fig. 5 plots the difference in payoffs, denoted by Δ, that a compliant server in each of these profiles would accrue by deviating to Oblivious. We also display the maximum deviation gain that a server in p_{guard} would achieve by switching to a compliant policy from Oblivious. A negative value of Δ means that the agent loses utility by deviating. Note that the gains Δ are bounded above by regret, so cannot be significantly positive in approximate equilibrium. As the attack probability increases, servers in p_{sC} and p_{sRC} lose considerably more by deviating from their compliant policies. Fig. 5 also demonstrates that p_{guard}'s Δ reaches the level of approximate equilibrium only for the highest value of q.

Environment Severe's results are consistent with the Moderate setting in Scenario 1, for sufficiently large attack probability values. In approximate equilibrium, the non-introducer nodes adopt either Compliant2 or RCompliant2 while the introducer plays Oblivious. Let p_{scC} (p_{scRC}) denote the profile where all non-introducer nodes adopt Compliant2 (RCompliant2). Fig. 5 confirms that when the introducer plays Oblivious, both the servers and clients have a stronger incentive to play compliant policies as q increases. Smaller values of q provide a less clear picture in which some approximate PSNE profiles have some non-introducer nodes playing Oblivious. Note that the possibility of false positives and negatives in detecting attacks in environment Severe, coupled with smaller values of q, makes it more difficult for nodes to effectively block potential attacks, rendering the compliant policies less desirable.

4.4   Network of Introducers

We conducted a further preliminary analysis of a more elaborate second scenario, with a network of introducers between clients and servers. For this scenario, we

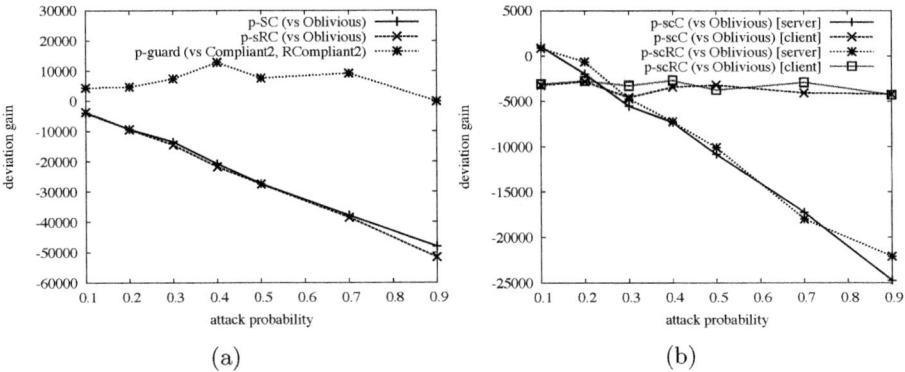

(a)   (b)

Fig. 5. (a) Servers' payoff gain in environment Moderate, when deviating to Oblivious in profiles p_{sC} and p_{sRC}, and by deviating to either Compliant2 or RCompliant2 in p_{guard}. (b) Payoff gains in environment Severe, when deviating to Oblivious in profiles p_{scC} and p_{scRC}. Results are shown for different values of the client attacker's q while the server attack probability is fixed at 0.1.

omit the RCompliant2 option, and find that all the servers adopt Compliant2 in all PSNE, under both Moderate and Severe environments. This observation reinforces the first scenario's conclusion that nodes gain substantial benefit from playing Compliant2 to protect themselves from attacks. Since a malicious client may pursue many introduction paths, it is more difficult for the network of introducers to shield the server from the need to maintain its own vigilance. While this provides appropriate incentive for the servers, it also suggests that Compliant2 policy settings may not be optimized for introducer performance. For example, note that in Scenario 2 a malicious client C_{mal} has multiple available paths of introduction to a given server S_1. When S_1 plays Oblivious, its proximal introducer I_1 essentially assumes the role of protecting S from C_{mal}'s attacks. However, given the indirect propagation of feedback, even if I_1 plays Compliant2 and detects the attack from one path, it may end up reintroducing C_{mal} to S_1 via a different path. A server can be introduced via three different paths that correspond to the three intermediate introducers in Scenario 2 illustrated in Fig. 4, thus allowing faster reintroductions of malicious nodes. By playing Compliant2 as well, S_1 uses reputation to track I_1's effectiveness as a shield, and may avoid accepting the second connection from C_{mal}.

4.5 Remarks

Our simulations of some simple network scenarios and environment settings, under different node policies, illustrate the possible roles of IBRP's reputation mechanism in discouraging malicious behavior. Through an empirical game-theoretic analysis, we find that the IBRP-compliant policies would be generally preferred over accepting all connection requests as in today's Internet protocol. The more hostile the environment, the greater benefit a node can obtain from adopting a compliant policy. Moreover, as others deviate by playing Oblivious, a node has greater incentive to protect itself by making reputation-based decisions. Overall, the experiments support the proposition that IBRP's reputation and feedback system enables and incentivizes nodes to adopt safer policies, thus contributing to improving network security under IBRP.

Our analysis is of course quite incomplete, and the empirical game-theoretic evidence should be regarded as supporting but preliminary. The most glaring limitation is our consideration of only three candidate policies thus far. A more comprehensive analysis would include policies that deviated from IBRP in particular ways, including selective use of reputation information, failure to propagate feedback, and false reporting of node activity. It would also include a broader palette of compliant policies, including more sophisticated ways to maintain reputation information and condition decisions on this basis. By including imperfect detection and malicious nodes, and considering a suboptimal compliant policy, we did attempt to deflect bias, but ultimately there is no substitute for the more in-depth study. This investigation should also employ much larger networks of more complex topology, and nodes with multiple roles as clients, servers, and introducers. Finally, we should also consider variations on rational behavior and their impact on IBRP performance.

5   Related Work

IBR participants use local trust assessments and policies to decide when to introduce and accept connections. In some respects, this resembles the "web of trust" paradigm employed notably by Pretty Good Privacy (PGP) [1, 32], in that entities rely on endorsements from trusted others in determining with whom to interact. PGP allows multiple parties to sign a given certificate, create a complex graph of trust. (PGP uses the term "introducer" to describe peer signatories.) Calculating reputation over a certificate trust-web has been extensively explored [18, 20, 26], and applied to social networks [8]. Trust-web mechanisms assume that the graph of trust relationships is generally accessible [17].

Distributed trust is used to control access in systems where centralized access control is unavailable, for example in peer-to-peer (P2P) environments [12, 13, 30]. Reputation systems [21] calculate and disseminate global reputation ratings [3, 4, 16]. Global reputation measures: i) depend on universally recognized identity and authentication for each node, ii) require uniform standards of good behavior, iii) are susceptible to attacks on reputation infrastructure, such as Sybil and ballot-stuffing [15, 25]. TrustGuard [24] uses models of misuse to resist some of the attacks to which a shared reputation system is susceptible.

Trust management systems such as KeyNote [2] allow one to specify access control and other policies with a well-defined language. A great deal of prior work on trust and reputation mechanisms have shown how authorization decisions can be made [11, 22]. Route integrity verification mechanisms focus on improving network accountability by auditing pairwise network connections to detect malicious data-package passing activities [14, 29].

Game theory has often been used to analyze reputation systems [7], in networking and other contexts. For example, Friedman and Resnick [6] establish inherent limitations to the effectiveness of reputation systems when participants are allowed to generate new identities (a tactic IBRP is immune to), and Srivastava et al. [23] survey a range of game-theoretic applications to wireless ad hoc networks. Increasingly, game-theoretic techniques are also finding application in security domains, including but not limited to information security [9, 10, 31].

In the *empirical game-theoretic analysis* (EGTA) approach [27], expert modeling is augmented by empirical sources of knowledge, that is, data obtained through real-world observations or outcomes of high-fidelity simulation. In our own prior work, we have applied EGTA to a range of problems, including for example auctions [28] and games among privacy attackers [5].

6   Conclusion

The Introduction-Based Routing Protocol takes an unorthodox approach to promote a more trustworthy Internet. Rather than control access via authentication and authorization, or otherwise attempt to render forms of misbehavior algorithmically impossible, IBRP creates disincentives for associating with misbehaving nodes. Rather than attempting to track the behavior or reputation of endpoints (which is neither scalable nor practical, given the ill-defined and fleeting nature of their relationship), nodes track the (aggregate) behavior of the supply chain of network neighbors that produced the set of communication partners.

We have provided preliminary evidence that IBRP can support a trustworthy Internet. Simulations of a 5000-node network demonstrate that IBR policies successfully insulate the network from a variety of attacks. We have also shown, for some modest-sized network models, compliant policies form a strategically stable configuration, and trust decisions based on the private reputation assessment of these compliant policies limit the impact of misbehavior. We have also shown that IBRP successfully operates with imperfect sensors, with the corollary that isolated acts of misbehavior will not cause a node to be disconnected from the network.

References

[1] Abdul-Rahman, A., Hailes, S.: A distributed trust model. In: Workshop on New Security Paradigms, Langdale, UK, pp. 48–60 (1997)

[2] Blaze, M., Ioannidis, J., Keromytis, A.D.: Trust management for IPsec. ACM Transactions on Information and System Security 5(2), 95–118 (2002)

[3] Buchegger, S., Le Boudec, J.Y.: Performance analysis of the CONFIDANT protocol. In: Third International Symposium on Mobile Ad Hoc Networking and Computing, Lausanne, pp. 226–236 (2002)

[4] Cornelli, F., Damiani, E., di Vimercati, S.D.C., Paraboschi, S., Samarati, P.: Choosing reputable servents in a P2P network. In: Eleventh International World Wide Web Conference, Honolulu, pp. 376–386 2002)

[5] Duong, Q., LeFevre, K., Wellman, M.P.: Strategic modeling of information sharing among data privacy attackers. Informatica 34, 151–158 (2010)
[6] Friedman, E.J., Resnick, P.: The social cost of cheap pseudonyms. Journal of Economics and Management Strategy 10(2), 173–199 (2001)
[7] Friedman, E., Resnick, P., Sami, R.: Manipulation-resistant reputation systems. In: Nisan, N., Roughgarden, T., Tardos, E., Vazirani, V.V. (eds.) Algorithmic Game Theory, pp. 677–697. Cambridge University Press, Cambridge (2007)
[8] Golbeck, J.A.: Computing and applying trust in web-based social networks. Ph.D. thesis. University of Maryland (2005)
[9] Grossklags, J., Christin, N., Chuang, J.: Secure or insure?: A game-theoretic analysis of information security games. In: Seventeenth International Conference on World Wide Web, Beijing, pp. 209–218 (2008)
[10] Jain, M., Pita, J., Tambe, M., Ordóñez, F., Parachuri, P., Kraus, S.: Bayesian Stackelberg games and their application for security at Los Angeles International Airport. SigEcom Exchanges 7(2), 1–3 (2008)
[11] Jøsang, A., Ismail, R., Boyd, C.: A survey of trust and reputation systems for online service provision. Decision Support Systems 43(2), 618–644 (2007)
[12] Kamvar, S.D., Schlosser, M.T., Garcia-Molina, H.: The Eigentrust algorithm for reputation management in P2P networks. In: Twelfth International Conference on World Wide Web, Budapest, pp. 640–651(2003)
[13] Lagesse, B., Kumar, M., Wright, M.: AREX: An adaptive system for secure resource access in mobile P2P systems. In: Peer-to-Peer Computing 2008, pp. 43–52 (2008)
[14] Laskowski, P., Chuang, J.: Network monitors and contracting systems: Competition and innovation. ACM SIGCOMM Computer Communication Review 36(4), 194 (2006)
[15] Levien, R., Aiken, A.: Attack-resistant trust metrics for public key certification. In: Seventh USENIX Security Symposium, San Antonio, TX, pp. 229–242 (1998)
[16] Levine, J.: DNS Blacklists and Whitelists. RFC 5782 (Informational) (February 2010), http://www.ietf.org/rfc/rfc5782.txt
[17] Maurer, U.M.: Modelling a public-key infrastructure. In: Bertino, E. (ed.) ESORICS 1996. LNCS, vol. 1146, pp. 325–350. Springer, Heidelberg (1996)
[18] Mendes, S., Huitema, C.: A new approach to the X.509 framework: Allowing a global authentication infrastructure without a global trust model. In: IEEE Symposium on Network and Distributed System Security, pp. 172–189 (1995)
[19] Pease, M., Shostak, R., Lamport, L.: Reaching agreement in the presence of faults. Journal of the ACM 27, 228–234 (1980)
[20] Reiter, M.K., Stubblebine, S.G.: Authentication metric analysis and design. ACM Transactions on Information System Security 2, 138–158 (1999)
[21] Resnick, P., Kuwabara, K., Zeckhauser, R., Friedman, E.: Reputation systems. Communications of the ACM 43(12), 45–48 (2000)
[22] Ruohomaa, S., Kutvonen, L.: Trust management survey. In: Third International Conference on Trust Management, Rocquencourt, France, pp. 77–92 (2005)
[23] Srivastava, V., Neel, J., Mackenzie, A.B., Menon, R., DaSilva, L.A., Hicks, J.E., Reed, J.H., Gilles, R.P.: Using game theory to analyze wireless ad hoc networks. IEEE Communications Surveys and Tutorials 7(4), 46–56 (2005)
[24] Srivatsa, M., Xiong, L., Liu, L.: Trustguard: Countering vulnerabilities in reputation management for decentralized overlay networks. In: Fourteenth International Conference on World Wide Web, pp. 422–431 (2005)
[25] Sun, Y., Han, Z., Liu, K.: Defense of trust management vulnerabilities in distributed networks. IEEE Communications Magazine 46(2), 112–119 (2008)

[26] Tarah, A., Huitema, C.: Associating metrics to certification paths. In: Second European Symposium on Research in Computer Security, pp. 175–189 (1992)

[27] Wellman, M.P.: Methods for empirical game-theoretic analysis (extended abstract). In: Twenty-First National Conference on Artificial Intelligence, Boston, pp. 1552–1555 (2006)

[28] Wellman, M.P., Osepayshvili, A., MacKie-Mason, J.K., Reeves, D.M.: Bidding strategies for simultaneous ascending auctions. Berkeley Electronic Journal of Theoretical Economics (Topics) 8(1) (2008)

[29] Wong, E.L., Balasubramanian, P., Alvisi, L., Gouda, M.G., Shmatiko, V.: Truth in advertising: Lightweight verification of route integrity. In: Twenty-Sixth Annual ACM Symposium on Principles of Distributed Computing, Portland, OR, pp. 156–165 (2007)

[30] Xiong, L., Liu, L.: Building trust in decentralized peer-to-peer electronic communities. In: International Conference on Electronic Commerce Research (2002)

[31] Xu, J., Lee, W.: Sustaining availability of web services under distributed denial of service attacks. IEEE Transactions on Computers 52, 195–208 (2003)

[32] Zimmermann, P.R.: The Official PGP User's Guide. MIT Press, Cambridge (1995)

Catching the Cuckoo: Verifying TPM Proximity Using a Quote Timing Side-Channel

(Short Paper)

Russell A. Fink[1,2], Alan T. Sherman[2],
Alexander O. Mitchell[3], and David C. Challener[1]

[1] Johns Hopkins University / Applied Physics Laboratory
[2] University of Maryland Baltimore County / Cyber Defense Lab
[3] Hammond High School, Columbia, MD

Abstract. We present a *Trusted Platform Module (TPM)* application protocol that detects a certain man in the middle attack where an adversary captures and replaces a legitimate computing platform with an imposter that forwards platform authentication challenges to the captive over a high speed data link. This *revised Cuckoo* attack allows the imposter to satisfy a user's query of platform integrity, tricking the user into divulging sensitive information to the imposter. Our protocol uses an ordinary smart card to verify the platform boot integrity through TPM quote requests, and to verify TPM proximity by measuring TPM tickstamp times required to answer the quotes. Quotes not answered in an expected amount of time may indicate the presence of an imposter's data link, revealing the Cuckoo attack. We describe a timing model for the Cuckoo attack, and summarize experimental results that demonstrate the feasibility of using timing to detect the Cuckoo attack over practical levels of adversary link speeds.

Keywords: TPM, Attestation, Timing, Quote.

1 Introduction

Despite the proliferation of personal computers and mobile devices, the public relies on kiosk computers for critical security applications such as *Automated Teller Machine (ATM)* banking, filling out tax forms in public assisted offices, entering health insurance information at hospital kiosks, and voting on electronic terminals in large precincts. Kiosk computers are vulnerable to undetected physical attack because they are not controlled as well as personal devices. The *Trusted Computing Group (TCG)* has created the TPM, an embedded cryptographic processor that can convince the user by *attestation* that the correct software was booted on the platform with cryptographic proof of software measurements signed by a private key. A user who knows the corresponding public key can verify the attestation measurements recorded by the TPM, useful for verifying the state of a public kiosk. Attestation, however, requires the user to trust a smart token to issue challenges to the kiosk on his behalf and verify the cryptographic

J.M. McCune et al. (Eds.): TRUST 2011, LNCS 6740, pp. 294–301, 2011.

results. Further, attestation does not detect the Cuckoo attack, defined by Parno in [7] as a corrupt platform forwarding attestation challenges to a machine that can emit the expected responses, leading the user into disclosing sensitive information to the attacker. Therefore, the two major problems with kiosk computing are the user trusting a token to attest the state of the TPM, and the user trusting the physical path between his token and the TPM—in other words, the user cannot confirm the proximity of the TPM that is answering the challenges easily.

In our work to mitigate the Cuckoo attack, we have discovered that a reliable timing side-channel exists with quote command processing through the TPM.[1] We have designed a protocol to exploit this side channel by using an ordinary smart card to issue a sequence of quote requests, measure the amount of time taken to receive the responses, and decide whether the time taken to respond to the quotes is consistent with the expected path components between the smart card and the TPM. In short, we propose using timing to detect the Cuckoo attack. Our contributions are:

- Design and presentation of a TPM quote and timing attestation protocol using an ordinary, inexpensive smart card
- A timing model for the Cuckoo attack and required adversary bandwidth
- Experimental results supporting the use of timing side-channels to verify TPM proximity, revealing the Cuckoo attack.

In this short paper, we define the problem being solved, present a security and timing model, describe our protocol, and give an overview of the experimental results we obtained that demonstrate the feasibility of our approach.

2   Security and Timing Model

The problem we solve begins when the user intends to interact with a specific *kiosk*, but the adversary wants him to interact with an *imposter*. The adversary kidnaps the kiosk and replaces it with the imposter, and forces the kiosk to answer challenges on behalf of the adversary, thereby fooling the user.

This *Man-In-The-Middle (MITM)* attack is described by Parno as a Cuckoo attack where an adversary redirecting attestation challenges to a remote TPM under his control [7]. Our revised model, shown in Figure 1, places the imposter directly in front of the user. The imposter forwards any *Platform Configuration Register (PCR)* challenges to the kidnapped kiosk computer to obtain signed PCR values that the user expects to see. Our revised attack assumes that the user knows the public AIK of the kiosk used to verify quotes, but cannot confirm the physical proximity of the TPM. The attack resists detection by exploiting the gap between the challenger and the verifier.

---

[1] A *quote* is a reading of the TPM *Platform Configuration Register (PCR)* values signed by an *Attestation Identity Key (AIK)* belonging to that particular TPM. It is cryptographic evidence that the platform booted the correct software.

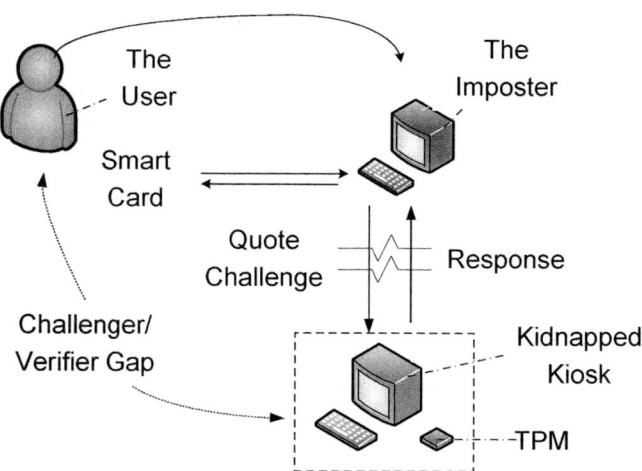

Fig. 1. In the revised Cuckoo attack, the user interacts with an imposter that forwards challenges to the legitimate kiosk, tricking the user into interacting with the imposter. This attack exploits a proximity gap between the challenger (user) and the verifier (kiosk).

We can detect Cuckoo attack by timing precisely an exchange of authentication messages between a smart card and a TPM. A notional timing model for this authentication sequence includes the time for the smart card to issue its challenge, the platform CPU to forward it to the TPM, and the time for the TPM to respond. Repeated trials of this exchange taken during a training phase will reveal some timing noise (measured as statistical variance) caused by network collisions, processor scheduling, card latency, and TPM load. In the Cuckoo attack, the adversary adds additional components to the model, potentially increasing the average transaction time. If we conservatively assume that the extra components in the Cuckoo case contribute no extra noise, then the attack succeeds without detection when the time added by the extra components is no greater than the noise time observed in training. We model the extra components in the Cuckoo attack in Figure 2.

Let the notional timing noise be ϵ, and the Cuckoo attack time be C. If we remove the imposter components from the model, and add back in the notional noise, the non-attack time becomes $C - 2(T'_N + T'_P) + \epsilon$; therefore, the Cuckoo attack cannot be distinguished from expected noise in the non-imposter case when:

$$2(T'_N + T'_P) \le \epsilon \tag{1}$$

Therefore, this model states that the adversary's connection speed in the hostage case varies linearly with the noise observed during the non-hostage training phase.

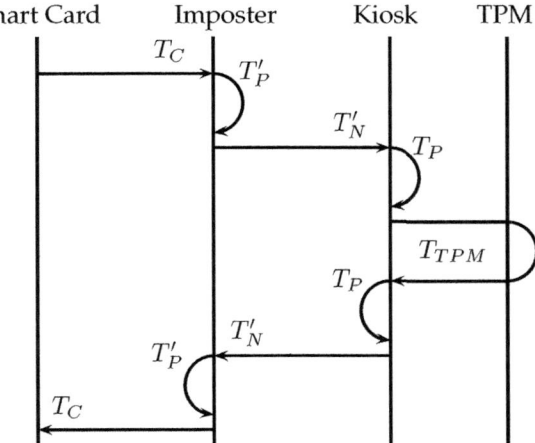

Fig. 2. Timing model for the revised Cuckoo attack. The smart card challenge takes time T_C to arrive at the imposter. The imposter takes takes T'_P to prepare the challenge and T'_N to forward it. The kiosk processes the message in T_P, and the TPM takes time T_{TPM} to respond.

3   Previous and Related Work

Parno [7] first described the Cuckoo attack as a user interacting with a kiosk tampered to forward challenges to the attacker's machine. Parno assumes that the user does not know any public keys of the kiosk TPM, enabling the attacker's (or anyone's) TPM to respond to attestation requests.[2] Our revised Cuckoo attack reverses the placement of the kiosk and the imposter. As with Parno, we assume that the user cannot confirm the physical proximity of the TPM. Unlike Parno, we require that the user knows the public AIK of the kiosk.

The Cuckoo attack is also called a Masquerade attack. Stumpf *et al.* proposed a TPM solution in [9] that establishes an encrypted session tunnel following attestation using a shared key exchanged during attestation, preventing interactions with the imposter. Goldman *et al.* proposed a similar system in [4]. While these are feasible when both communicating endpoints are computers, they do not fit the user-kiosk model where the human interacts directly with the host.

The TCG specifies the TPM, an embedded cryptographic processor and non-volatile storage device that can generate keys and use them securely according to policy. Our protocol uses the TPM to verify the correctness of platform identity and software state, and to keep accurate time for the smart card. The TPM is explained in specifications [10], and the software programming interface is explained in [11]. Challener *et al.* covers TPM application programming in [1]. Fink *et al.* give an example of TPMs enforcing election security policy using platform state in [2].

---

[2] While we disagree that distributing public portions of AIKs is difficult, we concede that *Public Key Infrastructure (PKI)* is often implemented incorrectly in practice.

Attestation involving cryptography is not practical for a human without assistance. Trusted computing supports attestation by using TPM to engage in a special challenge-response protocol with networked computers, called *Trusted Network Connect (TNC)*, described in [12]. However, TNC requires back-end infrastructure to verify challenges. We use a smart card in place of the back-end to let the user verify the platform.

We use timing side channels to verify TPM proximity to our smart card. Seshadri *et al.* created SWATT [8] that attests embedded software using timing. Gardner *et al.* uses memory access latency to attest software running on general purpose computers in [3]. These systems show the feasibility of using timing for attestation.

4   Protocol

Our authentication and proximity verification protocol uses a smart card to issue a fixed number of TPM_QUOTE requests to the local platform, measuring the time taken for these calls to complete as a group. The smart card verifies the quotes, and compares the aggregate response time with some clean room training set of timings and noise established previously. If the quote responses are correct and the response time is within the noise margin of the training times, the smart card releases a passphrase to the local platform indicating attestation success indicating the attestation decision of the smart card to the user. If either the timing or quote verification fails, the smart card releases a duress passphrase.

We assume that the adversary has a network of finite speed to connect his imposter to the kiosk. We assume that the adversary does not know the passphrases, nonces, or the AIK private key. We also assume that the TPM is working correctly. Figure 3 presents the protocol in more detail.

5   Experiments

We conducted experiments to verify our approach. The experiments timed the interactions between the operating system and TPM separately from the interactions between the smart card and operating system—this simplified setup allowed quick validation in lieu of a full end-to-end experiment. We calculated the average values and variances of the challenge/reponse times in each experiment, then combined the variances to compute the critical value of the one-tailed t distribution that dictates the required speed of the adversary's network.

5.1   OS to TPM

We created the experiment using a STmicroelectronics TPM running on a Dell OptiPlex 755. We developed two software programs for Linux, one using IBM's software TPM emulator and accompanying command-line utilities [6] and the other built on TrouSerS [5]. We collected data for runs that consisted of 200 challenge/response messages, and did several hundred runs to form the population. We terminated many extraneous operating system services during the runs.

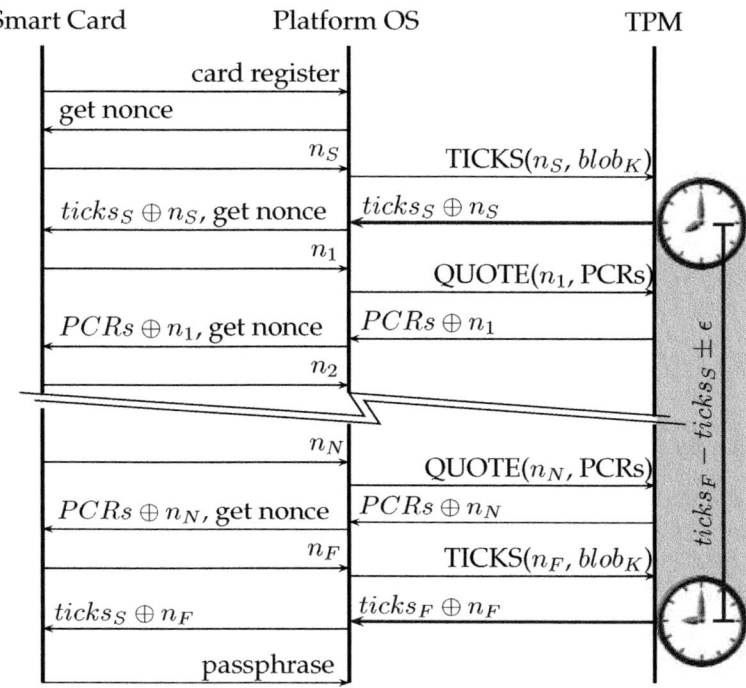

Fig. 3. A smart card issues a challenge nonce n_S to the TPM for an initial tickstamp, $ticks_S$, recording the start of the timed quote loop. The smart card issues unique nonces to obtain quotes. After receiving a final tickstamp, $ticks_F$, the smart card verifies the responses and loop time, then releases a positive or duress passphrase. The expected loop time is measured in an initial training phase. [$\oplus$ signifies cryptographic binding with the TPM's AIK.]

Table 1. Sample timing data, showing results for TPM (left) and smart cards (right). Times are of repeated challenge/response runs, expressed in seconds. OS (wall clock) time is compared with tickstamp time. Multi-modal harmonics (counts per group shown) differed by 0.004 secs for TPM and by 0.6 secs for smart cards.

Count	OS Time	Tickstamps
1	148.792325	149.934
351	148.800337	149.945
	148.800325	149.944
	148.800326	149.945
	. . .	. . .
45	148.804325	149.949
	148.804315	149.946
	148.804325	149.947
	. . .	. . .
1	148.808326	149.952

Count	OS Time
799	1.3997048
	1.3997401
	. . .
1	1.4006945
790	1.9997026
	1.9997082
	. . .
8	2.0000521
	2.0009368
	. . .

A summary of the TrouSerS data is presented in Table 1. The multi-modal clustering resembles *harmonics* that occur at intervals of 0.004 seconds; these are due likely to device interrupts and process scheduling of our test program by the Linux operating system.

5.2   OS to Smart Card

We timed different *Subscriber Identity Module (SIM)* Java cards running under Windows XP, and implemented a simple data collector using C#—we have approximated the timing variance of reading data from a program running on the card with that of reading a simple data value from the card. We timed 1,600 samples of 200 message transactions per sample. Data are shown in Table 1.

5.3   Analysis

Using the data from the largest harmonic groups, we computed the population standard deviation and used it to determine the one-tailed t test critical value. At the 95% confidence limit, our experiments a SIM variance of 3.2739×10^{-10} seconds and a TPM variance of 2.4925×10^{-7} seconds. The combined σ is 4.9958×10^{-4}, giving a critical value of 8.1931×10^{-4}. The attestation challenges consume 2,806 bytes per loop, for a total of 1.5 megabytes after adding in nominal packet headers. This requires the adversary to have a minimum network speed of 14.8 gigabits per second to avoid detection by our protocol.

6   Results and Conclusions

The predicted gigabit speed is faster than modern wireless technologies, meaning that the adversary must use wired, and possibly fiber, connections to carry out the Cuckoo attack. Such wired connections are both visible and expensive, and are revealed by simple physical inspection of the kiosk.

In conclusion, we have developed a protocol that works with an ordinary smart card and a TPMs to verify identity, state, and physical proximity of the platform. The protocol uses inexpensive technologies and enables practical proximity attestation for kiosk-style public computers. The attestation smart card is simple enough to be validated independently, *e.g.* in Seshadri [8].

7   Future Work

We must develop a full path, smart card to TPM experiment, and investigate environmental factors. We must characterize the probability of Type 1 errors.[3] A variety of smart cards should be tested, including identical models of the same cards. We should determine the optimal training time and number of loops to minimize the time needed for attestation.

---

[3] The timing harmonics are evidence that Type 1 errors are likely.

Acknowledgments

We thank Ryan Gardner for formative discussions, and also T. Llanso, F. Deal, B. Benjamin, E. Reilly, and members of the UMBC *UMBC Cyber Defense Lab (CDL)* for good suggestions. We thank April Lerner, gifted and talented coordinator for Hammond High School, for lending us a promising new researcher.

References

1. Challener, D., Yoder, K., Catherman, R., Safford, D., Van Doorn, L.: A practical guide to trusted computing. IBM press, Upper Saddle River (2007); ISBN 978-0132398428
2. Fink, R.A., Sherman, A.T., Carback, R.: TPM meets DRE: Reducing the trust base for electronic voting using trusted platform modules. IEEE Transactions on Security and Forensics 4(4), 628–637 (2009)
3. Gardner, R.W., Garera, S., Rubin, A.D.: Detecting code alteration by creating a temporary memory bottleneck. IEEE Transactions on Security and Forensics 4(4) (2009)
4. Goldman, K., Perez, R., Sailer, R.: Linking remote attestation to secure tunnel endpoints. In: Proceedings of the First ACM Workshop on Scalable Trusted Computing, pp. 21–24. ACM, New York (2006)
5. IBM Corporation: The Trusted Computing Software Stack (TrouSerS) software library (2008), http://sourceforge.net/projects/trousers/ (last accessed February 3, 2011)
6. IBM Corporation: Software TPM emulator (2010), http://ibmswtpm.sourceforge.net/ (last accessed June 23, 2010)
7. Parno, B.: Bootstrapping trust in a trusted platform. In: Proceedings of the 3rd Conference on Hot Topics in Security, pp. 1–6. USENIX Association (2008)
8. Seshadri, A., Perrig, A., van Doorn, L., Khosla, P.: SWATT: SoftWare-based ATTestation for embedded devices. In: Proceedings of IEEE Symposium on Security and Privacy, pp. 272–282. IEEE, Los Alamitos (2004)
9. Stumpf, F., Tafreschi, O., Röder, P., Eckert, C.: A robust integrity reporting protocol for remote attestation. In: Second Workshop on Advances in Trusted Computing (WATCâ06 Fall), Citeseer (2006)
10. Trusted Computing Group. TCG TPM specification version 1.2, revision 103 (2008), https://www.trustedcomputinggroup.org/specs/TPM (last accessed on March 15, 2008)
11. Trusted Computing Group. The TCG Software Stack (2009), http://www.trustedcomputinggroup.org/developers/software_stack (last accessed September 1, 2009)
12. Trusted Computing Group. The TCG Trusted Network Connect (2009), http://www.trustedcomputinggroup.org/developers/trusted_network_connect/ (last accessed September 1, 2009)

Group Distance Bounding Protocols

(Short Paper)

Srdjan Capkun[1], Karim El Defrawy[2,*], and Gene Tsudik[2]

[1] ETH Zurich
capkuns@inf.ethz.ch
[2] UC Irvine
{keldefra,gts}@ics.uci.edu

Abstract. Distance bounding (DB) protocols allow one entity, the verifier, to securely obtain an upper-bound on the distance to another entity, the prover. Thus far, DB was considered mostly in the context of a single prover and a single verifier. There has been no substantial prior work on secure DB in group settings, where a set of provers interact with a set of verifiers. The need for group distance bounding (GDB) is motivated by many practical scenarios, including: group device pairing, location-based access control and secure distributed localization. This paper addresses, for the first time, one-way GDB protocols by utilizing a new *passive DB* primitive. We show how passive DB can be used to construct secure and efficient GDB protocols for various one-way GDB settings. We analyze the security and performance of proposed protocols and compare them with existing DB techniques extended to group settings.

1 Introduction

Enabled by pervasive availability of location information, new wireless communication scenarios have emerged where accurate proximity information is essential for both applications and basic networking functions. Such scenarios require secure, reliable and efficient verification of distances between nodes. Distance Bounding (DB) addresses such scenarios by allowing one entity (verifier) to obtain an upper bound on the distance to another entity (prover) and, optionally, authenticate the latter. DB was introduced by Brands and Chaum [3] as a means of preventing so-called "mafia fraud" attacks on bank ATMs. Such an attack occurs if the adversary identifies itself to the verifier using the identity of the prover, without the latter being aware, i.e., man-in-the-middle attack. In [3], a user's smart-card (verifier) checks its proximity to the ATM (prover). DB has been recently implemented [17] using commercial off-the-shelf electronics with 15cm accuracy. It was also suggested as means of securely determining node locations in wireless networks [14,5,8,20]. In most prior work, DB was considered in the context of a single prover and a single verifier. Group Distance Bounding (GDB) is the natural extension of distance bounding to group settings with multiple provers and verifiers.

GDB is motivated by some emerging wireless applications. First is group device pairing, a procedure for setting up an initial secure channel among a group of previously unassociated wireless devices; e.g., several users establishing keys among their

---

* This work was conducted as an academic guest at the System Security Group at ETH Zurich.

J.M. McCune et al. (Eds.): TRUST 2011, LNCS 6740, pp. 302–312, 2011.

devices [7] or a single user with multiple devices in a home-area network [4]. In either case, GDB can help verify that the entire group of devices is clustered within a particular area. GDB is also useful in critical (e.g., military) mobile ad hoc network (MANET) settings where all nodes must track locations of, and authenticate, other friendly nodes [2]. Critical MANETs can operate in hostile environments where node compromise is quite realistic. GDB can be used for location based-access control, node tracking and location-based group key management.

We begin by showing that straightforward extensions of current single prover-verifier DB techniques to GDB is inefficient and insecure for localization, without synchronization between verifiers[1]. We then continue by exploring and constructing more efficient and secure GDB techniques. This work makes four contributions: (1) definition of Group Distance Bounding (GDB), (2) a novel one-way *passive DB* primitive, (3) a secure and efficient GDB protocol for several group settings and (4) security and performance analyses of the proposed protocol.

This paper is organized as follows: prior DB protocols, formulation of the GDB problem and our system and adversary models are discussed in Section 2. Passive DB, including its security analysis, is presented in Section 3. Applications of passive DB to the construction of GDB protocols are discussed in Section 4. Performance and security aspects of proposed GDB protocols are considered in Section 5. Related work is overviewed in Section 6, followed by future work summarized in Section 7.

2   Preliminaries

This section overviews DB protocols, formulates the GDB problem and presents our environmental assumptions.

2.1   Overview of Distance Bounding (DB)

Figure 1(a) shows a generic (Brands-Chaum-based) *one-way DB* protocol. The core of any distance bounding protocol is the distance measurement phase, in which the verifier measures a round-trip time between sending its challenge and receiving the prover's reply. The verifier's challenge is unpredictable and each reply needs to be computed as a function of the received challenge. Thus, the prover cannot reply before receiving a challenge. Consequently, it cannot pretend to be closer to the verifier than it really is (only further). First, the verifier and the prover each generate n b-bit nonces c_i and r_i ($1 \leq i \leq n$), respectively. In the Brands-Chaum DB protocol [3], the prover also commits to its nonces using any secure commitment scheme. The verifier sends all c_i to the prover, one at a time. Once each c_i is received, the prover computes, and responds with a function of both nonces, $f(c_i, r_i)$. The verifier checks the reply and measures elapsed time between each challenge and response. The process is repeated n times and the protocol completes successfully only if *all* n rounds complete correctly. Prover's processing time: $\alpha = t_s^P - t_r^P$ must be negligible compared to time-of-flight; otherwise, a computationally powerful prover could claim a false bound. This time might

---
[1] This was also pointed out in [8].

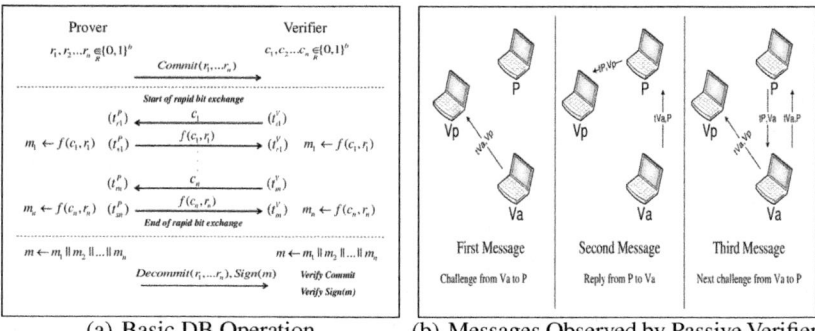

| (a) Basic DB Operation | (b) Messages Observed by Passive Verifier. |

Fig. 1. DB Operation and Messages Observed by a Passive Verifier

be tolerably small, depending on the underlying technology, the distance measured and required security guarantees: less than $1nsec$ processing time yields $0.15m$ accuracy [17].

Security of DB protocols relies on two assumptions: (1) verifier's challenges must be random and unpredictable, and (2) challenges traverse the distance between the two parties at maximum possible speed, i.e., the speed of electromagnetic waves. After running a DB protocol, the verifier knows that the distance to the prover is at most $\frac{t_r^V - t_s^V - \alpha}{2} \cdot c$, where α is prover's processing time and c is the speed of light [3]. DB protocols typically require $(2n + C)$ messages, where C is the number of messages exchanged in the pre- and post-processing protocol phases. Typically, $C << n$ and can thus be ignored.

In some applications, e.g., distributed localization, there is a need for mutual DB between two parties: P_1 and P_2. This can be achieved by modifying the one-way DB protocol such that each response from P_2 to a challenge by P_1 also includes a challenge from P_2 to P_1 (more details in [22]). If prover authentication is required, public key signatures can be used to sign challenges and responses. The verifier validates the signature in the last step, as shown in Figure 1(a). The protocol succeeds *only* if the signature is valid. Public key identification schemes, e.g., Schnorr or Fiat-Shamir can also be used, as described in [3].

2.2   Problem Statement and System Model

We first present the general GDB problem statement and its variants, then describe our system and adversary models.

GDB Problem Statement: GDB involves *one or more provers* interacting with *one or more verifiers*. Verifiers want to accurately and securely establish DBs to provers and, optionally, authenticate them. Provers are generally untrusted; they may behave maliciously by reporting false distances and identities. In the most general case, any device can be a prover, a verifier or both, corresponding to one-way or mutual DB. We consider three GDB cases: (1) N verifiers establish DBs to M provers (*MPNV*), (2) N verifiers establish DBs to a single prover (*1PNV*), and (3) a single verifier establishes DBs to M provers (*MP1V*). In mutual GDB, two special cases (*1PNV* and *MP1V*) are equivalent; we refer to them as 1-to-M. There is an additional case where N peer

Table 1. Notation

$DB(s)$	Distance Bound(s)
P	Prover
$V \quad (V_a, V_p)$	Active and Passive Verifier, respectively
$DB_{x,y}$	DB established by verifier x to prover y
$t_{x,y}$	Time of flight between x and y
$d_{x,y}$	Distance between x and y ($d_{x,y} = d_{y,x}$)
$n \quad (n_a, n_p)$	Number of active and passive DB rounds, respectively
d_a	Fraction of verifiers performing n_a active rounds
$H()$	Cryptographic hash function
$Pr_{ch}(X)$	Fraction of DB rounds where node X cheats

nodes need to establish mutual DBs, that we refer to as *mutual multi-party* GDB. This paper focuses on the one-way GDB settings.

System Model: Our assumption are as follows: (1) *Coverage:* all devices are within each others' transmission range.[2] (2) *Accuracy:* each device is capable of fast and accurate processing, on the order of nanoseconds. This is possible using off-the-shelf components [17] or UWB ranging platforms e.g.[1]. (3) *Interaction between Verifiers:* Verifiers know each others' locations or distances separating them. Assumptions (4) and (5) are needed only if authentication is performed. (4)*Keys:* each device has a public/private key-pair and a certificate binding the public key to its identity. (5) *Collusion:* colluding provers do not reveal their private keys to each other.

Adversary Model: We assume that the adversary is computationally bounded and can not prevent nodes within its radio range from receiving transmissions, i.e., is not using directional antennas. The adversary can compromise only provers. Verifiers trust each other. Our adversary model covers the following attacks (based on DB [3]):

1– Distance Fraud Attack: A dishonest prover claims to be closer than it really is, aiming to shorten the distance to one or more verifiers. Note that a prover can always claim to be further by delaying responses.

2– Mafia Fraud Attack: The adversary, posing as prover, interacts with the verifier. In parallel, it interacts with the actual prover posing as the verifier. The goal is to fool the verifier into believing that the adversary is the prover located closer to the verifier than the actual prover. We consider a GDB version of this attack where the adversary places one or more nodes between the prover(s) and one or more verifiers. The adversary aims to convince verifiers that these malicious nodes are real provers.

We assume that the DB protocols used in the construction of our GDB protocols are designed such that they prevent Distance Fraud and Mafia Fraud Attacks and further prevent Distance Hijacking attacks [9]. We do not consider Terrorist Fraud Attacks.

3   Passive DB

Whenever a prover and a verifier engage in a DB protocol, some information about their locations and mutual distance is leaked [13]. We use this observation in the presence of multiple verifiers and show that it is unnecessary for *every verifier* to directly interact

---

[2] This is a common assumption in all DB literature, e.g., [3,14,20,19,13,21].

with the prover (P) to establish a DB to that prover. If *at least one* verifier (V_a) interacts with P, any other (passive) verifier (V_p) can deduce the DB between itself and P by observing messages between P and V_a. We assume that V_p and V_a trust each other, know the distance separating them (or each other's locations) and both need to establish a DB to P. We address passive DB with untrusted verifiers in Section 5.3.

Figure 1(b) shows V_p observing the timings (T_i) of messages exchanged between P and V_a. V_p constructs three equations:

$$T_1 = t_0 + t_{V_a,V_p} \tag{1}$$

$$T_2 = t_0 + t_{V_a,P} + \alpha_p + t_{P,V_p} \tag{2}$$

$$T_3 = t_0 + 2 \cdot t_{V_a,P} + \alpha_P + \alpha_{V_a} + t_{V_a,V_p} \tag{3}$$

where α_P and α_{V_a} are processing times of P and V_a, respectively (ideally $\alpha_P = 0$) and t_0 is the protocol starting time. V_p can determine time of flight for signals between P and V_a thus computing the distance between them (where c denotes speed of light):

$$d_{V_a,P} = c \cdot t_{V_a,P} = c \cdot \frac{(T_3 - T_1) - \alpha_P - \alpha_{V_a}}{2} \tag{4}$$

For V_a (and V_p) to measure the distance between itself and P, α_P must be negligible (or constant and known)[3].

Overview: V_p uses time differences of arrival (TDoA) of three messages, its own and V_a's locations to construct the locus of P's possible locations (a hyperbola, similar to other TDoA techniques [11]). V_p then determines the distance between V_a and P (as shown in Equation 4) and constructs a circle with the radius of that distance. This circle intersects with P's location locus at two points (s_1 and s_2). V_p computes DB to P as the distance between itself and s_1 (or s_2)[4].

Passive DB Details: We show, among other things, that if P fools V_p with a shorter-than-real passive DB, then the active DB established by V_a *must* also be shortened. However, since V_a's DB can not be shortened, a passive DB is as secure as its active counterpart. Suppose V_a and V_p are located at (x_a, y_a) and (x_p, y_p), respectively. V_p knows both of these locations and the distance d_{V_a,V_p}). Without the loss of generality, we assume $(x_a, y_a) = (0,0)$ to be the origin of the coordinate system. It follows that:

$$d_{V_a,V_p} = \sqrt{(x_p - x_a)^2 + (y_p - y_a)^2} = \sqrt{(x_p)^2 + (y_p)^2} \tag{5}$$

We further assume that P is at (x, y). V_p also knows that:

$$d_{V_p,P} = \sqrt{(x - x_p)^2 + (y - y_p)^2} = \sqrt{(x)^2 + (d_{V_a,V_p} - y)^2} \tag{6}$$

$$d_{V_a,P} = \sqrt{(x - x_a)^2 + (y - y_a)^2} = \sqrt{(x)^2 + (y)^2} \tag{7}$$

---

[3] This is a common assumption in the literature [3,14,20,19,13,21].

[4] If V_p does not know V_a's exact location, but only its distance to V_a, then, instead of a sector of a circle, V_p obtains an area between two circles with radii corresponding to furthest and closest points to V_p on the hyperbola. In that case, the larger radius will be used as a DB to P.

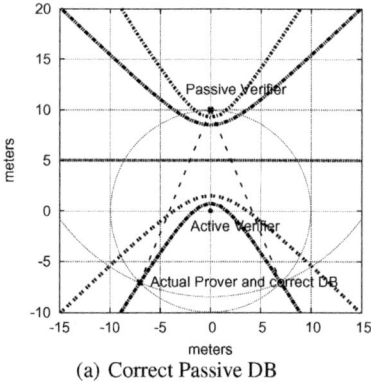

(a) Correct Passive DB

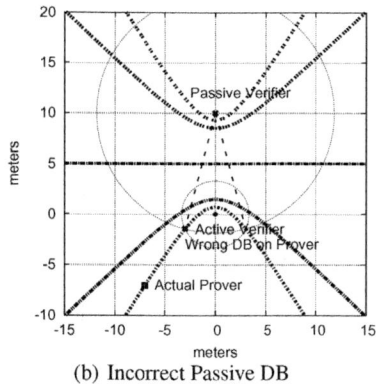

(b) Incorrect Passive DB

Fig. 2. Establishing a Correct and Incorrect Passive DB

If three messages in Figure 1(b) are received at times: T_1, T_2 and T_3, V_p computes $d_{V_a,P}$ as shown in Equation 4. V_p also computes:

$$c \cdot (T_2 - T_1) = c \cdot \delta_1 = d_{V_a,P} + c \cdot \alpha_P + d_{P,V_p} - d_{V_a,V_p} \qquad (8)$$

Where c is the speed of light. However, since $d_{V_a,P}$ (Equation 4) and d_{V_a,V_p} (verifiers know distances between them) are known, V_p obtains:

$$\Gamma = c \cdot (\delta_1 - \alpha_P) + d_{V_a,V_p} = d_{V_a,P} + d_{V_p,P} =$$
$$\sqrt{(x)^2 + (y)^2} + \sqrt{(x)^2 + (d_{V_a,V_p} - y)^2} \qquad (9)$$

This yields the following formula for the locus of P's possible location (on a hyperbola, due to TDoA [11]):

$$y = \frac{d_{V_a,V_p}\sqrt{(d_{V_a,V_p}^2 - \Gamma^2)} \pm \Gamma \cdot \sqrt{(4x^2 + d_{V_a,V_p}^2 - \Gamma^2)}}{2\sqrt{(d_{V_a,V_p}^2 - \Gamma^2)}} \qquad (10)$$

Note that $DB_{V_a,P} = d_{V_a,P}$ is an upper bound for the distance between P and V_a. Using $d_{V_a,P}$, V_p can construct another equation for the locus of P's possible location (a circle around V_a with radius $d_{V_a,P}$):

$$(x - x_a)^2 + (y - y_a)^2 = (d_{V_a,P})^2 \qquad (11)$$

V_p can now establish a passive DB using the intersection of both loci (i.e., solving equations 11 and 10). The computed DB is the distance between V_p's own location (x_p, y_p) and the intersection of P's loci described by equations 11 and 10. The end point of this DB ($DB_{V_p,P} = d_{V_p,P}$) lies within a sector of a circle, not within the entire circle, as in the case of active DB. Substituting $x = x_a + \sqrt{(d_{V_a,P})^2 - (y - y_a)^2}$ (from equation 11) into equation 10, the y-coordinate of P's location becomes: $y \propto (d_{V_a,P})$ (same for P's x-coordinate). For V_p to compute a wrong (shorter) DB to P, it has to have computed a shorter $d_{V_a,P}$. A shorter $d_{V_a,P}$ requires $DB_{V_a,P}$ to have been computed shorter than the actual distance between P and V_a (which is impossible, as shown in Section 2.1).

To better illustrate this, Figures 2(a) and 2(b) show an example scenario. P (labeled Actual Prover in the Figures) at $(-7, -7)$ is on one of several possible hyperbolas. The DB from V_a at $(0,0)$ to P is shown as a circle around V_a (labeled as Active Verifier) If P cheats, the circle drawn around V_p at $(0, 10)$ would intersect the hyperbola at a point $((-3, -1.5)$ in Figure 2(b)), close to V_p. This point would be inside the circle established by V_a. However, the DB computed by V_a would be shorter than the actual distance to P, which is impossible. If V_p engages in a DB protocol with V_a, it would obtain the circle shown around it in Figure 2(a). However, in this passive case, it obtains a sector of that circle defined by the arc connecting two points $((-7, -7)$ and $(7, -7))$ where the computed hyperbola intersects the circle around V_a. Section 2.1 shows that active DB prevents the distance fraud attack. Since passive DB is as secure as active DB, it also prevents the distance fraud attack. Adding authentication to passive DB prevents the mafia-fraud attack on passive DB since an attacker would be unable to authenticate itself to V_p unless it also does so to V_a. Both types of verifiers can use the same authentication mechanism, e.g., public key signatures (or public key identification schemes), as described in Section 2.1. All information (commitments, challenges, responses and signatures) required to authenticate provers also reaches passive verifiers. The only disadvantage is that V_p does not generate its own challenges. Therefore, passive DB remains secure as long as active verifiers are trusted. We assume that the active DB protocol also prevents distance hijacking attacks.

4   One-Way DB Extended to Group Settings

We focus on the most general one-way GDB case: M provers and N verifiers (MPNV). All other scenarios correspond to special cases. For comparison, we consider a GDB protocol where nodes sequentially engage in a naïve single prover single verifier DB. In each case, we propose an alternative approach based on passive DB. We assume that n rounds of DB are needed in all cases.

In a one-way MPNV setting, nodes act either as provers or as verifiers. In a naive MPNV protocol, each prover sequentially interacts with each verifier. This is repeated until *all* provers have interacted with all verifiers. The total number of messages is: $(2n \cdot N \cdot M)$. In this context, there are two parameters to consider: (1) number of active and passive DB rounds performed by each verifier and (2) selection of active verifiers (i.e., deterministic or probabilistic). The second parameter does not affect how nodes act, however, it impacts security if verifiers are compromised (see Section 5). Active verifiers can be selected at random or by any leader election protocol, e.g., [15]. The numbers of active verifiers and active rounds influence the number of messages required, the time to complete the protocol, the security of the DB. If all verifiers are treated equally, two parameters can describe a general protocol: (1) the number of active verifiers and (2) the number of active rounds by each verifier. If each verifier performs n rounds, let n_a and n_p ($n_a + n_p = n$) be the number of active and passive rounds, respectively. Let d_a be the fraction of verifiers which perform n_a active rounds. Each verifier has $(d_a \cdot (N-1) \cdot n_a)$ opportunities to execute passive DB with each prover. Two

Table 2. Number of Messages (# Messages) and Execution Time of One-Way GDB Protocols

Setting	Base Case # Messages	Our Protocol # Messages	Base Case Time	Our Protocol Time
MPNV	$2n \cdot N \cdot M$	$(2n_a + 1) \cdot (N \cdot d_a) \cdot M$	$2n \cdot \sum_{i=1}^{N} \sum_{j=1}^{M} t_{V_i, P_j}$	$(2n_a + 1) \cdot \sum_{j=1}^{d_a \cdot N} \sum_{k=1}^{M} t_{P_k, V_j}$
1PNV	$(2n + 1) \cdot N$	$(2n_a + 1) \cdot N \cdot d_a$	$2n \cdot \sum_{i=1}^{N} t_{P, V_i}$	$(2n_a + 1) \cdot \sum_{j=1}^{d_a \cdot N} t_{P, V_j}$
MP1V	$(2n + 1) \cdot M$	$2n + \sum_{j=1}^{M-1}(j + 1) \cdot (n - ((M - 1) - j))$	$2n \cdot \sum_{i=1}^{j} t_{V, P_i}, j \in 1, M$	$(n \cdot max(t_{V, P_i})) + \sum_{i=1}^{M-1} t_{V, P_i}$

interesting special cases are where (1) $d_a = 1/N$ and $n_a = n$ – one verifier interacts with all provers, and (2) $d_a = 1$ and $n_a = n/N$ – all verifiers interact with *all* provers. By varying n_a and d_a, we can obtain a protocol with the required security level and fewer messages than in the sequential pairwise interaction.

5   GDB Performance and Security Analysis

5.1   Performance

Table 2 compares number of messages in one-way GDB protocols based on passive DB to the base case of pairwise DB. Table 2 also shows total time required to compute all DBs. We compare with this base case since there are no prior GDB proposals. Our protocols require fewer messages and depend on the fraction of active verifiers and active rounds. MPNV requires $(n_a \cdot d_a)$ messages. For example, with 60 nodes (30 provers and 30 verifiers) and $d_a = 0.8$, 33% fewer messages are needed. Decreasing d_a to 0.6 saves more than 55% of messages. Similar savings are also attainable for lower and higher numbers of provers/verifiers.

5.2   Security with Trusted Verifiers

The probability of a single prover successfully cheating a single verifier decreases exponentially with the number of DB rounds. For n rounds, a prover has 2^{-n} chance of successfully guessing all challenge bits and sending responses ahead of time. This tricks the verifier into measuring a shorter round trip time of flight[5]. An active verifier (V_a) does not need to trust any other entity. In a group setting, where each prover-verifier pair engages in an active DB protocol, these security guarantees still hold. However, active DB in a group setting is insecure if used for localization. When a prover interacts with each verifier separately, it can selectively lengthen its distance by delaying messages. Verifiers would then incorrectly localize the prover. Secure localization schemes must therefore require *at least three* verifiers that interact with the prover *simultaneously*.

5.3   Security Untrusted Active Verifiers

Passive DB with untrusted verifiers is mainly useful in MANETs, where nodes continuously encounter new peers. Passive DB is secure if each V_a is trusted, as shown in Section 3. This is be the case in a fixed (or mobile) verification infrastructure with prior security association, or under control of one administrative entity. A malicious V_a could undermine security of passive DB as follows:

---

[5] 2^{-n} is the probability for Brands-Chaum protocol [3], whereas in other protocols (e.g., Hancke-Kuhn [12]), this probability is $(3/4)^{-n}$.

(1) Report Fake Location (or Distance): V_p requires the exact location of, or the distance to, V_a in order to construct the DB, as shown in Section 3. V_p will compute the hyperbola incorrectly (via Equation 10), if V_a reports an incorrect location or distance.

(2) Sending Early Challenges: Even if V_a reports its location or distance correctly, it can send new challenges prematurely. This would convince V_p that the prover is closer than it actually is, as shown in Figure 1(b). V_p would then compute $d_{V_a,P}$, intersecting incorrectly with the hyperbola, as shown in Figure 2(a), thus yielding a wrong DB.

We introduce a metric, *DB Correctness* (DBC), to illustrate the effectiveness of passive DB in the presence of such attacks:

$$DBC = 1 - 2^{n \cdot (Pr_{ch}(V_a)-1)} \tag{12}$$

where $Pr_{ch}(V_a)$ is the fraction of rounds where V_a cheats. If V_a does not cheat at all, $Pr_{ch}(V_a) = 0$ and $DBC = 1 - 2^{-n}$. If V_a cheats in all rounds, $Pr_{ch}(V_a) = 1$ and $DBC = 0$. Average correctness (DBC_{avg}) For a DB obtained by a V_p to a specific prover (in case of N active verifiers: $V_{a_1}, V_{a_2} ... V_{a_N}$, each engaging in $n_1, n_2 ... n_N$ rounds) average correctness (DBC_{avg}) can be computed as the average of individual DBC for each verifier:

$$DBC_{avg} = \frac{N - \sum_{i=1}^{N} 2^{n_i \cdot (Pr_{ch}(V_a(i))-1)}}{N} \tag{13}$$

For example, for 10 verifiers and 10 DB rounds, even if half of all V_a-s cheat in half of their rounds, DB would be established correctly $> 98\%$ of the time. Also, as long as less than half of V_a-s cheat in $< 90\%$ of rounds, DB would be correct $> 70\%$ of the time.

5.4   Combined Passive/Active DB Security

When a verifier performs n_a active rounds and n_p passive rounds both can be combined to obtain a more stable DB. We estimate the correctness in such a combined DB using a metric $(DBC_{a/p})$ as follows (note that both passive and active rounds have to result in the same DB):

$$DBC_{a/p} = 1 - \left(2^{-n_a} \cdot \frac{\sum_{i=1}^{N} 2^{n_{p(i)} \cdot (Pr_{ch}(V_a(i))-1)}}{N} \right) \tag{14}$$

If all other active verifiers cheat in all their DB rounds, $DBC_{a/p}$ becomes that of the active rounds performed by a verifier only, i.e., $1 - (2^{-n_a})$. Otherwise the correctness of the established DB increases with any additional passive round. As an example, consider the case of 10 verifiers. Even if only two rounds of active (n_a) DB are performed and as long as the fraction of rounds being cheated in is less than 1 correctness of the DB captured by $DBC_{a/p}$ increases. Even if the probability of cheating in passive DB rounds is as high as 0.5, $DBC_{a/p}$ will increase to over 0.95 if there are four or more opportunities to do passive DB.

6   Related Work

DB was introduced in [3], as mentioned in Section 2.1. Several DB optimizations and studies were done subsequently. In particular, [13] studied information leakage in DB protocols as a privacy problem. [22] proposed a mutual DB protocol by interleaving challenges and responses; between a single prover and a single verifier. [20], [19] and [5] investigated DB protocols in location verification and secure localization with three verifiers. [18] investigated so-called "in-region verification" and claimed that, for certain applications (such as sensor networks and location-based access control) in-region verification is better than location determination. [8] and [6] considered collusion attacks on DB location verification protocols. Other work, such as [23] looked at using time difference of arrival (TDoA) to determine location of transmitters. [23] proposed using TDoA in the context of Ultra-Wideband (UWB). DB was implemented using commercial off-the-shelf electronic components [17] and commercial off-the-shelf UWB ranging devices [21,14]. DB was also studied in the context of ad-hoc networks [22], sensor networks [16,5] and RFIDs [10,12].

7   Discussion and Conclusion

This paper presents the initial foray into group distance bounding (GDB). GDB is a fundamental mechanism for secure operation in wireless networks where verifying distances between, or locations of, groups of nodes is required. We investigated one-way GDB settings and constructed secure and efficient one-way GDB protocols. In doing so, we made minimal assumptions. However, there remain some open issues for future work, such as: (1) Can a passive verifier establish a DB without knowing the location of (or distance to) an active verifier, while perhaps knowing other information about distances to other nodes? (2) can passive DB be used to obtain mutual GDB protocols? (3) What can be done to address denial-of-service attacks in group settings (i.e., noisy environments)?

References

1. Multispectral Solutions Inc., Urban Positioning System (UPS),
   http://www.multispectral.com
2. RFC1677-Tactical Radio Frequency Communication Requirements for IPng,
   http://www.faqs.org/rfcs/rfc1677.html
3. Brands, S., Chaum, D.: Distance-bounding protocols. In: EUROCRYPT 1994 (1994)
4. Callaway, E., Gorday, P.: Home networking with ieee 802.15.4: a developing standard for low-rate wireless personal area networks. IEEE Communications Magazine (2002)
5. Capkun, S., Hubaux, J.: Secure positioning of wireless devices with application to sensor networks. In: IEEE INFOCOM (2005)
6. Chandran, N., Goyal, V., Moriarty, R., Ostrovsky, R.: Position based cryptography. In: Halevi, S. (ed.) CRYPTO 2009. LNCS, vol. 5677, pp. 391–407. Springer, Heidelberg (2009)
7. Chen, C., Chen, C., Kuo, C., Lai, Y., McCune, J., Studer, A., Perrig, A., Yang, B., Wu, T.: Gangs: gather, authenticate 'n group securely. In: ACM MobiCom (2008)
8. Chiang, J., Haas, J., Hu, Y.: Secure and precise location verification using distance bounding and simultaneous multilateration. In: ACM WiSec (2009)
9. Cremers, C., Rasmussen, K., Capkun, S.: Distance hijacking attacks on distance bounding protocols. Cryptology ePrint Archive: Report 2011/129 (2011)
10. Drimer, S., Murdoch, S.: Keep your enemies close: distance bounding against smartcard relay attacks. In: USENIX Security Symposium (2007)

11. Gunnarsson, F.: Positioning using time-difference of arrival measurements. In: IEEE International Conference on Acoustics, Speech, and Signal Processing (2003)
12. Hancke, G., Kuhn, M.: An rfid distance bounding protocol. In: IEEE SECURECOMM (2005)
13. Rasmussen, K., Čapkun, S.: Location privacy of distance bounding protocols. In: ACM CCS (2008)
14. Luecken, H., Kuhn, M., Tippenhauer, N.: UWB impulse radio based distance bounding. In: Workshop on Positioning, Navigation and Communication (WPNC) (2010)
15. Malpani, N., Welch, J., Vaidya, N.: Leader election algorithms for mobile ad hoc networks. In: ACM DIALM (2000)
16. Meadows, C., Syverson, P., Chang, L.: Towards more efficient distance bounding protocols for use in sensor networks. In: IEEE Securecomm (2006)
17. Rasmussen, K., Čapkun, S.: Realization of rf distance bounding. In: USENIX Security Symposium (2010)
18. Sastry, N., Shankar, U., Wagner, D.: Secure verification of location claims. In: ACM WiSe (2003)
19. Shmatikov, V., Wang, M.: Secure verification of location claims with simultaneous distance modification. In: Cervesato, I. (ed.) ASIAN 2007. LNCS, vol. 4846, pp. 181–195. Springer, Heidelberg (2007)
20. Singelee, D., Preneel, B.: Location verification using secure distance bounding protocols. In: IEEE International Conference on Mobile Adhoc and Sensor Systems Conference (2005)
21. Tippenhauer, N.O., Čapkun, S.: ID-based secure distance bounding and localization. In: Backes, M., Ning, P. (eds.) ESORICS 2009. LNCS, vol. 5789, pp. 621–636. Springer, Heidelberg (2009)
22. Čapkun, S., Buttyán, L., Hubaux, J.: Sector: secure tracking of node encounters in multi-hop wireless networks. In: ACM SASN (2003)
23. Young, D., Keller, C., Bliss, D., Forsythe, K.: Ultra-wideband (uwb) transmitter location using time difference of arrival (tdoa) techniques. In: Conference Record of the Thirty-Seventh Asilomar Conference on Signals, Systems and Computers (2003)

Author Index

GPSR Compliance

*The European Union's (EU) General Product Safety Regulation (GPSR)
is a set of rules that requires consumer products to be safe and our
obligations to ensure this.*

*If you have any concerns about our products, you can contact us on
ProductSafety@springernature.com*

In case Publisher is established outside the EU, the EU authorized
representative is:

Springer Nature Customer Service Center GmbH
Europaplatz 3
69115 Heidelberg, Germany

Batch number: 09490872

Printed by Printforce, the Netherlands